DREAM OF COMMONWEALTH, 1921 – 42

Also by Max Beloff

*BRITAIN'S LIBERAL EMPIRE, 1897–1921 (Volume 1 of IMPERIAL SUNSET)

PUBLIC ORDER AND POPULAR DISTURBANCES, 1660–1714

THE FOREIGN POLICY OF SOVIET RUSSIA (2 Volumes)

THOMAS JEFFERSON AND AMERICAN DEMOCRACY

SOVIET POLICY IN THE FAR EAST, 1944–51

THE AGE OF ABSOLUTISM, 1660–1815

FOREIGN POLICY AND THE DEMOCRATIC PROCESS

EUROPE AND THE EUROPEANS

THE GREAT POWERS

THE AMERICAN FEDERAL GOVERNMENT

NEW DIMENSIONS IN FOREIGN POLICY

THE UNITED STATES AND THE UNITY OF EUROPE

THE BALANCE OF POWER

THE FUTURE OF BRITISH FOREIGN POLICY

THE INTELLECTUAL IN POLITICS

THE GOVERNMENT OF THE UNITED KINGDOM (*with G.R. Peele*)

WARS AND WELFARE, 1914–1945

Edited by Max Beloff

THE FEDERALIST

MANKIND AND HIS STORY

*THE DEBATE ON THE AMERICAN REVOLUTION

ON THE TRACK OF TYRANNY

L'EUROPE DU XIXe ET DU XXe SIECLE (*with P. Renovin, F. Schnabel and F. Valsecchi*)

AMERICAN POLITICAL INSTITUTIONS IN THE 1970s (*with V. Vale*)

*Also published by Sheridan House

DREAM OF COMMONWEALTH
1921 – 42

Volume 2 of IMPERIAL SUNSET

MAX BELOFF

Emeritus Professor of Government and Public Administration
University of Oxford

SHERIDAN HOUSE

First published in the United States of America 1989 by
SHERIDAN HOUSE INC.
145 Palisade Street
Dobbs Ferry, N.Y. 10522

Library of Congress Cataloging in Publication Data

Library of Congress Cataloging-in-Publication Data
(Revised for vol. 2)
Beloff, Max, 1913 –
Vol. 2 published by Sheridan House, Dobbs Ferry, N.Y.
Bibliography: p.
Includes index.
Contents: v. 1, Britain's liberal Empire, 1837 – 1921.—
v. 1. Dream of commonwealth, 1921 – 42.
1. Great Britain—Foreign relations—20th century.
2. Great Britain—Colonies—History—20th century.
3. Commonwealth of Nations—History. I.Title.
DA566.7.B442   327.42   69 – 11480
ISBN 0 – 911378 – 92 – 8 (v.2)

Printed in Hong Kong

*For Rupert, Natasha, Nicholas,
Catherine and Jonathan*

CONTENTS

SOURCES AND ACKNOWLEDGEMENTS

In the first volume of the present work, I acknowledged the help I had received from many individuals and institutions, including access to and the right to quote from copyright material. I should like to repeat my thanks to all those individuals there named. In the twenty years that have elapsed since that volume appeared I have incurred further debts of gratitude which it is now my pleasure to record.

Access to the papers of the first Lord Lloyd at Churchill College, Cambridge was accorded to me by the late Lord Lloyd. I am grateful to Lady Lloyd, Dr John Charmley and the Archivist of Churchill College for permission to quote from them. I must also thank the University of Newcastle upon Tyne for allowing me to quote from the Papers of Walter Runciman, the 1st Viscount Runciman.

I am grateful to the Marquess of Salisbury for permission to quote from the papers of the fourth Marquess, at Hatfield House, and to Viscount Caldecote for permission to quote from the papers of the first Viscount Caldecote, deposited at Churchill College, Cambridge.

I must thank the Rt. Hon. Julian Amery M.P. for access to his father's diaries and for permission to quote from them here.

A letter of Joseph Chamberlain's is quoted by permission of Mr John Sparrow.

Extracts from Crown-copyright records in the Public Record Office and the India Office Library and Records appear by permission of the Controller of Her Majesty's Stationery Office. Extracts from the Halifax and Reading papers on permanent loan to the India Office Library and Records appear by permission of the Marquess of Reading and the Earl of Halifax.

The Australian Government Publishing Service gave permission for the quotation of material from *Documents on Australian Foreign Policy*.

I should like to record my thanks to the librarians and library staffs of the libraries in which I have worked during the preparation of both volumes: in Oxford, the Bodleian Library and Rhodes House Library, the Codrington Library, All Souls College and St Antony's College Library; in London, the London Library and the Library of the House of Lords; in Cambridge, Churchill College.

For financial assistance, I must thank the Rockefeller Foundation, the Ford Foundation, the Social Science Research Council (now the Economic and Social Research Council) and the Leverhulme Trust. The funds thus made available enabled me to call upon the services of successive research assistants: Mrs Margaret Croft, Mrs Mary Brown, Miss J.F. Maitland-Jones and Dr Richard Oliver; all provided indispensable assistance, but I am particularly indebted to Dr Oliver, without whose careful and well-organised labours my own original typescript would never have assumed a shape suitable for publication. I also wish to thank Dr Oliver for compiling the index.

Some of the ideas in this work were tried out in seminars at the Institute of Historical Research and at the London University Institute of Commonwealth Studies; for making this possible, I am indebted to Dr Alice Prochaska, Dr Kathleen Burk, Professor W.H. Morris-Jones and Dr Peter Lyon.

A number of fellow workers in this field of study or related subjects have answered individual queries or offered other advice; I should like to thank Dr C.M. Andrews, Dr David Carlton, Professor Isaiah Freidman, Dr Martin Gilbert, Professor Barry M. Gough, Dr. D. Harkness, Professor Elie Kedourie, Professor Paul Kennedy, Dr A.F.Madden, Dr G.C.Peden, Professor Kenneth Robinson, Mr Richard Symonds and Professor David Vital.

LIST OF ABBREVIATIONS

AJPH   *Australian Journal of Politics and History*
BL   British Library, Department of Manuscripts
C.I.D.   Committee of Imperial Defence
C.I.G.S.   Chief of the Imperial General Staff
DAFP   *Documents on Australian Foreign Policy*
DBFP   *Documents on British Foreign Policy*
DCER   *Documents on Canadian External Relations*
DDF   *Documents Diplomatiques Français*
DGFP   *Documents on German Foreign Policy*
FRUS   *Foreign Relations of the United States*
H.C. *Deb.*   *House of Commons Official Report* (Hansard)
HJ   *Historical Journal*
H.L. *Deb.*   *House of Lords Official Report* (Hansard)
H.M.S.O.   His/Her Majesty's Stationery Office
I.C.S.   Indian Civil Service
I.D.C.   Imperial Defence College
IORL   India Office Library and Records
JCH   *Journal of Contemporary History*
JCPS   *Journal of Commonwealth Political Studies*
JICH   *Journal of Imperial and Commonwealth History*
PRO   Public Record Office (London)
R.A.F.   Royal Air Force

EDITORIAL NOTE

An asterisk following a name indicates that a short biographical note will be found on pages 395 – 9 below.

PART I

THE ATTEMPT AT CONSOLIDATION: 1921 – 32

Chapter 1

INTRODUCTION

A long time has elapsed since the appearance of the first volume of this work[1] and the period has been marked by new attention from different perspectives to the history of the Empire-Commonwealth in the years covered. I have endeavoured to summarise these in the preface to the second edition.[2] But these additions to our knowledge and understanding have not significantly altered my own approach to the subsequent decades which are the subject of the present book. It remains my view that the rapid disintegration of the Empire-Commonwealth as a political system, which was one of the major consequences of the second world war was not something unexpected, still less desired, by the makers of British policy. If one observes the changing scene through their eyes rather than with the benefit of our contemporary vision we can see that while we may think it remarkable that the imperial view survived as long as it did, the British elite persisted in thinking that wise policy, tactful diplomacy and good administration could keep the system in being for a long time yet. Most of the best current writing on the subject starts from the same point of view and does not detect the defeatism which in the light of the true balance of forces, demographic, economic and military, might have been considered more realistic.[3] Nor was Britain unique among European colonial powers. The French Third Republic saw its colonial manpower and other resources as being of increasing importance and paid growing attention in its educational system to inculcating the benefits of Empire.[4] The reason for the

[1]Max Beloff, *Imperial Sunset*, vol. I, *Britain's Liberal Empire* (London, Methuen, 1969; New York, Alfred Knopf, 1970).
[2]*Britain's Liberal Empire*, 2nd ed (London, Macmillan, 1987).
[3]'The besetting sin of the policy-makers was not a galloping defeatism but if anything, an excess of confidence in their ability by a timely redeployment of the imperial factor to outflank those elements in colonial nationalism which demanded a complete separation from Britain and the repudiation of her claims to political, economic and strategic privileges. Sectional nationalism in the Dominions, the Zaghlulist coalition in Egypt, the Congress in India were all to be outmanoeuvred and disarmed by deft political and constitutional footwork.' John Darwin, 'Imperialism in Decline? Tendencies in British Imperial Policy between the Wars', *Historical Journal (HJ)* (Cambridge), vol. XXIII, (1980), pp. 657 – 79.
[4]Raoul Girardet, *L'Idee Coloniale en France* 1871 – 1962 (Paris, 1972).

choice of the fall of Singapore as the final event to be considered in this volume is the outcome of a conviction that it was only this shattering event that revealed the realities of Britain's weakness as against both the enemies of that time and her newly acquired principal allies. For the believer in Britain's might and right, the subsequent story is one of downhill all the way.

It could be argued that it would have been wise to accept the more conventional date of 1939 in that it was unthinkable that an imperial system so precariously poised could survive participation in a global conflict which would highlight the differences in the aspirations and combat-readiness of its different components. Such was indeed one of the most powerful arguments of the 'appeasers' of the 1930s. But to do this would again be to overlook the evidence of what was thought at the time. Winston Churchill did not take office in 1940 as a liquidator. More to the point is the fact that the relevance of Britain's role as an imperial power was actually seen to grow rather than diminish in the inter-war years. It was still possible to hold that, even where nations not of British or even European stock were concerned, the new constitutional formula of Commonwealth could help transform the whole system into one of consent.

It is perhaps necessary to remind oneself that whatever the worries about the imperial system and its capacity to hold its own against competitors, new and old, it did in fact operate as a system at the outbreak of war in 1939 as it had in 1914. Southern Ireland, or Eire as it was then styled, provided the only important exception. It was only the war itself and in particular the Japanese conquests and their impact upon India that made the later dissolution probable and perhaps inescapable. Given our knowledge of the outcome, it is not surprising that much attention has been paid by historians to the defence aspects of the period, even though actual military operations played a much smaller part during its first two decades than while the imperial system was being extended.

It has also been argued that it was Britain's failure to cope with the new threats in Europe in the 1930s that made possible the subsequent weakening of her world position, and that one reason for this inability had been a set of policies in relation to the recruitment, training and disposition of Britain's armed forces concentrated upon imperial defence.[5] Yet even this by now orthodox position has been

[5]The classic statement is in Michael Howard, *The Continental Commitment* (London, 1972).

4

challenged and the defence of the United Kingdom seen as the most important reason for the failure fully to meet a 'continental commitment'.[6] Since in the end what counted were relations of power, whether as between Britain and other states or between British rulers and the movements towards national independence, the present narrative will keep to the distinction, clear at the time, between countries effectively governed by fiat of the Imperial Parliament, or according to recently worked out conventions by the parliaments of the Dominions, and those where, whatever the degree of British economic penetration, sovereignty resided elsewhere. One might add in further justification of this approach, that the largest area of informal penetration, Latin America, had seen British influence largely replaced by that of the United States as one of the results of the first world war. And we are dealing with the Empire which as of 1921 stood at its maximum territorial extent, if we include with the home islands, the Dominions, Crown Colonies, Protectorates and Mandates. Parts of the system were no doubt more closely linked to the centre than others. But even the Dominions – three of which were themselves mandatory powers – had a direct interest in developments in the colonial world. Because of the migrations that had been a feature of imperial development, individual parts of the Empire had overseas interests themselves: India in South and East Africa, Canada in the Caribbean. The concern felt by Britain for the allegiance of its Indian Muslim subjects played a continuing role in determining policy in the Middle East. And although the civil services of the colonies were individually recruited (and separate from the Indian Civil Service) there was a considerable degree of mobility between them and the top levels. Service in Mauritius and Nigeria was a prelude to Sir Donald Cameron's* role as governor successively of Tanganyika and Nigeria; Sir Harold MacMichael* was less appositely translated from being governor of Tanganyika to the high commissionership in Palestine; Sir Harry Luke* from Palestine to Malta and thence to the governorship of Fiji. Lord

[6]'It was the direct defence of the United Kingdom, not overseas resources which absorbed most of the resources which might otherwise have been committed to the continent of Europe. Moreover...such diversion of military effort as there was to imperial defence need not have militated against technical innovation...although the Empire could make only a very limited contribution at the outbreak of war, the Empire was an important source of manpower and raw materials which could be mobilised in a long war.' G.C. Peden, 'The burden of Imperial Defence and the Continental Commitment Reconsidered', *HJ*, vol. XXVII, (1984), pp. 405 – 23.

Lugard*, both the practitioner and the theorist of 'indirect rule', was after his retirement a permanent member, from 1922 to 1936, of the Permanent Mandates Commission of the League of Nations, and as such with a remit to study Britain's handling of its responsibilities in countries as far apart as Palestine and Tanganyika. Lord Hailey*, whose official career had been wholly devoted to India and who retired as governor of the United Provinces in 1934, subsequently devoted himself to the study of Africa and his volume *African Survey*, published in 1938, had immense influence over colonial policy for the next decade and a half.

While the India Office and the Colonial Office (from which the Dominions Office was separated in 1925) were separate departments with their separate traditions, and while the periphery of learned societies and particular pressure groups that formed the penumbra of much policy making were normally specialised in their interests and clientele, it is hard not to be impressed by the evidence for the existence of a single system as seen through the eyes of the statesmen and officials of the period. Argument by analogy from one part of the Empire to another was in constant use; nor were the Empire's enemies restricted in their activity to individual territories; the long-standing connections between the Irish nationalists and the Indian national movement continued even after the establishment of the Free State.[7] The various anti-imperialist movements usually concentrated among expatriates brought together individuals from many different countries, and for a time in the 1920s were even linked through Marcus Garvey with the struggle for equality of the American negro.[8]

The whole complex appeared to form a single system from yet another point of view. It was possible in some quarters to regard the history of the original Dominions as providing a pointer to future constitutional advance, first for the Indian sub-continent, and in the fullness of time for other parts of the Empire as well – a time which white settlers in the Rhodesias and Kenya thought should not be long postponed, though only in a form to safeguard their predominance. Such a transition from 'Empire' to 'Commonwealth' had now come to form the staple doctrine

[7]An American historian prints a photograph of a Hindu demonstration in Detroit in 1931 backed by Sinn Fein protesting against the imprisonment of Gandhi: R.F. Betts, *Uncertain Dimensions: Western Overseas Empires in the Twentieth Century* (New York, 1985), p. 172.
[8]For Garvey and the impact of his movement see ibid., pp. 148-9.

of the Round Table group.[9] The accompanying assumption was that the kind of voluntary co-operation in matters of common concern that had proved practicable in wartime would be relevant in dealing with the problems of peace – men, money, markets. Some people harked back to Joseph Chamberlain's idea of a single mutually sustaining imperial economy, though this was always a minority view in Britain and for obvious reasons without much appeal overseas.

External threats, whether in the 1930s from the German pressure for the return of Germany's former colonies or from Japan's growing power in the Pacific, might enhance the argument for a common system of defence but the perception of the threats was an uneven one, and the priority attached to each of them different again.

To do more than improvise to meet contingencies as they occurred was the most of which practical men found themselves capable. British statesmen were dependent upon a home electorate at a time when its demands were for retrenchment in defence and overseas expenditure and for a greater concentration upon the promotion of domestic prosperity and improved public services.[10] It has been suggested that not only was interest in imperial affairs confined to a relatively narrow class but that politically it was a cause which in Britain (as in France) appealed only to the Conservative end of the political spectrum.[11] This may be an exaggeration in the light of the record of the two Labour governments of the period.[12] Imperial sentiment may indeed still have had a populist streak, but it was not the stuff of daily politics.

It would be wrong to claim that the upheaval of the war years had made no difference or that there were no changes of attitudes and expectations during the twenty years that followed its conclusion. The changes were however held in check by certain established principles of action that guided the official mind, with its concern for precedent and for established procedures. In constitutional matters these might be sought as far back as the middle

[9]See my article, 'Dream of Commonwealth', *Round Table*, (London), no. 240, (November 1970), pp. 463 – 70.
[10]My own approach to the domestic history of Britain in the inter-war period can be found in Max Beloff, *Wars and Welfare* (London, 1984).
[11]See Miles Kahler, *Decolonization in Britain and France: The Domestic Consequences of International Relations* (Princeton, 1984), pp. 72 – 3.
[12]On the Labour Party and the Empire, see Partha Sarathi Gupta, *Imperialism and the British Labour Movement* (London, 1975).

ages.[13] All the apparatus of constitution-making through Royal Commissions and other forms of inquiry and through Parliamentary enactments and Orders in Council had a long history behind it. If the British public felt itself little involved directly – only Ireland, Palestine, and above all India had important Parliamentary repercussions – it could be certain that relevant concerns were taken into account.

Another aspect of the official approach, if anything strengthened in this period, was the dominant role accorded to the Treasury. Never an enthusiast for colonial expansion, the Treasury had always clung to the view that in all circumstances colonies must pay for themselves and not be a burden on the British taxpayer. A criterion of this kind meant that the tax-collector had to follow the flag, with important consequences for the economies of hitherto undeveloped areas and for their patterns of employment and social organisation. It also ran counter to the notion of positive development in the shape of public services, which demanded a capital investment that few colonial territories could easily supply from their own resources. During the inter-war period, this attitude was to some extent modified when events in different parts of the Empire made people aware of the political dangers that stagnation might itself engender.[14] And by the time of the second world war, the language of development was beginning to be used rather more freely and a number of steps taken towards the ends it indicated.[15]

If one turns from policy-makers to those who executed their policies on the ground or were responsible for recommending courses of action to the home government, one other change is perceptible, though its beginnings can be traced earlier. In India, in the previous century, the westernisers had by and large won the day over those who would have preferred to see traditional society and its beliefs left intact. One element in the sense of cultural superiority which had made this position tenable was a belief in the superiority of

[13]See the preface by Frederick Madden to 'The Empire of the Bretaignes', 1175–1688: The Foundations of a Colonial System of Government, in Frederick Madden and David Fieldhouse (eds) Select Documents on the Constitutional History of the British Empire and Commonwealth, vol. 1 (Westport, Conn., and London, 1985).

[14]On this aspect of the subject see D.J. Morgan, The Official History of Colonial Development: vol. 1, The origins of British Aid Policy, 1924–1945 (London, 1980); Stephen Constantine, The making of British Colonial Development Policy, 1914–1940 (London, 1984).

[15]The total transformation of attitudes towards the colonial empire within a single generation is agreeably illustrated in the autobiography of Sir Kenneth Bradley, Once a District Officer (London, 1966).

Christianity over the religions of the east. But in the east, the masses of the King-Emperor's subjects remained wedded to the Hindu, Buddhist or Islamic creeds. In Africa, on the contrary, missionary activity had been a major aspect of imperial penetration for both the British and their European rivals.[16] By the 1920s religious issues in British politics and interest in missionary activity were on the decline while colonial administrators had become more aware that existing religious beliefs and practices were closely bound up with the whole fabric of society. 'Indirect rule', the attempt to administer colonies through traditional authorities, even to the extent of creating such authorities where none could be found, involved limiting the tasks of government and non-interference with current social practices where these were at least tolerable in western eyes. The new stress upon cultural anthropology with its emphasis upon the richness and complexity of what had been seen as undifferentiated primitiveness or even savagery gave intellectual backing to what was also an administrative convenience. The missionary gives way to the anthropologist.

The now accepted rule that empires can in the end only be ruled successfully if the imperial power can find appropriate collaborators – whether traditional as with Indian Princes or African chiefs, or based upon new political classes emerging as a result of the partial westernisation of indigenous societies – cannot be gainsaid in the light of experience. Even the devolution of power depended upon a willingness of local elites to work the new institutions. The American Revolution had shown the inevitable result of the loss of the sense of an identity of interests between a local elite and the imperial power.[17] In Canada with some difficulty arising from its bi-national composition and in Australia and New Zealand with much less, the handover of power to the local elites was by 1921 almost complete. A possible solution for the Irish question was gradually and painfully taking shape. Even more remarkable was held to be the achievement of having succeeded in South Africa in finding collaborators in the Boer community ready to assume governmental responsibilities within the imperial structure. Botha and Smuts had become the real jewels in the imperial crown.

[16] For the contrast between India and Africa in this respect, see D.A. Low, *Lion Rampant* (London, 1973), 120 ff.
[17] See R.W. Tucker and D.C. Hendrickson, *The Fall of the First British Empire - The Origins of the American War of Independence* (London and Baltimore, 1982).

Since the interests of non-white South Africans were given so little weight – it is a testimony to the way opinion has moved that the pro-Boer sentiment was still powerful in Liberal circles - South Africa provided no precedent for the possible development towards self-government and ultimately 'dominion status' for countries in which the only possible recipients would be non-white. In theory, the claims for the obvious superiority of the white race based upon the tenets of 'social Darwinism' had lost its hold over most educated opinion. In practice the belief that a proper fulfilment of imperial obligations involved the social self-segregation of the rulers was undiminished, and was perhaps even stronger than before, now that the physical conditions of life at home could more easily be replicated. Yet both the impediments which this created to free and continuous discussion between the representatives of power and local notables and the resentment of the western-educated members of local elites whose numbers were increasing made the rulers' task more difficult than it need have been.[18]

Such beliefs and practices did not necessarily impede genuine concern for the people over whom an individual district commissioner or higher authority might exercise power; and concern might at times include even affection. But this tempering of a sense of superiority by an affectionate paternalism was easier when the people in question were far removed in standard of living, style of life and mental perceptions from the rulers themselves. In India there was the preference for the 'martial races' against the educated urban middle classes; in Palestine for the fellaheen or still better the desert Bedouin – one sometimes feels that every colonial servant was a frustrated Colonel Lawrence – rather than for the often highly educated and sophisticated Jewish immigrant. I remember a distinguished Israeli who had been an important figure in the Jewish community during the British mandate remarking how hard it was for colonial service officers to get used to coming to his home and finding it full of books and other appurtenances of a civilised life. It was not what they were used to among those over whom they held sway. The

---

[18] Writing about the 1920s, Lord Garner remarked: 'It is one of the mysteries of the British Empire that the British, a people with a deserved reputation for tolerance and liberalism should have shown such insensitivity in relations with coloured people. To some extent they shared this prejudice with most other white people at the time, but the British arrogance had a peculiar edge to it and it cast long shadows.' J. Garner, *The Commonwealth Office, 1925–1968* (London, Heinemann, 1978), p. 3.

doctrine of paramountcy for 'native interests' first enunciated for East Africa was in essence a decision in favour of the paternalist and conservationist approach to local rule as against the initiative for change brought about by the Jews in Palestine and by 'white settlers' and the Indian immigrants in Africa.

Too much should not be made of the sentiments and prejudices of those who had to work the system; others placed in the same position might have reacted in the same way. Clearly, with air communications as yet embryonic, the opinions of the man on the spot counted for more in the subsequent and latest stages of colonial rule. What they conveyed to the centre by way of information and advice was an important element in the home government's policy making, but in the last resort decisions were made in London, and where necessary London could make sure that it was represented on the spot by those whom it could trust to carry out its wishes. That being so, the lobbying of ministers, civil servants and of those Parliamentarians who had an interest in such things was a fairly continuous process. It was carried out both by interests in Britain and overseas seeking advantages for themselves or to protect their own positions in the event of a change in policy, and by those who made themselves the voices of those who might have found direct access difficult – missionary circles on behalf of some Africans for instance, or the Government of India through the India Office for Indians in other parts of the Empire. The fact that Empire was a minority interest made such pressure politics more significant than in the case of other issues where opinion was canalised by parties and where major domestic interests were clearly at stake.

In view of the fact that nearly all colonial societies were composed of different elements, local or immigrant, the imperial government was almost always forced to take sides between them. Even Dominion status did not prevent some sections of the population from looking for protection to the Imperial power, and sometimes constitutional provisions gave such appeals at least a basis for argument even when the power to intervene was lacking. Occasionally the right of intervention was consciously safeguarded. Thus, when in 1922 an amendment was proposed to the draft constitution of the Irish Free State to give the Dail sole legislative authority, it was resisted by the Colonial Office. The precedent might be hurtful elsewhere.[19]

When policy changed or when it was decided to make concessions to local nationalisms, the lot of those who trusted in Imperial support might be an unhappy one. The fate of the Unionists of southern Ireland was not the first example.[20] And even more striking proofs of the ruthlessness of an empire in retreat can be found nearer our own day.[21] The attempt to deal with the problem of looking after the Empire's direct strategic and economic interests while handing over domestic responsibilities to a successor government was sometimes seen clearly enough by the minority in the British establishment who took an older view. As Lord Lloyd* wrote in reference to Egypt:

> Whether we are administering our colonial empire merely for the purposes of trade or merely with some high moral aim, the success of either must depend upon the welfare of the people. It can, in the long run, depend upon nothing else. Once that welfare is ignored every intelligible motive disappears. Independence with safeguards is to my mind a policy which fully justifies the criticism that all the enemies of our Imperial history heap upon us. It appears as an attempt to shirk the responsibilities of government and at the same time to take the profits.[22]

One can follow in minute detail in his correspondence the efforts of the Zionist leader Chaim Weizmann* to convince his colleagues that the British government could be trusted to fulfil the Balfour Declaration. In the end Lord Passfield's* hostile policy forced him out of the leadership.[23]

[19]Sir James Masterton-Smith, the Permanent Under-Secretary to the Colonial Office, wrote to Churchill on 6 October 1922: 'A specific renunciation of legal jurisdiction over one part of H.M. Dominions by the Imperial Parliament, would lead to further extension of the principle, and might be of practical importance when the time came to confer Dominion status on India.' See T. Towey, 'The Legislative Supremacy of the United Kingdom Parliament: An Aspect of Dominion status endangered in 1922', *HJ*, vol. XXVII, (1984), pp. 991 – 6.

[20]Commenting on the fate of the loyalists after the American war of independence, Joseph Chamberlain wrote: 'It is curious how often in our history we have made our terms with rebels and left our loyal subjects in the lurch. We have suffered less than we deserved for what is both a crime and a folly.' Letter to Lady Dilke, 24 February 1901, in the possession of Mr John Sparrow.

[21]The effects of the sudden withdrawal of imperial power in countries where substantial elements had identified themselves with British rule or relied upon British protection was a preoccupation of the writer John Connell, and was a theme stressed in his unpublished work, *Retreat from Empire*. He gave it fictional treatment in his novel *Time and Chance* (London, 1952).

[22]Lord Lloyd, *Egypt since Cromer*, vol. 2 (London, Macmillan, 1934), p. 359. Another instance was the grant of independence to Iraq in 1932 with its fatal consequences for the Assyrians and for the Jews of Baghdad. See E. Kedourie, *The Chatham House Version and other Middle Eastern Studies* (London, Weidenfeld & Nicolson, 1970), ch. X, 'Minorities'.

While in dealing with any issues that arose in the Empire, Dominion susceptibilities of different kinds might need to be taken into account, so too might the opinions of foreign governments.[24] It has been argued that one major line of division between policy makers in London was between those who saw the Commonwealth as mainly a source of extra weight to Britain's own international diplomacy and those who saw the maintenance of the Commonwealth itself and its evolution as the primary concern of British policy.[25] It is however the case that the precise weight to be attached to the Commonwealth factor is difficult to assess, not only in terms of military policy but also in relation to the diplomatic crises of the inter-war period. In part this is the result of the traditional separation between the study of 'foreign policy' or diplomatic history and the study of Commonwealth affairs. When the documents are brought together it would seem that the imperial or Commonwealth factor was a more powerful one than has often been allowed.[26]

One needs to remind oneself that while it is now correct to regard the British Empire as something in the past and the Commonwealth as an existing organisation, it was possible as late as 1943 for a major historian of the Empire-Commonwealth to use the two terms interchangeably, since he believed that the British Commonwealth should be seen as the whole Empire in the light of its progress towards self-government.[27] And with this in mind the view that in the inter-war period we are dealing with what those responsible for its guidance saw as a single system becomes easier to defend.

For most practical men, whether in Whitehall or at Westminster, one did what came to hand with whatever resources were available, and the same is true of the Dominion governments, for whom the Commonwealth connoted much more the nature of their relationships with Britain than those with its other members.

[23]See *The Letters and Papers of Chaim Weizmann*, Series A, Letters, vols X to XV (New Brunswick and Jerusalem, 1977 – 8).

[24]Arguing in May 1922 in favour of a judicial inquiry into the disorders in Ulster, Lloyd George remarked: 'We are not a Protestant or a Catholic or even, as some tried to make us, a Mohammedan Empire. We were bound to be sternly impartial. It was very important to carry the dominions with us, to carry America and to carry the outside world.' Cabinet meeting, 30 May 1922, Public Record Office (PRO) CAB 23/30.

[25]R.F. Holland, *Britain and the Commonwealth Alliance 1918–1939* (London, 1981).

[26]See e.g. Max Beloff, 'The Imperial Factor in Appeasement' in *Culture, Science et dévelopment: mélanges en l'honneur de Charles Morazé* (Toulouse, Privat, 1979).

[27]W.K. Hancock, *Argument of Empire* (London, Penguin, 1943), and *Survey of Commonwealth Affairs*, vol. I (London, 1937), pp. 60 – 1. See J.D.B. Miller, 'Hancock, Mansergh and the Commonwealth Surveys', *Historical Studies*, (Melbourne), vol. 13, no. 51 (October 1968).

Of Dominion leaders, only the ex-rebel Smuts had a view of the Empire-Commonwealth as a whole. And among British statesmen it was by and large only those whose experiences went back to the first world war or earlier who took an imperial view. Of course there were efforts to direct public opinion or at least informed opinion towards the Empire-Commonwealth. The Royal Colonial Institute, which became the Royal Empire Society in 1928 (and the Royal Commonwealth Society in 1958), put much effort into bringing the Empire and Commonwealth into the curriculum both at the university and the school level. The celebration of Empire Day was also an occasion for focussing interest in the Empire and its products. It is germane to the discussion of the nomenclature of this period that when in 1934 the London County Council proposed that it should be renamed Commonwealth Day, the chairman of the Royal Empire Society described this as a grave mistake:

> Commonwealth Day assumes that the British Empire is only composed of what is known as the Commonwealth of Nations, those great self-governing Dominions and eliminates from the mind of the child the fact that he or she is the trustee of the great heritage of your Crown Colonies, Protectorates and Mandated Territories.[28]

It is notable that India was not referred to at all.

The academic study of the Empire-Commonwealth was indeed expanded during this period, notably at Oxford, Cambridge and London. In Oxford in particular the visible evidence of Empire in the Indian Institute building dating from an earlier period (built with money from India and now abandoned to meaner uses), and the Rhodes House of Sir Herbert Baker, architect of the government buildings at Pretoria and of the Secretariat buildings in New Delhi, provided a background in which such studies could flourish even if only as a minority interest.[29]

[28]Trevor R. Reese, *The History of the Royal Commonwealth Society, 1868–1968* (London, Oxford University Press, 1968), pp. 157–8. The omission of India is the more curious since by that time the Society had a number of Indian members: ibid., p. 136. See also S.R. Mehrotra, 'On the use of the term Commonwealth', *Journal of Commonwealth Political Studies (JCPS)* (Leicester), vol. II, (1963), pp. 1–16.

[29]For Baker, see R.G. Irving, *Indian Summer: Lutyens, Baker and Imperial Delhi* (Yale University Press, 1981). For Oxford generally in this context, see F. Madden and D.K. Fieldhouse (eds) *Oxford and the Idea of Commonwealth* (London, 1982), and R. Symonds, *Oxford and Empire* (London, 1986).

At a bread and butter level, the Empire Marketing Board first concentrated on the British Market for imperial produce, and later upon propaganda for British trade overseas. But the economic difficulties of the early 1930s ensured that its life would be a short one.[30] Could so amorphous a system, economic as well as political, lend itself to purposeful projection? The answer would seem to be negative.

An amorphous system may nevertheless exist, and that there was a British world system no traveller by sea (or later air) was likely to forget. Even though self-government had been attained by some of its members by 1921 and was to be sought by others, the system was one throughout the period in which allegiance was owed by all to the British crown. And over much of the area in question, the British Parliament still claimed and exercised sovereign legislative power. For many purposes the judicial committee of the Privy Council remained the supreme tribunal. Since free institutions were thought to be what distinguished the British experience from that of its rivals and competitors, the idea of a gradual accession to self-governing status without a weakening of the capacities for common action was perhaps understandable. It was a hope that overlooked some aspects of the situation and the portents they conveyed. It was to be proved false by later experience, but for the present volume it does not seem inappropriate to look at the process as a 'Dream of Commonwealth'.

[30]On the Empire Marketing Board and subsequent developments in the projection of Britain abroad, see J.M. Lee, 'The Dissolution of the Empire Marketing Board 1933: Reflections on a Diary', *Journal of Imperial and Commonwealth History (JICH)* (London) I, (1972), pp. 49 – 57, and P.M. Taylor, *The Projection of Britain: British Overseas Publicity and Propaganda 1919-1939* (Cambridge University Press, 1981), pp. 102 – 9.

Chapter 2

THE EMPIRE IN 1921: INTERNAL STRAINS
AND EXTERNAL PRESSURES

Democracy and Empire

In 1915 the Royal Colonial Institute set as the theme for its research monograph for the year, the applicability of the claim by the Athenian demagogue Cleon, as recorded by Thucydides, that 'a Democracy cannot manage an Empire' to the 'present conditions and future problems of the British Empire, especially the question of the future of India'. The winning entry was published in the following year, by which time it was clear to the author, as to his countrymen at large, that the struggle in which the Empire was engaged would have major effects both upon Britain itself and upon its other constituent parts.[1] The text reflects both the mood of the time and the light the war had thrown upon Britain's lack of preparedness in some areas, and the extent to which it was possible to identify some at least of what would prove to be the major problems of the post-war years.

While history appeared to justify Cleon's dictum where past empires were concerned, the author was sufficiently heartened by the rallying of the Empire in support of the mother-country's struggle to look with some optimism to the future, provided only that the British democracy did not shirk from the tasks that Empire presented. Some of the author's prescriptions were removed from political reality both at the time and in respect of the future – the idea for instance that imperial defence and imperial fiscal policy could be taken out of the domain of party politics. Equally far from the attitudes developing in the Dominions was the idea of expanding the Committee of Imperial Defence (C.I.D.) into a permanent instrument for controlling part of the defence effort of the Empire as well as of Britain which might be pooled for common imperial purposes. Other passages showed an appreciation of what the problems were, without being able to provide solutions for them more precise than the spread of a better understanding

[1] A.E. Duchesne, *Democracy and Empire* (London, Oxford University Press, 1916).

16

through education and a widening of the imperial experience of individual citizens.

The author was particularly struck by the damage being done to the imperial idea by the strength and persistence of race prejudice which he thought of particularly as affecting actual or potential Indian emigration to other parts of the Empire: 'The citizen of the Empire must be taken by his fellow citizens at his worth as a man without any tinge of race, colour or creed prejudices.' For India's need for an outlet for her surplus population, he could only suggest that in East Africa and the Sudan 'there would be room for many millions of Indian workers who would add to the wealth of the tracts they occupied'.[2] If the question of mass emigration were settled, the Dominions might withdraw their objections to Indians and Chinese 'of standing' visiting or even settling in them. Meanwhile British emigration to the Dominions should be stimulated with vigour.

In dealing with the future of India itself, the author reflected the kind of thinking that was to inspire the Montagu-Chelmsford reforms a few years later. India and Britain had need of each other and this meant that, for the forseeable future, final authority in major matters must rest with the British government, though giving an increasing role to the Viceroy and his advisers on the spot at the expense of the Secretary of State. Indeed the war seemed to suggest a larger rather than a smaller role for the Indian element in imperial defence. On the other hand, Britain's role in India could not be justified unless it was for the good of the people. For this reason, complete fiscal autonomy should be accorded to her to help her to adjust to an imperial trading system for which Britain should work, even at the cost of abandoning her free trade prejudices. This assimilation of India to the position of the Dominions should be assisted by the creation of a separate department for the Dominions and India, with the Colonial Secretary only responsible for the crown colonies and protectorates.

For all the familiar reasons, the Dominion model was held to be inappropriate for India where its internal government was concerned. The structure of Indian society, which Britain was bound to respect, would make a mockery of direct elections on a broad franchise; nor, as experience showed, was majority rule possible in a country where such deep religious and caste divisions

[2] Ibid., pp. 33, 78 – 9.

existed. Yet since Indians were bound to claim, and rightly, a greater share in running their own affairs, an extensive measure of provincial autonomy represented the only way forward.

By the time of the Imperial Conference of 1921, it was possible to see the extent to which scepticism about the ability of a democracy to manage an Empire was finding new justification.[3] The democracies of the dominions were asserting their own individual needs and approaches and making it more difficult than ever to devise institutions and codes of conduct that would suit all alike. The degree of provincial self-government afforded to India had not detracted from but rather given new opportunities to claims for full political autonomy on a national scale; both the new acquisitions in the Middle East and sections of the population in the colonial empire at large were exhibiting the strength of national, racial and religious sentiments that would challenge, if at different levels of effectiveness, the ability of British governments to guide their policies in a common direction dictated by the needs of the Empire as a whole. Above all, the British democracy itself was less concerned with the management of Empire than with its domestic priorities. It was not so much a question of being able to manage an Empire as whether it wished to do so, or to make the sacrifices that such a vocation would demand.[4] It is not surprising that, looking back from the vantage point of half a century later, an historian is likely to pinpoint the weaknesses in what General Smuts had styled at the Imperial Conference, 'the greatest power in the world'.[5]

The British Empire: a Frenchman's view

If however we look at the British Empire not through the eyes of the statesmen, civil servants and soldiers who were confronting the magnitude of the tasks it presented to them but through those of an external if expert observer, we get a different impression. It was at

[3] For another attempt to look at how things stood in 1921, see Max Beloff, *Imperial Sunset*, vol. 1, *Britain's Liberal Empire* (London, 1969; 2nd edn, 1987), ch. VII, 'Apogee of Empire'.
[4] For the domestic background, see Kenneth O. Morgan, *Consensus and Disunity: the Lloyd George Coalition Government* (Oxford, 1979).
[5] See Corelli Barnett, *The Collapse of British Power* (London, 1972), pt. III, 'The Greatest Power in the World'. In pt. IV, 'An Imperial Commonwealth', the author elaborates his view that the Empire-Commonwealth was more of a drain on British resources than a contributor to them.

this time that a distinguished French geographer embarked upon a study of the British Empire and the relevant literature and produced a survey of its demographic, economic and political potential and problems.[6]

To this foreign observer, the British Empire with its original trading and maritime base enhanced by its recent territorial acquisitions, and with its capacity for common action increased through the development of the maritime cable network, the expansion of railway systems and now potentially through the new aerial routes, was still a formidable element on the world scene. He noted that there was indeed some evidence that the British people were now more concerned with domestic comforts than with pioneering under alien skies, but saw evidence in the other direction in the renewal of emigration to the Dominions. Naval strength was still supported by the possession of a high proportion of the world's merchant shipping, as well as of so many of the key points for supply and trans-shipment. London still possessed the means to raise the capital required for the major projects – railways and irrigation works – upon which other parts of the Empire relied for their economic advancement. In the light of these facts, and despite the political problems it created, the new Empire of the Middle East was seen as a natural extension of the defences of India, and as the strengthening of the bridge between Britain's long-standing presence in the Mediterranean and Indian Ocean, to whose command major importance should be attached.

Unlike some domestic observers, the Frenchman was impressed not by the indifference of the British to their empire but by the extent to which its existence was part of the daily experience of Britons in all walks of life. The Englishman suffers, he observes, if he feels his country taken up with the affairs of the European continent, and is content only when he looks out over the ocean. The will to maintain the Empire and even to strengthen it was not absent. The difficulty was that measures in this direction would run counter to the most obvious aspect of recent imperial history, the development of an individual outlook on the part of each of the Dominions. Indeed, he saw a paradox in the discussion of methods for strengthening the unity of the whole having come to the fore just at the time when facts were pointing in the opposite direction. He felt that the

[6] See Albert Demangeon, *L'Empire Britannique* (Paris, 1923).

19

discussion of European affairs at the 1921 Imperial Conference – the Silesian question for instance – signified a new departure. On the other hand, he rightly saw that the interest of the Dominions in European matters was a secondary one; what was important was not merely their nationalisms but their own local imperialisms – claims for territory or influence beyond their borders as individual nations; Canada in the West Indies, Australia and New Zealand in the Pacific, South Africa to its north. Indeed he took for granted that the destiny of the Rhodesias lay in incorporation in the Union.

While the future relations between Britain and the Dominions would rest upon consent, the case of India was fundamentally different since the ties of race and sentiment were absent and since British authority rested ultimately upon force. After the promulgation of the post-war reforms, it was clear that the process started by the grant of provincial autonomy was unlikely to end at that point. The author noted that the Indianisation of the administration would further isolate the remaining British civil servants and make it difficult to recruit their successors. How long in these circumstances British rule could survive and what form a post-British India might take were open questions. Nor indeed was the growth of nationalism likely to be restricted to India; it was already to be perceived in many other parts of the Empire and would receive an added impetus, particularly in the Middle East, from the new status accorded to Egypt. And with what was to prove a highly prescient remark, he pointed out that one should not ignore the increasing importance of the Islamic revival for an Empire which now incorporated the majority of the world's followers of that faith.

The British Empire: the insiders' view

For both a native and a foreign observer, it was possible to take apart the separate elements of the imperial problem, and subject them to analysis in the light of publicly known facts and of such historical analogies as seemed pertinent. But if one attempts to see how the issues presented themselves to those who had to make the decisions on a day-to-day basis – statemen, civil servants, the hard-pressed military – the impression is necessarily a different one. In the period between the dispersal of the Imperial Conference in August 1921 and the fall of the Lloyd George government in 1922, imperial problems fell to be handled along with the other international issues arising from the unfinished business of the peace conference, the challenge of the Russian Revolution and the negotiations in Washington for the limitation of naval armaments and for a new regime in the Far East. Anxieties over the economic situation at home and the actuality or threat of industrial action also pressed their claims for ministerial attention, as did events in Ireland both before and after the signature of the Anglo-Irish Treaty on 6 December 1921. The questions that came up before the cabinet or individual ministers could not be treated in the considered way that would commend itself to the academic mind. They were precipitated not by the government's own actions and policies but by events largely beyond its control or even its influence. All were urgent and some indeed so much so that the initiative had to be taken by the proconsul or other representative on the spot. It was not a tidy picture, and made even less so when party and personal rivalries also played a not insignificant part.

While there were of course differences in the outlooks of the principal figures – their imperialism came in very different shades – they had in common a commitment to maintaining the system and their own central role within it. Despite the fading of the hopes of 1917 – 18 that some system of co-operative decision making with the Dominions might continue into peacetime, they still assumed that they and the Dominion governments shared common interests and would if occasion arose be able to devise common strategies. They might differ as to the speed at which, if at all, a greater measure of self-government should be accepted for India and to what degree; none seriously considered that India should pass outside the imperial system. What further united them was a common appreciation of the inevitable interaction of one part of the system with another and the consequent need to reckon that a decision taken in relation to one part of it would inevitably create precedents to be appealed to by another. If the Irish Free State could enjoy Dominion status why not India? If white settlers in Rhodesia could be given a large measure of autonomy, why not white settlers in Kenya? Nor should one forget that this habit of thinking across geographical divides was fortified by the fact that the constitutions even of those Dominions most insistent upon their status as independent members of the

21

Commonwealth were the products of the legislative process of the imperial Parliament and still very largely subject to interpretation by the Privy Council in its judicial capacity.

What distinguished Britain from the other self-governing or partially self-governing constituents of the Empire-Commonwealth was precisely the fact that by and large the latter tended inevitably to take a narrower view. They had at the moment of crisis in 1914 rallied with different degrees of enthusiasm and commitment to the call of the King-Emperor from New Zealand at one extreme to South Africa at the other; they certainly felt that one advantage of the imperial link was protection against external enemies, but they did not see this as implying a permanent commitment of their own men or money to a common defence.[7] Still less were they prepared to modify their own internal policies – in economic matters or in questions of immigration and race relations – in order to avoid embarrassing a general imperial interest.

It had already been clear enough in wartime to a well-placed observer that this was going to be the case. The Dominions, wrote John X. Merriman, the former premier of the Cape, to Lord Bryce on 21 May 1917,

> will take anything you will give them but when it comes to the question of giving, either in kind or by way of surrendering their prejudices, you will find them kittle-kattle to deal with. Take the question of the British Indians. I question whether the patriotism of any single Dominion will stretch so far as to give these people the rights of British citizens, though they are quite conscious of the fact that every instance of harsh dealing may raise terrible difficulties in India itself. The same thing applies to the Mongolian races...[8]

On an issue of this kind even Smuts, who took a broader view of the Commonwealth's potential than other Dominion leaders, could not escape from the prejudices inherent in his upbringing.[9]

[7] In December 1918, the Australian Prime Minister W.M. Hughes had argued that Australian troops should take part in the occupation of Germany, but keeping their men overseas did not remain for long a desire of his own or other Dominion governments. See Keith Jeffery (ed.), *The Military Correspondence of Field-Marshal Sir Henry Wilson, 1918–1922* (London, 1985), 58–9.

[8] Merriman to Bryce, 21 May 1917, in P. Lewsen, (ed.), *Selections from the Correspondence of John X. Merriman*, vol. 4 (Cape Town, Van Riebeeck Society, 1969).

[9] For a recent study of Smuts emphasising his Boer heritage, see Kenneth Ingham, *Jan Christian Smuts: The Conscience of a South African* (London, 1986).

22

It was certainly not to be expected that Australians would modify the 'White Australia' policy in order to ease Britain's path in Far Eastern diplomacy, yet Australia was not prepared to take any major share in meeting the new calls upon imperial defence that Japanese hostility might entail; and even less could be expected from Canada even though the Canadians had been foremost in advocating the abrogation of the Anglo-Japanese alliance which Australia and New Zealand had regarded as the best guarantee of their security.

For these reasons as well as because of the priority attached to contingencies within the British Isles themselves, the principal questioning of Britain's world role, including the new imperial terrain in the Middle East, came not from politicians of the 'Little England' school, who were a minority even on the Left, but from the military. From the armistice to the fall of Lloyd George it was the conviction of Field-Marshal Sir Henry Wilson, Chief of the Imperial General Staff (C.I.G.S.) until the end of 1921, and his principal associates and confidants, including Lord Rawlinson, Commander-in-Chief in India from November 1920, that Britain's strength was too thinly stretched and that the Army was being asked to do more than was reasonable.[10] A useful though misleadingly titled recent work details the size, make up and equipment of the forces available for imperial purposes in the inter-war period and gives an account of the engagements in which they were concerned. Because the contingents were usually small and casualties relatively light, the extent to which actual fighting was going on at one spot or another and the degree to which the assistance of the military to uphold the civil power was required at home and abroad has generally been underestimated by historians of the Empire-Commonwealth.[11]

No doubt some of the alarmism was tactical, particularly in the light of the pressure for cuts in expenditure that came to a head with the Geddes Report of 14 December 1921. By then the combined efforts of the War Office, the Treasury and the India Office had put an end to the 'forward policy' for the defence of India with the withdrawal of British units from southern Russia and northern Persia. But the strain continued to be felt.

[10] Keith Jeffery, *The British Army and the Crisis of Empire, 1918–1922* (Manchester University Press, 1984).
[11] A. Clayton, *The British Empire as a Super-Power, 1919–1939* (London, 1986).

As always demands from one part of the system had their impact upon the remainder. In India the proportion of British to Indian troops had fallen during the war; it was now felt necessary to increase their numbers again in view of the political uncertainties there, as well as the external threat. At the same time the availability of Indian troops for service outside the sub-continent was becoming more difficult to assure. The Colonial Office was asked to look at the possibility of raising African troops as a substitute. Churchill at the War Office was favourable, although the mandate provisions were held to exclude Tanganykia as a possible source of recruits. Early in 1921 the matter was raised again in relation to the problem of upholding the British authority in Mesopotamia but met with strong opposition from the commander-in-chief on the spot who felt that it would be strongly resented by the Arabs. In the end some Indian troops together with Royal Air Force support proved sufficient for the task.

The Middle East and wider implications

The political futures of Egypt as well as of Trans-Jordan and Palestine all had their military corollaries; the demand for the repatriation of Indian troops from Allenby's command which embraced all three helped to increase the pressure for a political solution at least in Egypt. The concessions of formal independence by the Allenby declaration of 26 February 1922 reserved imperial responsibility for the defence of the country and for the Suez Canal whose importance in imperial communications had been stressed by Dominion representatives at the Imperial Conference. For the time being the British garrison was reduced to the pre-war level, but keeping it at this level depended upon political fair winds and no renewal of an external threat. And while Trans-Jordan presented no immediate problem, Palestine, the focus of conflicting claims and national aspirations, continued to demand a substantial military effort.

The reluctance to accept a situation in which imperial security depended upon negotiations with governments depending on nationalist opinion in South Africa and Egypt, and increasingly in India, was understandable. The Esher Committee on the future of the Army in India appointed in 1919 had reported in 1920 that the

Indian Army should be organised so as to fulfil imperial needs.[12] But by now such a view was politically unacceptable.

The correspondence of Field-Marshal Wilson illustrates to the full the animosity of some military chiefs to what they thought were political decisions that made unnecessary additional calls upon the military in the immediate aftermath of the war.[13] Some, like the intervention in Russia and the policing of Silesia, were to prove temporary. Some, like the preference shown by Lloyd George and the cabinet for the Greeks as against the Turks, ran into the contrary preference by the soldiers, to which the outcome of the confrontation at Chanak in 1922 was to give some backing. Wilson saw the possibility of the Turks and Afghans forming a useful block against Bolshevik pressures. He also deplored the retreat in Egypt and above all, with his Ulster background, that from Ireland, and felt that strength was being wasted upon the unnecessary extension to the Empire in the Middle East. Above all, Wilson and his friends, in whom anti-semitism and anti-Bolshevism combined to fortify their strategic assessment, deplored the Balfour Declaration and believed that the decision to support the building of the Jewish National home was a principal cause of the over-extension of British military strength. On the other hand, the idea that the army could be replaced in its imperial role by the Royal Air Force (R.A.F.) seemed absurd. Order could not be maintained through the threat of aerial bombardment, only by forces on the ground. Besides, the R.A.F. had no officers suitable for a mixed civil-military role; they were not really officers at all, 'only chauffeurs'.[14]

To differences of view over policy were added inter-departmental disputes and rivalries. The Foreign Office found itself as a result of the Cairo conference of March 1921 supplanted in respect of the new Middle Eastern acquisitions of the Empire by the Colonial Office, leading its prickly chief Lord Curzon to protest against the

---

[12] *Report of the Committee to inquire into the Administration and Organization of the Army in India*, (Cmd 943, 1920).
[13] Keith Jeffery (ed.) *The Military Correspondence of Field Marshal Sir Henry Wilson, 1918–1922*.
[14] Ibid., p. 283. For the reconstituting of the army in its post-war role, see Brian Bond, *British Military Policy between the Two World Wars* (Oxford, 1980), ch. 1. For the use of the R.A.F. for imperial policing duties, see Malcolm Smith, *British Air Strategy between the Wars* (Oxford, 1984), pp. 28–31.

assumption that the Colonial Secretary had the right to intervene in Egyptian affairs as well.[15]

Not only was there the friction between the War Office and the Air Ministry but also an unresolved problem of the position of the Colonial Office in respect of the troops used in Palestine, Trans-Jordan and Mesopotamia, since these came under the command of Allenby in Egypt and not under the civil representatives of British power in the mandates. Both the War Office and the Colonial Office saw this situation as an anomaly. But in respect of another matter they were at odds. Churchill's tenure of the Colonial Office was marked by strenuous endeavours to cut the cost of maintaining Britain's position in the Middle East. The substitution of local levies with air force backing for British troops was made with this in view. But the War Office felt that the savings should be used to help with other aspects of the military budget whereas Churchill argued that they should be treated as savings on the Colonial Office account. In this way he would be able to undertake some development in the tropical African colonies which he thought more worthwhile than expenditure on the barren sands and ungrateful people of the Middle East.[16]

None of the problems of administration, defence and expenditure could be isolated in an area so exposed to the currents prevailing in the wider world. To stabilise Faisal's rule in Iraq against internal discontents was one thing; to protect it against Turkey, now renewing its strength with Soviet help and not abandoning its claim at least on Mosul and the Kurdish lands was another. The policy of the powers in respect of Turkey might be a matter for the Foreign Office and the Prime Minister; but the Colonial Office could not but wish to have its say. Would Britain's authority among her Islamic subjects be enhanced more by defeating Turkish pretensions or by accepting them? In 1922 the Palestinian Arabs were reported to be encouraged

---

[15] Curzon, memorandum on 'The Situation in Egypt', 21 April 1921, in Martin Gilbert, *Winston S. Churchill*, vol. IV, *Companion*, vol. 3 (London, 1977), pp. 1443 – 7; and Curzon to Churchill, 13 June 1921, ibid., pp. 1503 – 4.

[16] Churchill to Sir Laming Worthington-Evans, 25 June 1921, 4 July 1921, 15 July 1921, ibid., pp. 1519 – 21, 1538, 1553 – 4. Churchill cabinet memoranda, 'Policy and Finance in Mesopotamia, 1922 – 1923', 4 August 1921, and 'The Reductions in the Military Garrison of Mesopotamia', 20 May 1921, ibid., pp. 1576 – 81 and 1471 – 2; Churchill to Lloyd George, 25 May 1921, ibid., pp. 1474-5.

by the Turkish victories over the Greeks and the subsequent allied abandonment of the Treaty of Sévres.[17]

In trying to balance these conflicting views and similar difficulties inherent in the pursuit of a new stability in world and imperial affairs, the political pressures at home were in one sense not too formidable. The revulsion on the left against the power politics that were thought ultimately responsible for the world struggle that had just ended was for the time being subsumed in adherence to the League of Nations ideal and did not for the most part affect attitudes towards Britain's own imperial role. Nationalist movements in India and elsewhere would be treated sympathetically by British politicians and publicists of a Labour or Liberal orientation, but except for a tiny minority on the far left mainly finding their home in the Communist Party of Great Britain, created in August 1920 under the auspices of the Third International, they did not seek to stimulate such movements or to direct their paths. They did not generally assume that the dismantling of the imperial system was something for the near future, nor had they made any systematic inquiry as to the likely impact of such a development upon Britain's own economic and social fortunes. In general therefore some degree of continuity seemed assured.

The real political problem, as Sir Henry Wilson and his friends realised, lay rather in the plea for economy and for the curtailment of government expenditure that seemed to statesmen of the right and centre the only way towards restoring the country's financial and economic health. Policies, however well argued, that seemed to imply continuing expenditure whether upon defence or upon developing the infrastructure of dependent territories were looked at with increasing mistrust, stimulated by the 'anti-waste' campaigns of the popular press. There was thus always an inducement to follow the line of concessions to both external and internal pressures, even if this meant achieving short-term alleviation for the Empire's problems at the expense of storing up trouble for the future. To those actually responsible on the ground, facing either foreign pressures or nationalist agitation the outlook often seemed bleak. Bonar Law was to herald his return to politics and ultimately his supplanting of Lloyd George by his letter to the *Times* on 7 October 1922 in which he wrote 'We cannot alone act as the policeman of the world', and

[17] General Tudor to Churchill, 22 October 1922, ibid., pp. 2090 – 1.

in this he was in accord with majority sentiment at home.[18] But for proconsuls who for the time being had to act as policemen matters looked very different.[19]

It was recognised that the British Empire had to rest upon a mixture of consent based upon a perception of the advantages to be accepted from its continuance, and of force so certain and overwhelming as to make overt challenges unlikely, and certain to fail if attempted. Both approaches were affected by the resources made available from the metropolis and by the continuous tradition in Britain's imperial expansion that all dependent territories should be self-supporting, and where possible contribute to the strength of the system as a whole. In so far as the politically aware classes in dependencies could be associated with the imperial regime this was looked upon as a source of strength. But this collaboration had been rendered more difficult by the excitement generated by the war which had stimulated nationalist movements, and by the uncertainties of those groups and classes who were used to such collaboration as to whether they could rely upon the support of the imperial power if challenged. British assumptions about the superiority of the British race, which tended to be enhanced through immersion in alien environments in Asia and Africa, were another factor of growing importance; but it would be wrong to see this factor as more than a contributing one. The difference of view between periphery and centre was equally to the fore in dealing with the already self-governing Dominions or with the claims of settler communities in East and Central Africa.

Ireland and imperial implications

In 1921, as the struggle for independence proceeded towards its temporary resolution in the treaty of 5 December, it was Ireland that best illustrated every aspect of the imperial dilemma.[20] The

[18] Robert Blake, *The Unknown Prime Minister: Andrew Bonar Law* (London, 1955), pp. 447 – 8.
[19] Even a non-imperially-minded press magnate could see this. Lord Northcliffe wrote in his diary on 31 January 1922: 'It has been my lot lately to stay in four houses in which my host has been labouring under intense anxiety – Government House, Ceylon; Viceregal Lodge, Delhi; Bombay, Cairo. This British Empire business is no easy job.' Lord Northcliffe, *My Journey Round the World* (London, John Lane, 1923), pp. 264 – 5.
[20] For the negotiations which led up to the Treaty see Frank Pakenham (the Earl of Longford), *Peace by Ordeal* (London, 1935); F.S.L. Lyons, *Ireland since the Famine* (London, 1971), 398 ff; Robert Key, *The Green Flag* (London, 1972), 651 ff.

settlement arrived at was based, like that in South Africa in 1910, upon the belief that some sacrifices were necessary if reconciliation was to be achieved. In the South African case this had meant abstention from further imperial intervention on behalf of its non-white communities; in the Irish case, it meant the abandonment of the southern unionists, whose political influence in London was large enough for reaction against the Treaty to be an additional factor in the fall of the Lloyd George government. Ulster unionism was however given the guarantee of territorial separation with its own political institutions and continued incorporation with the United Kingdom. In this sense there is a parallel between Ulster and what became the three High Commission territories in South Africa. Exclusion in both cases was expected to be temporary; the unification of Ireland would, like the absorption of the Territories into the Union of South Africa, be only a matter of time, to await the cooling of prejudices and the triumph of reason.[21]

The external impact upon the British negotiators of the Irish Treaty was an important one. No British politician could fail to appreciate the importance of the Irish-American vote at a time when so much depended upon achieving satisfactory arrangements with the United States over debts, disarmament and the Far East. But there was also a Commonwealth factor. Lord Beaverbrook supported conciliation in Ireland, he was to claim, because he was 'convinced that Empire Unity waited upon the reconciliation of Irish elements in Canada and Australia, who refused co-operation with Britain, until as they believed, Irish wrongs were put right'.[22] In respect of South Africa, where the Irish question was not to the fore, the important thing was believed to be a strengthening of the British element so as to perpetuate in office the coalition that Smuts and Botha had created and keep at bay the more dedicated nationalists under Hertzog*. For this reason the proper destiny of Southern Rhodesia as the South African Company's charter approached exhaustion was held to

[21] 'My earnest hope is that North and South may come together as the years pass by in some form or other which they will themselves devise.' Churchill to J.C. Robertson, 27 October 1922, Gilbert, op. cit., p. 2095. For the High Commission territories and South Africa's pressure for their incorporation, see R. Hyam, *Failure of South African Expansion 1908–1948* (London, 1972); M.Chanock, *Unconsummated Union – Britain, Rhodesia and South Africa* (Manchester, 1977).

[22] Lord Beaverbrook, *The Decline and Fall of Lloyd George* (London, Collins, 1963), p. 108.

be union with South Africa rather than a handover to settler rule. In 1921 the prospect of this being found acceptable seemed high; it was not held in London that the native population would suffer, and there were good financial reasons for wishing to get rid of this particular area of imperial responsibility.[23] But the elected members of the Legislative Council were pressing for full responsible government as their preferred outcome[24] and they may have been influenced by the belief that so far from the Rhodesians injecting a pro-British element into the politics of the Union, once inside it they might themselves be swamped by Boer immigrants. The defeat of the project of incorporation into the Union in the Southern Rhodesian referendum of October 1922 was thus foreshadowed.

In East Africa there was a clash between the Colonial Office as trustee both for the white settler communities and for the native peoples, and the Government of India with its continued interest in the welfare of the Indians settled there. By the time Churchill succeeded Milner as Colonial Secretary in February 1921, India had abandoned its hope of being chosen as the mandatory for Tanganyika, and the prospect of an Indian East African Empire disappeared.[25]

Although the 1921 Imperial Conference had accepted, over Smuts' objections, a resolution acknowledging 'an incongruity between the position of India as an equal member of the British Empire and the existence of disabilities upon British Indians lawfully domiciled in some other parts of the British Empire', and although Churchill during his first year in office attempted to act in East Africa in the spirit of this resolution, he acknowledged the strength of the local white opposition, and from the beginning of 1922 was to accept the priority of their interests.[26] The adverse impact upon India was

[23] Chanock, op. cit., pp. 152 – 3.
[24] Claire Palley, *The Constitutional History and Law of Southern Rhodesia, 1888 – 1965* (Oxford, 1966), 191 ff.
[25] The relationships between the Indian communities and other races in East Africa and between the Indian and the Imperial governments are fully set out in R.G. Gregory, *India and East Africa: a history of Race Relations within the British Empire, 1890 – 1939* (Oxford, 1971).
[26] 'The Indians in East Africa', he wrote, 'are mainly of a very low class of coolies, and the idea that they should be put on an equality with the Europeans is revolting to every white man throughout British Africa.' Churchill to Montagu, 8 October 1921, Gilbert, op. cit., p. 1644.

something which was well appreciated by those responsible for ruling her.[27]

Differences between the Dominions

A different source of imperial discord related to the distinction between the Dominions themselves in respect of Britain's future foreign and defence policies. South Africa, having secured the elimination of German military and naval power from the African continent, saw no need to involve herself in further international entanglements and was through Smuts – the only Dominion statesman with a strong influence on the British political elite – already casting itself as the voice of appeasement where Germany was concerned. Canada, satisfied with the protection of the United States and determined to align her policy upon that of her powerful neighbour, was likewise in favour of the maximum of British disengagement, though less prone to give her advice in any public way. Australia and New Zealand were in a different position. They had a greater interest in Europe, their principal market, and with the movement towards the abrogation of the Anglo-Japanese alliance had an interest in facilitating new measures of defence so as to ensure the support of Britain and her naval strength should Japan ever come to menace them.[28]

By 1921 it had been agreed that since finance did not permit the maintenance of a main fleet in the Pacific, it would be necessary to build and maintain a naval base at Singapore so that naval forces could be transferred to the Far East from home or Mediterranean waters. Indeed, the project was accepted

[27] e.g. Reading to Montagu, 6 February 1922, ibid., p. 1756. In relation to the position of Indians in South Africa itself, the Indian Government was prepared to act as the vehicle for Indian indignation and did so at the League of Nations Assembly in 1922. 'It was made clear to the League that India was free to express her own views and was not merely a mouthpiece of Her Majesty's Government. There was something rather piquant in the fact of one part of the Empire criticising another part and it gave reality to the proceedings.' Chelmsford to Peel, 3 October 1922, India Office Library and Records (IOLR), MSS EUR E.238/5.

[28] The Anglo-Japanese Alliance was allowed to lapse as a result of the conclusion of the Four-Power Far Eastern Pact at the Washington Conference of 1921 – 2. The view that the abrogation of the alliance titled the balance in Japan towards a more aggressive and expansionist policy is implicit in F.S.G. Piggott, *The Broken Thread* (Aldershot, 1950), and in Malcolm D. Kennedy, *The Estrangement of Britain and Japan* (Manchester, 1969). See also Ian H. Nish, *Alliance in Decline – a study in Anglo-Japanese Relations, 1908–1923* (London, 1972).

31

even when it was still hoped that the Anglo-Japanese Alliance could be kept in being.[29] From the beginning, Treasury opposition to the scheme was constant and unrelenting.[30] When agreeing in principle to build the base while accepting that no funds would be available for the next two years, the Cabinet was moved by political as much as by strategic considerations, since it was argued by Balfour that the scheme would not only assist with the defence of India and the Australasian Dominions and western Canada, but that the existence of such a scheme would counterbalance the American claim to be the protector of western civilisation and increase British influence with the Dominions.[31]

The most immediate and visible source of trouble for the dependent Empire remained the possibilities for Soviet subversion. The British withdrawal from Transcaucasia and Persia and the acquiescence in a Soviet presence in Afghanistan had been the effect of domestic financial and political considerations, not of any profound belief that Soviet hostility was no longer to be taken for granted. In late 1920, at the time of the negotiation of the Anglo-Soviet trade agreement signed in March 1921, it was Curzon's view that the 'renewed lease of life' which it would give the regime would be 'consecrated to no purpose more unswervingly than to the subversion and destruction of the British connection with the Indian Empire'.[32]

It was obvious that the British and Indian governments, with whatever assistance they could get from elsewhere in the Empire, would at least wish to maintain a watchful eye upon its agents. An imperial chain of intelligence with the Dominions had been inaugurated during the war and was later expanded to include colonial territories as well.[33] The intelligence services like the armed forces had then to substitute themselves and their own professional links for the political will to unity which was so often absent.[34]

[29] See Ian Hamill, *The Strategic Illusion – the Singapore Strategy and the Defence of Australia and New Zealand* (Singapore, 1981).

[30] See M. Beloff, 'The Whitehall Factor: The Role of the Higher Civil Service in 1919 – 1939', in G.R. Peele and C. Cook (eds), *The Politics of Reappraisal* (London, 1975).

[31] Cabinet conclusions, 16 June 1921, Public Record Office (PRO) CAB 23/26.

[32] R.H. Ullman, *The Anglo-Soviet Accord* (Anglo-Soviet Relations, 1917 – 1923, vol. III (Princeton, N.J., 1972), p. 472; memorandum of 14 November 1920, quoted ibid., pp. 416 – 7.

[33] See Christopher Andrew, *Secret Service: The Making of the British Intelligence Community* (London, 1985), pp. 242 – 7, 363.

In 1921, at the first Imperial Conference of the post-war era, all the familiar obstacles to the system acting as a single entity were plainly visible. Imperialists like Seeley had pinned their hopes on the federal principle uniting the mother-country with her own colonies of settlement; but this had been shown to ignore the fact that such colonies would develop quite different views of their own as to how their future should be seen. Nor had the vision taken in the fact that most of the Empire's population did not consist of British settlers and their descendants but of peoples of an infinite variety of colours, creeds and cultures. Above all, Seeley had like his successors failed to envisage a role for India in an Empire united on federal lines.[35] For British ministers, officials and military men, the assumptions of daily life were still those of a single system, and to the extent that each problem, economic, constitutional or military, interlocked with others, this was no more than a recognition of fact. What in the last resort, they asked, would the British taxpayer pay for or the British Parliament enact? But similar questions were being asked of their own taxpayers and legislators by the Dominion statesmen and increasingly by Indian Viceroys and colonial governors. Nor for most of these was there much support from an imperial element in the thinking of their electorates or their elites. They felt different pressures and responded in different ways.

[34] For the naval aspect see S. Roskill, *Naval Policy between the Wars*, vol. 1, 1919 – 1929 (London, 1968).
[35] See D. Wormell, *Sir John Seeley and the Uses of History* (Cambridge, 1980), ch. 6.

Chapter 3

BRITAIN AS A MIDDLE EASTERN POWER

PART I: THE FRENCH CONNECTION

Anglo-French imperial interdependence

The almost simultaneous collapse of the European overseas empires after the second world war must suggest to the historian that their ability to sustain themselves until then had to some extent rested upon a common world system that made such survival possible. On the other hand, the acquisition of overseas territories had been the fruit of rivalry only occasionally tempered by diplomacy, and one of the results of the first world war had been a redistribution of colonies to the advantage of the victors. Once the political map had been stabilised in 1921 – 2 with the allocation and entering into force of the mandates, the longevity of the surviving empires was not seriously called into question. The only immediate doubts were over the future of the Portuguese colonies in Africa, which were in fact to be among the longest to remain under European rule – a case of 'first in, last out'.[1]

What was of more immediate concern to European statesmen and their agents on the spot was whether the long-standing Anglo-French rivalries in Africa and the Far East would now be paralleled by new rivalries arising from the course of events in the Middle East.[2] It took

[1] It was not that the inhabitants of the Portuguese colonies in Africa were thought likely to be given independence but that the degree of misgovernment was held to be such that 'the conscience of the civilised world' would one day demand they be handed over to another Power – most probably South Africa. Memorandum of 10 April 1926 on 'The Foreign Policy of His Majesty's Government with a list of British commitments in their relative order of importance', *Documents of British Foreign Policy (DBFP)*, Series 1A, vol. I (London, 1966).

[2] On rivalry between Britain and France in China in the 1890s there is interesting material in a study of Paul Claudel's career in the French consular service. Gilbert Gadoffre, *Claudel et l'Univers Chinois* (Cahiers Paul Claudel no.8, Paris, 1968). A pioneer study of the rivalry between the two Empires in the Middle East is that of H.H. Cummings, *Franco-British Rivalry in the Post-War Near East* (London, 1938). The element of rivalry is underplayed in Ann Williams, *Britain and France in the Middle East and North Africa* (London, 1968). For the war and immediate post-war periods, see Jukka Nevakivi, *Britain, France and the Arab Middle East* (London, 1969).

an unusual degree of aloofness from popular prejudice to argue as did one eminent right-wing French historian and publicist that, contrary to the general belief, the two empires were mutually dependent.[3]

Much more common was 'that strange atavistic Schadenfreude which affects both French and English when discussing the failures of each other's colonial policy'.[4] For London-based British civil servant advisers it was obvious enough that one should not exaggerate 'the purely parochial importance of the Arab question at the expense of the maintenance of cordial relations with France'.[5] But this subordination of imperial considerations to European diplomacy was less welcome to the men on the spot. The prospect of the break-up of the Ottoman Empire had led to a jostling for influence among the various Arab nationalist groups between French and British agents even before the war.[6] It was not to be expected that the allocation of the mandates agreed upon at San Remo would put an end to such rivalries, the more so since some of the boundaries were poorly demarcated and did not in any event correspond to the actual distribution of the diverse religious and ethnic groups of the region. Furthermore, now that the British Hashemite protégé Faisal, expelled from Syria by the French, was King of Iraq and his brother Abdullah was Emir of Trans-Jordan, the French were always tempted to see Hashemite intrigues behind the various risings and plots that marked their rule in Syria and Lebanon. The attempt to murder the French High Commissioner General Gouraud in 1922 was launched by Syrian exiles in Trans-Jordan. And the revolt against French rule in the Hauran district of southern Syria was regarded by a French specialist in Middle Eastern affairs as part of the same struggle: 'clientèle Anglaise contre le mandat

[3]See Jacques Bainville, 'Les Puissances Coloniales sur la Defensive', where he writes: 'La France et l'Angleterre n'ont plus qu'une chose a faire: c'est de concerter et d'unir leur action pour garder leurs colonies asiatiques et africaines': La Liberté (Paris), 4 June 1927. In an article written in January 1931 he presciently remarks: 'L'Inde sans les Anglais, ce serait rapidement, l'Indochine sans les Fran,cais.' The articles and others are reprinted in Bainville, L'Angleterre et l'empire Britannique (Paris, 1938). A French historian of the era of 'decolonisation' has argued that the French demand for a zone of influence in the Middle East was largely the result of a wish not to see Britain establish itself there alone, together with a vague imperial sentiment and a surviving feeling for its former role as a protector of the Christian minorities, but was not productive of a policy suitable for the attainment of its ends. See Henri Grimal, La Decolonization, 1919–1933 (Paris, 1965), p. 24.
[4]Edward Mortimer, France and the Africans, 1944–1960 (London, Faber, 1969), p. 20.
[5]Memorandum by Sir Arthur Hirtzel, assistant under-secretary at the India Office, 14 February 1919, quoted by Nevakivi, op cit., p. 124.
[6]William I. Shorrock, French Imperialism in the Middle East: The Failure of Policy in Syria and Lebanon (Madison, 1976), pp. 115 – 135.

Francais'.[7] Many Syrians believed, according to the same authority, that France might abandon her ungrateful mission and cede the mandate to the British.

The French then and since have tended to see Colonel T.E. Lawrence as the source of hostile activities, and his own occasional anti-French outbursts gave some colour to this belief.[8] On the other hand more recent research suggests that while other British officers may have connived at the plotting in Trans-Jordan by Syrian opponents of French rule, Lawrence himself helped to dissuade Abdullah from supporting their plans for invading Syria.[9] Throughout the duration of the mandate the French regarded the British as a threat.[10] As late as the mid-1930's a member of the Syrian Parliament who wished to see the Arab world united under Saudi leadership, could refer to the regrettable separation of Syria and Lebanon from the rest of the Arab world, seeing Iraq, Palestine and Trans-Jordan as part of a British imperial economic system, with Haifa as Beirut's rival for the commerce of Iraq.[11]

The British statesmen, after their initial disagreements with the French over policy towards Turkey, were convinced that the need to work in harmony with them in Europe meant preventing Middle Eastern affairs from damaging their relationship. Thus Austen Chamberlain warned the Saudis against getting mixed up in Syrian affairs except through prior agreement with the French. And British officials in the Middle East were instructed to do their best to show understanding of France's problems and to dissipate any French suspicions of British behaviour.[12]

---

[7]B.G. Gaulis, *La Question Arabe* (Paris, 1930), pp. 157 – 8. For the general history of Syria and Lebanon in this period see S.H. Longrigg, *Syria and Lebanon under French Mandate* (London, 1958).

[8]'The French made our job as difficult as possible – if it is possible at all – by their wanton disregard of the common decencies observed between nations.' T.E. Lawrence to S.F. Newcombe, Amman, 8 November 1921, in D. Garnett, (ed.) *The Letters of T.E. Lawrence* (London, 1938), p. 336.

[9]See M. Larès, 'T.E. Lawrence and France: Friends or Foes?', in S.E. Tabachnik (ed.) *The T.E. Lawrence Puzzle* (Athens, University of Georgia Press, 1984). This article summarises M. Larès' University of Lille thesis, 'T.E. Lawrence – La France et les Français' (Imprimiere Nationale, Paris, 1980).

[10]A. Hourani, *The Emergence of the Modern Middle East* (London, 1983), ch. 13.

[11]E. Rabbath, *Unité Syrienne et Devenir Arabe* (Paris, 1937), pp. 283 – 4.

[12]Record of Conversations with the Emir Faisal, 11 October 1926, *DBFP*, Series IA, vol. II (London, 1948), pp. 824 – 5; Despatch of 1 November 1926 to H.M. Consul in Damascus, ibid., p. 825 n.

Looking back at the ultimate elimination of both powers from their positions in the Middle East, a distinguished French soldier could see the antagonisms deriving from their different conceptions of the mandate system as an explanation of their common failure. French public opinion had been unconvinced of the value of France's role in the Middle East.[13] The French enterprise could only be justified in prestige terms and no direct benefit to France itself could be claimed.[14] What persisted was the French view of the British as far more consciously imperialist than had ever been the case. Even literary studies confirmed this view.[15] French hostility to Zionism and to the National Home provisions of the Palestine Mandate was partly the fruit of French anti-semitism but was also based on the belief that Zionism itself was a tool of British imperial penetration.[16] And the Arabs of Palestine were encouraged by the French (as by the Italians) to express their hostility to the policy of the Balfour Declaration.[17]

Although the Anglo-French differences had on paper been resolved and the new structure in the Middle East accepted by the summer of 1921, the failure to achieve peace with Kemalist Turkey and the Turkish territorial claims on both Syria and Iraq as well as the possibility of some Arab opponents of western rule showing pro-Turkish leanings, meant that the region was still in some turmoil. Nor indeed were the mandates operative since they had not yet been confirmed by the League of Nations, partly because of the absence of a peace treaty renouncing Turkish rights, and partly because of the long drawn out opposition of the United States. The United States had not itself been at war with Turkey nor would it consider taking mandatory responsibilities for any part of the former Ottoman Empire, but it did claim the right as one of the Allied and Associated Powers to have a voice in the final settlement for that area. Its demands were no

[13]G. Catroux, *Deux Missions en Moyen Orient, 1919–1922*, (Paris, 1958), pp. 86, 132. Yet in order to preserve influence with the Roman Catholics of the Middle East, the French reestablished relations with the Vatican in 1921. The British had established diplomatic relations in 1914: Stelio Marchese, *La Francia et il Problema dei Rapport con la Santa Sede* (Naples, 1969).
[14]See on the general French indifference to imperialism at this time, Christopher M. Andrew and A.S. Kanya Forstner, *The Climax of French Imperial Expansion, 1914–1924* (Stanford University Press, 1981), also published under the title, *France Overseas and the Climax of French Imperial Expansion* (London, 1981).
[15]See M.F. Guyard, *La Grande Bretagne dans le Roman Francais* (Paris, 1954).
[16]Andrew and Kanya Forstner, op. cit., p. 18.
[17]See e.g. R. Meinertzhagen, *Middle East Diary, 1917-1956* (London, 1959), 58 – 9.

longer those of Wilsonian self-determination, but were essentially concerned with two material issues: an unwillingness to surrender to the consular jurisdiction of the mandatory powers the rights previously enjoyed by American citizens under the capitulations, and the maintenance of an open door for American commerce, including the interests of the oil companies.

American accusations that British interests were being given preference in Iraq and Palestine began early in 1920.[18] In November 1920 the United States government denied the British contention that the terms of the mandates could only be discussed by the League Council and the signatories to the Covenant since the transfer of power in these territories had been the result of a war in which the United States had participated and which gave the Associated Powers the right to participate in 'the rights and privileges secured under the mandates provided for in the Treaties of Peace'. Meanwhile since the Treaty of Peace with Turkey was unratified, the United States regarded the capitulations as still in force, despite their unilateral abolition by Turkey in 1914. The United States did not wish to be represented in negotiations with Turkey, but to be able to express its views since it had contributed to that country's defeat.[19]

The draft mandates for Syria and Lebanon were submitted to the League Council by the French on 1 December 1920 and the draft mandates for Mesopotamia and Palestine by the British on 6 December. Questions at issue between the two mandatories were settled in a convention signed on 23 December. But it remained unpublished since it now appeared that the mandates had not been dealt with by the League Council and might not be until the Turkish Treaty entered into force.[20]

The U.S. continued to press its claims for consideration in 1921, now adding demands for the protection of its educational and charitable as well as missionary enterprises – matters which in the view of the British Foreign Secretary could only be settled bilaterally.[21]

The delay and uncertainty caused in Palestine by the failure of the League Council to confirm the mandate was conveyed to the

[18]*Foreign Relations of the United States* (FRUS) (Washington), 1920, vol. I, 649 ff; DBFP, 1st Series, vol. XIII, (London, 1963), pp. 77, 322.
[19]Secretary of State to Curzon, 20 November 1920, FRUS 1920, vol. 2, 669 ff, 675 ff; ibid., vol. 3, 748 ff.
[20]*DBFP*, 1st Series, vol. XIII, 425. It was published on 17 March 1921 as Cmd 1195.
[21]*FRUS*, 1921, vol. 2, 106 ff.

Americans in a note by the Permanent Under-Secretary on 29 December 1921. Whereas Britain had been prepared to accept a non-discriminatory clause relating in the mandate for Tanganyika, this could not apply to Palestine. There, he points out:

> Article 11 of the mandate expressly provides that the administration may arrange with the Jewish Agency, mentioned in article 4, to develop any of the natural resources of the country in so far as these matters are not directly undertaken by the administration. The reason for this is that in order for the policy of establishing in Palestine a national home for the Jewish people should be successfully carried out, it is impracticable to guarantee that equal facilities for developing natural resources should be granted to persons or bodies who may be actuated by other motives.[22]

The British government were aware at the same time of the fact that American Zionist leaders were afraid that the mandate might make too little provision for preferential Jewish rights.[23]

In these circumstances Balfour, then representing Britain at the Washington Disarmament Conference, thought it proper to intervene in a letter to the American Secretary of State in which he pointed out that the task undertaken by the British in Palestine was one of 'extreme difficulty and delicacy' that he personally would have preferred to see discharged by the United States. This task could not be tackled by the civilian government now set up there unless its position was seen to be secure by all the populations and interests concerned. The delay in confirming the mandate was thus an important impediment to its work.[24] In his reply, Hughes said that while British suggestions about the access to courts with British judges would meet one of the United States' objections while the mandate lasted, it would be necessary for there to be a provision for the revival of the Americans' 'original rights [i.e. the capitulations] upon the termination of the the Mandate regime. Even in case a Jewish State should survive', he continued, 'it would still be necessary for the United States to reach a decision for itself on the question at that time'. While the use of the term 'Jewish State' rather than 'National Home', which figured in all the British

---

[22]Crowe to U.S. Ambassador, 29 December 1921, *FRUS* 1921, vol. 2, p. 117.
[23]Telegram from Sir Auckland Geddes, Washington, 14 October 1921, *DBFP*, 1st Series, vol. XIII, p. 358.
[24]A.J. Balfour to the Secretary of State, 13 January 1922, *FRUS* 1922, vol. 2, pp. 268 – 9.

communications on the subject, suggests some impact upon American official thinking by the American Zionists, the reference to the possibility of the Jewish entity not surviving suggests at this time an even greater fluidity of opinion in Washington than in London. For the rest Hughes reiterated the familiar American claims.[25]

Further correspondence between the two governments continued until May, leading to an agreement that the American claims would be met in a bilateral Treaty once the mandate had come into effect.[26] The mandate was passed by the League Council on 24 July 1922, and after the conclusion of the Treaty of Lausanne with Turkey on 24 July 1923, the Middle East mandates finally entered into force on 29 September 1923.

Although the final rounding off of the changes in the Middle East brought about by the war was not consolidated until the Treaty of Lausanne, Britain's new position had become clear somewhat earlier. There was some fear lest Turkey prove able to play one power off against another and of a possible Pan-Islamic move against the West in general, though the British fears in the immediate post-war period that the Bolsheviks might exploit the Pan-Turanian and Pan-Islamic movements were perhaps exaggerated, since these movements might also be seen as a threat to the Russians themselves.[27] More important, as the cabinet was reminded at more than one juncture, was the ability of an Islamic cause to awaken the susceptibilities of Indian Muslims, and for a time the Khilafat movement there did appear to embody a serious danger. But in March 1924 the Turks abolished the Caliphate and with this the Khilafat movement lost its motive power. The assumption of the Caliphate by Britain's protégé King Hussein of the Hejaz was not widely accepted; and he was soon to lose both his kingdom and the Caliphate when the Hejaz was added to the domains of Ibn Saud. Egyptian ambitions for the Caliphate also proved abortive

[25]Secretary of State to Balfour, 27 January 1922, ibid., pp. 269 – 71. The breach between Justice Brandeis and the Zionist leader Chaim Weizmann led to a falling off in American Jewish influence in the Zionist enterprise, and a lack of pressure on the mandatory power from this source as compared with the years leading up to the ratification of the Mandate.

[26]FRUS 1922, vol. 2, 268 ff, 292 ff. The issue was not settled even when the new Palestine constitution was set out by the British Order in Council of 1 September 1922. A convention was finally arrived at on 4 December 1924 and ratified on 5 December 1925. Its provisions included sending the United States a copy of the Mandatory's annual report to the League. FRUS 1923, vol. 2, 197 ff, 218 ff.

[27]John Darwin, Britain, Egypt and the Middle East: Imperial Policy in the Aftermath of War, 1918–1922 (London, 1981), p. 214.

and for the time being it was Arab nationalism rather than Islam itself that seemed to be the imperial powers' main interlocutor.[28]

Except for the situation in the Persian Gulf and to a lesser but increasing extent in Iraq, oil did not yet present the major interest of British policy-makers. What Britain was left with when the coalition government fell in October 1922 was a determination to safeguard the route to India, which meant preserving responsibility for the defence of the Suez Canal and the exclusion of other imperial powers except to the extent that France's place in the Levant had been accepted. Against this was the pressure at home for retrenchment forcing political skill and diplomacy into becoming substitutes for military power. In each of the four countries principally concerned, Egypt, Iraq, Palestine and Trans-Jordan, the tactics adopted were necessarily different but the objectives were the same.[29]

The British position in the four countries could not be separated from the continued close relationship with Saudi Arabia, which persisted even after Ibn Saud ejected the Hashemites from the Hejaz in 1925, nor from the continued concern with the Gulf states, whose original role as outposts of the Indian Empire was made more significant with the increasing importance of oil politics; nor indeed at the other end of the Arabian peninsula could the importance of another Indian outpost, Aden, be overlooked, both because of its role in the commerce of the Red Sea and as a link with East Africa.[30]

British policy needed to take into account not only domestic pressures and the relations between Britain and other western countries with an interest in the region – the Italians were not reconciled to their exclusion and even less so after the rise of Mussolini – but also and above all of developments in the outlook of the region itself. And here there were endless ambiguities which were to remain unresolved when the French and the British finally surrendered their positions.

[28]E. Kedourie, *The Chatham House Version and other Middle Eastern Studies* (London, Weidenfeld & Nicolson, 1970), ch. 7, 'Egypt and the Caliphate, 1915–1952'.
[29]When Abdullah was put in charge of Transjordan for a limited period it had been generally assumed that it would be reunited with Palestine. Lawrence seems to have been responsible for swaying the decision in favour of leaving Abdullah in place and this led to it being provided in the British draft mandate of 6 December 1920 in article 25 that the force of provisions 'inapplicable to existing local conditions' could be postponed or withheld. The obligations respecting a Jewish National Home were henceforth held not to apply to TransJordan, and this derogation was accepted by the League in September 1922. See Mordechai Nissan, 'The Palestinian Features of Jordan', in D.J. Eleazar (ed.), *Judea, Samaria and Gaza: Views on the Present and Future* (Washington, n.d.), and A. Klieman, 'Lawrence as Bureaucrat', in Tabachnik, op. cit.
[30]For a picture of Aden at this time, see David Footman, *Antonin Besse of Aden* (London, 1985).

The Arabs had been freed from the Turks by allied military success, in fact and in the general estimation, by their spontaneous efforts on their own. The possibility of a Turkish comeback was excluded. As a minimum there was the Turkish pressure for territorial concessions, met in Syria by the cession of the Sanjaq of Alexandretta in stages between 1936 and 1939, and where Britain was concerned, the ambition to annex Mosul from Iraq – important to the Turks because of their Kurdish problem, and to Iraq and hence to Britain increasingly as a source of oil.

In Arab eyes, the mandates were simply mechanisms by which their full access to political independence should be facilitated. The question was, in what form? Was the Middle East to become like the Balkans, a series of separate States with overlapping territorial claims and rivalries, or did the Arab world united by language and preponderantly by religion form a possible unity, and if so under what constitutional arrangements?[31] Was there an Arab nation or Arab nations? The answer would have a different accent in the different countries. Egypt in particular, while clearly related in many ways to the rest of the Arab world, was arguably a nation with roots that went back beyond the original Arab conquests. At different junctures it was bound to view differently the balance of interests and sympathies between its own nationhood and the general Arab cause. Saudi Arabia, particularly after its acquisition of the Muslim holy places through the conquest of the Hejaz, was both sufficient unto itself (and indeed very largely self-isolated) and an aspirant to wider leadership.[32] Even more complicated was the position in the fertile crescent where the rivalries between the Hashemite and Saudi dynasties were a constant factor, with the occasional irruption upon the scene of an Egyptian prince. In addition there were, especially among the more sophisticated Syrians and Lebanese, those who professed republican principles and did not wish to see the idea of Arab unity commandeered to serve dynastic interests. Each move in this direction, whether or not acceptable to the British, produced its own countervailing pressures. Even an issue such as the creation of the Jewish National Home, did not always result in concerted action since the future of Palestine was also an

[31] There is much material even for the earlier period in Yehoshua Porath, *In Search of Arab Unity, 1930–1945* (London, 1986). See also 'Pan Arabism and British Policy' in Kedourie, op. cit.
[32] See H. St John Philby, *Saudi Arabia* (London, 1955), ch. 10, and Clive Leatherdale, *Britain and Saudi Arabia, 1925-1939* (London, Cass, 1983).

issue that presented itself differently to the different parties: the protagonists of a 'greater Syria' were hardly congenial to the Hashemites. It must also be borne in mind, despite what happened subsequently, that the Zionist leaders themselves – or some of them – had not given up hope of reaching an accommodation with at least some of the Arab leaders, so that there was an undercurrent of Zionist diplomacy apart from Britain's own activity as the mandatory power.[33]

In seeking advice as to how to retain the essential of Britain's Middle East position at minimum cost, the British government could turn to its representatives in the different Arab countries who made valiant efforts to find their way through the tangle of ethnic, religious and dynastic rivalries. As is the way with ambassadors – and in some countries they had a proconsular status – they tended to identify themselves with the country in which they were stationed, and to seek understanding at home for its particular interests and needs. In the case of Saudi Arabia, something of the same role was played by St John Philby, a former member of the Indian Civil Service (I.C.S.), who after wartime missions in the Arabian peninsula became an unofficial adviser to Ibn Saud.[34] The familiar problems of trying to align the differing perspectives of the Foreign, Colonial and Indian offices and at taking into full account the military factor made the process of reaching decisions more complex than in relation to any other part of the imperial system. Nor was it an area in respect of which Parliamentary quiescence could always be expected, particularly as regards Egypt and Palestine.

Egypt

Egypt had since its occupation been seen as the key to the imperial position of Britain in the Mediterranean and as the essential defence of the Suez Canal, the principal route of the Empire's communications.[35] The status of the Sudan as an Anglo-Egyptian condominium was also the justification for British rule there, which with its cotton-growing capacity led the British government to regard it as 'potentially

[33]The principal printed source for Zionist diplomacy is *The Letters and Papers of Chaim Weizmann*, series A, letters, vols X and following (Rutgers University Press and Hebrew University of Jerusalem, 1977 and subsequently).
[34]See E. Monroe, *Philby of Arabia* (London, 1973).
[35]For an account of the British period in Egyptian history, see Peter Masefield, *The British in Egypt* (London, 1972).

an asset'.[36] But while the British had given themselves a free hand by the declaration of the protectorate in 1914, thus terminating the shadowy Turkish suzerainty, it was obvious that the nationalist demands for greater independence would not long be resisted. British rule did not find favour in any quarter nor, despite the view of a future pro-consul, Lord Lloyd can this be attributed to any large degree to a failure to make the welfare of the people a primary concern of imperial policy.[37] It was rather that there was no meeting of minds between the Egyptian propertied classes and elites who formed political opinion and controlled political parties and even the most high-minded British administrators. Nor were their differences confined to ideas as to what constituted the welfare of the people. It was also a fact that these elites looked not to England for education and inspiration as did nationalist leaders in the rest of the Empire but, like the Syrians, to France.[38] Sir Percy Loraine*, British High Commissioner from 1929 to 1933, wrote after he had left Egypt,

> The failure of England to make use of the forty years from 1882 to 1922 to create for herself a strong cultural position in Egypt is one of the most extraordinary phenomena of our illogical Imperial story. The net result is that the declaration of Egyptian independence in 1922 found France still predominant in the cultural field.[39]

The question was whether power could be handed over to an independent Egyptian government while Britain retained necessary military dispositions in respect of the Canal, and prime authority in

---

[36]Cabinet meeting, 11 July 1921, PRO CAB 23/26.

[37]Lord Lloyd, *Egypt since Cromer*, vol. II (London, 1934), pp. 4, 56. Lord Lloyd's point has been re-echoed by a later historian of the Middle East: 'The great justification of the British occupation of Egypt – which was carried out in order to protect British interests – had been that the British recognised a responsibility for the good government and welfare of its inhabitants. With this justification repudiated, the British position in Egypt was bound sooner or later to become untenable and indefensible.' E. Kedourie, 'The End of the Ottoman Empire', *Journal of Contemporary History (JCH)* vol. IV, no. 3, (1968), 1928, (quotation from p. 27).

[38]The fact was observed by Russell Galt of the American University in Cairo: 'In Egypt England had an army – the French an idea. England had educational control – France a clear educational philosophy. Because the French did have such an organised philosophy and the English did not the French pen proved mightier than the British sword.' Quoted by Frances Donaldson, *The British Council – the first Fifty Years* (London, Cape, 1984), p. 3.

[39]Quoted ibid., 22. It is not suprising that when Lloyd became chairman of the British Council in 1937, he concentrated its efforts on the Mediterranean and the Middle East.

the Sudan.[40] The first set of talks, those between Lord Milner and Zaghul Pasha, leader of the Wafd party, broke down in November 1920.[41] Renewed negotiations with a new Egyptian government under Adly Pasha which lasted from June to November 1921 were also fruitless.[42] It was now argued in some quarters that more generous terms should be offered and that the reasoning that had brought about the Irish treaty was applicable also to Egypt.[43] But in the intricate counterpoint of imperial debate, the opposite view could also be defended; having given way in Ireland, the coalition government could not afford to show weakness in regard to Egypt.[44] Lloyd George's view that past experience had shown that the Egyptians could not run their own affairs was widely shared; if therefore Britain withdrew, another European country would take her place.[45] There could be no settlement with Egypt, it was maintained, until Egyptians recognised the fact that the interests of the Empire and of Egypt herself 'demanded equally that Egypt should be at war when the Empire was at war and at peace when the Empire was at peace' and that 'Egypt should not be able to make war independently'.[46]

Pressure for a settlement came primarily from the High Commissioner, Lord Allenby*, concerned at the growth of political violence and the deterioration of the situation.[47] He backed up his plea to the Government with a threat of resignation, an eventuality which the weakening coalition could not afford to ignore.[48]

On 28 February 1922 the government finally took the plunge and issued a declaration putting an end to the protectorate, and recognising Egypt as an independent state, reserving security questions to be

[40]Labour and Conservative Foreign Secretaries were to go on looking for 'collaborators in Egypt who would shoulder the burden of ruling the country while leaving the British in possession of the Canal'. John Gallagher, *The Decline, Revival and Fall of the British Empire* (Cambridge, 1982), p. 109.

[41]See 'S'ad Zaghlul and the British' in Kedourie, op. cit.

[42]The successive rounds in Anglo-Egyptian negotiations are chronicled in vol. II of Lord Lloyd, op. cit.

[43]Valentine Chirol to Edward Grigg, 26 December 1921, Grigg Papers.

[44]A. Gollin, *Proconsul in Politics* (London, 1964), 594.

[45]Cabinet meeting, 4 November 1921, PRO CAB 23/27.

[46]Grigg to Chirol, 28 December 1921, Grigg Papers.

[47]'Armed resistance instinctively produces in an imperial power an unwillingness to capitulate to violence; yet capitulation happened all over the Middle East between the end of 1920 and the fall of the Lloyd George government at the end of 1922.' E. Monroe, *Britain's Moment in the Middle East* (London, 1963), p. 67.

[48]PRO CAB 23/29, meetings of 18 and 26 January 1922. On Allenby's role see Lord Wavell, *Allenby in Egypt* (London, 1943), 70 ff; John Marlowe, *Anglo-Egyptian Relations, 1800–1953* (London, 1954), pp. 244–9; Brian Gardner, *Allenby* (London, 1965), 239 ff.

settled in a future treaty. The question was not whether it was in Britain's interests to see that no other power could threaten the canal; everyone agreed upon that.[49] The question was why the security of the Empire should take priority of the sovereignty of a country that was not part of it. Some took the view that it was best simply to assert the imperial interest and make no attempt to disguise it.[50] Allenby was left with the task of finding an Egyptian government prepared to sign such a Treaty and with only a prospect of a lessening of the British military presence as a bargaining counter. But to try to secure a government of this kind meant getting involved in the faction fighting around the palace which was to be the principal feature of Egyptian politics until the end of the dynasty. From the British point of view, greater democracy was the best instrument even though western democratic theory made few allowances for the particular conditions of Egyptian political life. The Egyptian constitution of 1923 was only promulgated after Allenby had pressed for further concessions to democratic demands and had been fought off by an alliance between the King and Zaghlul and the Wafd.[51]

Allenby had in fact no alternative but to treat with whatever demagogues the political process had thrown up. Even if there had been the will to direct rule its instruments were lacking.[52] He himself had never been optimistic about the prospects of Empire,[53] and his experience confirmed his pessimism.

The return of Zaghlul to power and the advent of a Labour government in Britain might have been expected to permit the negotiation of the proposed treaty to cover the issues dividing the two governments.

[49]'We cannot allow any other Power to take our place. For control of the Canal would double its naval strength. Consequently if there is a breakdown ... we should have to go back.' John Dove to Robert Brand, 12 April 1922: Scottish Record Office, Lothian Papers, vol. 211.

[50]At a conference of ministers on 18 November 1921, Montagu said that it was desirable to draw a clear distinction between action taken in the interests of the British Empire which could not be abandoned and action of a benevolent and paternal kind taken for the good of Egypt; Egypt should be told that the army must remain for the protection of British interests. PRO CAB 23/27.

[51]'The Genesis of the Egyptian Consititution of 1923', in Kedourie, op. cit.

[52]Someone who had lived in Egypt as the child of a British official in the pre – 1914 era pointed to the deterioration in the quality of British administration brought about by the war: all the younger administrative British had gone away to fight the war, to be replaced not by Egyptians, because no-one had time to train them, 'but by other British who were older and more prejudiced and spoke no Arabic and had no knowledge of the country'. P. Napier, *A Late Beginner* (London, 1966), pp. 174 – 7.

[53]'I had a long talk with Allenby and our talk drifted far into the future; he thought the dissolution of the British Empire inevitable as the people we rule become more educated.' Diary entry, 6 January 1920, in Meinertzhagen, op. cit., pp. 67-8.

For MacDonald himself had given vocal support to Zaghlul when he passed through Cairo shortly before the 1922 declaration. But once in government things looked different. The Egyptians were pressing for complete control of the Sudan, while at the end of June it was announced that the British government had no intention of abandoning its position there. When Zaghlul came to London for talks in September 1924, his demands for the total withdrawal of British troops, officials and influence from Egypt itself, and for the abandonment of any British claim to provide for the defence of the canal or for the protection of Egypt's minorities were as unacceptable as ever.[54] Back in Egypt, Zaghlul did nothing to discourage the sporadic violence designed to weaken Britain's hold on the country and which culminated in November, after the fall of the Labour government, in the murder of Sir Lee Stack, governor-general of the Sudan and Sirdar of the Egyptian Army.[55]

Allenby responded, without waiting for instructions, with an ultimatum couched in the strongest terms, demanding the end of political agitation, and the removal of all Egyptian troops from the Sudan, in which British control was henceforth in fact to be exclusive; a paragraph about increasing the area of irrigation under the Gezira cotton-growing scheme could be interpreted as a threat to use the control of the Nile waters as a political weapon against the Egyptians. The Government did not disavow the High Commissioner and the immediate crisis was ended by the resignation of Zaghlul and the appointment of a caretaker administration sheltering under the authority of the High Commissioner. But the new foreign secretary, Austen Chamberlain, felt some mistrust of Allenby's judgement and sent out as his adviser a professional diplomat, Nevile Henderson*. Allenby, regarding this move as an indication of no confidence, tendered his resignation and despite urgings to reconsider his decision only agreed to postpone his departure until June 1925.[56] In the interim, the renewed success of the Wafd at the elections held in January despite the efforts of the Palace to prevent this from happening, and the consequent dissolution of the new Parliament in March gave no prospect of a settlement.

[54]Wavell, op. cit., pp. 83, 107; Gardner, op. cit., p. 245.
[55]Marlowe, *Anglo-Egyptian Relations*, 266 ff.
[56]Wavell, op. cit., 113 ff; Gardner, op. cit., pp. 248 – 54; Cabinet meeting 21 January 1925, PRO CAB 23/49.

Allenby's successor, Sir George Lloyd, was a man of a very different stamp, a positive paternalistically minded imperialist after the style of Cromer.[57] But no change of personnel could alter the fundamentals of the problem. On the one hand, it had been decided at a meeting of the Chiefs of Staff subcommittee on the very day of the Sirdar's murder that troops must be retained in Cairo itself, despite Trenchard's view that providing suitable bases were built, the troops necessary for defending the Canal could all be stationed in the Canal Zone itself.[58] Another British officer was appointed to command the Egyptian army, and the deadlock remained. Another general election was inevitable and the outcome a certain victory for Zaghlul. The cabinet accepted Lloyd's advice that he could not be permitted to resume office lest disorder flare up again.[59] While for the time being Zaghlul was prepared to allow a coalition government under another Prime Minister to function, this was clearly no long term solution.

The British government was unable to bring the facts of the situation into harmony with the ironically independent status of Egypt or alternatively to secure its own needs.[60] It opposed the dismissal of British officials and the appointment of nationals of other countries; it dissuaded Egypt from applying for membership of the League of Nations and reduced the size of Egypt's own forces, taking the view that there was no need to train or equip them to a European standard.

In 1927 divergences of approach began to appear as between Lloyd and the home government, which was unwilling to abandon the hope of a settlement which would permit some lightening of Britain's

[57]This chapter was written before the publication of John Charmley, *Lord Lloyd and the Decline of the British Empire* (London, 1987). This work details in considerable depth the hostility of the Foreign Office to Lloyd's appointment and to the policies he pursued and recommended. His dismissal by Henderson and the failure of Austen Chamberlain to defend him are shown to be the culmination of a virtual conspiracy in which the lead was taken by two successive Permanent Secretaries, Sir William Tyrrell (later Lord Tyrrell) and Sir Ronald Lindsay.
[58]Meeting of 20 November 1924, PRO CAB 53/1.
[59]Meeting of 2 June 1926, PRO CAB 53/2.
[60]Lloyd set out the position clearly in a private letter in 1927: 'We cannot carry on much longer as we are. We have magnitude without position; power without authority; responsibility without control. I must ensure that no foreign power intervenes in education, aviation, wireless communications, railway or army (where all seek to do so), and I must achieve this without upsetting the Parliamentary regime which we forced upon the country in the face of the King's wishes; without weakening the power or alienating the loyalty of the Monarchy which we set up, and without displaying that military power which is in fact our sole remaining argument. I must maintain and respect Egyptian independence, and yet justify our army of occupation... Is there *no* other way of defending the Canal; and even if there be, since Egypt has already become the very Clapham junction of Eastern and African long-distance flights, can we abandon it to others?' Quoted in C.F. Adam, *Life of Lord Lloyd* (London, Macmillan, 1948), p. 197.

burdens. Although Lloyd was supported in his objections to putting the Egyptian army wholly under the control of the Minister of War (a Wafdist), Austen Chamberlain used the occasion of an Egyptian State visit to London in August 1927 to begin negotiations for a new treaty – a move regarded as unwise by Lloyd, since he held that even if a treaty were reached, no non-Wafdist ministry would be able to carry it through Parliament, the more so since Nahas Pasha, who had succeeded Zaghlul as party leader when the latter died at the end of August, had much less control over the party. On the other hand Nevile Henderson was urging generosity in dealing with Egypt's demands.[61] Whether Chamberlain believed that he had made a breakthrough is unclear and not all his colleagues were at one with him in believing that the draft Treaty would be accepted as a final settlement. It did not in fact go very far, since the position of British troops was only to be reviewed after the elapse of ten years, with the matter being referred to the League Council in the event of there being no agreement at that time.[62]

Having failed to get opposition support, the Egyptian Prime Minister who had negotiated the Treaty resigned and was succeeded by Nahas, who was in turn dismissed by the King and replaced by a Minister of his own choice on whose advice Parliament was dissolved and the Constitution virtually suspended. But the British Foreign Office disliked the turn of events and still hoped that Britain's security needs could be obtained by a treaty with a friendly Egypt, nor did they share Lloyd's view that the existence of British business interests meant that a considerable measure of control should be maintained over Egypt's internal affairs.[63]

Some signs of hope appeared in the signature of a Nile Waters agreement on 1 May and, emboldened by the return of Labour to office, the Egyptians now thought the time ripe for demanding further

[61]'The problem is how we can reconcile Egypt's right to independence ... with our own right to self-protection. Give whatever you are going to give her generously and with an air of trust in her goodwill.' Henderson (Cairo) to Mr Selby, 21 October 1927: Cecil Papers, Hatfield, (Fourth Marquess of Salisbury), S(4)123/29.
[62]Meetings of 12 October and 11 November 1927, PRO CAB 23/55. It is worth noting that despite the importance attached to Egypt as a nodal point in imperial communications, the Dominions were not consulted about the Treaty: Arnold J. Toynbee, *Survey of International Affairs 1928* (Oxford, 1929), pp. 279 – 83.
[63]Marlowe, op. cit., pp. 280 – 4.

concessions.[64] Lloyd wrote to the new Foreign Secretary, Arthur Henderson, on 16 June that he had been assured that the Egyptian Prime Minister, who was about to visit London, would not embark on general negotiations which would give the Wafd an opportunity to attack him for selling out to the British. But he received a noncommital reply.[65] In fact talks were entered into and a new set of draft proposals were published on 8 August. Meanwhile Henderson seems to have become convinced of the rightness of the view of his Permanent Under-Secretary, Sir Roland Lindsay, that Lloyd's tenure of the High Commissionership was an obstacle to any agreement. Lloyd was therefore summoned to London, and after talking with Henderson felt he had no option but to submit his resignation.[66] In defending his action in the House of Commons Henderson referred to differences between Lloyd and his predecessor, Chamberlain. The government was not pressed to a division on this issue, but MacDonald felt that the proposals being considered with the Egyptians went too far, particularly in providing for an Egyptian unit to return to the Sudan.

Henderson, however, got his way. The draft proposals embodied a return to the situation before the upheaval of 1924, with British troops being withdrawn to the Canal Zone. But it was necessary in the cabinet's view for the proposals to receive Egyptian Parliamentary approval and this meant new elections in December 1929 which resulted in the return of Nahas and the Wafd to power. By now it was felt among British officials in Egypt that Lloyd's departure was a signal for a retreat and that it was anomalous that the British should stand out in Egypt more than in Iraq, Palestine or China. Nahas however returned to London demanding further concessions; the negotiations in the end broke down on the issue of Egyptian immigration into the Sudan.[67] Labour had thus proved no more able than the Conservatives to solve the Egyptian dilemma and Lloyd's successor, the

[64]David Carlton, *MacDonald versus Henderson: the foreign policy of the second Labour government* (London, 1970), ch. 8. The Labour government had decided to adopt the Option Clause about compulsory arbitration and not to accept the Foreign Office's wish to see reservations attached. If Egypt were specifically blamed it would show that the government considered Britain's position there legally indefensible. Ibid., p. 76. A similar view was taken by Viscount Cecil of Chelwood. Cecil also thought that the coming of the submarine and aircraft had meant that the Suez Canal would no longer be a vital link in case of war. Cecil to Henderson, 23 July 1929, Cecil of Chelwood Papers, British Library, Department of Manuscripts, (BL), Add MSS 51081.
[65]Henderson Papers, PRO FO 800/284.
[66]Lloyd's own account of these transactions is to be found in vol. II of his *Egypt Since Cromer*.
[67]Notes by the Marquess of Salisbury, loc. cit.

diplomat Sir Percy Loraine, found himself up against the same intractable set of issues as his predecessors.

Iraq

Iraq, as the mandate set up in Mesopotamia was known, was never seen as being as important to Britain as Egypt, but there were reasons that made Britain unwilling to sacrifice the position that had been gained there as a result of the war. Turkish claims to Mosul were one reason, apart from Lloyd George's philhellenism and the long-standing British interest in the Straits, for the inability to secure a peace with the new nationalist Turkey and for the tensions that this delay produced with France. The fall of the Lloyd George government as a result of the confrontation with Turkey at Chanak, and the return of a Conservative government first under Bonar Law and then under Baldwin, enabled Curzon in the long drawn out Conference of Lausanne (November 1922 to February 1923 and April to July 1923) to achieve a satisfactory treaty.[68]

The issue was not as straightforward as it might seem in retrospect. Bonar Law set up a committee under the new Colonial Secretary, the Duke of Devonshire, to examine the question of the retention of Iraq. The committee reported on 26 April 1923 opposing British withdrawal as likely to lead to Turkish infiltration and as possibly leading to 'a Bolshevik Persia'. If the Turks got back Mosul, they would go on to claim Syria and Palestine. But the committee also recommended that expenditure on Iraq should be progressively reduced, and that the mandate itself should be terminated within four years of the signature of a peace treaty with Turkey.[69] The cabinet's acceptance of this recommendation raised again the question of Iraq's frontier, since the League Commission that had recommended that Mosul go to Iraq had done so on condition that the mandate lasted for twenty-five years. But the Lausanne Treaty confirmed Iraq in possession though Iraq was told that unless she ratified the Treaty she would lose the area.[70]

[68]The documentation relating to the Treaty of Lausanne and its antecedents is to be found in *DBFP*, 1st Series, vols XVII and XVIII, (london, 1970 and 1972). On Curzon's own role see Harold Nicolson, *Curzon, the last phase* (London, 1934).
[69]Cabinet meeting, 26 April 1923, PRO CAB 23/45. The Report of the Committee is CP 167(23) in PRO CAB 24/159 and a memorandum on the report by Lord Salisbury is CP 182(23) in ibid.
[70]Britain's role in Iraq is analysed in detail in P. Sluglett, *Britain in Iraq, 1914–1932* (London, 1976).

In respect of relations with Iraq itself, the cabinet decided that the Treaty of Alliance entered into with King Faisal on 5 October 1922 should terminate when Iraq became a member of the League of Nations.[71] The retention of Iraq under British mandate was not a popular decision.[72] It was only secured against opposition from within the government because of the argument that the new methods of air-policing would enable fewer British or Indian troops to be used.[73]

The new importance attached to air links with the Empire was one element in deciding upon retention; but the most important was oil, since the Admiralty had been pressing since 1918 for this factor to be taken into account, though Curzon played down this aspect in his negotiations and insisted that Mosul, where the potential oilfields were situated, should go to Iraq on ethnic grounds.[74] The French had come to an agreement on oil matters, but the Americans claimed an interest both on commercial grounds and in view of their possible future security needs. It was decided that it would be necessary to allow American participation in the exploitation of the oil fields though the details took a long time to work out and a final settlement was only achieved on 31 July 1928.[75]

In one sense the problem in Iraq was not altogether dissimilar from that in Egypt — the question was how to find a basis in consent for the perpetuation of Britain's position.[76] Some British participants in the transactions that led up to the establishment of the monarchy believed

[71]Opposition in the cabinet was led by Sir Phillip Lloyd-Greame (the future Viscount Swinton). See J.A. Cross, *Lord Swinton* (Oxford, 1982), pp. 48 – 50.

[72]In *Back to Methusaleh*, written in 1922, Bernard Shaw makes Baghdad the future capital of the British Empire.

[73]The air force campaign in northern Iraq which put down Kurdish dissidence and so paved the way for the Treaty of Lausanne had an important impact on military thinking. See Lord Templewood, *Empire of the Air* (London, 1957). But this had been preceded by the use of aircraft against tribesmen on the north-west frontier of India in 1919 and in the campaign against the 'Mad Mullah' in Somaliland in 1919 – 20. The R.A.F finally took over responsibility for the defence of Iraq in October 1922, though the last Indian troops did not leave until late in 1928. See Andrew Boyle, *Trenchard* (London, 1962), pp. 354 – 6, pp. 365 – 9, 378 ff, p. 422, 450 ff, p. 570. On the use of air power to deal with insurrection in Iraq, see Charles Townshend, *Britain's Civil Wars: counter-insurgency in the twentieth century*, 93 ff.

[74]See Benjamin Schwadran, *The Middle East. Oil and the Great Powers* (New York, 1955).

[75]The question of Iraq explains Curzon's reluctance to have oil discussed at the Washington Conference on Naval Disarmament. Curzon to Balfour, 9 November 1921, Balfour Papers, BL Add MSS 49734. For the American role at the Lausanne Conference, see Joseph C. Grew, *Turbulent Era* (London, 1953), chs 38 – 40.

[76]See E. Main, *Iraq: From Mandate to Independence*, (London, 1935), 78 ff, and Helmut J. F. Mejcher, 'The Birth of the Mandate Idea and its fulfilment in Iraq up to 1926' (unpublished Oxford D.Phil thesis, 1970).

that Faisal had the support of the majority of the Arab population.[77] Others maintained that the whole structure was a wholly artificial one which forced Britain to become involved in the details of local politics simply to secure her own imperial interests. British influence, it has been powerfully argued, was used to

> create in Baghdad a centralised government ruling over a population disparate and heterogeneous in the extreme, whom no ties of affection, loyalty or custom bound to its rulers. To establish the authority of its rulers, therefore, the British following the logic of their choice had to exert their power and influence and eliminate all potential and actual resistance; and the fortunate Baghdad government found at its disposal the Royal Air Force to coerce and inhibit all opposition, and devoted British officials who used their prestige, ability and good name in its favour.[78]

From the beginning there was trouble both internal and external. A Constituent Assembly elected in the spring of 1924 objected to the draft Anglo-Iraqi Treaty on the grounds that the control retained by the British over both the army and the administration was too great and that the financial provisions were inequitable. But after a British ultimatum threatening otherwise to revive the original terms of the mandate, the Assembly gave way. The agreement was approved by the League Council in September and the Treaty finally ratified in November. In September, there had been a new Turkish incursion which was repulsed; thereafter Turkish claims were not pressed.[79]

The programme of maintaining the Hashemite rulers of Iraq and Trans-Jordan on their thrones while guiding their countries towards an independence reconcilable with British interests could now be pursued without any immediate prospect of foreign intervention. In Iraq's case the oil revenues also made it possible to pursue a policy of economic development unusual in British overseas policy at that time.

---

[77]Reader Bullard, *The Camels Must Go* (London, Faber, 1961), p. 118.
[78]E. Kedourie, *The Chatham House Version*, ch. 9, 'The Kingdom of Iraq: a retrospect', pp. 258 – 9.
[79]One difficulty was that Britain as the mandatory power had given the League undertakings that there would be a semi-autonomous status for the Kurds, a matter of genuine worry for the Turks with their own Kurdish minority problem. In the end the Turks gave way on the frontier issue in return for financial assistance. See *DBFP,* Series IA, vol. I (London, 1966), ch. V. This agreement helped in making for good relations with Turkey itself where there was no hostile reception to Britain's breach with the Soviet Union in 1927. Sir George Clark (Constantinople) to Austen Chamberlain, 5 July 1927, ibid., vol. III (London, 1970), pp. 769 – 72.

Preparations were also made for the Iraqi army to take over respon-sibility for the country's defence by introducing British officers into it. But it was not thought that the time for independence would arrive in the near future.[80]

Faisal's demands for a new Treaty were thought premature and likely to annoy the French because of their implications for Syria and Lebanon. It was argued that the declaration of Egyptian independence had been productive of much embarrassment.[81] Nevertheless a draft treaty was signed on 14 December 1927, though ratification was postponed pending conclusion of the accompanying financial and military agreements. The latter was of particular impor-tance since there had been tribal risings against Faisal and severe raiding across the border (as across the Trans-Jordan border) which was only checked by British military action.[82] Further fighting on the Iraq border in 1927 – 8 again involved British forces.

The advent of the Labour government in 1929 brought about a renewal of negotiations with Iraq, and a Treaty was agreed upon in the following year, with a consequential agreement on a new judicial regime, ending the old system of capitulations, in March 1931. In June 1931, the Mandates Commission reported favourably on Iraq's claim to League membership, and the mandate came to an end when Iraq became an independent member of the League in October 1932.[83] The pipe-line from Iraq to the Mediterranean which had been much discussed with the French and taken long to build was finally opened late in 1934 with terminals at both Haifa and Tripoli.[84]

Trans-Jordan

For Trans-Jordan, smaller and weaker and still formally part of the Palestine mandate, such a solution was not available. The British continued in a supportive role and put up with the Emir's ceaseless political and dynastic intrigues. It was indeed the British subsidy which kept the Emir's regime afloat by enabling him to equip and pay

[80]Meeting, 28 June 1925, PRO CAB 23/49.
[81]Meetings, 28 June, 7 August 1925, PRO CAB 23/49; 24 November 1925, PRO CAB 23/51; 3 March 1926, PRO CAB 23/52; 4 July, 23 November 1927, PRO CAB 23/55.
[82]On the revolt of the tribesmen of the Middle Euphrates, see Reader Bullard, op. cit., pp. 114 – 5.
[83]S. H. Longrigg, *Iraq 1900–1950* (London, 1953), ch. 6.
[84]S.H. Longrigg, *Oil in the Middle East* 2nd edn (London, 1961), pp. 76 – 9.

the British-officered Arab legion which could protect him against tribal revolts and put down would-be disturbers of the peace in Syria.[85]

Saudi Arabia and the Gulf

Relations with Ibn Saud were more tempestuous. The ending of the British subsidy in March 1924 may have emboldened him to go against British wishes and turn to the conquest of the Hejaz which began that autumn and was completed in the following spring. He was proclaimed King of Hejaz – Nejd on 1 January 1926.

Britain had remained neutral in the contest between the Saudis and the Hashemites, and in a new Treaty with Ibn Saud on 31 May 1927 accepted the establishment of his enlarged kingdom. The Treaty replaced that of 26 December 1915 which had been modelled on the treaties with the lesser Gulf States and was now considered inappropriate.[86] As has been seen, this did not at once put an end to trouble on the Iraqi border, and early in 1929 there was a rebellion against Ibn Saud himself. He succeeded now in establishing his authority over the whole country and the practice of trans-border raids came to an end. Meanwhile he had begun the process of dissociating himself from British influence by cancelling in 1928 his oil concession to a British firm. In 1932 the Kingdom took on the new name of Saudi Arabia and in 1933 entered upon a close relationship with the American oil company, Standard Oil. Thereafter the country moved steadily out of the British orbit and into that of the United States.[87]

U.S. oil interests had also begun to penetrate Bahrein in 1932 and Kuwait in 1933, but Britain remained alert to preventing Saudi expansion touching the Gulf Sheikdoms, where the new air routes as well as oil added to their former importance as outposts of the Indian empire. By the mid – 1920s the position in the Gulf had been stabilised and British control secured. When asked to look at the matter in 1928, a sub-committee of the Committee of Imperial Defence (C.I.D.) agreed with the Chiefs of Staff in their assessment of its vital importance to

[85]See P.J. Vatikiotis, *Politics and the Military in Jordan, 1921–1957* (London, 1967).
[86]For the foundations of British and Indian power in the Gulf, see B. C. Busch, *Britain, India and the Arabs* (Berkeley and London, 1971).
[87]For the U.S. oil interests in the Arabian peninsula see W.R. Polk, *The United States and the Arab World* (Cambridge, Mass., 1965), p. 238.

the defence of India.[88] The problem here was not only the Saudi claims but also the deterioration of relations with Persia.

Persia

The new regime set up by Reza Shah after the war was dedicated to getting rid of the degree of subservience to foreign powers and particularly Britain which had been true in the latter years of his predecessors. In 1921 he got rid of the South Persia Rifles, a regiment raised and officered by the British, and in 1922 replaced the country's British financial advisers with Americans. And these in turn were replaced by Germans in 1927. In the same year the capitulations, that emblem of less than complete equality of status, resented alike by Turks, Egyptians and Persians were abolished. Meanwhile, in 1926 new negotiations with the Anglo-Persian Oil Company were begun, leading to the cancellation of their contract in 1932.[89]

By 1926 the British were worried about the possibility of Persia either falling into chaos or under the control of some other power.[90] In the following year it was reported from Tehran that Russia was taking Britain's place through propaganda among the uneducated classes.[91] In 1928 the Persians put forward a demand for the cession of Bahrein.[92] At the other end of the Arabian peninsula, there was friction with the Imam of the Yemen over the boundaries of the Aden Protectorate, and the Chiefs of Staff emphasised the need to retain Aden and the importance of preventing any other Power from obtaining a foothold on the Yemeni Coast. In this case, the anxieties were directed towards Italy.[93]

It could be argued that by the beginning of the 1930s the British venture in the Middle East was proving successful. Even with Persia

[88]Meeting, 5 November 1928, PRO CAB 23/59.
[89]See L.P. Elwell-Sutton, *Modern Iran* (London, 1944), for a general account of Persian-British relations and their background in the country itself. For the persistence of British dominance in the 1920s see *The Memoirs of Lord Gladwyn* (London, 1972), 21 ff.
[90]See the correspondence and memoranda in *DBFP*, Series IA, vol. II (London, 1968), pp. 805 – 20.
[91]Sir R. Clive (Tehran) to Foreign Secretary, ibid., vol. III, 780.
[92]Ibid., vol. VII (London, 1972), 599 ff. Bahrein had belonged to Persia till 1789 when it was conquered by Arabs from the mainland. A British protectorate was proclaimed in 1906. On the position in the Gulf in general see John Marlowe, *The Persian Gulf in the Twentieth Century* (London, 1962).
[93]Chiefs of Staff subcommittee meetings of 3 November 1926, PRO CAB 53/1, and 14 March 1927, PRO CAB 53/2.

relations began to improve and were not giving cause for serious anxiety. Full diplomatic relations with Ibn Saud were established in December 1929. Relations with Italy over the two countries' interests in Arabia had been put on an even keel for the time being by the agreement reached in May 1927.[94] In the countries where British authority was buttressed by mandate or treaty its strength was regarded with some complacency by those who actually wielded the power: 'The British personnel in this area were still full of hope and confidence and the habit of authority which had its effect not only on their demeanour but on Middle Eastern acceptance of their orders.'[95] And in this area, in contrast to other parts of the world, many of the important figures were given a very long run in their respective countries: Sir Kinahan Cornwallis, Sir Alec Kirkbride, Sir John Glubb.[96] As later events were to reveal, there was a good deal of illusion mixed up in all this. The genuine British affection for the Arabs was unreciprocated; the British presence was only one factor in Arab politics to be exploited one way or another as events might determine. In seeking to explain the Arabs' ultimate repudiation of their British guides, and to explain difficulties that arose even before the eventual débâcle, British diplomats and soldiers and many politicians have been prone to put it all down to one cause – the blow to Arab hopes and alleged repudiation of promises made by the continuing British commitment to the idea of a Jewish National Home in Palestine. Of Arab objections to this policy there can be no doubt; but that its repudiation would have made the Arabs willing to subordinate their own views of the future to the requirements of a British (or any other external) world system seems highly improbable. Nor, given the shifting pattern of inter-Arab relations, was there a single Arab 'solution' for the future of Palestine itself. Nevertheless, the issue bulked so large in Britain's imperial concerns that it has to be looked at with special care.

PART II : PALESTINE

Palestine

British policy in respect of Palestine was confirmed by the Cairo Conference in March 1921. It was to be retained under British control

[94]See *DBFP*, Series IA, vol. VII, ch. IV.
[95]E. Monroe, *Britain's Moment in the Middle East, 1914–1956*, (London, Methuen, 1963), p. 74.
[96]Sir John Glubb, *Britain and the Arabs* (London, 1958), pp. 167 – 8.

and ruled by a civilian High Commissioner who would have as his task the reconciliation of the dual commitment to the Jewish National Home in the Balfour Declaration and the more general commitment to self-governing institutions as a prelude to the granting of independence, the common target for the Middle East mandates.[97] When Sir Herbert Samuel* took office as the first High Commissioner on 1 July 1920 he inherited an administration much influenced by the strongly anti-Zionist attitudes of most of the military who had been in charge of the country since Allenby's conquests.[98] While Samuel endeavoured to hold the balance in a more even fashion and was encouraged to do so by the Colonial Office at home, he met with opposition from within his own administration, and his opponents' hand was strengthened by the serious Arab riots in May 1921. Under their impact, Samuel felt obliged to give assurances that there would be no mass immigration of Jewish settlers and that the Balfour Declaration did not imply the creation of a Palestine governed by the Jews.[99]

Such concessions, which outraged Zionist opinion, did not satisfy the Arabs and the prospect of holding the ring between two irreconcilable elements in the population was not an attractive one.[100] Samuel's solution, to try to find at least a spokesman for the Arabs with whom political negotiations could be attempted by elevating to the position of Grand Mufti of Jerusalem, Amin Husaini, a member of one of the rival clans who between them shared much authority among the Arab population, if anything made matters worse.[101] It allowed 'the

[97] On the origins of the British position in Palestine and the Balfour declaration, see Isaiah Friedman, *The Question of Palestine, 1914–1918: British-Jewish-Arab relations* (London, 1973), and Mayir Vereté, 'The Balfour Declaration and its Makers' in E. Kedourie and S.G. Hain (eds), *Palestine and Israel in the Nineteenth and Twentieth Centuries* (London, 1982).

[98] On the strongly anti-Zionist (and occasionally anti-Semitic) crusade of the military, see Keith Jeffery, *The British Army and the Crisis of Empire, 1918–1922* (Manchester, 1984), and the same author's edition of *The Military Correspondence of Sir Henry Wilson, 1918–1922* (London, 1985).

[99] For the situation in Palestine in this period, see Bernard Wasserstein, *The British in Palestine: The Mandatory Government and the Arab-Jewish Conflict 1917–1929* (London, 1978), and the same author's *Wyndham Deedes in Palestine* (London, 1973). For Samuel's role, see Kedourie, *The Chatham House Version*, ch. 4, 'Sir Herbert Samuel and the Government of Palestine', and Neil Caplan, 'The Yishuv, Sir Herbert Samuel, and the Arab Question in Palestine, 1921 – 1925', in E. Kedourie and S. G. Haim (eds), *Zionism and Arabism in Palestine and Israel* (London, 1982).

[100] Churchill's suggestion that the auxiliary police no longer needed in Ireland after the Treaty might be used to keep the peace in Palestine, an effort to kill two birds with one stone, is an indication of how even a Zionist well-wisher, as Churchill was at that time, saw the situation in Palestine as essentially a colonial one. Martin Gilbert, *Winston S. Churchill*, vol. IV, *Companion*, vol. 3 (London, 1977), p. 1645.

[101] For the politics of the Palestinian Arabs and the rivalry between the Husaini and Nashashibi families, see Y. Porath, *The Emergence of the Palestinian-Arab National Movement* (London, 1974).

Husainis, already powerful enough in Palestine, to become the self-appointed, exclusive and irresponsible spokesmen of the Palestinians whose power their fellow-countrymen could, as the sequel showed, challenge only at their peril'.[102]

Samuel's speech of 3 June 1921 can be regarded as the basis of subsequent policy; further attempts were made to clarify and refine it by Sir John Shuckburgh of the Colonial Office in a memorandum of 17 December. The 'Churchill' White Paper of 30 June 1922 was based upon the Shuckburgh memorandum.[103] Yet this did little more than hold out the prospect of even-handedness between the two sides.[104] It was perhaps beyond the grasp of most of the British that neither side would tolerate mere even-handedness, since for both sides there were quite different and incompatible ideals at stake. For the Arabs, as successive delegations to London and pronouncements in Palestine made clear, there was no validity at all in the Jewish claims: Palestine was an Arab country and the Jews there had no right to more than a minority status, and no right to increase their numbers by immigration from Europe. For the Jews, their commitment to Zion had been recognised as a right by the international community. Its precise future might still be undetermined but it could not rightfully be sacrificed to the current Arab majority in the country. Over the next decade and even afterwards, this equal intransigence in theory was not paralleled in practice. The Zionists were prepared to make some concessions in the hope and expectation that in the long run the mandate was their best hope. But this was the view of the international leadership of Weizmann based in London. In Palestine itself, the leaders of the Yishuv tended to be more absolutist in their positions. Their mentality, like that of minorities of European settlers elsewhere, was coloured by the daily threat to their lives and well-being from an obviously irreconcilable enemy.[105] The Arabs on the other hand could see no benefit from going any part of the way to meet British wishes. For to accept any proposals based on the notion of even-handedness – an Arab Agency to parallel the Jewish Agency, elections to a legislative council which they would not be able to dominate – did

---

[102] Kedourie, op. cit., p. 69.
[103] See Michael Cohen, *Churchill and the Jews* (London, 1985), pp. 134 – 5.
[104] *Correspondence with the Palestine Arab Delegation and the Zionist Organisation*, Cmd 1700, 1922. W. K. Hancock, *Survey of British Commonwealth Affairs*, vol. I (London, 1937), 472 ff.
[105] The Weizmann Correspondence is the best source for this aspect of the matter. See Weizmann, op. cit., vols X and XI.

involve admitting that the Jews had some rights to be considered and it was essential to their case that they had none. Even the occasional direct contacts with the Jews had to be made in a form which could be repudiated. No Arab leader could be seen to give the Yishuv legitimacy.[106]

In Britain, the Churchill White Paper was not without its opponents. Indeed, on 19 June 1922 the House of Lords passed by 60 votes to 29 a motion calling for the postponement of the coming into operation of the mandate pending its amendment in a pro-Arab sense. On 4 July, the House of Commons did endorse the White Paper policy but only by 292 votes to 35, not a sign of overwhelming enthusiasm. The cabinet itself was exposed to external as well as internal pressures; the fear of antagonising the Indian Muslims was still a lively element in official thinking.[107]

The Conservative government that succeeded the Lloyd George administration might well have been expected to reconsider the whole question once again, particularly in view of its commitment to cutting public expenditure. It turned down in December 1922 a suggestion put forward by Samuel and his Chief Secretary, Wyndham Deedes, for trying to bring about a wider confederation of Arab states in which a Jewish National Home might find a place.[108] Therafter further pressure on the government brought about the appointment of a committee similar to that which had already considered the question of Britain remaining in Iraq. The Committee had before it a number of documents submitted by the Colonial Office, arguing in particular

[106] From the vantage point of many years later it seems remarkable that the British should have underestimated the religious factors in the situation. Jerusalem, it was often pointed out, was a city sacred to the three great monotheistic religions. But so far from this having a eirenic effect, it had the opposite, as it had had during so many centuries. Men had in the past been willing to face great risks and do terrible things for the sake of Jerusalem: why should anyone think it would be different in the twentieth century? See e.g. Jonathan Riley-Smith, *The First Crusade and the idea of crusading* (London, 1986).

[107] 'I may say that the Aga Khan is anxious that Palestine should be turned into an Arab State and that Jewish immigration should be stopped.' Peel to Reading, 15 October 1922, IORL MSS EUR E.238/5. It should be borne in mind that the Indian Army at this time supplied much of the garrison in Palestine. See Samuel's despatch of 8 December 1922, C.P. 4379, in PRO CAB 24/140. There were of course counter-pressures. It was reported to a cabinet meeting on 18 August 1921 that the Canadian and South African Premiers had let it be known that they would find British support for the Zionists politically helpful: PRO CAB 23/26. While in office, Churchill pressed the case for keeping American sympathy as a reason for going along with the Zionists: Cohen op. cit., p. 122.

[108] Curzon seems to have been an important figure in getting the scheme rejected. See Kedourie, op. cit., p. 78; Wasserstein, *The British in Palestine*, pp. 26 – 7. For the whole idea that the way to solve the Palestine question was to broaden it into general plans for the Arab world, see Y. Porath, *In Search of Arab Unity*.

that much of the opposition to Zionism emanated from anti-Jewish prejudice and that there were strong military reasons for remaining in Palestine, particularly if the recent changes in Egypt affected the problem of defending the Suez Canal. Indeed, Sir Gilbert Clayton, who had played a prominent part in Egyptian affairs, was quoted for the view that the policy now being followed in regard to Egypt would not have been recommended or accepted unless it had been thought certain that British control in Palestine would be maintained for at least a number of years. If the British failed to maintain their position and the League failed to find a new mandatory, the Turks would return and Britain would be seen as a Christian Power which had rescued the Holy Land from the Turk but lacked the strength or courage to guard what it had won.[109]

The military were less convinced of the advantages of remaining in Palestine. The Chief of the Imperial General Staff (C.I.G.S.) gave it as his opinion that if Egypt were attacked, for instance by the Turks in combination with a local rising, the British would be compelled to withdraw from Palestine and the Turks would return, producing unrest throughout the area. On the other hand, the Secretary of State for India pointed to its importance as a stage in the air link with India. Leo Amery*, the First Lord of the Admiralty, thought it advisable to remain in Palestine to keep out other Powers, particularly as the costs of doing so would not be great. He also supported Samuel's view that the important thing was to make it plain to everyone that Britain intended to stay; for only so would stability be achieved.[110]

The Report of the Committee pointed out that the existing policy could not be reversed without surrendering the mandate which would mean Britain being replaced by France or Italy or the return of the Turks; all would be equally injurious politically, and, despite the opinion of the C.I.G.S., strategically as well. On 31 July 1923, the cabinet accepted the committee's view that Palestine should be retained and the basic principles of the mandate upheld.[111]

It seems fairly clear that the decision to retain the mandate, which could not be a popular one, is what requires explanation, rather than the Balfour Declaration itself, which can fairly easily be accounted for in terms of the pressures of wartime. It would seem that, despite the

[109] C.P.4379, in PRO CAB 24/140; C.P.60(23), in PRO CAB 24/158; C.P.106(23), C.P.149(23), in PRO CAB 24/159.
[110] Meeting of 12 July 1923, PRO CAB 2/3.
[111] Report of the Committee on Palestine, 17 July 1923, PRO CAB 23/161; PRO CAB 23/46.

opinion of the C.I.G.S., the basic consideration was the strategic one; a reallocation of mandates and the general upheaval that this might cause was more than the government was willing to face at a time when it was trying to bring about greater stability in Europe. Once the decision was taken, the military arguments for it were to become more powerful. The R.A.F., whose opinions on imperial security were receiving more attention, was emphatic on its utility. By 1926 Trenchard* was arguing that the planned pipe-line from Iraq and the projected railway from Haifa to Baghdad were vital to the Baghdad-Cairo link, itself essential as a defence against a possible attack on Persia, and wished plans for the defence of Haifa in the event of war to be fully prepared.[112]

On the other hand, the Baldwin government when defending the decision to remain in Palestine, did not refer to the strategic considerations; indeed it was hard to see how it could without offending friendly powers. Instead, the government took its stand on the obligations it had undertaken towards the League of Nations. And this in turn helped the opponents of the policy, who argued that British blood and treasure were being spent to carry out the quixotic purpose of setting up a Jewish National Home which could not be regarded as a British national interest.[113]

In the day-to-day affairs of Palestine, questions of administration would inevitably bulk large. Because of the Arab determination not to co-operate, Palestine was an anomaly among the Middle East mandates. In Syria the highest posts were held by Arabs, with the real power, as everyone was aware, being in the hands of their French advisers. A similar situation, with the British in control, existed in Egypt and was being developed in Iraq and would be in Trans-Jordan. In Palestine some Arabs and Jews were employed by the government, though with the exception of Samuel himself none in the most crucial positions. It was run as a colony would be, by direct rule. And this was irksome for many of the Jewish settlers. They felt, with a good deal of evidence to support them, that the instincts of the administrators were to side with the Arabs as those most needing protection.[114] And those

[112] Chiefs of Staff subcommittee meeting, 2 April 1926, PRO CAB 53/2.

[113] This point is well made in Christopher Sykes, *Crossroads to Israel* (London, 1965).

[114] This typical attitude of the British in contact with colonial peoples was spotted early on by a shrewd Jewish observer: 'One young officer said to me 'The Jews are so clever and the Arabs so stupid and childish, that it only seems sporting to be for the Arabs'. Sporting. They don't consider the wide difference in numbers. I wonder if the public-school Englishman will ever get over his love affair with the Arabs'. Letter written in 1920 by Helen Bentwich, wife of Norman Bentwich

Jews who carried a heavy baggage of European culture did not relish being treated as 'colonials'.

More important was the disjunction between administration and politics. Each of the communities ran its own religious, social and educational institutions, negotiating with the mandatory government for such privileges and status as they required. In the Jewish case, the communal organisation had from early on a representative character including elected bodies, though it was of necessity interlocked with the world Zionist movement which was responsible for fund-raising and the recruitment of immigrants. In 1925, after some protest from the officials of the Colonial Office to whom the idea was an alien one, the institutions of the Yishuv were recognised by the British government as parallels to the Supreme Muslim Council, which had functioned as the accepted voice of the Islamic community since 1921.[115]

From another point of view, the quasi-colonial status of Palestine was of advantage to the Jews. It was the firmly held view in Whitehall that colonies should pay for themselves, and the best hope that Palestine would develop a suitable tax-base lay in the encouragement of a more efficient use of the land and the setting on foot of industrial enterprises based upon the country's few natural assets, the capacity for generating hydro-electric power and the chemical deposits of the Dead Sea. For such economic development Jewish capital and Jewish skills had to be encouraged, and the need for the latter balanced against the political demands to stop all immigration coming from the Arab leadership.[116] The concept of economic absorptive capacity

who until the end of the 1920s was as attorney-general the highest ranking Jew in the administration. Norman and Helen Bentwich, *Mandate Memories* (London, Hogarth Press, 1965), 57. Mrs Bentwich was right to wonder; sixty five years later, a British diplomat specialising in the Middle East, Sir Anthony Parsons, could still in his memoirs, *They Say the Lion* (London, 1986), show the same uncritical tenderness for Arabs.

[115] Wasserstein, op. cit., 135 – 6. The establishment and role of the Supreme Moslem Council is dealt with in Y. Porath, *The Emergence of the Palestinian Arab National Movement*.

[116] The question of the impact of this immigration upon the Arab population at large is a vexed one, particularly in view of the ideological hostility of Zionism to the employment, particularly in agriculture, of non-Jewish labour since part of the ideal of 'normalising' the Jewish position was to restore to Jewry pride in manual labour. The population figures for the mandatory period suggest that as elsewhere in the colonial world any economic development did attract labour from outside. The figures for Arab immigration into Palestine put forward by Joan Peters in her somewhat hysterical and bitterly anti-British book, *From Time Immemorial* (London, 1985), have come in for much criticism. A more sober inquiry suggests that rather over a third of the immigration into Palestine during the mandatory period was by Arabs. See Fred M. Gottheil, 'Arab immigration into pre-State Israel', in E. Kedourie and S.G. Haim (eds), *Palestine and Israel in the Nineteenth and Twentieth Centuries* (London, 1982).

used by the administration to regulate the issue of immigration permits was of course a highly subjective one, and the pressure for immigration varied with the changing economic and political conditions in Eastern Europe, the principal source of Jewish immigration. In addition, the ability of the Zionists to collect funds was affected by the split that had developed in the movement between the London-based Executive, of which Weizmann was the principal leader and spokesman, and the American branch of the movement. It is perhaps ironic that one reason for the Americans, led by Justice Brandeis, separating themselves from the main body of the movement was their objection to what seemed to be too close an identification of Zionism with Britain's imperial purposes.

Meanwhile, as was revealed in the discussion held with the Permanent Mandates Commission of the League of Nations, the degree to which the mandate should be administered in a positive spirit was still an open question.[117] It had become clear that the original expectation of some Zionists that the Arabs would come to accept the idea of Jewish settlement as a contribution to the revival of the Arab world after the lifting of the Turkish yoke, and that the Jews could be intermediaries between the cultures of west and east were doomed to frustration. The British as rulers were forced to make choices, and to external observers they often appeared to give priority to Arab claims.[118] One reason for this was the security issue which, always of concern to colonial administrators, was of particular relevance in a country so divided that neither community, it was held, could be trusted with basic policing functions. The Jews, subject to attacks upon their settlements from time to time, were bound to arm themselves in underground self-defence organisations, and the British had either to acquiesce in such activity or to risk appearing as conniving in Arab violence. In addition there was the sensitivity to communist subversion, to which in the 1920s colonial administrators and some politicians at home were keenly attuned. Some difficulties had been created at the beginning of the mandatory period by

[117] See the discussion in Ben Halpern, *The Idea of the Jewish State* (Cambridge, Mass., 1961), 312 ff.

[118] As in Egypt however, nothing was done to win over the cultural allegiance of the Arab elite. Nothing came of a Report by Sir James Headlam-Morley on the Anglican Schools in Palestine in which he suggested an Institute for Higher Studies co-operating with the Hebrew University of Jerusalem but providing for the non-Hebrew speaking population and competing with the American University of Beirut which was attracting students from Palestine and Trans-Jordan as well as Iraq, Egypt and the Sudan. M.S. in the possession of the late Agnes Headlam-Morley.

immigrants from Russia sympathetic to communism, and thereafter one of the main arguments against allowing further immigration was that it was likely to involve importing communists – an argument not much attenuated by the evidence for the Soviet Union's own increasingly overt hostility to Zionism.

The British Labour Party and Zionism

In considering British policy, it is worth recalling that of the earlier sponsors of the idea of a Jewish National home in Palestine, all except Balfour had been Liberals. Opposition had in the main come from the Conservatives, especially from the extreme right of the party. After 1922, with the declining force of liberalism in British politics, it was more important to know what attitude the Labour Party would take if it achieved power.[119] The British Labour Party, coming into existence after Jewish emancipation, had had less direct contact with the 'Jewish problem' than other European socialist parties.[120] It was however affected by the propaganda of the Labour branch of the Zionist movement, the Poalei Zion. The Labour Party's war aims, drafted by Henderson and Webb and issued in August 1917, that is before the Balfour declaration, had expressed the view that Palestine should be freed from the Turks and created a 'Free State under international guarantee, to which such of the Jewish people as desire to do so may return, and may work out their salvation free from interference by those of alien race or religion'. Although the declaration did not refer to autonomy or a 'National Home', it was important in paving the way for the admission of the Poalei Zion to the second international. The English branch of the Poalei Zion affiliated to the Labour Party in 1920 and ceased to function independently.

The *New Statesman* which had been pro-Zionist from before the war supported the Balfour Declaration but was guarded in its interpretation of what it implied. In 1919 the *New Statesman* supported Weizmann's moderation against the criticism of advocates of Jewish

[119] The changing attitudes of Liberal opinion over the years can be followed in the different attitudes of the editors of the *Manchester Guardian*. C.P. Scott was an intermediary between the Zionists and the Lloyd George government. His successor but one W.P. Crozier (1932 – 44) was a strong pro-Zionist while his successor A.P. Wadsworth (1944 – 56) was much more sceptical, though critical of Ernest Bevin's pro-Arab stance. By the late 1960s the *Guardian* (as it became) was distinctly unsympathetic to Israel. See D. Ayerst, *Guardian* (London, 1971).
[120] See for what follows Joseph Gorny, *The British Labour Movement and Zionism 1917–1948* (London, Cass, 1983).

statehood such as the novelist Israel Zangwill, pointing out that Jews were only ten per cent of the country's population and that while a National Home was possible a Jewish State would be a disaster. Thereafter the *New Statesman* continued to support moderate Zionism and selective immigration but showed an increasing concern for Arab fears, seeing as the solution a bi-national Palestinian State incorporating the National Home. The Labour Party itself gave general support to the policy of the Balfour Declaration and made this clear in a letter to Balfour on the eve of the San Remo Conference. On the other hand it was in favour of the withdrawal of Britain's military presence in Palestine as a contribution to the cutting of public expenditure.

Ramsay MacDonald toured the Middle East in late 1921 and wrote a pamphlet, *A Socialist in Palestine.* He combined a sympathetic view of the Yishuv with a savage denunciation of the Jewish 'plutocracy'. He saw the primary impulse to the Jewish desire for the National Home as a religious one, but suggested that more significant for the British working class than these historic ties were the new socialist experiments being carried out by the settlers. Nevertheless Jewish immigration was creating a situation of confrontation with the Arabs, and the Jews would have to guarantee Arab rights; he was thus in favour of restrictions on immigration.[121] In November 1922 Henderson enunciated the Party's policy as being support for the Balfour Declaration, provided its policy was carried out in an even-handed way. And Thomas*, the Colonial Secretary in the 1924 Labour Government, defined the government's policy in the same way. Weizmann expressed himself as satisfied with the assurances he had received from Thomas and other ministers and believed that the government's friendly attitude was getting more support from public opinion as the exorbitant demands of the Egyptians were increasingly understood. Palestine was now essential for the security of the Empire and people began to realise that it could only fulfil this role if Jewish enterprise were allowed free course: 'otherwise the Arabs would for a certain time enjoy the fruits of a British regime and then fall on the backs of the British, just as the Egyptians have done'.[122]

Such an identity of interests between the British Empire and the Jews was an assumption made on the whole by the Conservative

[121] For MacDonald's visit see N.Bentwich, *My Seventy Seven Years* (London, 1962), p. 76.
[122] Weizmann to Louis Marshall, 17 July 1924, in Weizmann, vol. XII, pp. 219 – 20.

government that came to power after MacDonald's defeat in the autumn of 1924. The Colonial Secretary was now Leo Amery, whose own sympathies were strongly Zionist. It was also the view powerfully expounded by General Smuts, now regarded as the senior statesman of Empire.[123] It was held by exponents of this view that the Arab threat had been exaggerated and that firm government would enable the British objective to be pursued without too much difficulty. In that respect, the choice as Samuel's successor of a soldier, Field-Marshal Plumer*, in 1925 was significant. Although the Zionists were not consulted about the appointment, he proved of all the successive British rulers of the country the most favourable to the Jewish cause and showed himself able to maintain the peace with relatively little force.[124] In these circumstances it was possible to envisage a permanent relationship between the Yishuv and the British Empire such as was espoused by Josiah Wedgwood* and his friends of the Seventh Dominion League.[125] Wedgwood himself believed that the Labour Party had shown insufficient understanding of the importance to the Jews of some form of political autonomy. At a dinner party in the House of Commons, Wedgwood embarked upon a discussion of the future of Palestine which, as Amery recorded it,

> became largely a discussion as to how to find a workable bridge from Crown Colony to responsible government. I answered Jos's question by saying that our ultimate end is clearly to make Palestine the centre of western influence using the Jews as we have used the Scots, to carry the English ideal through the Middle East and not merely to make an artificial Hebrew enclave in an oriental country. Secondly that we meant Palestine in some way or other to remain within the framework of the British Empire. Thirdly that on the constitution we must mark time hoping that experience in Ceylon and elsewhere will find us new lines of development to follow.[126]

[123] W.K. Hancock, *Smuts*, vol. II, *The Fields of Force* (Cambridge, 1968), 278.

[124] Sykes, op. cit., 101 ff. For a Jewish view of the Plumer years see Bentwich and Bentwich, op. cit., ch. 6.

[125] C.V. Wedgwood, *The Last of the Radicals: Josiah Wedgwood M.P.* (London, 1951), 181 ff; N. Rose, 'The Seventh Dominion', *HJ*, vol. XIV (1971), pp. 397 – 416. Among the Zionists the Revisionists under Vladimir Jabotinsky were keener on the idea than the official leadership; Jabotinsky's representative in London, Meir Grossman was in constant contact with Wedgwood and Commander Kenworthy (Lord Strabolgi), another enthusiast. (Information from Professor David Vital.)

[126] John Barnes and David Nicholson, *The Leo Amery Diaries*, vol. 1, *1896–1929* (London, Hutchinson, 1980), pp. 558 – 9. Ceylon had presented the British government with a typical example of the difficulties of introducing representative institutions among a people in which the

If Palestine was regarded as part of the imperial system it had in the view of Churchill, now Chancellor of the Exchequer, to be prepared to pay its full share of the system's expenses and he was clearly tempted by its budget surplus. When therefore Plumer established, as part of his reorganisation of local security, the Trans-Jordan frontier force, it was suggested that Palestine pay most of the cost, as well as the high proportion of Transjordan's administrative costs which had already been agreed to by Amery. Plumer argued that the burden being put on the Jewish taxpayers in Palestine was an unfair one at a time when there was in fact considerable unemployment in the community, but though some concessions were made, he was unable to carry the day. Nor, despite Balfour's support, was Amery able to persuade the cabinet to support the Zionists' request for an approach to the League to guarantee a loan for development which they would hope to raise.[127]

There were thus limitations on the British readiness to see the problems as the Zionists saw them, but it could reasonably be claimed that by the late 1920s Palestine was the quietest part of the Middle East.[128] The British seemed much more secure there than the French next door.[129] This did not mean that its problems had been solved – far from it – only that a point of equilibrium had been reached so that administration could take the place of policy-making. The uneasy triangle formed by Britain's imperial needs, the inchoate but mobilisable force of Arab feelings and the needs and longings of persecuted Jewry only needed to have one of the three sides submitted to external pressure for the balance to be overthrown. With nothing to hope for from a change in the constitutional position, it was the interest of the Zionists to co-operate with the British as far as they were allowed to, and to hope that where British officialdom was

main divisions were communal; this problem was recognised in its first constitution, that of 1920. See Hancock, *Survey*, vol. 1, 394 ff.

[127] Cohen, op. cit., pp. 153 – 4, 161 – 3.

[128] In 1925 Plumer had been so confident of the security situation that he dissolved the local gendarmerie. Townshend, *Britain's Civil Wars*, p. 92.

[129] The Foreign Secretary was as keen as ever to keep the French in good humour to assist his pursuit of objectives in Europe. In February 1926 Chamberlain and Amery successfully (though improperly) brought pressure to bear on Sir Frederick (Lord) Lugard, the British Member of the Permanent Mandates Commission, to prevent condemnation of the French handling of the Syrian revolt of 1925. See M. Perham, *Lugard*, vol. 2 (London, 1960), pp. 650 – 2. In 1927 the British government were thanked for the handling by the Trans-Jordan authorities of the situation caused by the presence of Druze refugees from Syria. Chamberlain to Crewe, 11 May 1927, *DBFP*, Series IA, vol. III (London, 1970), p. 286.

obdurate public sympathy could be reckoned upon. Whatever the feelings and wishes of the local administration might be, policy would continue to be made in London.[130]

It is nevertheless arguable that the next crisis in the affairs of the mandate was precipitated by temporary local conditions. It is possible that had Plumer still been at his post at the time of the Arab riots and attacks on Jews that began in August 1929, ostensibly as the outcome of a disagreement over Jewish access to the Western Wall (the 'Wailing Wall') which had been simmering since the previous September, the Arabs might have held their hand.[131] In fact, when the riots broke out, authority was in the hands of the Chief Secretary, Sir Harry Luke, in the absence of the new High Commissioner, Sir John Chancellor, who was at Geneva attending the annual meeting of the Permanent Mandates Commission.[132] Luke had also been responsible for the administration during the period that elapsed between Plumer's departure and Chancellor's arrival and had been negotiating with some of the Arab leaders for a constitutional advance towards self-government which had ended in June in a draft agreement for a nominated Legislative Council. While the Husaini faction had not been party to the negotiations – they had clearly been behind the riots – Luke does not appear to have wavered from his pro-Arab sentiments. He did of course call upon troops from outside to back up the security forces, but although Arab policemen had taken part in the massacres, he would not permit the arming of Jewish settlers for their own self-defence.[133] It is clear that both Chancellor and Luke took the view that these bloody events fortified the often expressed contention of the British administrators on the spot that they were being asked to execute an impossible and unjust policy and that the use of superior force could not be more than a temporary expedient.[134]

---

[130] On this point see Max Beloff, *The role of the Palestine Mandate in the period of Britain's Imperial decline* (Haifa, 1982).

[131] See Y. Porath, *The Emergence of the Palestinian-Arab National Movement, 1918–1929*, ch. 7. For the administration's handling of the dispute, see Wasserstein, op. cit., pp. 220–35.

[132] Although Chancellor had begun his career as a soldier he had retired from the army and had been a civilian governor in a number of colonies. It is interesting to speculate what the outcome would have been had General Smuts become high Commissioner rather than Chancellor. He was apparently approached with the suggestion but declined to be considered. Weizmann, *Letters and Papers*, vol. XIII, p. 480.

[133] For the security issue in Palestine as seen after the 1929 riots, see Townshend, op. cit., 99 ff.

[134] They thus gave ear to the somewhat preposterous idea of St John Philby that he could act as an intermediary between the British and the Palestinian Arabs, offered on the ground that he was an active member of the Labour Party and an intimate friend of the new Colonial Secretary.

Whether this view would now be acceptable to the home government would depend on the attitude of the Labour administration which had come into office in June. In this administration the Colonial Secretary was Sidney Webb, now Lord Passfield. There was some reason to doubt whether the new government would insist upon following the line of its predecessor. The discussions on Palestine at the Labour Conferences of 1925 and 1928 had shown a desire to see the principle of self-government applied to Palestine, and an unwillingness to accept the Poalei Zion arguments that if this were granted, it would mean enabling the Arabs to use their majority to shut the doors against any further Jewish immigration, and so stifle the National Home. Direct contacts with MacDonald suggested to the Poalei Zion that Labour was reflecting a general British view that Arabs were more important to Britain than the Jews, and that Britain's obligations to each must be given equal weight.[135]

MacDonald's reactions to the events in Palestine was somewhat confused. According to a report of his speech at the League Assembly in Geneva, he said that there was 'no racial conflict in what happened in Palestine the other day. There was no conflict between Moslems and Jews'.[136] On the following day the acting High Commissioner telegraphed to the Colonial Secretary: 'I should be glad to know if the Prime Minister has been misrepresented since the present disturbances, as you are aware, are essentially racial in origin and character'.[137]

While Passfield himself seems to have taken up office with no more than the general caveats about Zionism now common form in the Labour Party, his wife was a strong opponent of the National Home, the claim to which she regarded as 'sheer nonsense and hypocritical nonsense'.[138] It seems improbable that Passfield himself took kindly to admonitions from Beatrice Webb's nephew, Richard Meinertzhagen (one of the few strongly pro-Zionist servants of the Palestine administration in the mandatory period), who wrote to him on 29 August setting forth the Zionist case in the aftermath of the riots.

Chancellor also tried to convince the Colonial Office to renew the attempt at constitutional changes which had been thwarted by the August riots. See Y. Porath, *The Palestinian Arab National Movement*, vol. II, *From Riots to Rebellion, 1929–1939* (London, 1977), pp. 20 – 2.

[135] See Gorny, op. cit., pp. 32 – 46.

[136] *The Times* (London), 3 September 1929.

[137] Copy in IORL L/P&S/10/1032 P.5774.

[138] N. and J. Mackenzie (eds), *The Diary of Beatrice Webb*, vol. IV (London, Virago, 1985), pp. 190 – 2.

When he saw Passfield on 4 October the latter seemed 'rather tired of Zionism, having been subject to a ceaseless bombardment of complaint and suggestion' for the past two weeks.[139] Passfield had already made it clear to Weizmann that he would be following the advice of his officials and would not even consider the dismissal of Luke or his subordinate Archer Cust.[140]

The obvious immediate step was to appoint a Commission of Inquiry into the riots – the Shaw Commission – which was sent to Palestine. Its terms of reference were 'to enquire into the immediate causes which led to the recent outbreak in Palestine and make recommendations as to the steps to be taken to avoid a recurrence'. The Arabs, who wished to raise the whole issue of the mandate, were disappointed at this apparent restriction.[141] In fact, however, when the Report appeared at the end of March 1930, the Commission was found to have gone beyond its terms of reference and to have gone into the whole problem of Palestine in a way which appeared to call into question the attitude of both sides.[142] To the Jews it seemed that the Commission's view that too little had been done to make plain the rights of the non-Jewish inhabitants of the country, suggested a further watering down of the National Home concept.

Passfield's welcome for the Report confirmed the view that his own instincts were on the Arab side. Indeed, as the Zionist leader Ben Gurion had noted even before the riots, Passfield apparently regarded the Jews and the Arabs as he did the Whites and Blacks in the African colonies – he saw it as his duty 'to defend the natives against the threat of the settlers'. Ben Gurion's formulation is fully confirmed by Passfield's letters and his wife's diaries. An increasing hostility towards Zionism in the Labour press and the Labour Party was now obvious. Passfield himself disputed the validity of the Zionist concept of 'Jewish labour' and denied the existence of any room for mass immigration into Palestine: a nationalist movement was not a suitable instrument for constructing a socialist society.[143]

---

[139] Meinertzhagen, op. cit., pp. 140 – 4.
[140] Passfield to Weizmann, 20 August 1929. N. Mackenzie (ed.), *The Letters of Sidney and Beatrice Webb*, vol. III, 1912-1947, (Cambridge, 1978), pp. 315 – 18.
[141] Y. Porath, op. cit., p. 3.
[142] *Report of the Commission on the Palestine Disturbances of August 1929*, (Cmd 3530, 1930).
[143] Gorny, op. cit., pp. 58, 70 – 1. Beatrice Webb believed that the modern Jews were not Semites at all but Mongols and so had no ancestral connection with the Holy Land; and the Zionists being secularists could not put forward a religious claim either. *Diary*, vol. IV, 228.

If the whole question of policy in Palestine was to be looked at afresh, that further investigations would clearly have to be made. London in the spring of 1930 was thus the scene of much diplomatic and political manoeuvering, with Weizmann endeavouring to exploit MacDonald's former friendliness to the Zionists and to instigate pressure from the United States – perhaps counter-productively – and the Arabs sending a delegation both to try to push the government to make further concessions to their constitutional demands and to prohibit immigration, and to add their voices to the public propaganda of their friends. The Indian government once again expressed its concern about Palestine. 'It is difficult' ran an India Office Minute, 'to see what connection exists between the suppression of the riots and the Moslem situation in India, but the Government of India should clearly know what is going on'.[144] Arabs in Cairo appealed directly to the Indian Khilafatists. And the Viceroy expressed the fear lest a strong anti-British agitation might grow up in India, uniting Hindu and Muslim, such as had previously been the case in relation to Turkey.[145] On 21 April 1930 the All-India Muslim Conference telegraphed the Colonial Secretary to demand the ending of the Mandate. Attempts were made by Arab envoys to India to stimulate disturbances there to coincide with further riots in Palestine.[146]

The question of who would conduct the new inquiry which would clearly focus on the land question and immigration was obviously of great importance. Weizmann had hopes once again that the *deus ex machina* might be Smuts to whom he had addressed a powerful letter setting out his policy.[147] And it appears that he originally got his way with MacDonald, who may actually have asked Smuts to take on the task. But the Prime Minister was then persuaded that Smuts was too

---

[144] India Office minute, 25 August 1929, IORL L/P&S/10/1302.

[145] Reuters from Bombay, 28 August 1929, ibid.; Viceroy to Secretary of State for India, 1 September 1929, ibid., p. 5691. The Khilafat movement, which was probably at the root of the Viceroy's anxieties, had been bereft of its original cause when the Treaty of Lausanne was signed and the Ottoman Caliphate abolished. It had turned its attention to the Middle East and originally sided with the Wahabis against the Hejaz but turned against them after their invasion of that country and the damage to the Holy Places. It had also campaigned against France and Spain in connection with the Riff rising in Morocco. Note on 'Unrest' by J.W. Hose in 1925, India Office records, Departmental Memoranda, MSS EUR D.713. When the Khilafat movement leader Muhammed Ali died, he was buried in the precincts of the Al Aqsa Mosque in Jerusalem.

[146] IORL L/P&S/10/1034. The recurring Indian element in British policy towards Palestine is well brought out in G. Sheffer's unpublished Oxford D.Phil. thesis (1971), 'Policy making and British Policies towards Palestine, 1929 – 1939.'

[147] Weizmann to Smuts, 28 November 1929, in J. Van der Poel, ed., *Selections from the Smuts Papers*, vol. V (Cambridge, 1973), pp. 426 – 31.

pro-Zionist and fell back upon a retired colonial civil servant and Liberal M.P., Sir John Hope Simpson.[148] Weizmann believed that MacDonald had let him down both by allowing Passfield to appoint Hope Simpson without prior consultation and because he was deprived of the opportunity of seeing Hope Simpson before he left for Palestine where he would be bound to be over-influenced by the officials.[149]

In October, the Hope Simpson Report was published together with a Government White Paper, which while not overtly representing an obvious departure from previous policies nevertheless gave the impression that a further retreat from the basic commitment to the National Home was implicit in its analysis of the country's potential, seeing 50,000 as the maximum number of future immigrants.[150] The result was that Weizmann felt that his policy of co-operating with the British administration and of dampening down Zionist criticism of its behaviour was no longer sustainable against his critics. He therefore resigned from his Presidency of the Zionist Organisation and Jewish Agency.[151] This did not prevent him from endeavouring to get the language of the White Paper modified, and negotiations with MacDonald ensued, with the Prime Minister's son Malcolm* acting as the intermediary.

The internal politics of the Labour Party now became caught up in the storm created by the White Paper. A by-election was required in the Whitechapel constituency and it was hoped to find a seat for Stafford Cripps (another nephew of Beatrice Webb's) who had just been appointed as Solicitor-General. It was clear that no member of the government stood much chance in a constituency with a large Jewish vote – nor indeed was Cripps personally sympathetic to the Zionists. At this point, Ernest Bevin was approached; in view of his later record it is ironical that his selection should have been seen as likely to attract the Jewish vote. Bevin declined, but found a candidate from his own

---

[148] Beatrice Webb, *Diary*, vol. IV. pp. 212 – 3; Thomas Jones, Keith Middlemas, (ed.), *Whitehall Diary*, (Oxford University Press, 1969) vol. II, pp. 254 – 5; N. Rose, *Lewis Namier and Zionism* (Oxford, 1980), 46 ff.

[149] Weizmann, op. cit., vol. XIV, pp. 256 – 86.

[150] *Report on Immigration, Land Settlement and Development*, by Sir John Hope Simpson, (Cmd 3686, 1930); *Statement of Policy by His Majesty's Government in the United Kingdom*, 21 October 1930, (Cmd 3692). On 12 May the Colonial Office had instructed the Palestine administration to suspend the issue of immigration certificates. The Permanent Mandates Commission had been critical of British policy at its June meeting.

[151] Weizmann to Passfield, 20 October 1930, in Weizmann, op. cit., vol. XIV, p. 388; Passfield to Weizmann, 21 October 1930, in *Letters of Sydney and Beatrice Webb*, vol. III, p. 336.

union, and intervened to secure an assurance from the government which might satisfy Jewish voters. On 4 November he issued a statement saying that the government had no intention of altering the terms of the mandate, no intention of stopping Jewish immigration, and no intention of setting limits to the expansion of the National Home within the terms of the mandate. These assurances secured the return of the Labour candidate, though with a much reduced majority.[152] By the end of the year, it seemed clear that MacDonald's support for Passfield was wavering and that he now felt that both Shaw and Hope Simpson had been too pro-Arab. He had been shaken by the hostility to the White Paper in the House of Commons debate when Lloyd George, Samuel and Amery led the attack. In February he gave way, and read to the House of Commons a letter he had written to Weizmann which he stated to be an authorised interpretation of the White Paper. In it he declared that facilitating Jewish immigration and settlement was an obligation of the mandate and could be fulfilled without prejudice to all sections of the Palestine population.[153] The document appeared to be an indication that in the context of the support of British opinion the Zionists had proved successful. The interpretation of the White Paper contained in MacDonald's letter was denounced by the Arabs as proof that they had nothing to hope for from the British government and must rely upon the support of the rest of the Arab and Moslem worlds. In fact however there was no interruption to the attempt by the British government to seek some ground for co-operation with the less extreme factions among the Arab leaders, particularly in respect of development, and even Weizmann seemed to hope that there might yet be direct Arab-Jewish negotiations.[154] What was put aside for the time being was the idea of an elected Legislative Council which the Zionists had always seen as a threat, and against which Weizmann had always argued in his contacts with the Colonial Office. Once again the course of events in Palestine would depend upon what happened elsewhere. The period of Colonial Office domination of its affairs which had been a feature of the decade since the Cairo Conference was now coming to an end.

[152] Alan Bullock, *The Life and Times of Ernest Bevin*, vol. 1 (London, 1960), pp. 455 – 7; Gorny, op. cit., 91 ff.
[153] H.C. *Deb.*, vol. 245, cols 77 – 210, 17 November 1930, and ibid. vol. 248, cols 751 – 7, 13 February 1931. Text of letter in Rose, *Lewis Namier and Zionism*, Appendix III. On Zionism's political friends in Britain, see N. Rose, *The Gentile Zionists* (London, 1973).
[154] Porath, op. cit., 34 ff.

Chapter 4

EMPIRE INTO COMMONWEALTH
– THE IRISH ANOMALY

Dominion attitudes

When during the Imperial Conference of 1921 it was announced that there had been an agreement for a truce in the fighting in Ireland to enable negotiations to begin, Beatrice Webb commented in her diary: 'It is a blow to the government of Great Britain that it is the premier of South Africa, backed up by those of Australia and Canada and the foreign power of the U.S.A. to whom Ireland will owe her liberty of self-government, a sign that power to rule is passing from England to other English-speaking communities.'[1] It was of course true that power had shifted across the Atlantic but, with the growing isolationism of the United States, the direct impact of its government on British policy-making in the sphere of imperial relations was not for a long time to be of major importance. The role of the Dominions was a different matter. The war had given rise to feelings of similarity of purpose and readiness to co-operate which were already beginning to look somewhat overblown. It was one thing to seek security within a system dominated by the Royal Navy or to ask for preferential treatment in London's commodity or financial markets or to look to Britain in the first instance if immigrants were required. What the Dominion governments would not do was to sacrifice what they perceived to be vital national interests or affront national sentiment at home for the

[1] Mackenzie (eds), *The Diary of Beatrice Webb*, vol. III, p. 382. The Dominion governments were subject to domestic pressures as a result of immigration from Ireland. Some quarter of Australia's population were of Irish Roman Catholic origin; Borden himself was M.P. for Halifax where the Irish were an important element and where there were significant Protestant-Catholic differences; orangeism was strong in Ontario and Newfoundland.

sake of a wider whole. And by 1921 it was already clear that no constitutional changes were envisaged by any of them that would shift the locus of decision-making to London; though they might differ as to the extent to which they wished their own voice to be heard before London came to its decisions.[2]

Each of the four Dominions took up a position arising from its own individual character and history. New Zealand, economically and strategically the most dependent of them, was the least likely to cause trouble. W.F. Massey, Prime Minister from 1912 to 1925, regarded the Imperial War Cabinet of 1917 – 18 as the foundation of the independent status of the Dominions and regretted its demise. He also preferred the procedure of the Washington Conference of 1921 – 2 where the Dominions were represented in a British Empire Delegation, which acted as a unit, to the separate representation of the Dominions at the Paris Peace Conference and their separate signatures to the Versailles Treaty.[3] Australia had its own interests and sensitivities and, having failed to secure the prolongation of the Anglo-Japanese alliance in the face of American and Canadian pressure, was mainly concerned with what this portended for its future security, and for the 'White Australia' policy which was seen as the core of its national existence. For the most part, Australia was reluctant to see the development of an independent foreign policy based upon its own representation abroad, and was in that sense prepared to be a passive rather than an active partner.[4] South Africa had been put under much greater strain as a result of its participation in the war; many Afrikaners were unhappy at the degree to which it appeared to have accepted an imperial role and were more concerned with their economic and social future than with the wider issues which so

---

[2] For the development of intra-Commonwealth relations in the post – 1921 period, see Nicholas Mansergh, *The Commonwealth Experience*, 2nd edn (London, 1982), vol. II, part 1; H. Duncan Hall, *Commonwealth, A History of the British Commonwealth of Nations* (London, 1971); R.F. Holland, *Britain and the Commonwealth Alliance, 1918–1939* (London, 1981). Successive issues of the *Round Table* show a gradual shift on the part of its sponsors from continued insistence upon constitutional unity to accepting the new position of the Dominions and emphasising instead the need for better machinery of consultation so that the Crown would not receive 'conflicting advice'.
[3] R.M. Burdon, *The New Dominion: New Zealand 1918–1939* (London, 1965), pp. 183 – 5.
[4] See P.G. Edwards, *Prime Ministers and Diplomats: the Making of Australian Foreign Policy, 1901–1949* (Melbourne, 1983).

attracted their Prime Minister.[5] A veteran South African politician had seen the danger of trying to turn the wartime partnership into something closer: the Dominions, wrote John X. Merriman to Lord Bryce,

> will take anything you give them but when it comes to the question of giving, either in kind or by way of surrendering their prejudices, you will find them kittle-kattle to deal with. Take the question of the British Indians. I question whether the patriotism of any single Dominion will stretch so far as to give these people the rights of British citizens, though they are quite conscious of the fact that every instance of harsh dealing may raise a terrible difficulty in India itself.[6]

Canada presented a more complex problem; there had been in the Canadian thinking an imperial element of its own. The possibility of taking over the West Indian colonies had been mooted even before the war and by 1918 the prospect was enthusing some of the imperially-minded around Whitehall; Leo Amery envisaged 'a Greater Dominion of British North America, including Newfoundland, the Bermudas, the West Indies, and even, if you liked to have them thrown in, the Falkland Islands'.[7] A more equal partnership with Britain in such circumstances seemed not unthinkable. And it was Sir Robert Borden who had given most definite expression to the idea of perpetuating in some form the machinery of the imperial war cabinet. But by 1921, caution had set in. What would influence Canada would be the need to restore national unity damaged by the wartime conscription issue, a reluctance to become embroiled in issues arising from the peace settlement, and above all an unwillingness to adopt positions which might separate her from the United States.

By the Anglo-Irish Treaty of 6 August 1921 which recognised the Irish Free State as having the status of a Dominion, another and even more difficult member was introduced into the Commonwealth partnership. It was not in its own view a colony that had achieved self-rule but a subject nation that had at last been recognised, though only in

---

[5] For developments in South Africa see M. Wilson and L. Thompson (eds), *The Oxford History of South Africa*, vol. II, 1870 – 1966 (Oxford, 1971).
[6] P. Lewsen (ed.), *Selections from the Correspondence of John X. Merriman*, vol. 4 (Cape Town, Van Riebeeck Society, 1969), p. 296.
[7] P.G. Wrigley, *Canada and the Transition to Commonwealth: British-Canadian Relations, 1917–1926* (Cambridge, 1977), p. 49.

a truncated form. It was the only member of the Commonwealth with a territorial irredenta, and that a part of the United Kingdom itself. And before the new status was accepted – even as an interim settlement, as it was viewed by nearly everyone in southern Ireland – the government had to fight a difficult and vicious civil war against its recent comrades in the anti-British struggle. Even the victors could not afford to seem less than wholehearted in pursuit of their country's national goals.[8] Relations between the Irish Free State and the British government were envenomed by the fate of the Boundary Commission, provided for in the Treaty, to demarcate the definitive border between the two parts of Ireland. To the chagrin of the Free State it came up with the view that no departures from the provisional line could be accepted which would seriously damage the political integrity of Northern Ireland. The recommendations were not published or implemented. Instead, Cosgrave accepted a revocation of the Boundary Commission clause in return for an ending of the Free State's financial obligations under the Treaty. The hope that Ulster would prove to be unviable and that the unity of Ireland would come about in the end despite the acceptance of partition, which had much influenced the Irish negotiators, had been proved a vain one.[9] Furthermore, despite the fact that the Treaty included provisions for the retention by Britain of its naval bases in the South, the Free State was highly averse to any possible involvement in Britain's wars. Neutrality became part of the national creed.[10]

The Empire and the Chanak affair

The British cabinet in 1922 was to some extent oblivious of the kind of association into which the British Commonwealth was developing. They still presumed that, whatever the formal position, when it came to the point, the Dominions would rally round the mother-country as

[8] For Ireland in this period see F.S.L. Lyons, *Ireland since the Famine* (London, 1971); on the separation of Ulster, see T.G. Fraser, *Partition in Ireland, India and Palestine* (London, 1984), chs 2 and 3; on Anglo-Irish relations after the Treaty see David Harkness, *The Restless Dominion: The Irish Free State and the British Commonwealth, 1929–1931* (London, 1969); Paul Canning, *British Policy towards Ireland, 1921–1941* (Oxford, 1985).

[9] Robert Kee, *The Green Flag: A History of Irish Nationalism* (London, 1972), pp. 746 – 7. The whole matter was explored and the text of the Commission's Report finally printed in J.G. Hand (ed.), *Report of the Irish Boundary Commission* (Shannon, 1969).

[10] The origins and nature of the Irish commitment to neutrality are explored in Patrick Keatinge, *A Singular Stance: Irish Neutrality in the 1980s* (Dublin, 1984). Irish delegates emphasised their distance from Britain by addressing the League Assembly in French.

in 1914. The Chanak episode which brought down the Lloyd George government revealed the danger of making assumptions of this kind and created for its successors a more realistic mood even if they had yet to perceive the full implications of the Dominions' reactions to the call for assistance against the Turks.[11]

The British had by the autumn of 1922 got into a position in which neither the French nor the Italians were prepared to support them in preventing the Kemalist forces in Turkey from pursuing the defeated Greeks and from going on to take command of the Straits. Only the Dominions seemed to have forces to spare and it had not been grasped how unwilling they were likely to be to commit troops to support a policy which they had not had a share in making. The cabinet on 15 September authorised Churchill to cable the Dominion Prime Ministers for their assistance.[12]

Much of the blame for what ensued has been laid at Churchill's door, for his handling of the message and in particular for the fact that a government press communiqué setting out what had been done, and intended as a warning to Kemal, was in the papers in Canada, Australia and New Zealand before the telegrams themselves had been decoded for the Prime Ministers.[13] They thus had the feeling that they were being hustled into a decision before their governments could give the matter proper consideration. Furthermore it seems to have been assumed that equality of status implied that the telegrams must be identical, whereas the phrase 'securing firmly the Gallipoli peninsula' which meant a good deal to the Australians and New Zealanders was unlikely to make much of an appeal to South Africa or Canada. Churchill had therefore to send further telegrams to the South African and Canadian governments to explain that they were not expected to make a comparable effort to that of the Pacific Dominions.

The varied nature of the Dominions' responses carried a warning for the future. South Africa did not reply at all. In Canada, Mackenzie

[11] The diplomacy that led up to the Chanak crisis is fully covered in *DBFP*, 1st Series, vols XVII and XVIII. For the general background, see Howard M. Sachar, *The Emergence of the Middle East, 1919–1924* (London, 1970). The Chanak story itself is well told in David Walder, *The Chanak Affair* (London, 1969).

[12] For what ensued see Hall, op. cit., 485 ff. Churchill's role is dealt with in Martin Gilbert, *Winston S. Churchill*, vol. IV, (London, 1975), ch. 45. The relevant documents are in the *Companion* to this volume (London, 1977).

[13] For the muddle over the telegram and the Canadian reaction to it, see R. McGregor Dawson, *Mackenzie King*, vol. I (London, 1958), pp. 408 – 11. On the Australian side, see P.M. Sales, 'W.M. Hughes and the Chanak Crisis of 1922', *Australian Journal of Politics and History (AJPH)* (St Lucia, Queensland), vol. XVII, (1971).

King took what was to be his standard approach to developments in Europe: nothing could be done by Canada except on the authority of its own Parliament; no participation in European wars could be contemplated. No public statement was made.[14] The New Zealand ministers who happened to be together when the cable arrived agreed to send a contingent – a decision confirmed by the New Zealand Parliament three days later.

The Australian case was the most significant for the future. Hughes had taken the view that settling conflicts was a matter for the League of Nations and that, if it failed to fulfil this function, Australia might even contemplate withdrawing from it.[15] He now claimed that he had been put in a difficult position by the publicity given to the British government's request and that he had been left in the dark about what had led up to the crisis. Churchill was obliged to send him a telegram to put him more fully in the picture.[16] Hughes accepted in fact that if there had been a decision to resist the Turks, Australia would join in but felt that she should have been consulted earlier: 'Either the Empire is one and indivisible or it is nothing... If Britain', he continued, 'only consults the Dominions when they are committed then all talk about the Dominions having a real share in deciding foreign and imperial policy is empty air.'[17] The very tentative support of the Dominions was glossed over by the British government. General Harington, in command of the troops on the spot, was told that Chanak had 'now become a point of immense moral significance to the prestige of the Empire'.[18] For the remainder of the episode. Hughes did give overt support to the British government, for instance in a speech to the Australian Parliament on 29 September.[19] By this time agreement had been reached with the French and the Italians for a revision of the Treaty of Sèvres very much in the Turks' favour and

[14] Mackenzie King, who had become Prime Minister in December 1921, was to play the dominant role in the transformation of the Commonwealth in the inter-war period and during the second world war. His assiduity as a diarist makes his career the best documented of that of any Commonwealth statesman of the period except Churchill. But he remains to some extent an enigma. On his private life and in particular his involvement with spiritualism, see C.P. Stacey, *A Very Double Life – the Private World of Mackenzie King* (Toronto, 1976).

[15] Balfour to Curzon (from Geneva), 20 September 1922, *DBFP*, 1st Series, vol. XVIII, pp. 35 – 6.

[16] Churchill to Hughes, 20 September 1922, in Gilbert, *Companion*, vol. IV, pp. 2002 – 3.

[17] Mark Arnold-Forster, 'Chanak rocks the Empire', *Round Table*, no. 240, April 1968, pp. 169 – 77. Hughes had similarly protested about the failure to consult Australia before the Milner recommendations about Egypt in 1920. R.F. Fitzhardinge, *William Morris Hughes*, vol. 2 (Sydney, 1979), pp. 461 – 2.

[18] War Office to Harington, 21 September 1922, *DBFP*, 1st Series, vol. XVIII, 62.

[19] Hall, op. cit., pp. 486 – 92; Fitzhardinge, op. cit., 484 ff.

when they refused to accept what was now offered, General Harington was ordered to present what amounted to an ultimatum. But his cool diplomacy prevented there being a test of armed strength and on 11 October the immediate crisis was ended by a Greco-Turkish convention ending hostilities. A new Conference at Lausanne would work out a definite peace settlement for Turkey. The feeling that Britain had been led into dangerous courses was the proximate cause of the fall of the Lloyd George government.[20]

Bonar Law as Prime Minister did not fulfil Beaverbrook's hope that 'here was a leader who would turn his back to Europe and his face to the Empire'.[21] In dealing with European problems, both Bonar Law and his successor Baldwin had to bear in mind the lack of Dominion appreciation of France's need for security and their unwillingness to see Britain involved in giving it a guarantee.[22] But Baldwin, who took over the premiership on 22 May 1923, gave the European settlement a clear priority over imperial affairs.[23] It could be and was argued that there was no incompatibility between the pacification of Europe and the preservation of the Empire: 'There is no doubt', wrote Lord Robert Cecil, whom Baldwin had brought into the government to deal with League of Nations affairs,

> that in another world war would lie the greatest danger to which the security and maintenance of the British Empire could be exposed. The recent war strained its resources to the uttermost... a recurrence of a similar catastrophe would provide both our discontented subjects and foreign enemies with an unequalled opportunity to break up the imperial system. It is not too much to say that it would also place a severe, perhaps a too severe strain upon the relations of the mother country with the Dominions.[24]

One major difficulty however which faced Cecil and his fellow enthusiasts for a security system based upon the League was that the

[20] On the domestic repercussions of Chanak, see Michael Kinnear, *The Fall of Lloyd George: The Political Crisis of 1922* (London, 1973). The volatility of public opinion is shown by the fact that when Kemal brought on a fresh crisis through the occupation of Constantinople the firm stand taken by the new Conservative government under Bonar Law would actually seem to have helped their cause in the subsequent general election: ibid., pp. 166 – 7.

[21] Lord Beaverbrook, *The Decline and Fall of Lloyd George* (London, Collins, 1963), p. 180.

[22] See Hancock, *Smuts*, vol. II, 132 ff.

[23] 'We've got to settle Europe', he told Thomas Jones on 28 May 1923, 'we can't wait for migration and Empire development.' Thomas Jones, ed. Keith Middlemas, *Whitehall Diary*, vol. I, (Oxford University Press, 1969), pp. 237 – 8.

[24] Note by Lord Robert Cecil, 6 June 1923, Cecil of Chelwood Papers, BL Add MSS 51103.

Dominions did not see things in that way. Sir Eric Drummond, the League's Secretary-General, told Cecil that he had made a splendid case for the League at the 1923 Imperial Conference and that the response of the Dominion premiers appeared to be excellent.[25] In fact, however, Canada, in the person of Mackenzie King, was adamant against giving the League a greater role, and this view was shared by some of the Conservative opposition including its leader Arthur Meighen.[26] At the first League Assembly in November 1920, Canada had tried to get Article X struck out of the Covenant altogether and was responsible for an interpretative resolution passed at the 1923 Assembly which would allow countries to be judges of their own contribution to dealing with an aggressor.[27]

It could be and was held that the Chanak affair had demonstrated that 'British statesmen were not sufficiently interested in relations with the Dominions to provide a basis for the co-operative diplomacy that people like Sir Robert Borden had looked forward to'. And the Canadians were content to allow a minimum of consultation to take place provided it was clear that Canada was not bound to follow Britain's lead. It should not be concluded from this that Mackenzie King was not in a sense a man of Empire, believing that in the last resort Canada would have to stand with Britain, even if his principal adviser O.D. Skelton had an unabated suspicion of British 'imperialists' and their assumed desire to centralise all authority.[28] King's dominant concern, and understandably, was the unity of his own country, which could be threatened by an activist foreign policy.[29] The Australians, both Hughes and Bruce* who succeeded him early in 1923, took a more positive view: Australia could not avoid involvement, and therefore should be consulted. One difficulty was how to bring this about. Hughes had not believed that the Prime Ministers could meet regularly in peacetime nor that Australia would be assisted by keeping a cabinet minister in London. Developments in air travel and wireless communications would in time provide the

---

[25] Drummond to Cecil, BL Add MSS 51110.

[26] Dawson, *Mackenzie King*, vol. I, pp. 402 – 5, 427 – 8.

[27] A. Gordon Dewey, *The Dominions and Diplomacy* (London, 1929), vol. II, pp. 220 – 4.

[28] C.P. Stacey, *Canada and the Age of Conflict*, vol. 2 (Toronto, University of Toronto Press, 1984), 31; ibid., pp. 178, 234.

[29] Two historians, one Canadian and the other British, gave their assessment of Mackenzie King's role as an Empire statesman in a seminar at Canada house, London in November 1978: Norman Hillmer, *Britain and Canada in the Age of Mackenzie King*, pt. I, 'The Outstanding Imperialist'; David Dilks, ibid., pt. II, 'Britain, Canada and the Wider World'.

technical solution.[30] Where the British government was concerned, the position was a more equivocal one. In public, there was still the language which suggested unity of action as the keynote. On 10 November 1924, Austen Chamberlain, who had just resumed charge of the Foreign Office after Labour's defeat in the general election, made the customary Guildhall speech:

> The first thoughts of any Englishman on appointment to the Office of Foreign Secretary must be that he speaks in the name not of Great Britain only, but of the British Dominions beyond the seas and that it is his imperative duty to preserve in word and deed the diplomatic unity of the British Empire. Our interests are one. Our intercourse must be intimate and constant, and we must speak with one voice in the councils of the world.[31]

Problems of a common Empire foreign policy

In practice the difficulties of arriving at an agreed position for joint negotiations were such that 'the Foreign Office was in favour of a common Empire foreign policy only in so far as it was a policy both decided and administered in Whitehall. If it involved consultation with the Dominions the Office greatly preferred a system under which Britain would pursue her own foreign policy and the Dominions would pursue their's.'[32] But this retrospective judgement is based upon a consideration of a series of events in the 1920s, of the outcome of which no-one at the time was fully certain. It is arguable that the Lausanne Conference rather than Chanak marks the true watershed in imperial affairs between the wartime centralisation of decision-making and the subsequent era of separate paths.[33] What should not be overlooked is that what Chamberlain's formulation meant in practice was that in framing its independent policy, the government of the

---

[30] Chanak may also have contributed to the defeat of Hughes in the subsequent Australian general election. Bruce succeeded him as head of a coalition including the Country Party brought into being to keep the Labour Party out of office. There was an under-current of pacifism in the Labour Party throughout the inter-war period, mainly stemming from its large quota of Irish Roman Catholics, who had strongly turned against Britain after the Easter Rising. Fitzhardinge, op. cit., p. 76, 419 ff.

[31] Quoted by Sir Charles Petrie in *The Life and Letters of Austen Chamberlain* (London, Cassell, 1940), vol. 2, p. 251.

[32] Stacey, op. cit., p. 71.

[33] Fitzhardinge, op. cit., p. 495.

United Kingdom would still be guided by the wish to do nothing which would put the ultimate unity of the association to further strain.

The British government had in fact suggested that the Dominions might themselves be individually represented at Lausanne. The French objected to this suggestion and countered with the view that in that case Tunis, Algeria and Morocco should be represented also. The British government then proposed that the United Kingdom should be considered as speaking for the Dominions as well, as had been the case when the Treaty of Sèvres had been negotiated.[34] All the Dominions except New Zealand raised objections, though not identical ones, to this course. Canada did not wish to be represented although Meighen had thought Mackenzie King should use the opportunity to press upon Britain the need to minimise her European commitments.[35] The Canadian government let it be known that although the United Kingdom government would be signing the eventual Treaty on behalf of the Empire as a whole, Canada itself would judge to what extent it would be bound by it, nor was it moved by the suggestion that the Canadian Parliament could consider or approve the Treaty prior to British ratification. Peace with Turkey was a British not a Canadian matter.[36]

Hughes on the other hand protested against Australia's exclusion. Canada and South Africa might be prepared not to participate in the negotiations since they had been unwilling to fight at Chanak. Australia, which would be bound by the consequences of the Treaty whether it signed it or not, was in a different position: 'This habit of making Australia agree to do things when they are done and cannot be undone, when there is only one course open to us in practice – and that is to support Britain – is one which will wreck the Empire if persisted in.'[37]

In the end Canada did not obstruct ratification since otherwise she would still have been technically at war with Turkey, but Mackenzie King used the occasion to make clear that in respect of any 'interimperial obligations' arising from the treaty, Canada would not be bound by anything except what its own Parliament might accept. His diary reveals that he believed he had helped 'to make history' by defining in this way the equality of status between the different parts

[34] Meetings of 1 and 16 November and 19 December 1922, PRO CAB 23/32.
[35] Roger Graham, *Arthur Meighen*, vol. 2, (Toronto, 1962), pp. 214–18.
[36] W.K. Hancock, *Survey of British Commonwealth Affairs*, vol. I, (London, 1937), pp. 254–5.
[37] Quoted by M. Arnold-Forster, loc. cit. See also Fitzhardinge, op. cit., pp. 493–5.

of the Empire: 'The British foreign office have been trying to impose a sort of Imperial right superior to our national right – but have begun the wrong way this time.'[38] And he confirmed his interpretation of the issue in a letter to Ramsay MacDonald who had become Prime Minister by the time the ratification issue arose.[39]

In making this point, Mackenzie King was also looking back at the Imperial Conference that had sat in October and November 1923, during which Curzon referred to the Conference as a 'cabinet'. This could not be the case, argued Mackenzie King, since what were represented were governments each responsible to its own parliament.[40] Bruce had once again claimed a voice for Australia in the making of the Empire's foreign policy as he had done on the occasion of his first appearance as Australian Prime Minister before the Australian Parliament.[41] The Irish Free State, making its first appearance, was close to the Canadian viewpoint, but Smuts was too concerned with the chaos in Europe to take so negative a view, holding that nations that had done so much to win the war should take part in the peace-making.[42]

The Imperial Conference itself gave formal recognition to the new position that had been reached by passing a resolution on 'the Negotiation, Signature and Ratification of treaties' which confirmed the right of Dominion governments to appoint their own negotiators and recommend the ratification of the treaties so reached according to their own constitutional processes.[43] If the Dominions were thus recognised as separate states in their external relations the only constituted identity possessed by the Commonwealth would be that of the common allegiance to the Crown.[44] But the important question

[38] Speech in Canadian Parliament, 9 June 1924, quoted in W. Blair Neatby, *William Lyon Mackenzie King*, vol. 2, (Toronto and London, Methuen, 1963), p. 37; ibid., p. 36.

[39] Mackenzie King to Ramsay MacDonald, 23 April 1924, ibid., p. 34.

[40] Dawson, *Mackenzie King*, pp. 453 – 80.

[41] Cecil Edwards, *Bruce of Melbourne* (London, 1985), 85. Bruce was also concerned with the success of the Imperial Economic Conference which was being run in tandem with the Imperial Conference, itself dealing with constitutional, defence and foreign policy issues. Ibid., pp. 100 – 1.

[42] Harkness, op. cit., ch. 4. Smuts' view of South Africa's role was set out in a speech to the South Africa Club in London on 23 October 1923. Text in *Smuts Papers*, vol. V, pp. 192 – 205.

[43] As so often, what was being done was no more than a formal recognition of what had already happened. Earlier in the year Canada had negotiated and signed the 'Halibut Treaty' with the United States without a British signature, though at that stage the Foreign Office had only gone along with the procedure to dissuade Canada from carrying into effect a proposal for independent representation at Washington. See Wrigley, op. cit., p. 173.

[44] Smuts made it clear in a speech to the Conference on 24 October that the common crown did not imply unity of citizenship; a British subject could not claim equality of rights in any part of

was to what extent unity in action could still be assured even without formal machinery. And here the 1923 Conference in its handling of defence issues showed how far apart was thinking in Britain from the outlook of at least the majority of the Dominions. Even when, as in some questions of foreign policy, there was no reason to suppose that there would be unbridgeable difference of opinion, the Dominion sensitivity at being taken for granted was ever on the alert. Thus when Curzon sent a note to Washington about the proposed inquiry into German reparations and related topics on 19 October 1923, while the Conference was sitting, it created trouble because the impression was given that the Dominions had been consulted when they had not. Further objections were raised to messages sent to Paris, Rome and Brussels which appeared to commit the Dominion governments to proposals upon which their opinion had not been asked and which, in fact, both Smuts and Bruce were said to dislike.[45]

The internal discussions within Whitehall at this time show that there was a difference between the attitudes of the two departments mainly involved, the Foreign Office and the Colonial Office. The former was ready to see Dominion governments negotiate and sign bilateral treaties of a technical kind without British participation and a British counter-signature; but the treaties would apply only to that Dominion, and it alone would be responsible for carrying them into effect. The Colonial Office believed that this concession would undermine the diplomatic and legal unity of the Commonwealth.[46]

Labour and the Empire

The fall of the Baldwin government and the coming into power of Labour in 1924 affected Commonwealth relations largely because of

the Commonwealth to which he might migrate. See Jones, *Whitehall Diary*, vol. 1, p. 251.

[45] Derby to Baldwin, 22 October 1923. Randolph Churchill, *Lord Derby, 'King of Lancashire'* (London, 1959), pp. 520 – 1. The correspondence with Washington printed in the relevant volume of Foreign Office documents does not disclose any attempt to commit the Dominions but the instructions from Curzon to the ambassador in Paris could be taken in this sense: Curzon to Crewe, 19 October 1923, *DBFP*, 1st Series, vol. XXI (London, 1978), pp. 574-6. Smuts was strongly opposed to what he saw as British acquiesence in France's hard line over reparations. For his attempt to act as an intermediary with the German statesman Gustav Stresemann, see Beloff, *Wars and Warfare*, 114 fn.

[46] Wrigley, op. cit., pp. 184 – 5. The view of the Foreign Office that the diplomatic unity of the Empire must be maintained is discussed in Norman Hillmer, 'The Foreign Office, the Dominions and the Unity of the Empire, 1925 – 1929', in D. Dilks, (ed.), *Retreat from Power*, vol. 1 (London, 1981), ch. 3.

the 1923 election defeat of protectionism upon which some hopes of closer union within the Empire had been built. In other respects, as in regard to foreign affairs in general, continuity prevailed. Indeed the new Labour Colonial Secretary, J.H. Thomas, was robust in his conviction that Labour must be ready to show that it intended to maintain the Empire.[47] As for the Prime Minister, it may be somewhat hard on him to say that his 'blundering in imperial relations verged on genius'.[48] Apart from economic issues, the main immediate questions were concerned with the League of Nations. Although Labour was not as unequivocally committed to the League and 'Collective Security' as the Liberals, the government did depend upon the Liberals for Parliamentary support.[49] The 'Draft Treaty of Mutual Assistance' presented to the League Assembly in September 1923 would have given additional powers to the League Council to designate an aggressor and decide upon appropriate sanctions. MacDonald was no enthusiast for such proposals. Lord Robert Cecil, the President of the League of Nations Union and regarded as the Opposition's expert on these matters, reminded MacDonald in a memorandum on the Draft Treaty that the Prime Minister had advanced against it the argument that it could not be subscribed to by Britain without Dominion consent, which would never be obtained. He argued that a constitutional rule that Britain could not enter into any engagement of any importance without the assent of each of the Dominions was not sustainable. 'I suggest', he continued,

> that the most extreme doctrine of Dominion right cannot go further than to say that before any international agreement of importance is made the Dominions should be consulted, and that any one of them may refuse to undertake any obligation involved in such an agreement. Even that is further than I myself should be disposed to go. I

[47] Apocryphal perhaps is the story that Thomas introduced himself to his officials by saying: 'I'm here to see that there is no mucking about with the British Empire.' R.W. Lyman, *The First Labour Government: 1924* (London, n.d., ?1958).

[48] Neatby, op. cit., p. 39; the specific reference is to Canada's exclusion from the Conference on Reparations that sat 9-16 August 1924. It is however fair to say that MacDonald did not go out of his way to seek Dominion opinion. The recognition of Soviet Russia, his most important positive step, was taken without consulting the Dominions, and he was originally ready to have no Dominion representation in a Conference on Reparations. Hall, *Commonwealth*, p. 547.

[49] For the cross-currents in Labour foreign policy see Henry R. Winkler, 'The Emergence of a Labour Foreign Policy in Great Britain in 1918 – 1929', *Journal of Modern History* (Chicago), vol. XXVIII, (1956), pp. 247 – 58; C.A. Cline, 'E.D. Morel and the Crusade against the Foreign Office', ibid., vol. XXXIX, (1967), pp. 126 – 37. For the taking-up by the Liberals of the League cause, see M. Cowling, *The Impact of Labour, 1920–1924* (Cambridge, 1971), p. 284.

think that the Imperial Government has in the last resort full responsibility for the Foreign Policy of the Empire, and although every possible consideration should be given to the Dominions and every effort should be made to meet their views, it is for the Imperial Government in the end to decide what should be done.[50]

The British rejection of the Draft treaty was based on more general grounds and on 4 September MacDonald himself, in a speech before the League Assembly, put forward a different approach, making a country's willingness to submit to arbitration the test of aggression; the link between compulsory arbitration and the reduction of armaments was the foundation of the 'Geneva Protocol' of 4 October, by which, in contrast to the Draft Treaty, the duty of individual countries to comply with a call for sanctions was severely limited.[51] The Dominion delegates at Geneva were not kept fully in the picture about the negotiations and the Dominion governments were only informed about the Protocol on 27 September when they were assured that it would not be accepted until they had been consulted.[52] But their objections to it were to prove no less strenuous than to the Draft Treaty, which may have had an effect on MacDonald's subsequent attitude.[53] Meanwhile he had suggested in June the holding of another Imperial Conference to discuss measures for improving 'consultation with other self-governing parts of the Empire on matters of foreign policy and general imperial interest'.[54] It was certainly not a matter which the 1923 Conference could be said to have dealt with to the satisfaction of the Dominions.[55] But the suggestion of a further meeting evoked no enthusiasm. The Australian reply did propose that the Dominions should have permanent representation in London,[56] but this does not seem to have been of great interest to the other governments. Desultory correspondence about a new Conference was still in progress when the government fell and it was left to the new

[50] Cecil to MacDonald, 23 June 1924, Cecil of Chelwood Papers, BL Add MSS 51081.

[51] See F.S. Northedge, *The Troubled Giant: Britain among the Great Powers, 1916–1939* (London, 1966), p. 241.

[52] Hall, *Commonwealth*, pp. 544 – 5.

[53] MacDonald to Gilbert Murray, 12 September 1927, Gilbert Murray Papers, Cecil Correspondence.

[54] Cmd 2301 (1924).

[55] For Canada's views see Wrigley, op. cit., 185 ff.

[56] At the invitation of the Bruce government, Alan Leeper of the Foreign Office had visited Australia and suggested the creation of a separate Department of External Affairs with a permanent head and a liaison officer in London. The original idea had been that such a liason officer should be attached to the Foreign Office. But the new Colonial Secretary suggested that he

Colonial Secretary, Leo Amery, to bury the idea.[57] The new government soon took a decision not to proceed with the Geneva Protocol, partly because of the hostile view taken of it by the Committee of Imperial Defence, and partly because of the opposition of the Dominions and the Indian government.[58]

Among the decisions made by the incoming Conservative government was the creation on 11 June 1925 of a separate Dominions Office out of the Dominions department of the Colonial Office, though both departments for the time being shared the same Secretary of State. It was largely because of Amery's interest in the possibilities of active colonial development rather than a recognition of the new constitutional position that prompted the move.[59] It was not that the atmosphere was particularly conducive to concentration upon imperial affairs; Baldwin's priorities remained the pacification of Europe and domestic recovery. Nor was public opinion much excited over imperial issues. The Royal Commonwealth Society remained a somewhat elitist body and the *Round Table* a journal of even more limited appeal.[60] The members of the Round Table now differed as between the movement's original commitment to closer union and those who took into account the new situation and in particular the effect of the League of Nations and of the new commitments to

would be better placed in the cabinet office where Hankey could regard him 'as his confidential Australian assistant in imperial policy making, rather than as a prying foreign diplomat'. The first incumbent of the post was R.G. Casey*. See Edwards, op. cit., 70; *The Leo Amery Diaries*, vol. 1, pp. 392 – 3. Casey, whose tour of duty lasted from 1924 to 1931, was critical of the Colonial Office and subsequently of the Dominions Office for failing to make any critical comments on the views or actions of the Dominions, believing that the lack of leadership this indicated would lead to disunity. Lord Casey, *The Future of the Commonwealth* (London, 1963), pp. 54 – 5. His correspondence with Bruce does however provide an important source for British policy in this period as seen through the eyes of a friendly but external observer. See W.J. Hudson and J.North, eds, *My Dear P.M.: R.G.Casey's letters to S.M.Bruce, 1924–1929* (Canberra, 1980).

[57] A. Gordon Dewey, op. cit., vol. 1, pp. 193 – 7.

[58] Meeting of 2 March 1925, PRO CAB 23/49.

[59] Amery had secured Baldwin's agreement very soon after taking office, and that of the cabinet on 18 March 1925: PRO CAB 23/49. The successive steps can be followed in *The Leo Amery Diaries*, 394 ff. Explaining the move to the Imperial Conference of 1926 Amery said that it was only reasonable to relieve the Colonial Office of the task of corresponding with the Dominions because of the growth of its other tasks: 'The whole work of colonial administration in the topics ... inevitably calls for a much greater degree of supervision, and in many directions of initiative, on the part of the central department which guides those territories.' *Imperial Conference of 1926: Appendices to Summary of Proceedings*, Cmd 2769 (1927).

[60] The membership of the Royal Commonwealth Society dropped from over 15,000 in 1920 to only 14,400 in 1927. It rose again to a new peak of 18,000 in 1930 but dropped again during the depression. It was up again to 20,000 in 1939. T.R. Reese, *History of the Royal Commonwealth Society* (London, 1968).

Europe which, after the new government's rejection of the Geneva Protocol, were given form by the Treaty of Locarno in 1925. The language of the pre-war period such as that of the Empire Day movement seemed out of harmony with the more sceptical tone of the 1920s.[61]

The question where the Dominions were concerned was one of whether co-operation would be assisted if a way were to be found of formulating the new position so as to satisfy all the members of the group that their fears of centralisation were ill-founded. It was felt in some quarters that any attempt at definition would reveal the absence of a consensus among the members of the Commonwealth.[62] And in July 1926 the cabinet did in fact agree that any attempt to formulate the constitution of the British Empire was to be deprecated.[63]

In spite of these reticences, the constitutional issues were the subject of another Imperial Conference that sat from 19 October to 23 November 1926.[64] By this time the Locarno Treaties signed on 16 October 1925 had provided further material for illustrating the new position, since the Dominions had neither been represented at the negotiations nor consulted about the line Britain should take, though it was indicated that the Dominions could if they wished at some later date associate themselves with the guarantees Britain had given.[65]

[61] See J.O. Springhall, 'Lord Meath, Youth and Empire', in *JCH*, vol. V, no. 4, (1970), pp. 97 – 111; J.M. Mackenzie, *Propaganda and Empire* (Manchester, 1984), and J.M. Mackenzie, (ed.), *Imperialism and Popular Culture* (Manchester University Press, 1986). On the other hand, so imperialist and to some extent racialist a text as C.R.L. Fletcher and Rudyard Kipling, *A School History of England*, published in 1911, was still in print in 1930. Works like H.B. Marshall's *Our Empire Story* and the novels of G.A. Henty were avidly read by the present writer as a schoolboy in the 1920s, and he was not alone.

[62] J. Eayrs, *In Defence of Canada*, vol. 1 (Toronto, 1964), p. 17.

[63] Meeting of 21 July 1926, PRO CAB 23/53.

[64] For a general survey of constitutional issues see Hancock, *Survey*, vol. I, ch. V. For the 1926 Conference see Holland, *Britain and the Commonwealth Alliance, 1918–1939* (London, 1981), ch. 4.

[65] 'The present Treaty shall impose no obligations upon any of the British Dominions, or upon India, unless the Government of such Dominion, or of India, signifies its acceptance thereof.' Article 9 of the Locarno Treaty: A.B. Keith, (ed.), *Speeches and Documents on International Affairs, 1918–1937*, vol. 1 (London, 1938), 116. The negotiations leading up to Locarno and the Conference itself are documented in *DBFP*, 1st Series, vol. XXVII, (London, 1986). Hertzog disagreed with the criticism made in the House of Commons that the Dominions should have been consulted over Locarno. It demonstrated that they were free nations whose co-operation with Britain was a matter of choice: 'It is here where I fundamentally disagree with General Smuts, who seems to labour under the impression that if we are to stand and hold together, something in the nature of a super-state is required to bind us as a Commonwealth.' Hertzog to Amery, 18 December 1925: copy in Baldwin Papers, vol. 96. E2, p. 34. Bruce had taken the view that a security pact was itself dangerous since it was impossible to get the Australian government to endorse it and since Britain acting by herself would mean a blow to the principle of an Empire

The impetus to come to a constitutional definition was provided by South Africa, now, under Hertzog*, the most suspicious of any possible centralising tendencies in London. 'You have no conception', wrote Hertzog to Amery, 'what irreparable harm is being done to Empire co-operation through the policy of secrecy pursued in an atmosphere of constitutional fog.'[66] The Irish were to claim that they had made the running at the Imperial Conference and this has been echoed by some subsequent historians.[67] This view has however been challenged, on the ground that the Cosgrave government was concerned to keep relations with Britain out of Irish politics and content itself with establishing a reputation for efficient government.[68] The most recent historian of Anglo-Irish relations in this period comes to the conclusion that the Irish were in fact content to follow the South African lead 'from the sidelines rather than adopt any independent initiatives themselves'.[69] Indeed, to some extent they were to be found in the role of mediators along with Mackenzie King, who was somewhat reluctant to see a general definition of the Commonwealth system, to which he would have preferred piecemeal adjustments to the role of Governor-General, and to questions of Dominion representation. It was this Irish-Canadian combination that in the Canadian view convinced Austen Chamberlain and Birkenhead, the Secretary of State for India, that some action was required despite Amery's continued objections to a definition of Dominion status.[70]

When Balfour presented the draft report of his committee of the Conference which dealt with inter-imperial relations, he stressed that the need for it had arisen from the charges of subservience to British wishes brought in the Dominions against their own Prime Ministers: the task of the committee had been 'to make the practice of the Constitution conform to the reality of the position'.[71] The formula that put Britain and the Dominions on a par by defining them as

Foreign Policy. It would be better for European security to be left to the continental powers with Britain playing the part of an 'honest broker'. Bruce to Amery, 6 May 1925, Baldwin Papers, vol. 115.F.2(B), 76 ff.

[66] Hertzog to Amery, 26 July 1926, PRO DO 117/32.

[67] See Harkness, The Restless Dominion, ch. 6.

[68] Holland, op. cit., p. 153.

[69] Canning, op. cit., p. 111.

[70] Ramsay Cook, 'A Canadian Account of the 1926 Imperial Conference', JCPS, vol. III, (1965), pp. 50–63; Neatby, op. cit., pp. 176–87. Amery himself professed pleasure in the ultimate outcome: The Leo Amery Diaries, vol. 1, pp. 482–3.

[71] Meeting of 17 November 1926, PRO CAB 23/53.

'autonomous communities within the British Empire equal in status, in no way subordinate to one another, in any aspect of their domestic or external affairs although united by a common allegiance to the Crown, and freely associated as members of the British Commonwealth of Nations' was unequivocal and acceptable to all.[72] It was to be the basis upon which the new situation would be embodied in statutory form in the Statute of Westminster in 1931.[73] Anomalies were still present in that, for instance, Commonwealth constitutions were acts of the United Kingdom Parliament and in some cases repatriation would be a lengthy affair. Since however communities that are freely associated must be free to dissociate, the old ambiguities about the meaning of Dominion status which had worried the Irish in 1921 could now seemingly be set aside. The Irish, with their insistence upon symbols, were also agitated about the royal title, since the description of the monarch as king of the United Kingdom of Great Britain and Ireland seemed to compromise Ireland's position as a Dominion; on the other hand the separate mention seemed desirable so as to allow for the future abolition of partition. The Dominions Office was not disposed to object and indeed felt that it would be useful to have the Free State's relationship with the Crown given formal recognition.[74] The result was the formula embodied in the Royal and Parliamentary Titles Act of 12 April 1927 in which the monarch was described as king of 'Great Britain, Ireland and of the British Dominions beyond the seas'.[75]

Channels of communication

Of more practical significance was the question of how the recognition of autonomy and, as the Balfour Report put it, of equality of status though not of function could be a foundation for the degree of co-operation or at any rate of mutual understanding that was generally accepted as being desirable. This problem went beyond the question of negotiating powers which was of particular interest to Canada.[76] It

[72] Report of the Inter-Imperial Relations Committee, Imperial Conference 1926: A.B. Keith, (ed.), *Speeches and Documents on the British Dominions, 1919–1931*, (London, 1932), pp. 161 – 70.
[73] The Statute of Westminster 1931, ibid., pp. 303 – 7. For the legal aspects of these developments, see R.T.E. Latham's chapter 'The Law and the Commonwealth' in Hancock, *Survey*, vol. 1.
[74] Casey to Bruce, 25 March 1926: *My Dear P.M.*, p. 155.
[75] Harkness, *The Restless Dominion*, pp. 104 – 6. The change was of course unpopular in Ulster.
[76] See Wrigley, op. cit., pp. 266 – 83.

was in part the question that had worried Hughes: how did the governments of Commonwealth countries communicate with each other? The right of Dominion Prime Ministers to correspond directly with the Prime Minister of the United Kingdom without going through the Colonial Office had been accepted since the creation of the Imperial War Cabinet. But this could hardly be a regular channel of communication.

Before the war, the Governor-General in each Dominion had acted as the main channel of contact, in additional to his ceremonial role as the representative of the monarch. As early as 1922, Lionel Curtis had pointed out that the entry of Ireland into the Commonwealth had precipitated the need for change. The Irish would want to have one of their own people as Governor-General and he would not be a suitable person to act as a channel for the views of the United Kingdom government. The same situation was bound to arise in other Dominions.[77] The matter was brought to a head in Canada after Lord Byng's active role in the constitutional crisis leading to Mackenzie King's temporary replacement by Arthur Meighen in June 1926. Byng had in fact rejected Mackenzie King's suggestion of consulting Amery in his role as Dominions Secretary, though he did send a report on what had passed which came before the British cabinet.[78] Amery felt that Byng had gone too far in the direction of separating his role as the King's representative from his relationship to the Dominions Office, having given Amery the minimum of information while writing freely to George V, though he agreed that this had worked well in the recent crisis.[79] Before the crisis, Mackenzie King had thought it a major step forward that Lord Byng had banished from the public mind and the minds of Canadian ministers any suspicion that he regarded himself as 'the representative of the government of Great Britain or of any of its Departments rather than as the representative of His Majesty'.[80]

[77] Lionel Curtis to Sir James Masterton Smith, 23 May 1922, PRO CO 537/1035.
[78] Neatby, op. cit., 130 ff; meeting of 28 July 1926, PRO CAB 23/53.
[79] Diary entry, 26 July 1926: *The Leo Amery Diaries*, vol. 1, pp. 458 – 9.
[80] Mackenzie King to Baldwin, 16 April 1926, quoted in Neatby, op. cit., 146. On Byng's handling of the crisis see E.A. Forsey, *The Royal Power of Dissolution in the British Commonwealth* (Toronto, 1943). After Byng's relinquishment of the post, Mackenzie King had intimated the importance that had come to be attached to the views of the Government of Canada on the choice of a Governor-General. Amery asked Baldwin to approve a telegram to Mackenzie King which would enable him to have 'the pleasure of thinking that he is initiating the arrangements necessary for the appointment of a successor to Lord Byng'. His choice was the Marquess of Willingdon, whom George V had insisted on including in the list: he was neither Amery's nor Baldwin's preference. See the correspondence of February – March 1926 in Baldwin Papers, vol. 96.E.2, p. 49.

But if not the Governor-General, then who? One could clearly not rely on the occasional set-piece Imperial Conference, and Amery's suggestion of an annual subsidiary Imperial Conference to dicuss foreign affairs did not find favour with his colleagues.[81] The original idea of regular Dominion representation on the Committee of Imperial Defence had not been revived when that organisation came to life again after the war, though Dominion representatives did attend a meeting while the Imperial Conference of 1926 was in session.[82] Nor, despite Amery's hopes, was there any chance of the Dominions agreeing to a secretariat for the Commonwealth being set up, as had been mooted before the war.[83] The only answer seemed to be some form of diplomatic representation for the Dominions in London and vice-versa. Australia led the way with the establishment in London of an external affairs branch of the High Commissioner's office in 1924. And other Dominions followed this example. But, particularly in Canada's case, there was the fear that communications would flow largely one way and that the High Commissioners would simply reflect British policy. Mackenzie King himself was convinced that the Baldwin government intended to form 'a sort of central council, advisory or otherwise, of the British Dominions' and to that he was unalterably opposed. It was not for the British government alone, in King's view, but for each of the governments to decide upon which matters it wanted to be consulted or have discussed at conferences, and the Canadian government would wish in each case to decide for itself whether to make its wishes known informally through its High Commissioner by a formal communication.[84]

[81] Meeting of 21 July 1926, PRO CAB 23/53. Amery had argued that League experience had shown the possibility of very frequent meetings which did not have to wait upon the convenience of major statesmen. Special efforts to get 'the really big people' need only be made occasionally. Why not the same in the Commonwealth? Amery to Sir Charles Davis, 15 December 1925, PRO CO 537/1113. When it was suggested in 1928 that the Expert Committee on the Operation of Dominion Legislation and the sub-conference on Merchant Shipping Legislation, both offshoots of the Imperial Conference, might meet at Ottawa, the idea was successfully resisted by the President of the Board of Trade on the ground that Ottawa was less convenient than London for the experts and for the representatives of South Africa and the Irish Free State: meeting of 28 November 1928, PRO CAB 23/59.

[82] The meeting was on 11 November and dealt with the state of negotiations on disarmament. *DBFP*, Series IA, vol. II, p. 478.

[83] Amery, diary entry, 16 July 1926, (not printed).

[84] King to Peter Larkin, the Canadian High Commissioner, 12 December 1924, quoted in Neatby, op. cit., p. 41; Mackenzie to Larkin, 15 December 1924, ibid., p. 42.

Such suspicions continued to exist in Canada.[85] When Mackenzie King went to London for the 1926 Imperial Conference he suggested to Austen Chamberlain that the proper thing would be for diplomatic links to be established similar to those which existed between nations. Chamberlain was averse to calling the High Commissioners ambassadors as this might cast doubt upon the essential unity of the Empire but agreed that there would be advantages in British representation in the Dominion capitals.[86] Meanwhile, Amery found that the High Commissioners were not good at attending his regular meetings and when they did come they were unwilling to raise major issues of policy.[87]

The use of the High Commissioners as the normal channel for consultation was not a very satisfactory one. Amery's weekly meetings with them were allowed to lapse because of Mackenzie King's objections to the High Commissioners being regarded in this way. The Foreign Office appears to have been moving towards the view that the Dominions Office could not be expected to handle matters of foreign affairs and that consultation with the Dominions should be a matter for itself.[88] Lord Cecil argued that the position was not a tolerable one. The British government could not make a move in international affairs without consulting the Dominions, but they left all the initiative to the United Kingdom government: 'They send indifferent High Commissioners, and on the whole make but little effort to get to grips with the international situation so that they can give quick effective replies.' Australia and New Zealand were the most helpful, but 'Canada practically took the impossible attitude that she would not consult but she complained bitterly if she were not consulted'.[89] Even allowing for Cecil's personal bias, in that his resignation from the Baldwin government in 1927 had been due to its failure to adopt a strong pro-League stance which it had blamed on the Dominions, the general argument seems quite compatible with that derived from other observations of the situation respecting consultation at this time.

[85] 'What a joke it is for the Dominions to call themselves Sister Nations when we know in our hearts that the last word is always with the man who is acting as Colonial Secretary or Secretary of State for the Dominions here.' Larkin to King, 6 July 1926: Eayrs, *In Defence of Canada*, vol. 1, p. 15.
[86] Mackenzie King diary entry, 25 October 1926: Neatby, op cit., p. 182.
[87] Amery diary enties, 30 June 1925, 29 March 1927, (not printed).
[88] Casey to Bruce, 23 February 1928, *My Dear P.M.*, p. 299.
[89] Casey to Bruce, 7 June 1928, ibid., p. 369.

Casey* was correct in attributing the end of the High Commissioners' meetings to Mackenzie King, for he had already expressed his dislike of the device. He disliked the meetings themselves:

> These conferences are either official or they are not. If they are not, they should be avoided as liable, sooner or later, to create in the minds of someone an erroneous impression as to the obligations arising therefrom. If they are official, it would appear that by continuing to countenance them, our Government would be helping to build up in London, in conjunction with the Secretary of State for the Dominions, a sort of Cabinet... the members of which will have had from their Governments no instructions of any kind and with respect to the doings of which their Governments, in the nature of things, will have no knowledge.

This mistrust and Mackenzie King's consequent unwillingness to delegate authority to his High Commissioner was responsible in 1928 for the appointment of the first British High Commissioner to Ottawa.[90]

The difficulties from the British side were technical rather than political. In 1925 Amery argued that a communication to the United States government about a proposed conference on the limitation of naval armaments should only be made with the concurrence of the Dominions. Chamberlain accepted the principle but sharply protested against the Colonial Office holding up his despatch for a week so as to be able to propose amendments to it.[91] In February 1927 it was necessary to explain to the Americans that the reason for the delay in replying to a communication from them on this subject was due to the slowness with which the Dominion governments replied to requests for their views.[92] During the critical exchanges with the Soviet government in 1927, Amery pointed out that the Dominions should be consulted before a threatening note was sent. Chamberlain demurred, saying that it was impossible to conduct policy in this way and referring to the difficulties he had had over getting answers from the Dominions on naval disarmament.

[90] King to Amery, 22 March 1927: Neatby, op. cit., 42 – 3; ibid., p. 187.
[91] Amery to Chamberlain, 17 February 1925; Chamberlain to Amery, 23 February 1925: University of Birmingham, Austen Chamberlain papers, Box 52.
[92] Note by Mr Campbell of the Foreign Office, 12 February 1927; Howard (Washington) to Chamberlain, 17 February 1927; Chamberlain to Howard, 25 Feburary 1927: DBFP, Series IA, vol. III, pp. 571, 576 – 7.

'Salisbury', Amery noted, 'was almost the only member of the cabinet who seemed to realise that our foreign policy has got to become leisurely in its methods and accept the limitations of the new Imperial system.'[93]

The real problem was not of course ignorance on either side of the other point of view. There existed in addition to the formal machinery of consultation many unofficial channels. It was that perceptions were in fact different. Britain's worries about European security and her own growing vulnerability to attack from the air could not seem as immediate to the Dominions. As a Canadian historian has pointed out: 'The Great War brought Canadians to Europe, but left Europe remote to Canadians.'[94]

Europe for the Dominions was either a menace or a distraction. As early as 1920, the Canadian Under Secretary of State for External Affairs had written: 'Canada's true policy right now is to develop her resources and leave European affairs such as the Bessarabia frontier etc. to our Imperial statesmen and the trained experts of Downing Street.'[95] While some of the other Dominions were less isolationist than Canada, they wished to be the judges of what issues were of actual concern to them. Bruce told the 1926 Imperial Conference that Australia's interest in the security of India made it impossible to ignore Afghanistan. But when it came to such a question as the responsibilities assumed by Britain in Iraq, 'the people of Australia might take a great deal of persuading that it was a question which vitally interested them and it would have to be linked up with some other Imperial interest or the safety of some part of the British Empire before the people of Australia would regard it as a question in which they had any interest at all'.[96] If the Middle East where Australians had fought and was on the main imperial route seemed remote to Australians, how much more remote were European questions. The complicated balances in Europe seemed to Dominion statesmen as they did to Americans, a token of Europe's suicidal depravity rather than part of a system on which Britain's security and the Empire depended.

For all the Dominions, of course, there were some external problems of direct local interest. South Africa was clearly sensitive to

[93] Diary entry, 23 February 1927: *The Leo Amery Diaries*, vol. 1, p. 498.
[94] Eayrs, *In Defence of Canada*, vol. 1, p. 3.
[95] Diary of Sir Joseph Pope, 11 December 1920, ibid., p. 11.
[96] Annex to letter from Birkenhead to Irwin, 4 November 1926, IORL MSS EUR C.151/2.

anything that touched upon racial issues in Africa and hence the old problem of what would happen if Portugal failed to keep a grip on her colonies. If there were to be a partition, would South Africa be able to put forward a claim?[97] But could they then rely wholly upon the British foreign office and British diplomats to forward Dominion interests?

Secession, inter-se and Dominion independence

Independent representation at international conferences was by now taken for granted.[98] So was the right to negotiate and sign treaties.[99] In the matter of diplomatic representation at capitals other than London, the recognition of the right outstripped practice.

Alongside the idea of having diplomatic representation in foreign countries went that of having separate external affairs departments. Australia originally intended to make permanent a foreign affairs section in the Prime Minister's department but, after the 1921 – 2 Washington Conference, confidence in the Imperial government's intentions was restored, the study of Japan abandoned, and the attention of the section confined to League of Nations affairs.[100] By the end of 1923 the section had ceased to exist. The department set up after Leeper's visit in 1924 long had rather a tenuous existence. It was not until 1935 that the Department acquired its own Secretary.[101] In New Zealand it was only in 1926 that J.G. Coates, Massey's successor as Prime Minister, established a Prime Minister's department which was to advise the Prime Minister on foreign affairs among other matters. Its staff, which included an 'Imperial Affairs Officer', provided the Prime Minister with notes for his participation in the Imperial Conference of 1926.[102] Neither Australia nor New Zealand were

[97] *DBFP*, Series IA, vol. I, p. 854.
[98] In respect of a proposed Washington Conference on the limitation of armaments, it was agreed that invitations should be sent to the Dominion governments 'through the channels of the British government'. Meeting of 25 March 1925, PRO CAB 23/49.
[99] Dominion negotiators would sign in the name of the King and inform any other Commonwealth governments which might be indirectly concerned as to what had been done. Neatby, op. cit., pp. 188 – 9.
[100] J.R. Poynter, 'The Yo-Yo variations: Initiative and Dependence in Australia's External Relations, 1918 – 1923', *Historical Studies Australia and New Zealand* (Melbourne), vol. XI (1970), pp. 231 – 49. The fullest account of the development of Australia's machinery for dealing with external relations is in the editor's introduction to *My Dear P.M.*
[101] Edwards, op. cit., pp. 70 – 92.
[102] F.L.W. Wood, The New Zealand People at War (Wellington, 1958).

represented in foreign capitals until late in the 1930s. In this respect the initiative was taken by the Irish Free State which appointed a minister to Washington in 1924; Canada followed her example in 1927. It did not appear that Imperial unity was thought to have been breached by these actions. In December 1928 Chamberlain informed the cabinet that Sir Esme Howard*, the British Ambassador in Washington, had told him that 'the presence of diplomatic representatives of Canada and the Irish Free State at Washington so far from doing any harm had rather strengthened the general position in that capital... so far from any rift having appeared in the British Empire, the United States government found that the three representatives were constantly holding similar language.'[103]

It is not surprising that Mackenzie King was the most influential Dominion statesman of the period just as Canada was clearly the senior Dominion. King was premier from December 1921 to June 1926, from September 1926 until June 1930, and from October 1935 until after the second world war. As has been stressed, his priority was national unity and to prevent any attraction towards the United States which he believed would happen if Canada was drawn into the European arena.[104] Even when Canada become a member of the League Council in 1927, its suspicions of the organisation were not much diminished. If French Canadians should demand their share of representation, there might come a point where Canada would side against Britain on some issue and the result would be political trouble in Canada.[105] The Department of External Affairs was not given much additional strength although Canada did extend its diplomatic service to include posts in Paris and Tokyo in 1928.

It may be that the feeling that Canada was still dependent on Britain for so many of its contacts with the rest of the world that made Mackenzie King so sensitive to reports of his unpopularity in Britain.[106] He himself was particularly hostile to politicians of an

---

[103] Meeting of 5 December 1928, PRO CAB 23/59. The Irish Free State established a mission in Berlin in 1929.

[104] For a general view of Anglo-Canadian relations at this period see Max Beloff, 'Britain and Canada between two world wars: A British view', in P. Lyon (ed.) *Britain and Canada: Survey of a Changing Relationship* (London, 1976). On Mackenzie King's trusted and deeply anti-British adviser O.D.Skelton see Norman Hillmer's essay in the same volume, 'The Anglo-Canadian Neurosis: The Case of O.D. Skelton'.

[105] Mackenzie King diary entry, 8 June 1927, Neatby, op. cit., p. 194.

[106] At a dinner with Amery, the Canadian High Commissioner complained about the hostile attitude of the British press to King: 'We could hardly say', noted Amery, 'that people here know King to be a slippery customer and very weak in his imperial faith.' Diary entry, 26 March 1926,

imperial stamp such as Amery and Birkenhead. And Stanley Baldwin's visit to Canada in 1927 did not do much to sweeten relations.[107]

Mackenzie King's suspicions of British 'centralism' were encouraged by the High Commissioner in London, Larkin, and by Loring Christie, who had served as secretary to both Borden and Meighen. Christie had been committed to the view of a sharing by the Dominions in foreign policy and had been a member of the Round Table group. During a prolonged stay in England after resigning from the Canadian public service (to which he was to return in 1935) he had become disillusioned with British policy, which he regarded as too Europe-centered, and came to advocate a new Canadian constitution which should get rid of the obligations to the Commonwealth and the League of Nations which diminished Canada's sovereignty.[108] Larkin had come to work with the South African High Commissioner, Smit, in opposition to the more imperially-minded Australians and New Zealanders.[109]

In respect of the successive attempts to find a new security regime for Europe culminating in the Locarno agreements, Canada was not, as has been seen, out of step with the other Dominions. The exemption of the Dominions from the obligations of Locarno was fully accepted in Britain.[110] When Chamberlain was attacked by Lloyd George for this breach in the unity of the Empire he responded that 'what might be possible for an Empire which existed in a different hemisphere was not possible for an Empire, the heart of which lay in Europe.'[111] It may be that the Foreign Office still hoped the Dominions would come round and add their support.[112] Others, like Philip Kerr, argued that it would be unwise to try to persuade them. If the time came the Dominions would be willing to act as in 1914, but it was

---

(not printed). For Byng's low view of Mackenzie King, see entry of 15 October 1926, *The Leo Amery Diaries*, vol. 1, p. 471.

[107] Keith Middlemas and John Barnes, *Baldwin* (London, 1969), 377.

[108] For Loring Christie's change of views, see A.I. Inglis, 'Loring C. Christie and the Imperial Idea, 1919 – 1926', *Journal of Canadian Studies* (Peterboro, Ontario), vol. VII (1972); J.L. Granatstein, *The Ottawa Men: The Civil Service Mandarins, 1935 – 1937* (Toronto, 1982), 63 ff.

[109] Casey to Bruce, 23 February 1928, *My Dear P.M.*, p. 299.

[110] It has been claimed that the clause was included on Canadian insistence at the time: Eayrs, op. cit., p. 7. But the Foreign Office pointed out that the same thing had been done on the advice of Sir Robert Borden in respect of the abortive treaty with France of 28 June 1919. Memorandum of 13 November 1925, *DBFP*, Series IA, vol. I, pp. 142 – 6.

[111] H.C. *Deb*, vol. 188, cols 419 – 542, 18 November 1925.

[112] See Memorandum respecting the Locarno treaties, 10 January 1926, *DBFP*, Series IA, vol. I, pp. 1 – 17.

wrong to try to convert a moral obligation into a contractual one. If one insisted on the matter being put to the Dominion parliaments, neither Canada nor South Africa would sign; New Zealand probably would, and Australia might. But once countries had refused, then when the time came the anti-imperialists would use this as an argument against action: 'If you try to make the dominions commit themselves against their judgement, you will strike a serious blow at the real foundation alike of Crown and Empire.'[113]

In the event it became clear that only New Zealand would be prepared to submit the Treaty to its Parliament, and when the question of Dominion adherence was raised at the 1926 Imperial Conference, Mackenzie King's assertion that the Canadian Parliament would not approve ended the discussion.[114] It was therefore found preferable to allow the Conference simply to indicate its approval in general terms.

In 1928 – 9 the Kellog-Briand Pact raised once more the question of whether the Empire was one or many.[115] The Dominions and India were invited to be individual signatories, and all acceded. The question was one of ratification. The British government, when asked in January 1929 to ratify the Pact as the U.S. Senate had done, was keen that the ratifications by all members of the Commonwealth should be simultaneous but feared that their parliamentary procedures made this unlikely. In fact their parliaments acted at different times over the next three months. New Zealand considered that it had already approved the pact by including such approval in a motion in reply to the Address in July 1928.[116] The Briand proposals for European unity produced a Foreign Office memorandum stressing the importance *inter alia* of doing nothing to weaken 'political co-operation with the other members of the British Commonwealth', and the reply to the French was declared to be tentative because of the need for consultation with the Commonwealth.[117]

---

[113] Kerr to Chamberlain, 5 June 1925, Austen Chamberlain Papers, Box 24, 99b.

[114] Neatby, op. cit., pp. 179 – 80.

[115] The text of the Pact 'The treaty for the Renunciation of War' of 27 August 1928 is given in Keith, éd., *Speeches and Documents... 1918–1937*, vol. II, pp. 154 – 6.

[116] Austen Chamberlain to E. Howard (Washington), 17 January 1929, Austen Chamberlain papers, Box 50; *Journal of Parliaments of the Empire* (London, 1929).

[117] David Carlton, *MacDonald versus Henderson* (New York, 1970), pp. 85 – 6. The text of the Briand 'Memorandum on the Organisation of a System of European Federal Union' of 17 May 1930 is given in Keith, op. cit., pp. 198 – 203.

If the Commonwealth could provide a reason or excuse for inaction, this did not imply that the views of the Dominions would always be taken into account in the working out of Britain's own policies. The Australians were not consulted in what Casey regarded as a Foreign Office plot to get rid of Lord Lloyd in Egypt so as to pursue a line closer to the demands of the Egyptian nationalists. He pointed out that the C.I.D. had been deliberately excluded from the Egyptian issue, which the Foreign Office had taken straight to the Cabinet. At the C.I.D. Australia could have been represented.[118]

By the time of the Imperial Conference in 1930, when MacDonald was again in office, Commonwealth relations had been affected by the onset of the world depression. Furthermore, Britain was more deeply involved than ever in European questions. But even constitutional questions were still provocative of controversy, despite the preparations that had been made to forestall disputes.[119] It was feared that South Africa under Hertzog might be tempted to explore the right of secession which appeared to flow from the phrase 'freely associated' in the Balfour formula. It was also feared that the Irish Free State would bring pressure to bear in pursuit both of this objective and of other specific aims: changes in the concept of common citizenship arising from the allegiance to the Crown and the replacement of appeals to the Privy Council by a new Commonwealth tribunal.[120] The right of secession was not raised at the Conference, but on other issues it was the Irish who made the running, not uninfluenced by the fact that the opposition under de Valera* was growing in strength and that the Irish government felt it desirable to outbid him for the support of nationalist sentiment.[121] Hertzog indeed was a relatively moderate figure at the Conference, since he also had politics at home to consider and was trying to bring about a measure of agreement between Afrikaans and English-speakers in the light of the country's even more serious racial and economic problems. The Conference undertook

[118] Casey to Bruce, 18 July 1929, *My Dear P.M.*, p. 539. The proposed new Treaty was in fact communicated to the C.I.D. at the end of July. See S. Roskill, *Hankey, Man of Secrets*, vol. 2 (London, 1972), p. 479.
[119] On what follows, see Holland, op. cit., ch. 7, 'The 1930 Imperial Conference'.
[120] On the role of the Irish Free State, see Harkness, op. cit., ch. 8, 'The Imperial Conference 1930'.
[121] On Anglo-Irish relations between the two Imperial Conferences, see Canning, op. cit., pp. 110 – 17. There had been some reluctance to put the Irish on the same footing as the other Dominions where foreign affairs were concerned; only from 1927 did the Irish Prime Minister receive the Foreign Office papers routinely circulated to the other Dominion Prime Ministers.

some discussion of defence, though nothing serious emerged, and despite the original intention of MacDonald to avoid economic issues, which were bound to split opinion in Britain, some discussion of economic matters as well.

The Dominion office hoped to secure assent to the Report of the 1929 Conference on the operation of Dominion legislation which had sought to work out the consequences in terms of law of the Balfour formula on Dominion status.[122] It was also concerned to preserve the *inter-se* principle, that is to say, that relations between members of the Commonwealth were not to be regarded as on the same footing as those between foreign states, and that arrangements should be made to provide an alternative to the League in the event of any disputes arising between them.

The issues involved had included the avoidance of any League procedures by which an individual member of the Commonwealth might be made an object of sanctions and the others be obliged to participate in sanctions against it. More recently the question of *inter-se* had been raised by the wish of the new British Labour government to sign the optional clause of the International Court. The Australians wanted disputes between members of the Commonwealth to be excluded from the Court's jurisdiction, and the Foreign Office's legal adviser upheld the view that the constitution of the Empire was such as to exclude this possibility. The South Africans objected to the notion that disputes between two Dominions were not 'international'. The Irish went further, and signed the Optional Clause in a way which would have allowed *inter-se* disputes to come before the Court; South Africa declared that in the view of its government the Court did have jurisdiction, but that for the sake of uniformity of action it would not in practice bring disputes with other Commonwealth members before it. The other Dominions all signed with reservations as to *inter-se* disputes as well as of matters falling within their domestic jurisdiction.[123]

The British chairman of the constitutional subcommittee was hostile to the Report and hoped to get the Conference to modify it. In this he came up against the intransigence of the Irish delegation, whose principal delegate had objected to the use of British in the title

---

[122] Report of the Conference on the Operation of Dominion Legislation and Merchant Shipping Legislation, Cmd 3479, (1929), in Keith, *Speeches and Documents*, 173 ff.
[123] Hall, op. cit., 676 ff.

of the Commonwealth. While Hertzog was fairly passive and the Australians uninterested, the Canadians – though now represented by the Conservative Bennett – supported the Irish over the report for reasons of his own apparently connected with his disapproval of Britain's response to his economic proposals. With New Zealand alone giving the United Kingdom support, the 1929 Report was accepted. No progress was made on the *inter-se* doctrine or with respect to the position of the Privy Council and the suggestion of an imperial tribunal. On the other hand, although the atmosphere had not reproduced the geniality of 1926, it was also true that none of the Dominions wished at the moment to make use of their right of secession. The Commonwealth remained a conceivable unit with which to face the depression.

Chapter 5

THE ECONOMIC ARGUMENT

The nature of an 'imperial' economy

Critics of 'imperialism' have made much of its economic content. And it is of course the case that the expansion and retention of Empire has always been seen by some individuals and companies as offering opportunities for careers and profits that would not otherwise have existed, and this not in the metropolis only. For at a given stage of the development of a dependency access to a metropolitan market for exports or development finance may also be seen as essential to its own economy. Yet an economy diverse enough to sustain a role as the centre of an imperial system is likely to be too diverse for any single interest or set of interests to dominate its government's policies. Private interests may help to sway or even distort the process of policy-making, but that process is best seen as an attempt to mould reality to a particular vision of the present and future.[1]

The most serious difficulty in endeavouring to place economic policy in its proper context in the story of Britain's imperial decline is that few if any of the country's leaders in the inter-war period gave total priority to the imperial aspect of their policies, any more than this had been possible for Joseph Chamberlain or Lord Milner. They also had to take into account the more immediate needs and attitudes of the home country and its electorate upon whom they depended for attaining or retaining office. If they argued the case for action on an imperial scale they had to do so in terms which suggested direct benefits to the British themselves greater than any sacrifices they might have to make on behalf of the wider imperial purpose. And what was true of British

---

[1] The most impressive introduction to the subject remains W.K. Hancock, *Survey of British Commonwealth Affairs*, vol. II, *Problems of Economic Policy, 1918–1939* Part 1 (London, 1940), and Part 2 (London, 1942). The studies in the two works by the Canadian economist Ian M. Drummond, *British Economic Policy and the Empire, 1918–1939* (London, 1972), and *Imperial Economic Policy, 1917–1939: Studies in Expansion and Protection* (London, 1974), give a different perspective, and the former contains some useful documentary illustrations.

statesmen was even truer of their Dominion counterparts and of the government of India, which although formally an emanation of the British government had obvious reasons in such matters to insist upon the need to recognise India's own needs.[2]

It is also the case that economic and political motives for action are not always easy to separate. Migration to a Dominion or a dependency might serve the purpose of finding employment for individuals whose prospects would not be as good at home, but if properly directed it might also fulfil a political aim such as strengthening the British component in a country's population.[3]

The ideas that were dominant among the imperially-minded in Britain during and immediately after the war continued to revolve around the triple theme of 'men, money and markets'. Britain should facilitate the emigration of suitable settlers to what were seen as the empty spaces in the Dominions and to such areas in the colonial empire as seemed climatically suited to white settlement. It should provide the finance by which other parts of the Empire-Commonwealth could furnish themselves with a suitable infrastructure to enable settlement to proceed; the currencies that circulated within the Empire should have sterling as their base and management of the financial system should remain with the City of London. Britain should continue to provide a ready market for the produce of all parts of the Empire-Commonwealth and should in return expect to see the Empire as a principal market for its exports and a principal client of its merchant marine and burgeoning air routes.[4]

If such a system could be achieved and its prosperity guaranteed, then it would be possible for Britain to recover from the economic burdens imposed upon her by the war and be in a position to provide the main sinews of imperial defence. It could not be expected that an Empire of this kind would remain without rivals and even enemies; and the dependence of the system upon trade and hence upon

[2] See in particular B.R. Tomlinson, *The Political Economy of the Raj, 1914–1947: The Economics of Decolonization in India* (Cambridge, 1979).

[3] In 1927 Amery wrote to Baldwin about the South African Protectorates and Rhodesia: 'If we can get [settlers] out from England in the next 4 or 5 years we shall have carried the British element beyond Natal right up to the eastern border of the Union and made its position secure against swamping by the policy of giving all the land to poor Dutch whites when transfer takes place.' Amery (from Cape Town) to Baldwin, 24 September 1927, Baldwin Papers, vol. 96.E, p. 121.

[4] For the development of air routes as a conscious instrument of imperial integration, see J.A. Cross, *Sir Samuel Hoare, A Political Biography* (London, 1977), 100 ff.

communications suggested that its security would always present a major problem more readily perceived at the centre than at the periphery.

It was of course possible to argue that any policies directed towards creating an imperial economic system were to be deplored because they meant artificially diverting what would be the natural directions for the flow of people, goods and capital. Let individuals decide whether or not they wished to seek new homes overseas, let businessmen decide for themselves where their best hopes for profit would lie, let the capital market determine the nature and pace of investment and the balance between home and overseas. To this standard recapitulation of the classical free trade argument the standard reply was that in a world where other closed systems existed or were being created, Britain could not go on behaving as though it could afford to ignore this fact and frame its policies in terms of a world that did not in fact exist. But this real world included Britain's own economy and it was argued that Dominion development loans for instance might cause difficulty in upholding the gold standard to which Britain had returned with Dominion approval in 1925.[5] The issue was an important one both for the Dominions and for Britain, where the the study of development loans to the Dominions was taken over from the Treasury by the new 'Committee of Civil Research' in 1925.[6]

A variant of this approach, though one that commended itself to an old free-trader like Churchill, was to say that what mattered, or would matter in the end, was the prosperity of the British economy, and that this depended upon maximising trade and maintaining the value of the currency. It also meant a regime of low taxation, taxes being a prime burden upon industry. Most of what the enthusiasts for Empire wanted – whether in the encouragement of emigration, or in propaganda in favour of British exports, or in expenditure on colonial development – demanded additional expenditure. In the conflict during the second Baldwin government between Amery at the Colonial Office and Churchill at the Treasury the two viewpoints found their most telling expression.

Even those who put first the development of the British economy were themselves divided between the free-traders and the advocates

---

[5] See Amery to Baldwin, Baldwin Papers, vol. 193, p. 136.
[6] See Middlemas and Barnes, *Baldwin*, p. 313.

of industrial protection; and the two camps, protectionist and imperialist, were sometimes aligned but sometimes pursued separate goals, as was to be made evident in the fate of the Empire Crusade in 1929 – 31.[7] It was also the case that a system of preferences, which seemed the only way inter-imperial trade could effectively be stimulated, could have the effect of exacerbating relations between Britain and the Dominions as negotiators clashed over individual items. Yet preferences could also help countries to extend their area of land settlement, as in the case of Australian fruit and wines.[8] Above all the debates were not conducted in a vacuum but had constantly to take into account the changing world economic situation and the policies of other major industrial nations. In particular there was the continued American insistence on the desirability of a world of equal trading opportunities based upon non-discrimination in commercial treaties and the application of the most-favoured-nation clause. It was argued in imperialist quarters that unless the Empire could negotiate as a unit – and all the indications were against this – Canada in particular might find itself drawn into the American rather than the British orbit.[9]

The main issues were all ventilated at the long awaited Imperial Economic Conference which eventually came together simultaneously with the Imperial Conference itself in October 1923. The leader of the British delegation was Sir Philip Lloyd-Graeme, (later known as Sir Philip Cunliffe-Lister, and later still as Lord Swinton*), an enthusiast for imperial preference, although Bonar Law's pledges in the 1922 election seemed to stand against the kind of preferences on food that the Dominions would be seeking.[10] In the upshot there was agreement on all three parts of the package – men, money and markets – with preferences as the instrument to make possible the level of trade necessary to justify the development expenditure involved. Specific proposals on preferences of a kind believed

---

[7] See G.R. Peele, 'St George's and the Empire Crusade', in C. Cook and J.A. Ramsden, eds, *By-elections in British Politics* (London, 1973). This article is particularly important, since the books by Drummond do not deal effectively with the domestic political background to these arguments.

[8] Drummond, *British Economic Policy and the Empire*, pp. 26, 53.

[9] W.A. Hewins, *Apologia of an Imperialist* (London, 1923), vol. 2, p. 271.

[10] Sir Philip Lloyd Graeme, subsequently Sir Philip Cunliffe-Lister and subsequently Lord Swinton, was President of the Board of Trade in Baldwin's first administration. For his role in the 1923 Imperial Economic Conference, see J.A. Cross, *Lord Swinton* (Oxford, 1982), 53 ff.

not to violate the party's undertakings would be put before Parliament. But this modest programme was shelved by Baldwin's decision to go to the country on a full tariff reform and preference platform.

The defeat of the Conservatives by Labour and a temporarily reunited and rejuvenated Liberal Party showed how strong was the free trade tradition in British politics and how potent despite all reassurances, the fear that any further instalment of tariffs or preferences would raise the cost of living.

The Labour government which took office in January 1924 was dominated in these matters by Philip Snowden, the Chancellor of the Exchequer, a free-trader of a dogmatic kind. The government thus decided not to fulfil its predecessor's undertakings to introduce the new preferences, while professing that the new Government was 'not one whit behind the Opposition in their desire to promote the best interests of the Empire'.[11] They solved their diplomatic dilemma by duly putting the preferences agreed upon to the House but with a recommendation that they be rejected.[12]

Another feature of the 1923 Conference which had even fewer results was the attempt to follow up the point that Churchill had urged during the 1921 Imperial Conference, namely that the Dominions should be asked to take a constructive interest in the future of the Colonies. In a speech to the 1923 Conference the Colonial Secretary, Devonshire, was reported as saying:

> Although the destinies of these great dependencies of the Crown are the immediate responsibility and trust of the British Government, it would be wrong if it were to be supposed that the moral and material progress and development of these large areas were not of increasing importance to all the partners in the British Empire, and it is the constant aim and endeavour of the Colonial Office to foster the interest of the Overseas Dominions in those great territories and so to stimulate interimperial trade.[13]

[11] H.C. *Deb*, vol. 172, col. 1597, 29 April 1924. The draft of the budget speech including this phrase had been approved by the cabinet that morning: PRO CAB 23/48.

[12] This manoeuvre very nearly failed of its purpose: 'The Government only defeated those of the proposals which involved more than the increase of preferential margins in relation to taxes already existing by a few votes, six in the narrowest instance. This was due to the fact that practically all the Lloyd George Liberals and one or two of the Labour Party voted with the Tories while the Clyde showed their dislike of both sides by abstaining.' P.J. Grigg, *Prejudice and Judgement*, (London, Cape, 1948), p. 139.

[13] *Imperial Conference 1923. Appendix to Summary of Proceedings*, Cmd 1988 (1923).

But although the summary of the Conference's proceedings said that great stress was laid by the representatives of the Dominions and India on the 'value to the Empire as a whole of the great tropical territories in East and West Africa and in Eastern Asia',[14] nothing seems to have come of Devonshire's declaration, and the subject did not figure in the debates in the Dominion Parliaments when the delegates returned home.

Baldwin's appointment of Amery as Colonial Secretary in his second administration brought to the Colonial Office a man whose own ideas had departed from the view that the economic integration of the Empire was primarily a means of 'strengthening the sentiments of mutual affection and of a common patriotism upon which the existence of the Empire and the furtherance of Imperial unity' depended.[15] By the time he became Colonial Secretary he saw the matter more in economic terms: protection at home would restore the British market to British goods and the loss of foreign markets would be made up by developing imperial ones. Unemployment would also be tackled by encouraging migration to the Dominions.[16] Yet with a Prime Minister unwilling to renew the free trade debate which had cost him office in 1923 and general indifference to imperial issues in Parliament and public opinion, the chances of making major steps towards imperial economic unity were never very high.

Amery returned to the theme of the 'marriage of tropical production to the industrial production of the temperate regions' at the Imperial Conference of 1926, and to the importance of collaboration between the colonies themselves as brought out in the West Indies Conference of 1925, and the ties between the East African colonies, as well as the need for the Dominions to share in colonial enterprises as in Canada's links with the West Indies. He stressed the number of individuals from the old Dominions occupying posts in the colonies: an Australian running the Nigerian tin mines, a Canadian governor of the Gold Coast where the director of the geological survey was an Australian, (as was the holder of the same post in Tanganyika), a Canadian as general manager of the Nigerian railways, and many Canadians, Australians and Irishmen serving in the medical and

[14] *Imperial Conference 1923. Summary of Proceedings*, Cmd 1987, (1923).
[15] L.S. Amery, *Union and Strength* (London, 1912), p. 236.
[16] L.S. Amery, *National and Imperial Economics* (London, 1924), p. 51.

veterinary services.[17] But once again there was no echo from the Dominions to these ideas.

Nor was there much sympathy for the ideas of a partnership in development between Britain and the colonies in Britain itself. For anything concrete to be done required expenditure and came up against the Treasury view that all such expenditure was liable to be a breach of the general rule that colonies should be self-financing. The most they were prepared to contemplate was temporary assistance through small grants or loans with a view to putting the territories in a situation where they could pay their way. Meanwhile the acceptance of financial aid meant the application to the colony in question of stringent and detailed financial controls. Amery's assumptions in pressing for money for colonial development were constantly challenged by the Treasury:

> Mr Amery's financial philosophy is based upon the assumption that idle funds are available for Colonial investments, and that the exchequer has surplus cash for subsidies to attract them into enterprises which offer no early return. From these assumptions it follows that if Mr Amery is given a free hand, the land will flow with milk and honey.[18]

The Treasury view was fully supported by Churchill as Chancellor of the Exchequer, and his Labour successor Snowden was equally adamant against pleas for development money by Amery's successor Passfield. Both defence questions, as already noted in respect of the Middle East, and the advantages of moves towards more self-government were looked at by the Treasury in terms of Gladstonian parsimony.

At the 1926 Imperial Conference, which should have been the high point of Amery's tenure of office, economic questions were overshadowed by the constitutional debate. But there was no enthusiasm on the part of most Dominions for any development of common action in the economic sphere. Mackenzie King in particular opposed all moves in this direction and the Canadians claimed credit for having destroyed proposals for a permanent imperial shipping committee with statutory powers, the Board of Trade's proposals for collecting

---

[17] *Imperial Conference 1926. Appendix to Summary of Proceedings*, Cmd 2769, (1927).
[18] Minute by Mr Upcott, 7 January 1929, PRO T 161/291/S.33978.

Empire statistics, proposals in respect of Empire patents and for a permanent Imperial Economic Committee.[19]

Amery's period at the Colonial Office was thus marked by more gestures towards imperial development than concrete achievements. Of these symbolic achievements, the most obvious was the separation between the Colonial Office and the Dominions Office, which could be regarded as a recognition of the Colonial Empire as a distinct part of the imperial structure alongside the Dominions and the Indian Empire, as well as of the unsuitability of the Colonial Office as an instrument for handling communications with what were now the totally autonomous governments of the Dominions. But the Colonial Office did not become in his time or that of his successor an instrument for carrying into effect the ideas of colonial development with which he was associated. Cunliffe-Lister took over the Colonial Office in the National Government in 1931, and later recalled the situation he found:

> No one had ever attempted to make an economic survey of the colonies; there was no Economic Department. There were no records or statistics of the amount which different countries took from the Colonies or the relative importance of these markets, or where the imports to these Colonies came from. There was no assessment of the actualities much less the potentialities of mutual trade.[20]

During Amery's tenure of office, assisted by Sir Samuel Wilson who was transferred from the governorship of Jamaica to being Permanent Secretary in 1925, important developments did take place within the Colonial Office itself, particularly in the direction of creating more functional departments dealing with issues common to many parts of the Empire instead of the almost purely geographical organisation which had been the rule. The new arrangements gave a stimulus to research, and research itself was a contribution to economic development.

The Empire Marketing Board

If the Empire was to produce more, its goods would need to be sold

[19] Hall, *Commonwealth*, p. 515.
[20] Viscount Swinton, *I Remember* (London, Hutchinson, 1948), p. 65.

and, in the absence of further preferences, other ways of encouraging inter-imperial trade would need to be found. In 1924 the idea was thrown up that the £1,000,000 which it was reckoned the Dominions would have gained if the 1923 agreements had been adhered to should be put into an annual fund for the encouragement of the sale of Empire products in Britain. The plan was announced in December 1924 but nothing happened until January 1926, when Amery pressed for action. Churchill, who had originally backed the scheme, now opposed it.[21] But in the end Baldwin was persuaded to support it, and the creation of the Empire Marketing Board to administer the fund was announced in March. It was also agreed that the financial arrangements would be such that any part of the grant not spent in one year could be carried forward. Even so, the representation of the Treasury alongside other departments on the Board, and its responsibility to the Secretary of State, was unacceptable to Bruce of Australia, who wished to see the grant in the hands of an independent commission reporting to the heads of all the Commonwealth governments. But, in spite of Amery's sympathy, he failed to get changes made.[22] While the new Board both aided research and engaged in publicity for Empire products, it is difficult to be positive about its achievements in stimulating trade. The Board could quote examples of record sales of certain products but insofar as the general share of the Empire in British trade was concerned there was already in progress something of an upturn. From 1929 on all trade was affected by the depression and, subsequently, imports from the Dominions dropped at the same rate as those from foreign countries, while if India and the colonies are taken into account, the Empire share of the British market actually declined.[23] Throughout its brief life – the Empire Marketing Board was dissolved in 1933 – it was a target of Treasury hostility, and reductions were made in its grant. Amery was clear where the blame lay: writing of Cunliffe-Lister and Churchill, he noted: 'The real trouble is that both of them hate the EMB and want to wreck it. Neither of them, and as far as I can make out, very few of

---

[21] The idea seems to have come from an inter-departmental committee which had prepared the 1923 Imperial Conference and produced a paper on the subject in 1924: Baldwin Papers, vol. 93, Imp.9, 96 ff. Amery's battle for the idea can be followed in his diary: *The Leo Amery Diaries*, vol. 1, 440 ff. Cf Amery, *My Political Life*, vol. II, (London, 1953), p. 346.
[22] Amery Memorandum, C.P.112(26), including telegram from Bruce, 6 March 1926, in Baldwin Papers, vol. 93, Imp. 24, 233 ff, pp. 321 – 2.
[23] *Board of Trade Statistical Abstracts for the U.K.*, 1933 (Cmd 4233); *ibid.*, 1939, (Cmd 5903).

the Cabinet attach any importance to the fact that this money fulfils a pledge to the Dominions.'[24]

The Labour government that came into office in 1929 was made aware of the greater importance attached to the Empire Marketing Board by the Dominions, and Thomas suggested at the 1930 Imperial Conference that it should be converted into a 'trust fund' supervised by all the Dominions, but in the end the British delegation backtracked on the idea and the Conference agreed only to extend its marketing activities to include British goods and to an agreed minimum annual income.[25] And the latter undertaking was revoked in the following year under the pressure of the financial crisis.

It is clear that the Treasury never relinquished its opposition to the Empire Marketing Board, in part because it distrusted all expenditure on imperial development and in part because it feared that the principle of allowing money to be carried forward from year to year might be extended to colonial development expenditure as envisaged in the Colonial Development Act of 1929. And its suspicions of the way in which the Empire Marketing Board managed its finances were shared by the House of Commons Estimates Committee.[26]

It could of course be argued that any contribution to awareness by the British public of the economic potentialities of the Empire was to be welcomed, and in that sense the Empire Marketing Board did no more than follow on from the Wembley Exhibition in 1924 – 5, the cost of which had also alarmed financial purists, but in that case there had been considerable Dominion contributions as well. The Dominions also made possible the survival of the Imperial Institute which was in a parlous financial condition in the early 1920s, and which was amalgamated with the Imperial Mineral Resources Bureau in the Imperial Institute Act of 1925. It is also worth noting that the Empire Marketing Board played an active role in the development of the

[24] Diary entry 28 November 1928, *The Leo Amery Diaries*, vol. 1, 373. It has been argued that the Empire Marketing Board was the victim of the Ottawa agreements, since protection and preferences made such propaganda unnecessary: Stephen Constantine, 'Bringing the Empire Alive – the Empire Marketing Board and Imperial Propaganda, 1926 – 1933', in John M. Mackenzie (ed.) *Imperialism and Popular Culture*, (Manchester, 1986), p. 220.

[25] Memorandum by Thomas, 'The Imperial Conference', 27 October 1930, C.P.366 (1930), in PRO CAB 24/216; Report of Conference Committee on Economic Co-operation, PRO CAB 32/100; meetings of U.K. delegation 3, 11 November 1930, PRO CAB 32/85; meeting of Prime Ministers and Heads of Delegations, 13 November 1930, PRO CAB 32/79.

[26] 'Your committee are not satisfied that the proposals for expenditure placed before the Empire Marketing Board are in all cases submitted to sufficiently close financial criticism.' *Second Report of the Select Committee on Estimates* (H.C. 71 – 114 1928).

British film industry through its sponsoring of documentary films. The commercial needs of the industry, facing severe American competition, were met by the Cinematograph Films Act of December 1927. But there was also an imperial consideration, the availability of British films for colonial audiences, which occupied part of the attention of a Colonial Office Conference in 1927.

Positive action whether by government or by private firms was more likely where a clear need was felt for the production in the Empire of a particular commodity. Despite the relative fall in Britain's cotton exports in this period in face of competition from elsewhere, Lancashire cotton textiles still represented an important component of British industry and one with considerable weight because of its geographical concentration and the importance of Lancashire Conservative seats. Attempts to lessen dependence upon United States supplies had been made from early in the century. In 1921 the British Cotton Growing Federation was formed with the backing of a government grant together with the proceeds of a voluntary levy on spinning firms. It was presided over by the Earl of Derby, the major political figure in the county.[27] It did succeed in stimulating cotton growing in Uganda, Nigeria and Tanganyika in addition to the Gezira irrigation scheme in the Sudan. On the other hand the growth in assured cotton supplies was of no use unless markets could be found and held, particularly against Indian and Japanese competition. And this again meant fiscal measures which were ruled out for political reasons.

What was true of cotton was equally true of other industries, where British hopes of increasing exports to the Empire faded in the light of Britain's lack of competitiveness and in some cases the growth of production in the Dominions themselves.[28] The argument for an imperial trading area foundered on the rocks of economic reality.

The attempt to assist migration to the Dominions, which also had a pre – 1914 history, came up against equally hard facts.[29] Between 1919 and 1922 the British government provided free passages for selected

[27] See Randolph Churchill, Lord Derby, 'King of Lancashire', (London, 1959).
[28] For the chemical industry see W.J. Reader, Imperial Chemical Industries, vol. I (London, 1970), vol. II (London, 1975). An essay at explaining Britain's economic weakness and its impact upon imperial policy and its failures is B.R. Tomlinson, 'The Contraction of England: National Decline and the Loss of Empire', J.I.C.H., vol. XI, (1982), pp. 58 – 72. For an attempted sociological and cultural explanation of the weaknesses of British industry in the inter-war period see Corelli Barnett, Audit of War (London, 1986).
[29] See Reese, The History of the Royal Commonwealth Society, 162 – 6.

ex-servicemen desirous of emigrating to the Dominions. A Conference was held early in 1921 with representatives from Canada, Australia and New Zealand, and the proposals which were approved by the Dominion Prime Ministers resulted in the Empire Settlement Act of 1922, authorising the British government to make loans for a period of up to fifteen years to meet half the cost of transporting settlers overseas, with the Dominions furnishing the other half. Nevertheless most migration within the Empire continued to be on a private basis. When the 1923 Imperial Conference examined the result of the Empire Settlement Act it expressed disappointment, while recognising that any 'redistribution of the white population of the Empire' would depend on the rate at which the Dominions could successfully absorb newcomers. By 1928 both Canada and Australia were curtailing the opportunities for immigration in response to their own economic difficulties, though Canada actually took its largest number in the inter-war period in 1929. 1930 was the true turning point. The total emigration to the Empire, which had always topped 100,000 in every year since 1924, fell to just over 59,000 in 1930 and to less than half that in 1931.[30] Indeed, with the onset of the depression, there was a greater flow of immigrants from the Dominions into Britain than in the reverse direction.

India

Economic relations with India were in many ways more important than those with any other part of the Empire and were also affected by the anomalous and changing constitutional status of the Indian government. In 1913 India was the largest single market for British goods, which provided over 60 per cent of her total imports. In addition to her importance as a market for cotton textiles and engineering products, India also provided an important place among the recipients of British investment. Finally, because India had a strong positive trade balance with North America and continental Europe in particular, the British deficit in overseas trade was to a large extent made up through her own positive balance with India.[31]

[30] The figures are given for each year from 1924 to 1937 in table 15 of *Board of Trade Statistical Tables, 1938–9*, (Cmd 5903, 1939).
[31] Tomlinson, *The Political Economy of the Raj*, ch. 2 – 6. The analysis in this chapter owes much to this work.

The general picture did however conceal particular instances of gain and loss and was looked at differently by Delhi and London respectively. For the Indian government the development of the Indian economy on the basis in particular of further industrialisation was essential even if its intervention was not always methodical. It was important to be able to raise enough taxation to pay both for the local expenses of government and for those parts of it that reflected its position within the Empire. The Indian Government wished to see Indian entrepreneurs feel at home within the existing structure and not identify themselves too far with the nationalist movement. It did not regard it as its business to support the claims of British firms to preferential treatment. On the other hand the British government, of which the Secretary of State for India was a member, was vulnerable to electoral pressure in favour of safeguarding the economic position that British exporters and investors had built up. And apart from questions of protection, there was also, since so many of India's external payments and receipts passed through London, the complicated question of the rupee – sterling relationship in which the Treasury and the Bank of England had an interest. In the course of the period after the war, the previous separation between Indian and expatriate business interests was also partially broken down through various forms of partnership, so that the British business community might find itself closer to its Indian competitors than to the Indian government itself. And in a period of increasing industrialisation this development was of some significance.

In general terms, the ability of the Indian government directly to affect industrial development was weakened by the constitutional reforms of the Montagu – Chelmsford period, since industry was treated as a provincial subject and the portfolio made available for Indian ministers. What remained was tariff policy. By the Fiscal Autonomy Convention of 1919, the Government of India would normally act in fiscal matters where they were in agreement with the Legislative Assembly without the intervention of the Secretary of State. And although the Fiscal Convention had been accepted by the Imperial government as part of a new general system for the strengthening of imperial commercial ties, it soon appeared that imperial preference did not appeal to the Indian government and that its general policy would be one of straight tariff protection for Indian industries. The import substitution effect of protective tariffs was further enhanced by the increased reliance of the Indian government on customs duties, which tended further to raise the price of imported products. Purchasing policy giving preference to local purchases in rupees as against purchases in London in sterling also had some effect. Since during the 1920s the Indian government tended to use its Tariff Board to protect itself against internal pressures and to help it preserve some neutrality between them, the total effect of these policies was not as decisive as some might have expected. But it was sufficient to create alarm and anxiety among some of India's traditional suppliers in Britain, which might lead them either to demand a reassertion of imperial control and to oppose further constitutional change or to abandon an interest in India altogether. The economic as opposed to the political and strategic argument for retaining British rule in India was thus now substantially weakened.

The impediments created for the business community by the difficulty of fixing an appropriate rate for the rupee which should balance the problems of overseas payments against the need for credit both on the part of local industry and on the part of the Indian government itself, and in respect of the problems of the stagnating agricultural sector also divided Indian opinion, until the matter was dealt with by a gold standard settlement in 1927. The depression made this position untenable and in 1931 the rupee was aligned with sterling. The actual effect of this decision, which had not been foreseen, was to put a premium on gold, and India in the 1930s was able to pay its way through gold exports.

The autonomy in respect of fiscal policy and in the control of currency that the Indian government enjoyed from 1921 on gave some reality to the partial recognition of India's status in the imperial and international arena. It was clearly not a dependency in the sense that applied to most colonial territories. Furthermore, the agreements through which the British rather than the Indian taxpayer was to meet the expenses of the employment of Indian forces overseas also contributed to the perception that India, even with its limited measure of internal self-government, was a Commonwealth partner rather than a possession. But just as among nationalists it was still held that India's interests were being sacrificed to Britain's need so in Britain the logic of the new situation made only uneven progress in the worlds of commerce and politics.

In part, the reactions in Britain reflected an unwillingness to come to terms with the facts. It is the case that India's industrial imports fell during the inter-war period taken as a whole, but she remained dependent upon imports in vital sectors of the economy. It was Britain's share in those imports that began to decline after 1921, (despite some limited preferences granted in 1927), a decline that accelerated after 1929. The trade gap in Britain's favour, still considerable in 1921, was almost wiped out by 1932 and was thereafter until the war in India's favour. It was to prove to be the case that even when British exports began to pick up after 1932, it was Japan and the United States that continued to expand their position in the Indian market. The tariffs imposed after 1921 did not for the most part discriminate between overseas suppliers, and it was once again lack of competitiveness and commercial skills, not the Fiscal Autonomy Convention, that told against British trade.

Successive British governments had to learn to cope with the situation and the conflicting pressures upon them. During the discussions at the 1923 Imperial Conference, the Indian government showed its opposition to a general system of imperial preferences, both because of its wish to develop a protectionist system and because of its antipathy to the policies in other areas of some Dominion governments. To the British government this came as a disappointment.[32]

When Labour came into office in 1924, the new Secretary of State, Olivier, pointed out that the Fiscal Autonomy Convention did not rule out the responsibility of the Secretary of State for safeguarding imperial interests. But he did not in fact disallow protectionist measures, though voicing the view that protection was not in India's best interests. In 1925 the Indian government went still further in assisting Indian as against Lancashire cotton interests by recommending the repeal of the cotton excise duty which had been the compensation for the duty on cotton imports.[33] One reason for the tepid reaction in Britain to the repeal was the realisation that both British and Indian textile interests were now being affected by Japanese competition.

[32] Reading, *Rufus Issacs first Marquess of Reading*, vol. 2, p. 277. 'I was discussing this subject the other day with Amery who said that he thought this country had not a very good record with regard to Lancashire trade and fiscal policy in India ... [but] even the Labour members with all their professed willingness to grant self-government to India have pressed this subject. Just at this juncture with our million and three hundred thousand of unemployed the attempt of India to give us preference in her markets would calm a hundred acerbities.' Peel to Reading, 17 January 1923, IORL MSS EUR E 238/6.

[33] Drummond, op. cit., pp. 125 – 6.

The prospects for some co-operation with the rest of the Empire-Commonwealth in trade matters seemed more hopeful at the time of the 1926 Imperial Conference. The Indian government was happy that a general scheme of preferences was not on the agenda and was prepared to co-operate in examining the possibility of individual voluntary arrangements. The brief for the Indian delegation also included the following passage:

> It is desirable that the Indian delegation should take advantage of this opportunity to do what is possible at the present Conference to encourage the development of trade with other parts of the Empire and particularly with the self-governing Dominions. Close commercial ties it is thought would not only be of mutual advantage economically but might also ease the political difficulties inherent in Indian membership of the Commonwealth.[34]

But the same document went on to show that trade with the United Kingdom was actually diminishing in both directions, that with the rest of the Empire stagnating, and the only increase was with foreign countries. It was suggested that Commonwealth countries might be asked to pay more attention to the Indian market and give voluntary preferences to Indian goods. In a Conference dominated by constitutional issues such suggestions were unlikely to come to anything. It was still the relationship with Britain that dominated India's economic policies.

Early in 1930 the Viceroy informed the British government that India's financial needs, and the difficulties that the Bombay mills were running into, made a raising of the tariff essential, though there would be a modest and temporary concession of a measure of preference for British cotton goods.[35] When the Cabinet faced the issue and the likely political repercussions, it was pointed out by the Secretary of State that while the government was entitled to make its views known to the Viceroy, he must regard himself as responsible for the welfare of India and that the Fiscal Autonomy Convention must be observed. The Cabinet limited itself to calling the Viceroy's attention to the parlous state of the Lancashire cotton trade and the adverse effect that the duties would have.[36] While this incident reveals how even British

[34] IORL, 1290.E and O.1375.
[35] Drummond, op cit, 127.
[36] Jones, *Whitehall Diary* vol. 2, pp. 242 – 3.

employment prospects had to give way before the political realities of the relationship, it also helps to explain how it was that Churchill's resignation from the Opposition Business Committee (the shadow cabinet of the time) at the beginning of 1931 was followed by the building up of support in the country and more particularly in Lancashire, which after the 1931 election was represented wholly by Conservative members, except in four mainly mining constituencies.

Chapter 6

IMPERIAL DEFENCE AND ARMS CONTROL: THE ROLE OF THE UNITED STATES

PART I: DEFENCE POLICY AND ARMS CONTROL

Military planning and Disarmament

The pressure under which the British military and naval chiefs felt themselves to be in 1921 did not much diminish in subsequent years; while ways were found to cut down on some of the commitments, others proved more enduring. Political demands for the reduction of military expenditure, whether on economic or pacifist grounds, continued to be felt, and made it impossible for any government to give up the search for disarmament by agreement, and this in turn depended upon the achievement of some form of collective security which itself might require an element of British military commitment. And in so far as both Europe and the Middle East were concerned, such guarantees were unacceptable to most of the Dominions. British statesmen and service chiefs had to reckon with the fact that in peacetime certainly, if not in war, it would be Britain itself that would bear most of the burden.

In the early post-war years with potential enemies disarmed, or like Russia in the throes of revolution, immediate measures of a major kind did not seem necessary. The rivalry in the air with the French was a factor in the distribution of the British defence efforts but was diminished in importance as time went on. It was possible therefore to follow the guidelines laid down by the cabinet on 15 August 1919 that no major war was likely for ten years.[1] The consequence of this assumption where land forces were concerned was that the priority of

[1] For a general view of the problem see Michael Howard, *The Continental Commitment* (London, 1972), and N.H. Gibbs, 'British Strategic Doctrine', in M. Howard (ed.), *The Theory and Practice of War* (London, 1965).

122

imperial commitments had to be accepted: the Cardwell system of an army so organised as to meet the demands for small detachments to go overseas.[2] For such operations in mountains or jungles, specialised equipment was called for, and this also would be different from that which renewed continental warfare might require.[3] It is not surprising that Britain did not stand in the forefront of innovation where land and air warfare were concerned or that first-rate minds did not find careers in the armed forces particularly attractive.

It was not however merely the demands of Empire that directed the scope of Britain's military preparations. Many of those in leading positions were convinced that Britain's acceptance of a major role in continental warfare between 1914 and 1918 had been an error, if an unavoidable one; they were averse to any repetition of it. What they wanted was to go back to the traditional strategy of relying on seapower to blockade an enemy and facilitate flanking attacks against her; it was for continental allies to bear the brunt of fighting by land. But the technical, demographic and financial conditions which had made this strategy possible in the eighteenth century no longer prevailed.[4]

The military of course appreciated that this was the case and knew that in the last resort, in relation to Britain's commitments as they stood after Locarno, a small expeditionary force could only be a token of Britain's readiness. The complete apparatus for military expansion and industrial mobilisation would need to be ready in case of war.[5] Since it was difficult to envisage such preparedness in the immediate post-war years, service chiefs tended to fall back on the view that there was no necessary connection between their requirements and foreign policy. In 1924 the C.I.G.S., the Earl of Cavan, said that it was practically impossible to make adequate preparations for war against possible enemies without their identity becoming known to various ambassadors in London.[6] And when in 1926 the Foreign Office tried to get some military commitment from the chiefs of staff in order to

---

[2] B.H. Liddell Hart, *The Tanks* (London, 1959), vol.1, p. 271. The same author's *Memoirs*, vol.1 (London, 1965), give a valuable if idiosyncratic view of the military controversies of the period.
[3] W.J. Reader, *Architect of Air Power: the life of the first Viscount Weir of Eastwood, 1877–1959* (London, 1968), p. 182.
[4] Peter Dennis, *Decision by Default: Peacetime Conscription and British Defence, 1919–1939* (London, 1972), p. 6.
[5] Chiefs of Staff Review of Imperial Defence, 1926, C.I.D. 701-B, in PRO CAB 4/15.
[6] Cavan to Salisbury, 10 January 1924, Salisbury Papers, S.(4) 108/43.

convince European powers of the sincerity of Britain's attachment to the Locarno Treaties, their reply on 26 June ran:

> The size of the forces of the Crown maintained by Great Britain is governed by various conditions peculiar to each service, and is not arrived at by any calculations of the requirements of foreign policy nor is it possible that they ever should be so calculated.[7]

It would seem, in the light of subsequent experience, that foreign policy, military, and industrial considerations could only have been brought together had a Ministry of Defence been created, as was suggested during the discussions on defence organisation in 1923. But the idea was turned down, largely owing to the influence of Haldane and Hankey, who preferred to revive the old Committee of Imperial Defence, reinforced by the Chiefs of Staff subcommittee.[8] This system had among other advantages, it was suggested, that of being particularly well-suited to the structure of the Empire, since the Dominion Prime Ministers could take their places on it 'under the only leadership they [were] permitted by their people to acknowledge'.[9]

As has already been noted, this argument was fallacious. The Dominions did not wish for regular representation on the C.I.D., which remained a United Kingdom affair. Where army and air force planning was concerned, the British authorities had to work on their own with what manpower the United Kingdom and to a limited extent India could supply.[10] Contacts with the armed forces of the Dominions – other than their navies – were at a purely professional level.[11]

The naval situation was different and more complex. The abrogation of the Anglo-Japanese alliance and the conclusion of the Washington Treaties meant that the British accepted the view that competitive

---

[7] Quoted in Howard, op. cit., p. 94.

[8] Churchill revived the idea of a Ministry of Defence in 1926, again in vain: C.I.D. meeting, 10 June 1926, PRO CAB 2/4.

[9] 'The Direction and Staff Work of Imperial Defence', paper by Viscount Haldane, 2 April 1923, Paper N.D. – 9 in PRO CAB 16/47. Hankey to Haldane, 7 August 1923, Churchill College, Cambridge, Hankey Papers 4/15.

[10] In disarmament negotiations there was the question as to whether air units in the Dominions and India could be counted as part of Britain's strength. Statement prepared by R.A.F. representative at Geneva for Lord Robert Cecil, 2 April 1927, Cecil of Chelwood Papers, BL Add MSS 51113. On the relation of the Dominion air forces to the RAF, see Hilary St George Saunders, *Per Ardua: the Rise of British Air Power, 1919–1939* (London, 1939).

[11] The Chiefs of Staff were emphatic on the need for common training: meeting of 4 October 1923, PRO CAB 53/1.

building with the United States was impossible and that parity was the best that could be hoped for in the future. In view of the dominance of isolationist sentiment in the United States, this did not mean that Britain could rely upon U.S. naval strength to assist her in the tasks of imperial defence, particularly if Japan were to become a hostile power. The defence of the sea-lanes and the ultimate reinforcing of the Australasian dominions, the colonies, and perhaps even India were British responsibilities. Here it could hardly be said that the objectives were of interest only to the United Kingdom. So, as before 1914, the main debates over defence within the Commonwealth in the 1920s were over possible Dominion contributions to the Empire's maritime forces, and once again the argument was complicated by the Admiralty's desire to centralise control of the forces raised and the Dominions' preference for having their ships under their own control. It was true that for the time being there was not the pressure for concentration in home waters that the German Grand Fleet had provided; but both France and Italy were important naval powers, and, given the continued significance of the Mediterranean, their fleets' sizes and roles had to be taken into account. In addition the importance attached by the Admiralty to commerce protection produced demands for cruisers which the United States regarded as unacceptably high. Friction between Britain and the United States over naval disarmament and associated issues was thus endemic in the first postwar decade and contributed to Canadian anxieties.[12] British officials might speculate about the possibilities of war with Japan or France or a revived Germany.[13] But nearly all of them would, like Austen Chamberlain, have placed first and foremost among British responsibilities 'the free communications by sea throughout the Empire'.[14] And of this commitment the planned base at Singapore was to be the symbol, and its vicissitudes the most relevant indicator of British and Dominion attitudes.[15]

[12] Christopher Hall, *Britain, America and Arms Control, 1921-1937* (London, 1986), is a valuable study of its subject, particularly where the technicalities of naval disarmament were concerned, but pays no attention to the Dominions aspect of the negotiations.

[13] Note by Hankey accompanying C.I.D. minutes of 20 November 1924, PRO CAB 2/4.

[14] C.I.D. meeting, 22 July 1926, PRO CAB 2/4.

[15] The decision to build a base at Singapore had been taken in 1921 before the abrogation of the Anglo-Japanese alliance, and as late as 1925 the Foreign Office believed that there was no substantial cause to regard Japan as a potential enemy. Ian H. Nish, *Alliance in Decline: A study in Anglo-Japanese Relations, 1908–1923* (London, 1972), pp. 389–90.

If then it was agreed that 'the maintenance of the superiority at sea of the Naval forces of the British Empire over any combination of forces likely to be arrayed against them' was the 'basis of the system of Imperial Defence',[16] it was here that Dominion assistance would be sought. The Washington Conference seemed to the Admiralty a reason for more rather than less effort.[17] It had been agreed at the 1921 Imperial Conference that while the Empire must on its own maintain at least a single-power standard, the contributions of its individual parts were a matter for the separate Parliaments. At the Imperial Conference of 1923, Amery, then First Lord of the Admiralty, urged that national navies should be merged into a general defence scheme, quoting existing outlays as being twenty-five shillings annually *per capita* for the United Kingdom, eight shillings for Australia, and only one shilling each for Canada and South Africa.[18]

The result was a clash between Amery and Mackenzie King on the relative merits of centralisation and co-operation. Mackenzie King was particularly irked by the publication in Canada of an Admiralty memorandum urging increased Canadian naval expenditure, as being an attempt to influence public opinion over the head of the Canadian government.[19] Amery, undaunted, invited Mackenzie King to the fleet inspection at Spithead. 'Standing on the bridge with the Prime Minister, I could not help saying to Mackenzie King: "That is why you are Prime Minister of Canada, and not at best one of the Senators of the American State of Ontario".[20] The differences over inter-imperial relations in general are thus only to be understood in the light of the differences in interest and perception as between Canada and the Australasian Dominions. It was quite obvious, wrote the Prime Minister of Saskatchewan,

> that Australasian and British imperialistic propagandists... are straining to stampede us into a participation in big naval expenditures (& so commit us to Imperial Wars, *irrevocably*), so as, primarily, to secure Australia and New Zealand in the 'mandated'

[16] C.I.D. paper 257-B in C.I.D. minutes, meeting of 31 October 1921, PRO CAB 2/3.
[17] C.I.D. meeting, 30 November 1922, PRO CAB 23/29.
[18] Eayrs, op. cit., pp. 166 – 7, 181; *Journal of the Parliaments of the Empire*, vol. VI, (July 1925), pp. 445 – 6.
[19] Eayrs, op. cit., pp. 89 – 90, 179.
[20] Leo Amery, *My Political Life*, vol. II (London, 1953), p. 276.

territories which they have acquired in the Pacific up to the equator thus bringing them into direct and dangerous contact with Japan.[21]

During the lifetime of the second Baldwin government, the argument for the ten year rule appeared less cogent to those who gave first priority to defence and were sensible of the growth of Japanese power. In 1925 Baldwin suggested that the one-power standard could be maintained if the British fleet, wherever situated, was equal to the fleet of any other country, provided that arrangements were made from time to time to 'enable local naval forces to maintain the situation against vital and irreparable damage pending the arrival of the main fleet and to give the main fleet on arrival sufficient mobility'.[22] This would give an individual role to Dominion forces. But this formulation was objected to by Churchill in his economising stance as Chancellor of the Exchequer, since it was capable of being interpreted as meaning that Britain should be able at the end of the ten year rule period to fight Japan single-handed.[23]

The threat was not an immediate one and under the 1925 building programme it was reckoned that Britain would be superior in submarines to the United States, Japan and France, inferior in destroyers to the United States, but still the strongest power in the world in cruisers.[24] At the same time there was pressure from the Americans, and the sympathies of those who were desirous of coming to terms with the United States if at all possible and were not hostile to the American concept of the freedom of the seas.

Anglo-American Differences

What was clear after Washington was that Britain and the United States had needs and attitudes that were difficult to reconcile, since they arose from considerations of the national interest and a different view of the world. On the face of it, the Americans were interested in extending the idea of disarmament by agreed ratios of strength in categories of vessels as widely as possible. But this was the understandable attitude of a power which thought of its fleet as something that might have to be matched with others in war, but in peacetime was

[21] W.M. Martin to Mackenzie King, 14 September 1923, quoted by Eayrs, op. cit., p. 178.
[22] C.I.D. meeting, 30 March 1925, PRO CAB 2/4.
[23] C.I.D. meeting, 2 April 1925, PRO CAB 2/4.
[24] Chiefs of Staff review of Imperial Defence, 1926, in PRO CAB 4/15.

largely a matter of prestige. The British believed that the cohesion of the Empire and the security of their trade routes could be translated into an absolute definition of naval needs, particularly in cruisers, and that here no compromise was possible. The size and nature of the French fleet was almost as important in the 1920s, when France and Japan were the only two powers against whom a possible war was contemplated; and Italy became important, first because of its competitive stance as against France, and then as its ambitions increased in its own right. The Americans were seriously concerned only with Japan.

The Americans, unsympathetic to the Imperial argument and unimpressed by the alleged absolute requirements of trade protection, at times also suspected the British of more far-reaching and even aggressive designs, and attributed both their post-war cruiser programme and their diplomacy to preparations for carrying them out. The fact that this diagnosis overlooked the pessimism that underlay so much British thinking and the disparity between British and American resources, and the unlikelihood of other countries assisting to recreate a British hegemony – all this did not prevent the case from being powerfully argued in American naval circles:

> The United States is the present rival of Great Britain in world trade and commerce. The American protective tariff and protective coastwise laws impede British expansion of world trade and shipping. British interests for the last seven years, with the powerful backing of the League of Nations, have been slowly consolidating, and may be expected to continue the effort to consolidate a combine in which are to be included continental powers and Japan, for the purpose of breaking down, eventually, the American protective system.[25]

For this reason any discussions on naval disarmament were entered into by the Americans with the feeling that the British would be insincere and self-seeking.[26]

[25] Memorandum by Rear Admiral William W. Phelps, 15 July 1925, in the archives of the General Board of the Navy; quoted in R. O'Connor, *Perilous Equilibrium: the U.S.A. and the 1930 London Naval Conference* (Lawrence, Kansas, 1962), pp. 13 – 14.

[26] 'There are powerful elements in the British Government that will see that the British lion comes out of any conference unscathed. The great Conservative body of opinion of the aristocracy, the Admiralty, the War Office and the Air Ministry, will at the right time see that Great Britain gets a quid pro quo over everything that is sacrificed.' Report by U.S. naval attache in London, 2 March 1926, quoted ibid., p. 14.

The argument over the 'freedom of the seas' is even easier to understand in the light of the differing assumptions of the two governments and navies. It was assumed first of all by the Americans that, in any future war involving naval powers, they would be neutral. It was assumed therefore that their interest would lie in giving the maximum force to neutral rights against a Britain that would be using the weapon of blockade. It was the same argument that made them so hostile to any strengthening of the League of Nations. The British questioned the American assumption that they would or should be neutral in such a war – and given the tension between the United States and Japan, their scepticism was natural. But if there were a war, for instance against a European power, they certainly had no intention of giving up their most important weapon – the more important in that prevailing military theory precluded the idea of fighting another land-war on the continent.

It had been the hope of the British government that the discussions with the United States at the time of the peace conference had settled the right of Britain to use its sea-power in any future conflict without challenge from the United States. The rumour therefore that the State Department intended to support a series of claims by American nationals arising out of the operations of the blockade before the Americans entered the war caused an instant reaction in Whitehall. Chamberlain expressed himself very strongly to the American Ambassador:

> the United States claims went to the roots of our rights as a belligerent Power... they struck straight at our naval strength and at our power to defend ourselves. In fact, they would open up all the questions which had been covered by the German cry of the freedom of the seas, which at one time received some support from President Wilson, but which, after inquiry, had been abandoned by him at Versailles. It seemed to me inconceivable that these questions should now be reopened, and I saw no possibiliy of any compromise on the question of principle.[27]

On this occasion it did ultimately seem possible to reach an agreement, and a statement by the two governments was issued to the press a little while before the opening of the Geneva naval conference in

[27] Chamberlain to Howard (Washington), 3 November 1925, *DBFP*, Series IA, vol. II (London, H.M.S.O., 1968), pp. 867 – 8.

1927.[28] But it was not by any means the end of the story where the 'freedom of the seas' was concerned.[29]

In the light of such mutual suspicion, the advocates of a close alignment with the United States in world affairs generally were naturally put in the position of arguing that Britain could afford to give way on some naval issues so as to lay the foundations of a joint policy for the future. Lord Astor reported the American Secretary of State, Kellogg, as saying that war between the United States and Britain was unthinkable and that therefore neither country should aim at superiority. His policy would mean Britain giving up her cruiser supremacy and the United States giving up her destroyer supremacy. Astor thought the policy should be accepted; it would not stop there, but could lead to a method of separating differences between the two countries and of co-operation against external aggression.[30]

In the mid – 1920s the British sense of injustice was still lively. As Sir Austen Chamberlain told the Imperial Conference in 1926, while Britain had never been so generally popular with the American people as now, it was 'regrettable though not surprising' that in Britain feeling towards the United States was 'less friendly than at any time since the American civil war'.[31]

At the end of the following year, after the failure of the Geneva Naval Conference, the Cabinet was informed that Anglo-American relations were deteriorating under the shadow of an approaching Presidential election, and that to secure any permanent improvement was difficult. It was pointed out that in respect of the Irish Treaty, the abandonment of the Anglo-Japanese alliance, several of the provisions of the Washington treaties and the funding of the debt, it had been believed each time that a settlement would make for friendlier relations. These failures should be borne in mind in connection with the current issue of belligerent rights at sea.[32]

[28] *The Times*, 2 June 1927. See *FRUS*, 1927, vol. II, pp. 745-55. The negotiations leading up to the agreement were informally and secretly conducted by Robert Vansittart: Hankey to Balfour, 12 January 1928, Balfour Papers, BL Add MSS 49705.
[29] At the time there was some optimism in British quarters: 'I cannot conceal my own feeling of gratification that the principle of the blockade has been protected from effective challenge by the Government of the United States, and that a fruitful source of possible misunderstanding between the two countries has been finally removed.' Howard to Foreign Office, 3 June 1927, *DBFP*, Series IA, vol. II, p. 918.
[30] Astor to Kerr, 3 September 1926, Lothian Papers, Box 188.
[31] *DBFP*, Series IA, vol. II, p. 955.
[32] PRO CAB 23/55, meeting of 21 December 1927. Almost a year later, Hankey was saying virtually the same thing: 'We played up to America over the Covenant of the League, the

The discussions at Geneva in 1926 had suggested that while technical agreement on disarmament questions might be reached, there were always possibilities of political divergences making agreement impossible.[33] One such difficulty was the preference of Americans for settling naval questions apart from questions of general disarmament. Proposals for a naval agreement between the United States, Great Britain and Japan alone, put forward by President Coolidge in February 1927, were thus received with caution on the British side. The British were well aware that a large section of French opinion had 'always regarded the Washington agreement as riveting on the world a British naval supremacy in Europe, an American naval supremacy in American waters, and complete world supremacy of the two English-speaking peoples if they should act together'.[34]

American hostility could not be countered in the traditional sense of competition in armaments or by building up alliances. In urging that the strength of the United States should not be taken into account in deciding upon Britain's own needs, Sir Esme Howard wrote to Chamberlain:

A war between the British Empire and the U.S.A. is, I believe, physically impossible. I say 'the British Empire' and not 'Great Britain' for the reason that if ever by some unlucky chance we were forced against our will into war with U.S., it would be impossible for Canada to be other than neutral... If Canada declared her neutrality as she would be bound to do, since she could not defend herself and we could not defend her, would not this be the beginning of the break-up of the Empire? Is it not more than likely that one or two of the other great Dominions would follow her example?[35]

It could be argued, Howard admitted in a further letter, that with Japanese help the navy could hold its own against the Americans:

abandonment of the Japanese Alliance, the Washington Treaties, debt settlement, Irish settlement, liquor treaty (limits of territorial waters); always making concessions and always being told that the next step would change their attitude. Yet they are as a result more overbearing and suspicious against us than anyone else.' Hankey to Jones, 11 October 1928, Thomas Jones (ed.), Keith Middlemas, *Whitehall Diary*, vol. 2, (Oxford University Press, 1969), p. 147.

[33] Memorandum by Cecil (Geneva), 24 September 1926, *DBFP*, Series IA, vol. II, pp. 396 – 7.

[34] Memorandum by Cecil, Cecil of Chelwood Papers, BL Add MSS 51103.

[35] Howard to Chamberlain, 23 June 1927, *DBFP*, Series IA, vol. III (London, H.M.S.O., 1970), p. 615.

I don't know whether these views are entertained in the Navy or at the Admiralty by any number of persons. To me they seem only suitable for a Lunatic Asylum, because they show a complete lack of understanding of the sentiment of the Dominions. It would certainly be impossible to imagine anything more calculated to produce the secession of Canada and South Africa – to say nothing of Australia – than a war with the United States carried on *in alliance with Orientals*.[36]

The difficulty was that this reality did not conform to what was still, even after the 1926 Imperial Conference, a fixed attachment to the notion that externally the Empire was one: no-one in London, wrote Chamberlain, 'will or can consent to admitting the hypothesis that, in a war in which The King is engaged, any part of his Empire can be neutral. Each of the Dominions may make as great or as little effective effort in support of his arms as they please, but neutrality is not compatible with either the theory or practice of Imperial unity.' To this Howard perforce agreed, but pointed out that the contrary belief was bound to be held by anyone who knew Canada.[37]

There was the further difficulty that just because both were world powers, Britain in virtue of the Empire, the United States in virtue of its position on two oceans and its Far Eastern interests, they were bound to be affected by any conflict that broke out, whether or not they were directly implicated. There were, as Kerr pointed out to an American correspondent, no questions of a political kind on which the two countries would go to war. But a war in Europe would almost certainly involve Britain and one in the Far East would involve the United States:

Any war therefore, is liable instantly to precipitate an Anglo-American crisis... The United States and Great Britain, therefore, are living on the edge of a volcano in the sense that however friendly their relations may be, if two nations in any part of

---

[36] Howard to Chamberlain, 1 September 1927, ibid., pp. 736 – 7.
[37] Chamberlain to Howard, 10 August 1927, and Howard to Chamberlain, 1 September 1927, ibid., pp. 729, 737. A year later Thomas Jones, hostile to Hankey's policy on naval questions, was telling Baldwin that Hankey underestimated the United States and the importance of relations between Canada and the United States. Diary entry, 1 November 1928, Jones, *Whitehall Diary*, vol. 2, p. 155.

the world start fighting, they almost inevitably precipitate an Anglo-American row as well.[38]

But did this mean that there could be no partnership for the solution of international problems while the Empire survived?

The prospects for Anglo-American collaboration

Some British political figures believed this to be a situation that was capable of remedy and that it was possible to choose and follow a policy that would command both Empire and United States support, at the expense indeed of the League of Nations and of an active role in Europe.[39] It would involve the building up of the economic strength of the Empire through a positive policy of development and the full application of a 'British Monroe Doctrine' to the Middle East provided that it did not affect American interests. If this were done, ran a memorandum by the indefatigable Amery, 'there is no inherent reason why the British Empire should not be developed into something as far ahead of the United States in economic power fifty years hence as they are ahead of Great Britain today'.[40] What Amery did not see clearly was that while it was possible to reach local agreements, as had been done in regard to American oil interests in the Middle East, the master-plan would not be acceptable to the Americans, whose every political instinct and economic doctrine ran against the perpetuation of Empires and the carving out of areas of preferential trading or financial relations. For this reason it was in banking and financial circles , where the British on the whole held to the same universalist line of thought, that Anglo-American collaboration proceeded most smoothly.[41]

---

[38] Kerr to Raymond Buell (of the Foreign Policy Association, New York), 4 June 1929: Lothian Papers.

[39] 'Neither Austen and still less Cushendun are anywhere near realising that it is USA friendship and Empire approval versus Geneva. All this nervous deference to the US and fear of ever saying anything that might annoy them is futile and mischievous: what is needed is a self-respecting attitude but a policy which they can understand and sympathize with.' Leo Amery diary, 7 December 1928, (not printed).

[40] Memorandum by Amery on Anglo-American relations, written in 1928: C.P. 367(28) in PRO DO 117/125.

[41] Montagu Norman, who as Governor of the Bank of England from 1920 to 1944 exercised unparalleled influence in the City, worked very closely with Benjamin Strong, the powerful Governor of the Federal Reserve Bank of New York from 1914 to 1928.

The evolution of the Empire into the Commonwealth was little understood or admired by Americans. At times there was a tendency to expect that the Dominions would follow the road trodden by the Americans and arrive at total independence or, in Canada's case, at that incorporation in the United States which seemed to be manifest destiny.[42] Others might believe that the Dominions, while remaining within the system, would outgrow the mother country and end by dominating her.[43] But for the most part Americans, and particularly official Americans, took the view that the formal status of the Dominions was still that of dependencies and that their independent international existence, for instance as members of the League of Nations in their own right, was a sham or a Machiavellian device for increasing British influence.[44] It was even harder to believe British protestations about any degree of independence in international matters being exercised by the Government of India.[45]

Although American policy was hostile to the reinforcement of Commonwealth ties, the Dominions individually tended to favour good relations with the United States, and this had to be taken into account by British statesmen. It was even true of Australia, once the

[42] 'The Imperial Conference', reported the Washington Embassy on 5 November 1926, 'is exciting considerable interest. At first there was a tendency to expect open defiance on the part of South Africa and to a somewhat lesser extent Ireland, and even Canada. Now this has developed into a feeling that there will be no unpleasantness and that when the conference breaks up the commonwealth of nations will remain on as sound, if not a sounder, basis, than before. I feel that Mr Mackenzie King's emphatic denial of the existence in Canada of any desire for amalgamation with the United States was a most salutary pronouncement.' *DBFP,* Series IA, vol. II, pp. 899 – 900.

[43] 'Grandmother England is growing old. The war tired her, with its killed and wounded, its billions of debts, with millions of unemployed and disastrous strikes following. The Dominions are young, strong and growing. Now each Dominion is made officially the equal of Great Britain. The Colonies and Britain form an alliance, not an empire with Britain ruling. But the colonies are only officially Britain's equals. They will outgrow and dominate her in time and old England will come to be the European banking office and banking centre of brains in South Africa and Australia.' *The New York American,* quoted by the Washington Embassy in despatch of 26 November 1926, ibid., p. 906.

[44] A British lawyer reading the Senate debates on the Versailles Treaty was struck by the tendency to treat the legal relations between the imperial government and the Dominions as though they represented the constitutional situation: 'They continually insist on the power of the Imperial Government to amend or revoke the Dominion Constitutions and the power of the Imperial Government to control, through the "Governor-General, the Dominion Executives. They argue accordingly that the Dominions are dependencies". This fallacy which appears to be honestly entertained is remarkable and accounts for much.' J.H.Morgan to John Dove, 30 June 1926; copy in Lothian Papers, Box 186.

[45] A row developed at the Opium Conference of 1924 between the American and Indian delegations and spilled over into Anglo-American friction: 'Unfortunately it is believed that Great Britain entirely controls India.' Drummond to Cecil, 28 November 1924, Cecil of Chelwood Papers, BL Add MSS 51110.

Japanese alliance had been abrogated, since the importance of the United States as a possible protector against Japan was now undeniable.[46] Canada's views on the desirability of British non-involvement in Europe, while resting mainly on internal political considerations, were also powerfully influenced by a desire not to be separated from the United States in time of danger. The matter was however complicated by the fact that Canada had its own problems to settle with the United States and had always to be on its guard against the powerful economic influences pulling it into the American orbit.

In 1928 it was possible to hope that Canada would step in to help solve the naval dispute with the United States.[47] But the violent language used in the United States over British cruiser building caused a hostile reaction among Canadian Conservatives, particularly since it came at a time when the Americans were about to raise their tariff in ways likely to damage Canada, and Mackenzie King feared that the Opposition leader Bennett would win support on a programme of retaliation. His own concern was to prevent Canadian hostility against the United States from developing; he tried to turn Hoover (though not publicly) from his tariff proposals by threatening non-cooperation in the St Lawrence seaway project. But even he had to envisage the possibility of lowering duties on British goods if the Americans did not give way.[48] In July 1930 the Conservatives returned to power in Canada on a platform of economic nationalism which was bound to have an anti-American edge to it. But the fact that since 1927 Canada had had its independent representation in Washington was not without importance in giving Canada a degree of independence of action where relations between the United States and the Commonwealth were concerned.

It is perhaps worth asking whether a more imaginative handling of the problem of Britain's own representation at the American capital

[46] A memorandum on Anglo-American relations drawn up on 12 November 1928 by Craigie of the Foreign Office includes the pro-American feeling of the Dominions among the reasons for maintaining good relations with the United States, and quotes the remark of Hughes when Prime Minister of Australia: 'I hail with joy the laying down of every new American battleship.' PRO CAB 24/198.

[47] Kerr to Smuts, 20 March 1928, Lothian Papers, 189. On 3 December the Acting Secretary of State for Foreign Affairs suggested to Amery that Mackenzie King should be asked for his advice. Cf Amery to Chamberlain, 6 December 1928, PRO DO 117/125. See also the correspondence between Sir Robert Borden and Balfour in January 1929 arising out of an attempt by an American professor, W.K. Stewart, to try to get Canada (through Borden) to mediate between the United States and Britain by getting Britain to accept the American view of neutral rights. Balfour Papers, BL Add MSS 49697, 49736, 49738, 49749.

[48] Neatby, *Mackenzie King*, vol. 2, pp. 282 – 6.

might not have proved productive. From the retirement of Sir Auckland Geddes in 1924 until the arrival of Lord Lothian in 1939 the post was treated as a normal Foreign Office career appointment and no particular attempt was made to develop its political or public relations aspects. In June 1929 there was a rumour that Gilbert Murray, the eminent scholar and leading figure in the League of Nations Union, would be nominated to the post. But after MacDonald's successful visit to President Hoover it was thought that the situation had so changed that a professional diplomat could carry on better with the detailed work arising.[49]

Inter-imperial co-operation

Some issues of imperial defence did not raise important issues of principle: helping with the development of Dominion air forces,[50] and the consideration by the British Chiefs of Staff of South Africa's defence needs.[51] At the 1926 Conference emphasis was laid on the development of the air forces, on the importance of standardising training and the interchange of personnel, and on the use by the whole Empire of the newly established Imperial Defence College (I.D.C.).[52] Even in Canada there was no objection to the I.D.C., and postings to its courses were regarded as a high favour.[53] The Canadian Army, trained on British lines, could play an imperial role without difficulty and the Canadian military were indeed in favour of a single 'truly Imperial army' with quotas from the different countries.[54]

[49] Gilbert Murray to Isobel Munro Henderson, 25 October 1929, in Gilbert Murray Papers, American correspondence. MacDonald had himself previously visited Washington in 1927 when Leader of the Opposition: 'It was very useful for the American capital to see that a socialist politician was not necessarily equipped with horns and a tail. There was no very strong bond of sympathy between MacDonald and the trade union hierarchy in the United States. He was amazed at their conservatism and affluence.' Vincent Massey, *What's Past is Prologue* (Toronto, Macmillan, 1963), p. 150.

[50] Memorandum on the Development of Dominions Air Forces, approved by C.I.D. 12 October 1923, in minutes of Chiefs of Staff sub-committee, 4 October 1923, PRO CAB 53/1. The development of civil air routes was an important factor in the development of thinking about relations between air power and imperial defence. See Robert Higham, *Britain's Imperial Air Routes, 1918–1939* (London, 1960).

[51] Chiefs of Staff sub-committee, 25 January, 18 October, 19 December 1927, PRO CAB 53/1 and 53/2.

[52] Amery, op. cit., vol. 2, p. 383.

[53] The first course in 1927 included two Australians, two Canadians (one of whom was to command the Canadian troops in the United Kingdom in the Second World War) and one New Zealander. One of the two members from the Indian army was the future field-marshal Auchinleck.

[54] Eayrs, op. cit., pp. 81 – 90.

How to work out a common imperial position on defence was in any event a problem. In May 1928 Hankey noted that while Australia, New Zealand and South Africa had agreed to allow their High Commissioners to take part in the affairs of the I.D.C., nothing had been heard from Mackenzie King.[55] Indeed, the Canadian Prime Minister had asked for an explanation of the title 'Chief of the Imperial General Staff', which implied to him executive authority over the Canadian section of the staff. On supply there was agreement about the desirability of decentralisation. The Dominions and India were reported to be planning the supply of their own forces, and Canada was expected to be self-supporting.[56]

A problem existed with respect to Ireland. It was important to keep in with the Irish, since the Chiefs of Staff attached importance to the ports made available to Britain under the 1921 Treaty.[57] But when in 1929 it was proposed that Irish officers should be admitted to the I.D.C., the proposal was rejected on the ground that the Irish General Staff, if indeed it could be said to exist, was not in as close touch with the War Office as were the other Dominions General Staffs, and was in closer contact with West Point. When the matter was raised again, Trenchard urged a more generous view on his colleagues and a decision was postponed until the Dominions Secretary could be present. Lord Passfield, who held this office as well as that of Colonial Secretary during the first year of the second MacDonald government, emphasised the principle of equality between all the Dominions. But Admiral Madden, the chief of the naval staff, replied that Ireland could not be placed on the same footing because she had not co-operated during the war. It was agreed that secret army manuals and places at staff colleges should be withheld but contacts at lower levels encouraged. It was noted that the Irish Free State did not receive certain documents that went to other Dominions, though the Dominion requirements differed according to the forces they maintained. An appearance of equality was to be preserved by drawing up a list of service manuals not to be issued outside the United Kingdom.[58]

[55] Hankey to Balfour, 16 May 1928, Balfour Papers, BL Add MSS 49705. One South African attended the 1928 course. He was the first and last.
[56] Meetings of Chiefs of Staff sub-committee 2 April 1928, 1 March 1928, PRO CAB 53/2.
[57] Chiefs of Staff subcommittee, 5 November 1925, PRO CAB 53/1. For the Irish Treaty ports see Canning, op. cit., ch. 9.
[58] Chiefs of Staff subcommittee meetings of 14 October, 26 November and 16 December 1929, PRO CAB 53/3. See also Canning, op. cit., p. 112. The cabinet's anxieties about secrecy extended beyond Ireland. There was a fear that if the Dominions appointed service attaches in foreign

When in 1932 concern was expressed at the flagging attendance by Dominion officers at the I.D.C., there was reluctance to give full facilities to either the Irish Free State or South Africa.[59]

These imperial problems formed part of the background to the increasingly difficult relations between Britain and the United States in the period 1927 – 1930, beginning with the Geneva naval talks in the summer of 1927. The Americans insisted, as we have seen, on regarding the British Empire as a single unit for purposes of calculating naval armaments, and this was the line taken by other Powers. When, for example, a scheme was tabled at Geneva for limiting naval effectives, this was regarded as a possible source of trouble with the Dominions. If, for example, at any moment Australia wished to increase her naval effectiveness, either Britain or another Dominion would have to make a corresponding reduction.[60] Arrangements were therefore made to see that the Dominions were represented in the British Empire delegation during the Conference, and the Empire did in fact present a united front.[61]

At one point in the conference it was suggested by the British Ambassador in Washington that it would have a good effect on American public opinion if the Dominion governments would publicly announce that they supported the British stand on cruisers.[62] But the British delegation counselled delay, though the suggestion would be borne in mind if the American attitude were to harden. They did not wish to give the impression either that the British were unconvinced of the justice of their cause or that they were dragging the Dominions at their heels. In any event the negotiations themselves must have made it clear that Britain did have the support of the Dominions.[63]

---

capitals, the countries concerned would be able to post attaches to Dominion capitals, so as to obtain secret information by putting questions in different ways in different places and comparing the answers. Cabinet meeting, 19 October 1927, PRO CAB 23/55.

[59] Chiefs of Staff subcommittee meeting, 4 February 1932, PRO CAB 53/4. In 1932 one Canadian officer was the only Dominion member of the course. Australia and Canada were both represented from 1933 to 1936. In 1937, 1938 and 1939 New Zealand officers also took part. British officers from the Indian Army took part in every pre-war course. See *The Imperial Defence College Register 1927–1970*, published in 1971 by its successor, the Royal College of Defence Studies.

[60] Memorandum by Mr Kirkpatrick, Foreign Office, 1 April 1927, in *DBFP*, Series IA, vol. III, p. 171.

[61] Chamberlain to Howard, 5 April and 10 August 1927, ibid., pp. 588 – 9, 731.

[62] Chamberlain to Mr London (Geneva), 12 July 1927, ibid., p. 671.

[63] London (Geneva) to Chamberlain, 13 July 1927, ibid., p. 675.

The Geneva Conference broke down, in effect, on the cruiser issue. Britain wished to restrict limitation to the heavy crusiers which the United States favoured, but leave unlimited the number of light cruisers, the preferred type of vessel for trade route protection. The Admiralty felt that if the Americans insisted on parity in both types, each country should be asked to state openly what they needed and why. The Cabinet was divided on how far to go. Balfour was in favour of such a statement, but not without making a declaration in favour of the principle of parity. Hankey, taking his usual line, argued that to begin by granting the principle would give way to the 'heavy barrage' put down by the U.S. 'big navy' men.[64]

The service point of view was upheld by the First Lord, Bridgeman.[65] Churchill was clearly torn between a desire not to accept inferiority to the United States and an unwillingness to see Britain forced into an expensive naval programme. At this time economy predominated in his outlook and it was in line with this cast of mind that he secured in 1928 the agreement from his colleagues that the 'ten year rule' should advance from day to day; that is to say, all plans should be made on the assumption of no major war for ten years.[66] The publicity surrounding the Conference and the suspicions fostered on the American side that the whole thing was the outcome of a British desire to go back on the principle of equality of sea-power made the experience a damaging one on both sides.[67] After the breakdown, advocates of Anglo-American understanding got busy again trying to seek some wider understanding on the prevention of war which might reduce the naval question to its proper proportions.[68]

The Cabinet discussion in 1927 seems to have ended with a decision to maintain the broad claim for belligerent rights but to try to get

[64] Hankey to Balfour, 29 June 1927; Balfour to Hankey, 30 June 1927: Balfour Papers, BL Add MSS 49074. C.I.D. meetings, 20 May and 14 July 1927, PRO CAB 2/5.
[65] Bridgeman to Salisbury, 5 August 1927, Salisbury Papers, General Correspondence.
[66] C.I.D. meeting, 5 July 1928, PRO CAB 2/5.
[67] Material in Balfour Papers, BL Add MSS 49699. The disarmament enthusiasts tended to blame both sides for using arguments which would justify all countries adding to their armaments on land as well as sea. See Philip Noel-Baker to Gilbert Murray, 25 July 1927, Gilbert Murray Papers.
[68] e.g. Kerr to Balfour, 11 August 1927, Balfour Papers, BL Add MSS 49797. Viscount Grey (Sir Edward Grey) believed that more should be made of the argument that while parity was a bad principle as leading the competitiveness, the British did not intend to build against the United States or alter their programmes upwards by reason of any American action. Grey to Murray, 3 September 1927, Gilbert Murray Papers, Grey Correspondence.

agreement with Americans as to their exercise by private negotiation. Hankey was still anxious, telling Balfour that he could not have cons-cientiously remained secretary of the C.I.D. if belligerent rights had been surrendered. He feared that to restart negotiations might mean either than the Americans would have to stick to their position and the Cabinet break off the talks, which would be a repetition of the Geneva situation, or there would be an agreement like the Declaration of Paris or Declaration of London which would not hold when war came.[69] At the same time the Americans were making it clear that they would proceed with their own naval building programme.[70] Neither side seemed to accept the view of the advocates of partnership that the American navy was really 'a reinsurance of the British Empire', and the British navy a 'reinsurance of all that America cares about... one of the most powerful practical arguments behind the Monroe Doctrine ever since 1823'.[71]

Anglo-American discord

The American conduct at Geneva seriously worried the British: 'We may earnestly hope the occasion... may never arise', wrote the British Ambassador,

> but should it do so and should Great Britain ever again be involved in a European war, it is far from unlikely that we may have to choose between prosecuting a blockade of the enemy as we did from 1914 to 1918 and finding the United States associated with the enemy in a war against us on the one hand, or the benevolent neutrality of the United States on the other.[72]

In a further letter Howard wrote that, according to Colonel House, 'Republicans and Democrats are at one on this point of never again allowing American neutral shipping to be interfered with as in 1914 – 1917'. Chamberlain, in a memorandum to the Cabinet, argued that an American general was not exaggerating when he said 'that any attempt by us to enforce our rights in a future war where the U.S. were neutral, as we enforced them in the late war, would make war between

[69] Hankey to Balfour, 12 January 1928, Balfour Papers, BL Add MSS 49705.
[70] Chamberlain to Howard (Washington), Austen Chamberlain Papers, AC.50, 1928.
[71] Kerr to D. Lloyd (Washington), 20 March 1928. Lothian Papers, Box 189.
[72] Howard to Chamberlain, 12 August 1927, *DBFP*, Series IA, vol. III, p. 734; Howard to Tyrrell, 15 September 1927, ibid., vol. IV, pp. 360 ff.

us "probable".[73] So strong was the resentment on both sides that Baldwin gave up his intention of visiting New York and Washington after his tour of Canada that summer.[74]

The situation was made worse by a Franco-British compromise worked out at the session of the Preparatory Commission on disarmament that began in March 1928, and made public on 28 July. Since it gave the British the substance of their requirements by extending limitation only to heavy cruisers and allowing them to build an indefinite number of lighter ones, and since the announcement was accompanied by well-founded rumours that the *quid pro quo* for France had been the exclusion of trained reserves from the draft convention on land disarmament, it is not surprising that the American reaction was a sharp one. The proposals themselves were rejected by the United States on 28 September and the Americans almost reached the point of abandoning the peace pact talks.[75]

Hankey regarded the American note as 'extremely unfriendly in tone' and as ignoring the British Empire's needs.[76] Writing to Thomas Jones, a constant upholder of a pro-American standpoint, he explained his view:

> The root difficulty is that there is no denominator common to all the Powers. The naval problem of America and Japan is a deep-sea problem, requiring large sea-going vessels. That of Italy is a narrow-sea problem, requiring smaller vessels. France has mainly a narrow-sea problem though she has a secondary deep-sea problem also owing to her distant colonies.
>
> Our problem is both. We cannot afford to be inferior in either. Our communications, vital to our existence, run through the deep seas and the narrow seas. We must be able to defend either. Global tonnage parity is therefore impossible to us. If we make ourselves sufficiently secure on the deep seas, we shall run risks in the narrow seas, and vice versa.
>
> You speak of the Dominions. But neither Australia nor New Zealand, our most loyal Dominions, are willing that we should let down our sea-power.
>
> As regards France, she is the only nation that can deal us a blow

---

[73] Memorandum by Chamberlain, 26 October 1927, ibid., pp. 415-6.
[74] Middlemas and Barnes, *Baldwin*, pp. 371 – 3.
[75] O'Connor, *Perilous Equilibrium*, 21; Middlemas and Barnes, *Baldwin*, pp. 373 – 4.
[76] Hankey to Balfour, 25 October 1928, Balfour Papers, BL Add MSS 49705.

at the heart, unless she becomes so weak that her territory can be used by some other power (as in the late war) for the same purpose; or so unfriendly as to allow some friendly power to use her territory to strike us. What we need is a strong France, but a friendly one, strong enough to keep her enemies beyond the frontier, for which she needs our help. Our interests here coincide. I don't think we have really gone beyond the bounds which are justified by our experience of ten years ago and our mutual interests.

To sum up, then, I would continue our good relations with France, using the privileged position it gives us (as at Locarno) to get a settlement of all the outstanding questions with which our other friends Germany and Italy are concerned. I would drop the attitude of sycophancy towards the USA 'ganging our own gait' but in as friendly a manner as possible.[77]

Others expressed alarm at the new breach with the Americans, which might lead to still further competitive building.[78] Kerr expostulated strongly to Balfour.[79] The latter showed his letters to Hankey, who challenged his interpretation of the Washington agreements as covering all classes of ships, and argued that the Dominions were less inclined to favour the Americans and more understanding of Britain's interest in the Low Countries and consequently in European affairs than Kerr believed. It was not a question of choosing between Europe and America: 'we must interest ourselves in Europe, and we must be as friendly as we can to America... that is the policy that is forced upon us'.[80]

Hankey continued to worry that the Cabinet, and in particular Austen Chamberlain, were weakening on the freedom of the seas. He pointed out that Chamberlain had not discussed the matter with Salisbury, the Lord Privy Seal, who was chairman of the Committee covering 'all three great branches of our Anglo-American difficulties,

[77] Hankey to Jones, 11 October 1928, Jones, *Whitehall Diary*, vol. II, p. 147.
[78] Walter Lippmann, the eminent American journalist, wrote to Lady Astor on 23 October that American hostility to the Anglo-French entente would lead the Big Navy men to claim a two-power standard. Ibid., p. 151. Arthur Salter told Jones that Churchill had smashed the 1927 naval conference in his desire to keep Britain's naval supremacy. The Foreign Office was still, he asserted, dominated by the nineteenth century tradition of dealing with Europe through France and of forgetting the U.S.A. 'I did not tell him', Jones noted, 'what is the fact that this Anglo-French business was put through without consulting the American department at the F.O.' Ibid., p. 157.
[79] Kerr to Balfour, 30 October and 7 November 1928, Balfour Papers, BL Add MSS, 49797, 49705.
[80] Hankey to Balfour, 12 November 1928, ibid. 49705.

namely the cruiser question (Disarmament), the renewal of the Arbitration Treaty and Belligerent Rights'. Churchill was suggesting that as a gesture to the Americans the order for the proposed new cruisers might be put off.[81]

On 19 December 1928 the Cabinet decided that a *rapprochement* with America on naval limitation should be given priority over the development of the Singapore base.[82] Meanwhile Kerr had put forward a scheme by which belligerent rights would be classified as either 'public', i.e. in League of Nations wars, or private. Hankey thought the idea had some merit since the European countries might support Britain over it, but still preferred no discussion at all.[83] Kerr was also active in informal Anglo-American contacts.

The new U.S. Navy Act of 12 February 1929 included a reference favourable to a 'treaty with all of the principal maritime nations regulating the conduct of belligerents and neutrals in the war at sea, including the inviolability of private property thereon'.[84] By now the discussions had to focus on the renewal of the Anglo-American arbitration Treaty, first suggested in 1927, and partly put aside to see whether such a treaty might not be rendered superfluous by the Briand-Kellogg Peace Pact. The Cabinet Committee were reported to be in their majority willing to allow questions of belligerent rights to be subject to arbitration. The majority included Salisbury*, Hailsham, Austen Chamberlain, Cunliffe-Lister and Cushendun; but a minority consisting of Bridgeman, Peel and Amery were fighting to have the matter put off until after the election.[85]

A report of a subcommittee of the C.I.D. dealing with the renewal of the Arbitration Treaties was made available on 13 February.[86] Meanwhile the C.I.D. continued to look at the belligerent rights question, as did Balfour in his correspondence with Sir Robert Borden set off by the American Professor Stewart.[87] On 19 February Chamberlain reported a conversation he had had with the American

[81] Hankey to Balfour, 18 December 1928, ibid.

[82] PRO CAB 23/59.

[83] Kerr to Hankey, 12 December 1928, Hankey to Kerr, 14 December 1928, Hankey to Balfour, 20 December 1928: Balfour Papers, BL Add MSS 49705.

[84] O'Connor, op. cit., 22. An American correspondent of Kerr's told him that the British Ambassador had told Senators to vote for the bill as a move towards peace. He felt that he must have been made nervous by anti-British propaganda. Lothian Papers, Box 215.

[85] Note in Balfour papers, BL Add MSS 49705.

[86] Paper B.R.62. in Austen Chamberlain Papers, A.C.41.

[87] Balfour Papers, BL Add MSS 49697, 47705.

Ambassador, in which he had told him that neither naval disarmament nor the arbitration treaty could be discussed without reference to the problem of belligerent rights. A general conference for the codification of maritime law was to be avoided since it would be difficult to get agreement between the Americans and the Europeans. The first step should be an Anglo-American agreement.[88]

The C.I.D. Committee report had concluded that it was still Britain's interest to press for 'high' rather than low belligerent rights; in a future war, reliance would be almost entirely on British tonnage, and Britain would therefore gain nothing by having neutral ships protected. Dominion opinion, especially the comments of New Zealand and South Africa, had shown support for this position; in this respect the interests of Britain and the Dominions were identical since Empire trade was carried in British, not neutral ships.

The Chief of Naval Staff had pointed out that if Britain lost the power to enforce a blockade, she would have no means of 'ending a war except by raising an army on a continental scale'. Every restriction on maintaining the control of the sea diminished the influence of naval powers and enhanced that of military powers.

Balfour's proposed letter to Borden was circulated to the Cabinet shortly afterwards. He felt that the argument was not so much about the right of the Americans to use their sea-power as the American assumptions of the circumstances in which it might come into play:

> I do not myself believe in a new Armaggedon. But should it recur, why are we to assume that while one branch of the English-speaking peoples is fighting for some great cause to the limits of its capacity, the other will be disputing with it over belligerent rights and neutral claims?

American history showed that perspectives altered as countries became either neutrals or belligerents. He was also sceptical of the possibility of devising a logical and workable system of arbitration, which would be necessary if it were to become universal and

---

[88] Chamberlain to Howard, 19 February 1929, A.C.50. Kerr was now suggesting that the right thing would be to accept Wilson's definition of the freedom of the seas provided that the United States were willing to share responsibility for deciding when and how naval power was to be used for 'police purposes'. Kerr to Robert Cecil, 15 February 1929, Lothian Papers, Box 221. The suggestion was remote from the realities of the American position and of American public opinion, as should have been clear from the hostile reaction of the Americans to any suggestion of giving 'teeth' to the Kellogg – Briand Pact.

compulsory. Both the United States and the British Empire had made reservations in recent treaties; who would interpret the reservations? The countries themselves?[89]

In his comment on the Balfour draft, Chamberlain deprecated publication, as he thought it unwise to stimulate further public controversy. He believed that it should be possible to reach agreement on the cruiser question after the election, since the speech by the American representative Gibson on 22 April at the sixth session of the preparatory commission seemed to suggest a way round the difficulty. He also hoped for a new Arbitration Treaty. Chamberlain defended the decision of a majority of the Cabinet committee not to seek the exclusion of belligerent rights from its scope in order to get from the Americans the maximum of recognition for Britain's claims; what Britain needed was not very far from what the Americans included in their own naval instructions and the decisions of their courts:

> As we cannot in fact press the rights of a belligerent beyond the point where their exercise would convert American neutrality into hostility, our purpose must be to secure from America the recognition of those rights on the highest possible scale.[90]

The London Naval Conference of 1930

The movement of American governmental opinion towards agreement paved the way for action by the MacDonald government, which took office on 5 June, along the lines thus laid down by its predecessor. Preliminary discussions showed that the principal British anxiety in respect of the limitation of armaments was a high American figure for heavy cruisers, which would give the Japanese the possibility of raising their quota above the British figure, and thus force the British into further expenditure. Sufficient progress was made to enable invitations to be issued for a Conference in London the following year. It was agreed that the Conference would limit itself to the limitation of naval

[89] Balfour Papers, BL Add MSS 49705, 49749.
[90] Chamberlain to Balfour, 10 May 1929, ibid. 49736. Cecil also thought publication unwise and that it would be unfortunate to discuss the subject of arbitration at a time when the Americans were considering joining the Court of International Justice, as Balfour's argument would be seized upon by opponents of the Court to show that an important section of British opinion also mistrusted the idea. Cecil to Balfour, 19 June 1929, Balfour Papers, BL Add MSS 49738. The United States did not in fact join the Court.

armaments and not discuss the 'freedom of the seas'. But when MacDonald visited the United States early in October for talks with President Hoover, he found that new topics were being raised. The Americans advocated a much larger scrapping of battleships than the British considered acceptable. Furthermore, Hoover raised the question of the immunity of private property in time of war and the exclusion of foodstuffs from any blockade. Any temptation on MacDonald's part to give way on the 'freedom of the seas' was checked by the resolute opposition of his Foreign Secretary, Arthur Henderson, and the chiefs of staff, basing themselves on the C.I.D. subcommittee report. And MacDonald refused to be drawn on the subject while the Americans did not press the point; nor did they press the question of constructing further British naval bases in the western hemisphere, or the offer made verbally by Hoover to purchase Bermuda, Trinidad and British Honduras as part of a debts settlement.[91]

The overt success of Macdonald's visit now produced in reverse the situation in the previous year; it was now the French (as well as the Italians and Japanese) who suspected the Anglo-Saxon powers of having come to an agreement at their expense.[92] MacDonald had made it plain to the Americans that one limitation on British policy was the need to get agreement with the Dominions,[93] but they had not been given a full account of the MacDonald – Hoover conversations.[94] The problems to be addressed at the Conference were made known to the Dominions, all of whom (including Ireland), as well as India, sent delegations to the Conference itself, and were kept informed of what went on between the Five Powers principally involved.[95] At a plenary session Australia and New Zealand supported the British proposals for the abolition of all submarines. But their main concern was with the ratio between the British and the Japanese

[91] O'Connor, op. cit., pp. 31 – 48; Carlton, op. cit., pp. 116-7.

[92] The constant interlocking of the naval theme with the question of British policy in Europe is well illustrated by the fact that even so fervent an advocate of disarmament as Cecil, who was consulted by MacDonald on these matters, was opposed to drastic naval cuts: 'Until we have advanced much further on the lines of disarmament a relatively weak British Army must be balanced by a relatively strong British Navy, least an undue share of international authority should pass into the hands of the Continental Powers.' MacDonald to Cecil, 5 August 1929, Cecil to MacDonald, 17 December 1929: Cecil of Chelwood Papers, BL Add MSS 51181.

[93] MacDonald to Ambassador Dawes, 1 August 1929, FRUS 1929, vol. I, 171 ff.

[94] PRO DO 117/173. The general rule about circulation of papers was that they went only to the Dominions actually represented at the meeting in question. Roskill, Hankey, vol. II, p. 480.

[95] For the London Naval Conference see Roskill, Naval Policy between the Wars, vol. II, ch. 2; Christopher Hall, op. cit.; O'Connor, op. cit. The British documents are in DBFP, Series IA, vol. I, chs 1 – 3; the text of the Treaty of 22 April 1930 is given in an appendix to this volume.

fleets, and according to the U.S. records of the Conference they threatened to build up their own naval strength if dissatisfied with the outcome. In the end, thanks to Britain reducing its demand for cruisers from 70 to 50, agreement was reached with the United States and Japan; France and Italy refused to adhere to the Treaty and a solution to their problems was left to be considered at another Conference in 1935.

After the Conference was over, the British sea lords reconsidered the position of the Dominion navies, when it was agreed that the British government should for financial reasons encourage the Dominions to have their own warships, even though it was objected that this would weaken the unity and freedom of movement of the 'Empire' fleet by comparison with the unitary structure of the U.S. navy.[96] The general defence issue was further discussed at the 1930 Imperial Conference, but at only three of the plenary sessions. Most of the discussions took place between experts in the visiting delegations and their Whitehall counterparts.[97] The subjects for discussion had been set out in a series of documents circulated before the Conference to the Dominion governments.[98] In fact no important progress was made, though New Zealand undertook to continue to maintain two light cruisers. New Zealand had been less isolationist in spirit than Australia had become after the war, and preferred making a contribution to the Royal Navy to building up a fleet of its own, hoping for a broadly based Pacific Defence Organisation as the only remedy for its defence needs.[99] Hankey tried to get more done, and was allowed to circulate the Chiefs of Staff Annual Review to the Dominion governments, but a paper he wrote on 'The Association of the Dominions with the C.I.D.', prepared for a meeting of the C.I.D. on 28 November with the Dominion Prime Ministers present, was never circulated, in deference to the new Canadian Premier, R.B.Bennett*, who was as wary as Mackenzie King about foreign policy or defence entanglements for Canada.[100]

The differences in the attitudes of the Dominions remained what they had been a decade earlier. Canada had a sense of security that depended upon her position as a North American country remote

[96] Roskill, op. cit., p. 66.
[97] Hall, *Commonwealth*, p. 292.
[98] Roskill, *Hankey*, vol. II, pp. 524 – 5.
[99] B.K. Gordon, *New Zealand becomes a Pacific Power* (Chicago, 1960), pp. 54 – 5.
[100] Roskill, op. cit., pp. 528 – 9.

from any of the potential storm-centres in world politics. South Africa was restricted in vision to the continent of which she formed part. For Australia and New Zealand it remained true that a potential threat from an expansionist Japan was always present, and that distance from potential assistance was an ingredient in their thinking. Had the possibility of American assistance been seen as a realistic one, it would have been different. But so far from American and British attitudes being aligned on Far Eastern questions, the gap between them was fully visible.

PART II – SINGAPORE

The fall of the Singapore base has been taken as the appropriate point to conclude the present study, since it was a blow against the material and psychological basis of the British Empire from which ultimate recovery proved impossible.[101] The story of how it came to be built and the incompleteness of the preparations to defend it are illustrative of the interaction between British defence policy and inter-imperial relations at its most concrete.[102] When Admiral Jellicoe visited the Pacific Dominions in 1919, his recommendation was that there should be an Imperial Pacific Fleet comprising elements from the British, Australian and New Zealand navies, and commanded by a British admiral from a base to be established at Singapore.[103] The rejection by the Dominions of the idea of an imperial fleet was accepted by the Admiralty. Henceforward the basis of all plans for the defence of the Pacific Dominions was that the main British fleet should sail to their rescue when needed, and that this would require bases to receive it, originally at Sydney and Singapore, and later at Singapore only.

A conference of British and Dominion naval officers was held at Penang in March 1921 and the Singapore scheme was accepted. The decision to construct the base was announced at the 1921 Imperial

---

[101] For a valuable summary of the whole story see S. Woodburn, *Singapore: the Chain of Disaster* (London, 1971). The possibility of an attack from the land had not been overlooked and appeared as a likely scenario in an Imperial Defence College 'war game'. But these 'games' were not given much attention, if any, by the policy-makers. See R. Higham, *The Military Intellectuals in Britain* (New Brunswick, 1966).

[102] See in particular I. Hamill, *The Strategic Illusion: the Singapore Strategy and the Defence of Australia and New Zealand* (Singapore, 1981).

[103] Roskill, *Naval Policy between the Wars*, vol. I, 275 – 82; the documents on Jellicoe's mission are in A. Temple Patterson (ed.), *The Jellicoe Papers* (London, 1968).

Conference, and confirmed by the British government in February 1922.[104] But from the beginning there was Treasury opposition, and it had been decided in June 1921 that there should be no major expenditure for two years. While the defence of the Pacific Dominions remained the principal argument developed in favour of the base, more attention was given to its role in the defence of India and even of the Malay peninsula itself.[105]

The Bonar Law cabinet accepted its predecessor's policy, and the necessary land was made available by the Singapore authorities in July 1923. The Imperial Conference in that year welcomed what had been done, but doubts about the base surfaced in Parliamentary debate.[106] Amery had to play down the cost of the base and claim that it was far enough away from Japan not to constitute a menace to that country.[107] Doubtful M.P.s may have derived comfort from the knowledge that the Treasury was strongly opposed to the whole idea, and had been from the beginning, and that not on grounds of expense alone. The Treasury official involved with the project argued that Britain's distance from Japan should be taken as an advantage not to be thrown away, and that the idea of an attack on the Empire with the Americans remaining neutral was 'an almost impossible hypothesis'. The direct responsibilities that Britain might have in relation to the Dominions and indeed to the colonies was ignored in these submissions.[108] And Barstow's opposition was maintained in 1923 with the powerful support of Sir Warren Fisher, the Permanent Secretary to the Treasury. The Pacific Dominions however continued to support the project, with the added hope that it might also facilitate U.S. naval operations in the western Pacific, if the Americans could be drawn into a

---

[104] Roskill, op. cit., pp. 289 – 91, 347 – 9.

[105] Hamill, op. cit., pp. 35, 39. On 30 November 1922 Beatty told the C.I.D. that, even during the war, the Japanese had been in touch with Indian agitators: 'Japan might fall to a similar temptation for the future when by encouraging revolt in India and raising the banner of Asia for the Asiatics, it would be no exaggeration to say that Japan would be able to wrest from us our position in India.' PRO CAB 2/3.

[106] Smuts was a critic of the project, arguing that it would give the appearence of being directed against Japan, and was anyhow strategically unsound. A base would not be secure without a fleet on the spot and could be captured by an enemy before a fleet could arrive from a distance. Japan would be unlikely to move without European support and in that case Britain, with a fleet limited by the Washington Treaties, would not be able to afford the ships to send.

[107] H.C. *Deb*, vol. 163, 1 May 1923, cols 1263 ff.

[108] Memorandum by Sir G. Barstow, 15 June 1921; Reservation (undated) by Treasury Representative to the Overseas Defence Committee; Barstow to Col. S.H. Wilson (Secretary of the Overseas Defence Committee), 18 June 1921: PRO T161/800/S.18917/1

defensive combination against the Japanese.[109] The Canadians took their usual line of treating the matter as one wholly for the U.K. government, while Smuts objected to the scheme as likely to offend the Japanese and as being unnecessary in view of the accords reached at the Washington naval conference. It would appear that throughout the Admiralty was reluctant to go into details of its plans with the Dominion governments, even with those directly interested.[110]

The incoming MacDonald government received further hostile memoranda from the Treasury, but its decision, announced on 18 March 1924, not to proceed with the base was defended on the ground that to go ahead would raise queries about Britain's commitment to the League of Nations system and to disarmament, and invite suspicions about its intended role in the Far East.[111] The Cabinet had taken their decision on 5 March, and communicated it to the Dominions and the government of India. Smuts expressed his approval and India, Canada and the Irish Free State their lack of interest, but there were protests from both Australia and New Zealand: the New Zealand government had actually offered a financial contribution, and now Australia offered to help as well.[112]

The Conservative opposition attacked the abandonment of the base, stressing that without it all talk of naval co-operation with Australia and New Zealand was meaningless. When Baldwin returned to office, the question was raised at the Committee of Imperial Defence, when the Foreign Office argued in favour of the scheme, though admitting that in some circumstances it would not be possible to send a fleet away from home waters. Churchill felt that, with three strong naval powers in the world, one would not attack another while the third (the U.S.) remained neutral and could threaten it. The idea of winning over opinion in Britain as well as in the Dominions was referred to by Samuel Hoare*, who, with this in mind, suggested the partial dismantling of Hong Kong, a suggestion strongly opposed by Curzon.[113] A review of imperial defence by the Chiefs of Staff in 1926 took into

[109] Speech by Bruce, 24 July 1923. The possibility was also discussed by the Chiefs of Staff in London on 31 January 1924, when they suggested that it might be easier for the United States to send forces to the Far East via the Atlantic and the Mediterranean than across the Pacific. PRO CAB 53/1.
[110] Hamill, op. cit., pp. 67 – 8, 32.
[111] Barstow memoranda 26 February, 1 March 1924: PRO T161/800/S.18917/2. H.C. *Deb.*, vol. 171, 18 March 1924, Cols 314 ff.
[112] Hamill, op. cit., pp. 86 – 8.
[113] C.I.D. meeting, 5 January 1925, PRO CAB 2/5.

account only the possibility of hostilities with Japan and gave as its priorities the completion of the Singapore base and the arrangements for the defence of Hong Kong as part of the defence of Britain's Far Eastern trade routes.[114] They had before them a Foreign Office memorandum which declared that Japan, weakened by the great earthquake and industrial troubles, was not in a bellicose mood, but that if the military spirit were reawakened, it was more likely that she would attack the United States than Britain. The Singapore base would deter aggression, as well as Japan's knowledge that if she did attack the United States, Britain would intervene on the American side.[115]

It had already been made clear that work on the base would be resumed, and that the Dominions were being consulted about possible contributions to the cost. It was however stated that, since Australia had meanwhile gone ahead with naval expenditure of her own and since New Zealand was building a second cruiser, it was unlikely that their governments would now agree to contribute. It has been suggested that one reason for the Government's willingness to shoulder the cost and proceed with building the base was the fear that the two Pacific Dominions might otherwise be drawn increasingly into the American orbit.[116]

The opposition to the project continued to be voiced in Parliament, and the discussions there were mirrored at the 1926 Imperial Conference. Baldwin pointed out that, apart from Hong Kong and the Federated Malay States, no financial assistance had been given, and it was now for the Dominions with Pacific interests to shoulder the burden. Canada and South Africa were again silent; the Maharaja of Burdwan, speaking for India, declared that India's own defence expenditure made it impossible for her to contribute. Bruce pointed to Australia's expensive defence programme, undertaken after the British Labour government had suspended work on the base, and said that this made impossible a commitment to help finance the base. The New Zealand Prime Minister took the same line. In fact, Australia did not contribute, though New Zealand voted a contribution of £1,000,000 spread over eight years. It has been suggested that it was

[114] C.I.D. paper 701-B, 22 June 1926, in PRO CAB 4/15.
[115] Memorandum, 'The Foreign Policy of His Majesty's Government', PRO CAB 4/14.
[116] H.C. *Deb.*, vol. 179, 9 December 1924, cols 83, 87 – 8, 163, 171; Hamill, op. cit., 135 – 7.

only the colonial contributions that kept the project alive between 1926 and 1929.[117]

To some extent in Australia and to a lesser extent in New Zealand the issue was largely a party one. Australian Labour was in favour of territorial, not imperial, defence, and hence of concentrating on ground and air, not naval forces. The left in New Zealand was fearful of giving provocation to the Japanese.[118]

When Labour returned to power in Britain in 1929, the question was reconsidered, with the Treasury returning to its attack and claiming that it was not enough to slow down the work, which was what the government had decided to do, and that outright cancellation was the only proper course.[119] The Dominions, who had been kept out of active participation in naval planning, were dissatisfied with what was happening.[120] Both Australia and New Zealand were represented when the C.I.D. considered the matter on 25 July 1929, a meeting at which the Chancellor of the Exchequer refused to accept the view that Australia's naval expenditure should be taken as a contribution to the base.[121] While MacDonald was willing to give assurances that the British government were fully alive to Dominion interests, it is not suprising that, when a Parliamentary answer later in the year seemed to indicate that the government was in fact moving towards cancellation of the project, New Zealand should have protested about the failure to consult.[122]

The agreements reached at the London Naval Conference in 1930 gave the Treasury grounds for renewing its plea for cancellation. Sir Warren Fisher himself went into the attack:

> You are aware of my views about the Singapore base, I never could see any justification for it. Japan is not going to attack the British Empire single-handed let alone if aggression by her were to bring in

[117] *Imperial Conference 1926: Appendices to Summary of Proceedings*, Cmd 2769 (1926), and see Hall, op. cit., 568 ff. The Baldwin Papers contain extracts from the report of a speech by a member of the New Zealand House of Representatives arguing for a generous New Zealand contribution on the ground that Britain's position in India was threatened by a possible collusion between Japan and Russia, and that the loss of India would be a fatal blow to the Empire. He also called attention to the opposition to the building of the base by tin and rubber interests in Malaya who objected to the British government paying trade union rates for the work. Baldwin Papers, vol. 2.D.1.3, p. 117.

[118] Hamill, op. cit., pp. 146 – 9.

[119] Memoranda by A.P.Waterfield, 11 and 16 July 1929, PRO T 161/800/S.18917/6.

[120] Hamill, op. cit., p. 162.

[121] C.I.D. meeting, 25 July 1929, PRO CAB 23/62.

[122] Cabinet conclusions, 13 November 1929, PRO CAB 23/62.

the U.S.A. on the British side, and as regards Singapore itself it is not a white man's country and the demoralising effect of the climate on ships' crews is a factor of real importance to take into account. If a Pacific base is required, it is only people blinded by prejudice or obsessed by Japan who can deny it should be found in an Australian port.[123]

On the other hand, it was now realised that cancellation would involve paying back the contributions that had been made by the Dominions, and this might be more expensive than cancellation. It was hoped that the whole question could be settled by holding a meeting of the C.I.D., with Dominion representation, during the forthcoming Imperial Conference, a suggestion opposed by the First Lord of the Admiralty on the ground that the base should only be discussed with the Dominions directly interested and with those colonies which had made contributions.[124]

In the event, the Imperial Conference accepted the Treasury view that the existing contract for a graving dock should be completed, but that there should be no further expenditure and that no decision about the ultimate completion of the base should be made. There appears to have been no reaction from the Dominions and, as already noted, defence played little part in the deliberations of the conference.[125]

The Singapore record reveals how incohate were ideas of imperial defence in the Far East in this period, and how inadequate was the machinery for reaching a consensus with the Dominions, and, on the Admiralty's part, how weak a will existed to bring such a consensus about. At no time was it made clear what strategy the base was meant to serve and how it fitted into other commitments, whether on the part of Britain or of the Dominions. It was this lack of clear and consistent thinking at the political level which gave the Treasury its opportunity to concentrate on cost alone, an issue which arose in a new form when the Air Ministry argued at the Overseas Defence Committee that a

[123] Minute by Fisher for Chancellor of the Exchequer, 12 May 1930.
[124] C.I.D. meeting, 29 September 1930, PRO CAB 2/5. For this phase of the story see also Roskill, *Hankey*, vol. II, 496 ff. The apparent indifference of British ministers to Dominion anxieties did not pass unnoticed. Lord Bledisloe, the Governor-General of New Zealand, wrote to J.H. Thomas (who had just replaced Passfield as Dominions Secretary): 'I sometimes wonder whether Great Britain deserves an Empire, so callous does she seem about her fair daughters' requirements.' Hamill, op. cit., 193.
[125] In 1931 New Zealand secured British approval for spreading her contribution over a longer period. PRO T161/513/S.18917/07 and following files.

Japanese battle fleet would be accompanied by aircraft carriers and that Britain would need a strong air component at Singapore, both to defend the base and perhaps even as the main instrument of deterrence. The Admiralty retained its preference for heavy guns, and the Treasury was fearful that it might end up being committed to both.[126] In 1929 it found itself in this position, and unsuccessfully opposed an Air Ministry scheme to send to Singapore an experimental squadron of torpedo-armed aircraft.[127] In 1932, when the controversy came to a head, it supported the C.I.D.'s preference for guns, as cheaper in the long run.[128] The Coast Defence committee had quoted Admiral Mahan's dictum: 'Permanent works, established in quiet moments on sound principles, have the advantage that they cannot be shifted under the influence of panic.' Mahan did not say that they could not be taken.

---

[126] Minute for Sir G. Barstow, 1 January 1925, in PRO T 161/800/S.18917/3.
[127] PRO T161/210/S.18917/014, especially Air Ministry's notes on Treasury views, 20 December 1929.
[128] C.I.D. paper 370 – C, 24 May 1932, in PRO T161/560/S.18917/016.

Chapter 7

THE INDIAN AMBIGUITY

The challenge to the Raj

At the heart of the Imperial government's preoccupations lay the problem of India, which had not been altered either by the war or by the constitutional innovations of the Montagu-Chelmsford reforms. It has been pointed out that the imperial commitment, as seen from London, meant three things in practice: no barriers to the free flow of British exports to India; a sufficient income for the Indian government to meet its obligations in London, (the repayment of interest on loans and the upkeep of the India Office, the payment of the pensions of civil servants and military personnel, and the rest of the 'Home Charges'); and that the Indian Army should be made available for use overseas for imperial purposes, but at India's expense.[1] On the other hand, all constitutional development, upon which was felt to depend the existence of a sufficient consensus to enable the Raj to be maintained, was bound to put into positions of increased authority, or at least influence, men whose perspective would be much more the product of attention to India's own needs as they saw them.

Such perspectives were not only those of Indian members of the administration or of Indian politicians; they tended also to become those of the Viceroy and the British administrators through whom he governed. While their constitutional position was different from that of Dominion Prime Ministers, responsible to their own Parliaments, on questions of supporting imperial foreign policy strategic initiatives, or on the protection of India's own economy and its tax base, the spokesmen for India, like their Dominion counterparts, took a national rather than an imperial stance. Nor was there in India the counterbalance of a political party or parties who for sentimental or historic reasons were concerned to preserve the imperial tie for its own sake. The larger the political class called into being by

[1] B.R. Tomlinson, *The Indian National Congress and the Raj 1929–1942* (London, 1976), p. 8.

representative institutions in the provinces or, more slowly, at the centre, the harder to bring it to the support of the imperial outlook.

To some extent the fragility of the relationships between Britain and India was masked by the language of constitutional development, inevitably seen by Indians and by many in Britain as presaging an eventual assimilation to the status now conceded to the Dominions. It was also disguised by the international recognition, on British insistence, of India's national personality and separate government. India was represented at the Paris Peace Conference, and was a founder-member of the League of Nations. Its representatives took part in Imperial Conferences. This position, given the ultimate authority of the Viceroy, and behind him of the Secretary of State for India and the British cabinet, was a highly ambiguous one.

Two additional elements in the situation need to be taken into account. The first was the question of race. In India itself the association of Indians with the government of the country and in various fields of private activity did not bridge the social gap between Indians and British officialdom or the resident British commercial community. In part this reflected the position taken up by many of those responsible for policy in India, that the necessary degree of deference, upon which rested the ability to govern India without the constant use of force, depended on maintaining a distance between the rulers and the mass of the ruled. In part on the British side it was the outcome of the inevitable tendency of those working for a time in strange and uncongenial climes to seek the company of their own kind. On the Indian side this separation was reinforced by the taboos of religion, which put difficulties in the way of easy mixing. While such a degree of remoteness played its part in exacerbating nationalist feelings in the Indian elites, the difficulty from the point of view of the Imperial government was to offer the kind of life in India that would tempt men to seek service there at a time when India no longer acted as the magnet it had been. Even more important was the discrimination against Indians where they had attempted to settle in the Empire, either through the direct prohibition of such immigration or, as in the South African case, by discrimination against those already there.[2]

[2] W.K.Hancock, *Survey of British Commonwealth Affairs*, vol. I, ch. 4, 'India and Race Equality'. An agreement between the Indian and South African governments announced in February 1927 lowered the tension, at least for the time being. See H. Tinker, *Separate and Unequal: India and Indians in the British Commonwealth, 1920–1950* (London, 1976).

The second element was the growth of political organisation among Indians themselves, to some extent in reaction to the opportunities provided by the proliferation of elected bodies, and to some extent as an instrument of action looking ultimately to independence. Of these organisations the most important was the Congress, which had received a renewed impetus from the political activities of Gandhi in the post-war years.[3] But while Congress was to prove an important instrument in breaking down the consent upon which British authority rested, it was not capable of acting as an instrument for framing an alternative to British rule through negotiation, because of its own divisions and of the fact that there were important interests in Indian society which it failed to represent. From the British point of view, the most important of these was the Muslim community; the importance attached by Britain to the Indian Muslims had been illustrated in relation to Britain's new responsibilities in the Middle East.[4] To a large extent, though not exclusively, this was connected with the important role that Muslims played in the Indian Army, upon which, in the last resort, imperial rule depended.[5]

The impact of the war upon India had been severe and had given rise to considerable hardship. The Indian nationalist movement had been an obvious target for German propaganda and the greater ideological appeal of communism looked like providing it with a more attractive instrument.[6] Intelligence intercepts revealed Soviet subversion in the U.K., Ireland, Egypt and Iraq even while negotiations for a commercial agreement were proceeding in London in 1920.[7] By the summer of that year Soviet subversion in India and on its borders was thought more worrying than in Britain itself and definite contacts between Moscow and the Indian revolutionaries can be traced from October 1921. The so-called Curzon ultimatum of May 1923,

[3] See Judith M. Brown, *Gandhi's Rise to Power, 1915–1922* (Cambridge, 1972).

[4] See Peter Hardy, *The Muslims of British India* (Cambridge, 1972).

[5] For the limitations of recruitment to the Indian army in provincial terms and the preference given to the 'martial races', which gave a special status to Muslims and Sikhs in particular, see Stephen P. Cohen, *The Indian Army: its contribution to the development of a nation* (Berkeley and London, 1971), and Philip Mason, *A Matter of Honour: an account of the Indian Army, its officers and men* (London, 1974).

[6] The transfer of Indian hopes from Berlin to Moscow is graphically illustrated in *M.N. Roy's Memoirs* (Bombay, 1964). See also J.P. Haithcox, *Communism and Nationalism in India – M.N. Roy and Comintern Policy 1920–1939* (Princeton, N.J., 1971).

[7] Christopher Andrew, *Secret Service: the making of the British Intelligence Community* (London, 1985), pp. 262 – 7. On Soviet propaganda in the Empire and its impact on Anglo-Russian relations see Stephen White, *Britain and the Bolshevik Revolution: a study in the politics of diplomacy, 1920–1924* (London, 1979).

threatening to denounce the existing trade agreement, was mainly concerned with the subversion being carried out against India and her neighbours. On 14 January 1924 the Soviet Politbureau decided to instruct its representative in Kabul 'to work for the establishment of a united Empire of Muslim India and Afghanistan which should liberate millions of Indians from under the foreign yoke'.[8]

The Comintern entrusted the direction of communist movements throughout the Empire, including India, to the Communist Party of Great Britain, so that there was a close connection between the worries of the Indian and British governments. Both governments were also concerned with Afghanistan, where Soviet emissaries were particularly active in 1925. In India itself, attempts to set up an Indian Communist Party were less successful than the bringing about of contacts with Congress, represented by Jawarhalal Nehru* at the Brussels meeting of the 'League against Imperialism' in February 1927. The Nehrus then went on to Moscow. Some Soviet funds also went to local 'workers and peasants parties' under communist leadership from 1925 to 1927.[9]

It was the knowledge that the Raj faced subversion supported from without as well as the more or less constitutional opposition presented by the Indian political elite that explains the dominance of defence considerations in the handling of Indian questions over the next few years.

India showed itself sensitive to what was going on elsewhere in the Empire, in Ireland as well as in the Middle East. But what should be done about India was of more concern to British soldiers and statesmen than to the British electorate; and it was feared that if unrest continued the popular sentiment at home would be in favour of withdrawal.[10] On the other hand, those who were fully aware of the heterogeneous nature of Indian society, and believed that the country's progress could only be assured if unity were maintained, could argue that British rule was its only possible guarantee.[11] It had been intended that Parliament should play an active role in the

[8] Andrew, op. cit., pp. 277, 304 – 5.
[9] Ibid., pp. 326, 335. See also Haithcox, op. cit., p. 90.
[10] 'The temper of democratic countries such as ours is increasingly against remaining in a country where we are not wanted and we have either got to make our peace with the Indians, or as the educated classes grow we shall find a strenuous desire to get rid of India and all its bother.' Montagu to Lord Willingdon, Governor of Madras, 9 September 1920: quoted in S.D. Waley, *Edwin Montagu* (Bombay, Asia Publishing House, 1964), p. 235.
[11] Grigg to Clive Wigram, 8 February 1922: Grigg Papers.

implementation of the Montagu – Chelmsford reforms, but the standing joint committee which was set up did not seriously interfere with the discretion of the Secretary of State and the Viceroy.[12]

Lord Reading, Chelmsford's successor, was determined to see the reforms in operation, and hopes were placed on the visit of the Prince of Wales in November – December 1921 as a means of rewarding Indian loyalty to the Crown. But a boycott by the nationalists much diminished its effectiveness. On the eve of the Prince's visit to Calcutta the situation was thought so serious that Reading suggested that the Government agree to the nationalists' demands for a further conference on their constitutional demands. Despite the support of Montagu, the suggestion was rejected by the cabinet on the grounds that it would be wrong to sacrifice long-term policies to make a success of a royal visit.[13] It has however been argued that Reading was 'within an ace of having to concede Responsible Government for the Provinces' in place of the Montagu – Chelmsford 'dyarchy', and was only saved by Gandhi's failure to grasp the opportunity offered, partly because of his commitment to the Ali brothers and the Khilafat movement, which was outside the main stream of Indian politics.[14] Despite the boycott there were those who saw the Prince of Wales' visit as a success.[15] But the new political class, republican and democratic in sentiment, was not to be moved by such symbolism, though some people in England took a long time to learn the lesson.[16]

India's international status

Despite the reduction in India's external responsibilities and the abandonment of the idea of an Indian Empire in East Africa, the importance of India's role outside the sub-continent was fully taken

---

[12] Its original terms of reference, which were very broad, were changed in 1924 so as to confine it to matters referred to it by Parliament or the Secretary of State. It made a number of reports in its early years but ceased to function actively after 1925 and came to an end in 1928. Lord Hailey, *African Survey*, (London, 1938), p. xxviii.

[13] Conference of Ministers, 21 December 1921: PRO CAB 23/27.

[14] D.A. Low, *Lion Rampant* (London, Cass, 1973), p. 165.

[15] Grigg to Godfrey Thomas, January 1922: Grigg Papers.

[16] 'If the high line had been taken of telling India that she could not expect a visit from the Prince of Wales until she had proved herself worthy of such an honour and of receiving H.R.H. in the proper spirit, I am told this would have gone far towards making the loyal element bring its influence to bear upon the disloyal, while the sense of being neglected by the Crown, for a reason obvious to all, in the family of the British Empire would have had a wholesome effect upon all classes.' Lord Cromer to Grigg, 1 January 1922: Grigg Papers.

into account in London, while the development of the constitutional and political struggle in India was directly affected by the demands its external defences placed upon it.[17] India's interest in the Arabian peninsula as a whole was partly due to the concern of Indian Muslims with access to the Holy Places.[18] From the middle of the nineteenth century until 1917 the political control of Aden and the Aden protectorate was exercised by the Indian government acting through the Governor of Bombay. In 1917 political control was conceded to the Foreign Office and in 1921 to the new Middle East department of the Colonial Office, though civil administration was still directed from Bombay. Transfer to the Colonial Office was held up by disagreement over the financial terms of transfer, and Indian opinion also seems to have hardened against it. The C.I.D. view was that Aden, whose garrison was maintained by the War Office, was of more importance to imperial communications generally than to India.[19]

The Indian government had also from time to time entered into agreements with Kuwait, Bahrein and the Sheiks of the Trucial Coast. Again there were moves to make this a Colonial Office responsibility, but the Indian Government continued to bear most of the expenditure in connection with the imperial presence on the littoral, and maintained close relations with the Sultanate of Muscat.

More pressing was the problem of Afghanistan where Russian penetration was, as has been seen, of growing concern, and this in turn had a direct connection with the primary objective of the Indian government, retaining the loyalty of the Muslims. Ever since the 1890s the Indian government had been troubled by the tribal ties across the frontier with Afghanistan.[20] Now these fears became linked with those aroused by the Khilafat movement, arising from the threat to the position of the Sultan-Caliph.[21] The Third Afghan War in 1919 was the

[17] On the Indian connection with East Africa, see H. Lüthy, 'India and East Africa: Imperial Partnership at the end of the First World War', *JCH*, vol. VI, no 2, (1971), pp. 55 – 85; R.G. Gregory, *India and East Africa* (Oxford, 1971).
[18] 'British expansion in Asia and around the Indian Ocean had in fact been the expansion of British India, planned and generally initiated in India, often in the teeth of opposition from London, and executed with the autonomous material, financial, human and military resources drawn from the huge Indian empire which were not subject to British parliamentary control.' Lüthy, loc. cit., p. 69.
[19] C.I.D. meeting, 23 January 1923, PRO CAB 2/3. The transfer of Aden out of Indian jurisdiction, a process only completed in 1937, was opposed by its merchant community of about 7000 Indians, who regarded the Indian government as a more reliable protector. Lüthy, loc. cit.
[20] Hardy, *The Muslims of British India*, pp. 118, 176 – 7, 182, 189 ff.
[21] See meeting of Prime Minister with Indian Khilafat delegation on 19 March 1920: C.H. Philips, *The Evolution of India and Pakistan, 1858–1947: Select Documents* (London, 1962), pp.219 – 20.

result of an attempt by King Amanullah to take advantage of the Indian government's difficulties by renewing Afghanistan's claims to the disputed areas, and while the war itself was not of long duration, tension on the frontier continued over Afghanistan's harbouring of disaffected Indians from the Khilafat movement and other issues, until a new Treaty was signed on 21 November 1921. Amanullah made a further attempt at creating trouble in the north-west in 1923 – 4; but although this was put an end to by an agreement in May 1924, the Russians now began to show an increasing interest in the country, culminating in a treaty of neutrality and non-aggression on 31 August 1926.[22]

The winter of 1921 – 2 was thus a crucial time in India, since the followers of Gandhi were taking part in a non-cooperation movement, the Khilafat movement was at its peak, and there was an armed rising of the Moplahs in the Malabar territory of Madras from August to September.[23] It explains in part the increasing vehemence of Montagu, eventually made public, against the anti-Turkish attitude of the British government, which led to his dismissal by Lloyd George on 9 March.[24] In fact, however, the outbreaks of violence disturbed Gandhi's hopes for attaining home rule (Swaraj) by peaceful means, and in February 1922 the non-co operation campaign was called off.[25] The Moplah rebellion was put down and the Khilafat movement was not supported by the entire Muslim community, but indeed alienated important sections of it, with the result that it also faded away with the arrest of its leaders.[26] The departure of Montagu did not mean that concern for the Muslims was reduced. As Reading wrote to his successor Lord Peel*: 'We must get back to the position of Britain, the friend and protector of Moslems... whatever considerations may be thrown in the scales against us they are all outweighed by the supreme consideration of maintaining our position in India'.[27]

---

[22] See Louis Adamec, *Afghanistan, 1900–1923: A Diplomatic History* (Berkeley, 1967); W.K. Fraser Tytler, *Afghanistan* (3rd edn, London, 1967). Britain remained neutral during the 1929 rebellion and civil war: ibid., pp. 218 – 9.

[23] Brown, *Gandhi's Rise to Power*, pp. 228 – 31; A.Clayton, *The British Empire as a Super-power, 1919–1939*, pp. 180 – 3.

[24] Waley, op. cit., pp. 271 – 4.

[25] P. Moon, *Gandhi and Modern India* (New York, 1969), pp. 109 ff.

[26] Brown, op. cit., pp. 346 – 7.

[27] Reading to Peel, 21 September 1922: IOLR Reading Papers, MSS.EUR.238/5. Although relations with Afghanistan were conducted through the British minister in Kabul they were in fact primarily those of the Indian government; its political department supplied the personnel of the legation and paid all the expenses involved. Memorandum of 1924 by L.D. Wakely of the India Office political department, IOLR MSS.EUR.D.713.

The Khilafat movement and the Moplah rebellion with its accompanying massacres of Hindus helped to widen the gulf between the
Muslims and Hindus,[28] and the Muslims themselves lost interest in
the question of the Caliphate when it was abolished by the Turks in
1924. In the Indian nationalist movement itself the two communities
began from the summer of 1922 to follow their separate paths, and by
the end of the year it was in serious disarray. Nevertheless the bringing
into effect of the reforms was not an easy one, and was made more
difficult, as at other junctures of British rule in India, by the repercussions of the political debate in Britain itself. This impatience had
manifested itself even before Montagu's resignation, when some of his
colleagues expressed opposition to Indian claims.[29] On the other
hand, it was felt that Labour Party pronouncements were encouraging
Indian extremists.[30] In the cabinet itself, Churchill was the exponent
of the view that concessions leading inevitably to Home Rule would
not solve the problem of maintaining Britain's position:

> The fruit of a policy of introducing democratic institutions into
> India was that Indians turned against us at every stage... opinion
> would change soon as to the expediency of introducing democratic
> institutions to backward races which had no capacity for self-
> government... It would be preferable to extend the system of native
> states which would be in harmony with the ideas of Indians to
> whom European democratic institutions were generally
> repugnant.[31]

[28] E. Thompson and G.T. Garratt, *Rise and Fulfilment of British Rule in India* (London, 1934), pp.
613 – 4. Extracts from the official report on the Moplah rebellion (Cmd 1553, 1921) are in Philips,
op. cit., p. 221.
[29] 'The fact of the matter is, Rufus, that people here are fed up with India, and it is all I can do
to keep my colleagues steady on the accepted policy, let alone new instalments of it.' Montagu
to Reading, 1 February 1922, IOLR, Reading Papers, MSS. EUR.E.238/4. Later in the year an ill-
judged speech by Lloyd George and a rather bizarre suggestion that he and the Viceroy should
meet in Egypt cast doubts on the government's commitment to its announced Indian policy. See
John Vincent (ed.), *The Crawford Papers: the journals of David Lindsay, 27th Earl of Crawford and
10th Earl of Balcarres* (Manchester, 1984), pp. 432, 436 – 7.
[30] At a conference of ministers on 13 February 1922 Montagu attacked the socialists' attitude:
'They were completely ignorant of India and lost no opportunity of expressing sympathy with the
most outrageous demands of the extremists, and so caused a false impression as to opinion in this
country.' PRO CAB 23/29.
[31] For a discussion of the nineteenth century view that India's inherent backwardness would
always prevent her from achieving self-government within the Empire see E.G. Hutchins, *The
Illusion of Permanence* (Princeton, NJ, 1967), ch. X, and Anil Seal, *The Emergence of Indian
Nationalism* (Cambridge, 1968).

Indianisation and its impact upon recruitment in Britain

It was not however only a question of what responsibility could be transferred to representatives of an Indian electorate; here was also the problem of eligibility for employment in the administration. The Montagu – Chelmsford Report had indicated that the Indian Civil Service was destined to be increasingly Indianised, and that the role of British officials should be thought of largely in terms of the training of their successors. Yet there was still strong suspicion as to how officials, whether British or Indian, would be handled by the new provincial ministers elected under the system of 'dyarchy'. Safeguards were devised for their protection, resting ultimately upon the authority of the Secretary of State.

In 1923 a new Royal Commission was appointed to look into the public services, and in the following year it recommended important transfers of functions from the centre to the provinces while the scale of Indianisation was speeded up.[32] But what seemed slow progress to Indians was becoming an impediment to getting the right quality of recruits from Britain itself. And existing members of the services were found by Reading to be suffering under a strong sense of grievance because the Assembly would not vote them higher allowances to make up for the increased cost of living.[33] The Prince of Wales took a hand in the argument during his tour:

> I make it my business to talk to as many of our people as I can; soldiers, civil servants, and more especially the police who from the nature of the work, can usually give a more accurate picture of the whole situation out here than any one else... they one and all say the same thing – they won't let their sons come out here to earn their living in the Indian Army, Indian Civil Service etc etc... and that not now would they even recommend these services to any good fellow. The reason for this is that India is no longer a place for a white man to live in.[34]

[32] *Report of the Royal Commission on the Superior Civil Services in India*, (The Lee Commission, Cmd 2128, 1924). The fall in British recruitment was the main reason for the appointment of the Commission, which saw considerable differences of opinion between its British and Indian members. See Alan Clark (ed.), *A Good Innings: The Private Papers of Lord Lee of Fareham* (London, 1974), chs 22 – 5. For administrative developments generally see B.B. Misra, *The Administrative History of India: General Administration* (Bombay, 1970).

[33] G.R.Isaacs, *Rufus Isaacs, First Marquess of Reading* (London, 1942), vol. II, pp. 208 – 10.

[34] Prince of Wales to Montagu, 1 January 1922: Waley, op. cit., p. 262.

How far this discontent was due to the strains on government servants at a time of particular difficulty, and how far the feeling was coloured by apprehension that in the near future Britain would abandon India and leave them with no prospects, is not easy to discern.[35] The main effect of the Lee Commission's recommendations was to put an end to British recruitment for the provincial services, which had the effect of giving an increased importance to the provincial governments and their Indian ministers.[36]

The Indianisation of the Army was an even more difficult matter. The dual role of external defence and the maintenance of internal security was fully understood; but in addition there was the problem of the extent to which it would be possible to use Indian forces for general imperial purposes. During the war the previous preponderance of British troops in India had been reversed to give a large majority to Indian forces, as the British were withdrawn to take part in campaigns elsewhere. After the war, with internal tensions high, the situation changed again, so that by the summer of 1921 there were actually more British than Indian battalions committed to internal security.[37] By the later months of the year, when the authorities were confident that the civil disobedience movement was going to fail, and that Gandhi and his collaborators could safely be imprisoned, it was possible for soldiers to think that things could return to out and out direct rule: 'Once the die is cast we shall proceed to govern, but it means of course that the Montagu Reforms will go by the board and that we shall return to pre-war methods of government in India and push any idea of swaraj to the dim distant future.'[38] A similar harking back to previous conditions was to be found in the Esher Report, which had recommended in 1920 that the army in India should be reorganised to suit the needs of an imperial reserve.[39] The political pressures were all in the other direction, and the Esher report was set aside.

Indians objected to bearing the costs of a large defence establishment and external commitments, and wanted both reductions in the

---

[35] The impact of the war on British rule in India is treated critically in Algernon Rumbold, *Watershed in India, 1914–1922* (London, 1979).

[36] Tomlinson, *op cit*, pp. 17 ff.

[37] Jeffery, *The British Army and the Crisis of Empire*, pp. 101 ff.

[38] General Lord Rawlinson, Commander-in-Chief in India 1921–5, to Sir Henry Wilson, 15 November 1921: *Military Correspondence of Field Marshal Sir Henry Wilson*, pp. 306–7.

[39] *Army in India Committee, 1919–1920*, Cmd 943 (1920).

strength of the Indian Army and its Indianisation. For the Indian government itself, Indianisation had the appeal of cheapness.[40] But it raised the question of whether British officers would be willing to serve under Indians or whether 'Indianisation' should be a matter of setting up wholly segregated Indian units.[41] It was further complicated by the difficulty of finding Indian candidates suited to the training demanded of future officers, and whose families would willingly see them embark upon a military career. In addition, the prejudices of British officers and non-commissioned officers were given full weight, and British universities refused to allow Indian undergraduates to enter the Officers' Training Corps.[42]

In 1922 a subcommittee of the C.I.D. laid down future policy. It recognised the financial burden on India, but could see no way of relieving it by cuts in military expenditure. The organisation of the forces in India should give the maximum authority to the Indian government itself. Instead of the Commander-in-Chief India being appointed by the C.I.G.S., as the Esher Commitee had recommended, it was provided that the King would make the appointment on the recommendation of the Secretary of State for India after consultation with the Secretary of State for War. Indianisation would be restricted to an experiment with the efficiency of Indian-officered units. The report was accepted in an amended form on 23 January 1923.[43]

The timing of Indian self-government

Meanwhile the process of constitutional reform, even with its future goal undetermined, went ahead, and in the summer of 1923 elections were held for the Legislative Assembly, which met on 30 January 1924. By then the Labour Party, with its record of sympathy with the Indian nationalists, was about to take office in London. The post of Secretary of State for India had been coveted by Josiah Wedgwood, who had had long-standing contacts with the nationalists.[44] But he had to be content with the chancellorship of the Duchy of Lancaster,

[40] On the financial aspect of the Indian defence problem see Anne Orde, *Great Britain and International Security, 1920–1926* (London, 1978), pp. 178 ff.
[41] See Mason, *op cit*, pp. 453 ff.
[42] For Cambridge see S.C. Bose, *An Indian Pilgrim* (Bombay, 1965), p. 91.
[43] IOLR, Reading Papers, MSS.EUR.E.238/63b; PRO CAB 16/38/1.
[44] See P.S.Gupta, *Imperialism and the British Labour Movement, 1914–1964* (London, 1975), pp. 38 – 51, 102 – 118, and C.V.Wedgwood, *The Last of the Radicals* (London, 1951), pp. 140 ff.

while the India Office went to Sydney Olivier*, a former governor of Jamaica.[45] Like his new colleagues, Olivier agreed with the Viceroy that the 1919 Act should for the time being be allowed to stand.[46] Writing to Chelmsford, who also figured in the new government, Reading had argued that the thing to do was to strive to make the reforms effective: 'You and I know that firmness, accompanied by patience and tolerance and regulated by the determination to do right will win in the end, the 'Lost Dominion' notwithstanding.'[47]

The essence of such a policy was that Indians should be found to co-operate in making it work. But this was difficult when so much vocal Indian opinion was hostile to the very premises of British rule. In the first place, so far from recognising the significance of defence, it saw the need for defence as the consequence only of the British presence. An independent India would have no quarrel with her neighbours.[48] Now the Swarajist Party, which had been formed out of Congressmen who had rejected Gandhi's tactics and decided upon fighting elections, and which had become the largest party in the Central Assembly, demanded full responsible government, and by withdrawing co-operation put an end to ministerial rule in two provinces. Olivier therefore abandoned his previous position and suggested a meeting of a delegation from the Assembly with a committee of M.P.s to try for a new agreement on constitutional matters.[49] The proposal was strongly opposed in the Secretary of State's Council in London,

---

[45] Bernard Shaw, a fellow Fabian, explained his appointment: 'When the new Labour Party reached the Treasury Bench under the banner of socialism but under the thumb of Trade Unionism, its lack of representation in the House of Lords compelled it to hand out peerages to presentable members within its reach who were not needed in the House of Commons: and Olivier being eminently presentable and more aristocratic than most of the hereditary nobles became Lord Olivier. Being also the only available overseas Diplomat he was made Secretary of State for India.' Sydney Olivier, *Letters and Selected Writings*, ed M.Olivier (London, Allen and Unwin, 1948), preface.

[46] Georges Fischer, *La Parti Travailliste et la Décolonization de l'Inde*, (Paris, 1966), pp. 156 – 8.

[47] Reading to Chelmsford, 22 May 1924: IOLR, Reading Papers, MSS.EUR.238/63b. He is referring to the book *The Lost Dominion* by A.Carthill (London, 1924). Carthill was the pseudonym of B.C.H.Calcraft-Kennedy, (1871 – 1935), a former member of the ICS. His book was an expression of the view that Britain had betrayed her trust in India by abandoning its peoples to the rule of local demagogues.

[48] In 1921 the Congress party resolved that the Government's policy had been 'traditionally guided by considerations more of holding India in subjection than of protecting her borders... that India as a self-governing country can have nothing to fear from her neighbouring states...' It therefore urged states 'having no ill-will against the people of India' not to enter into any treaty with the Imperial Power. Neville Maxwell, *India's China War* (London, Cape, 1970), pp. 67 ff.

[49] Issacs, *op cit*, vol. II, pp. 281 – 97; S.R.Mehrotra, *India and the Commonwealth, 1880–1929* (London, 1963), pp. 127 – 9.

where the view was taken that this surrender to 'extremism and sedition' would be deeply humiliating, and alienate loyal Indians.[50] Wedgwood believed that Reading, whose hostility had caused the plan to be dropped, was in fact in favour of it and had been sabotaged by Olivier. Indian nationalists also tried to cultivate MacDonald directly.[51] It had been hoped that ministers would use their contacts with the Indian nationalists to prevent them pushing the government too hard, but this did not prove to work. It is worth noting in the light of later events that the Labour Party's contacts were almost exclusively with Hindus and that its spokesmen showed little sympathy for the Muslim case.[52]

The Government accepted as a substitute for Olivier's initiative a suggestion of Reading's that there should be a committee of inquiry in India itself, with official and non-official members, to see what more could be done within the framework of the 1919 Act. Although boycotted by the Swarajist leader Motilal Nehru, the committee began its work in August and was still in existence when the government fell, completing its work only in the following year.[53]

One element in the situation where Reading had sympathy with Indian aspirations was in respect of India's international position.[54] 'There is no doubt', he wrote,

> that in India the feeling is gradually manifesting itself that it should take its own place at the table of Empire, free to speak its own views through its own government, or at least its own representatives, instead of through the voice of the Secretary of State who is a British cabinet minister and whose position in this respect may, and at times has, become inconsistent with the representation of the true interests of India as a British dependency aiming at the status of a Dominion. Equally in foreign affairs there is the feeling that the Dominions have much more to say and are more freely consulted than India.[55]

[50] Olivier to Reading, 26 June 1924: IOLR, Reading Papers, MSS.EUR.E.238/7.
[51] Wedgwood to Reading, 26 March 1924; Olivier to Reading, 8 May 1924; ibid, MSS.EUR. 238/63b.
[52] M.Cowling, The Impact of Labour (Cambridge, 1971), p. 378; K.K.Aziz, Britain and Muslim India (London, 1963), p. 378.
[53] Report of the Reforms Enquiry Committee, under the chairmanship of Sir Alexander Muddiman, Cmd 2360, (1925): extracts in Philips, op cit, pp. 282 – 6.
[54] In 1923 India was represented at the League Assembly by a former member of the Viceroy's Council, but actually nominated by the British Treasury. Eric Drummond to Robert Cecil, 18 August 1923, Cecil of Chelwood Papers, BL Add MSS 51110.
[55] Reading to Olivier, 24 July 1924, IOLR, Reading Papers, MSS.EUR.E.238/7.

But these matters were of concern only to the few. The real question was whether the time was ripe for further authority at home to pass into the hands of elected Indian politicians. Of those consulted, the Governor of Bombay doubted whether any change was possible which would satisfy the extreme elements; meanwhile the very discussion of possible changes created uncertainty.[56] The governor of Assam was equally blunt:

> Except for the enlarged expectations of a few advanced politicians and for a somewhat larger acquaintance with the details of public business on the part of a few persons, India has really not moved one iota since [1919 – 20]. The obstacles in the way of a real move forward are precisely what they were then; the intense ignorance and apathy of the real people, the religious dissentions, the presence of important minority interests... which we are in honour bound to defend; the complications which will arise by bringing autocratic Indian States into relation with Parliamentary control in the Provinces or Government of India; and above all the supreme problem of the defence of India.[57]

Against this, Olivier's suggestion that the nationalists' reliance on direct action might have been 'schooled by the example of die-hard action in Ulster and Kenya' was not very consoling.[58] More importance was attached by the Government of India to increased Soviet propaganda which had been assisted, in its view, by the Labour government's recognition of the Soviet Union.[59]

While the government held firm, the Swarajists were beginning to see the limitations of their return to non-cooperation. Some of the ministries still functioned, and there was a move towards participation in the Councils' activities by some of the older leaders, though the younger ones sought ways to direct action. Gandhi, who had been released from prison earlier in the year, was for the time being outside the political mainstream. So though there was still violence in Bengal, it was decided that emergency powers need not be invoked.[60]

[56] Sir Leslie Wilson to Reading, 1 July 1924, *ibid*, MSS.EUR.E.238/49.

[57] Sir William Marris to Reading, 8 September 1924, *ibid*.

[58] Olivier to Reading, 14 August 1924, *ibid*, MSS.EUR.E.238/7. For the background to terrorist violence in Bengal, particularly from 1923 to 1927, see Townshend, *op cit*, p. 145.

[59] India Office to Foreign Office, 17 April 1924, IOLR L/P&S/10/1108.

[60] P. Spear, *A History of India*, vol. II, (London, 1965), 196; cabinet meeting, 22 September 1924, PRO CAB 23/48. A special ordinance was promulgated for the arrest and trial of suspected terrorists.

While the new Conservative government inherited a relatively peaceful scene in India, the underlying differences of outlook were more pronounced than ever. It was not just the degree and direction of change that was at issue; the nationalists now challenged the right of the British to decide upon either. The Indian leaders held that it should lie wholly with them to define India's future, and to decide whether or not the existing institutions could be used to help them achieve their goals. If not, and they again proceeded to measures of non-cooperation, the line between passive and active resistance would be hard to draw, if as in the past the authorities themselves attempted to put down illegal action. If Congress's pressure was to become irresistible, the Indian leaders would need to take all the country's major communities, including the Muslims, with them. On the other hand, the advantage that the country's rulers derived from the divergences between the communities was being enhanced by the provincialisation of politics and the impact of this upon attitudes at the centre.

It has been argued, on the basis largely of literary sources, that the 1920s were a period in which most of the earlier British selfconfidence was lost and in which there was increasing acceptance of the belief that Britain's role in India was coming to an end.[61] But there is little sign that those in responsible positions, however much they looked forward to India's becoming a willing self-governing member of the Commonwealth, took this view. It would be for Parliament to decide how and when Indian self-government should come about. Furthermore it would be necessary under the new dispensation for other members of the Commonwealth, some of whom had differences with India, to agree to her Commonwealth role. And in some cases it was made clear that they might prefer a united Commonwealth without India to a diluted Commonwealth of which she remained a member.[62] Commonwealth figures were often even more prone than the British to see the issue in racial or cultural terms. They saw the Commonwealth relationship as one between a family of English-speaking peoples to which India could not properly claim to belong:

---

[61] A.J.Greenberger, *The British Image of India* (London, 1969), pp. 110, 201 – 3.
[62] See the letter to Grigg of 22 August 1922, from E.ff.W. Lascelles, a New Zealand member of the Round Table: Grigg Papers.

'India is a great historic accident and remains the insoluble anomaly of the British Empire.'[63]

The new Secretary of State, Lord Birkenhead, came to his post with no previous experience of India and its problems; but his instincts were closer to those of the die-hards than Reading's or Peel's.[64] He made this clear in his early correspondence with the Viceroy.[65] Following discussions with Reading when the Viceroy visited England in the summer of 1925, Birkenhead made it plain that while constitutional changes could be considered if Indians could agree among themselves, he could not foresee a moment when Britain could, with a view either to its own safety or India's, abandon its trust.[66] Birkenhead's immediate task was to find a successor to Reading and the suggestion of Lord Irwin (the future Earl of Halifax*) was welcomed by him, though their divergences in policy and temperament became increasingly apparent.

For the time being it was the day to day decisions that had to be made in governing India that took precedence. The economic aspects of Britain's relationship with India at this time, growing out of the fiscal autonomy convention, have been described. Economic development was at no time high on the list of the Indian government's priorities. The growing class of Indian entrepreneurs were of some support to the nationalist movement, though others were fearful of some of its more extreme tendencies and proved to be a conservative force.[67] From the point of view of the masses of the population, agriculture was the most important area of economic activity, but despite the recommendations of a Royal Commission in 1928, the need for substantial expenditure for any extensive programme of

[63] John Dafoe, quoted in Cook, *John Dafoe and the Free Press*, 183. Dafoe found it quite natural to talk of Canada as an 'English-speaking' nation.
[64] His son wrote that he had a 'feel' of the country unusual in one who had never visited it, which he attributed to an intensive reading of Kipling. Lord Birkenhead (second Earl), *F.E.*, (London, Eyre and Spottiswode, 1959), a revised version of the same author's *Life of the First Earl of Birkenhead*, (London, 1935).
[65] He wrote that to him it was frankly inconceivable that India would ever be fit for Dominion self-government: 'In ultimate analysis the strength of the British position is that we are in India for the good of India. The most striking illustration of the truth of this position is supplied by the infinite variation of nationality, sect, and religion in the sub-continent. The more it is made obvious that these antagonisms are profound, and affect immense and irreconcilable sections of the population, the more conspicuously is the fact illustrated that we, and we alone, can play the part of composers...' Birkenhead to Reading, January 1925: Birkenhead, *op cit*, II, pp. 245 – 6.
[66] For the Birkenhead-Reading discussion see C.P. 310(25) in PRO CAB 23/50. For Birkenhead's speech in the House of Lords, see H.L. *Deb*, Vol 61, cols 1069 – 72, 7 July 1925.
[67] A.K.Bagchi, *Private Investment in India* Cambridge, 1972), 194 ff.

agricultural betterment and the lack of any dramatic political appeal in such activities made the provincial governments reluctant to move.[68]

The recommendations of the Lee Commission were followed through with the creation of a Public Service Commission, which assumed its duties on 1 October 1926. Some alleviation of the financial position of British recruits to the I.C.S. was introduced, and the Indian Political Service remained a separate affair recruited from army officers rather than the I.C.S. Its responsibilities in the princely States loomed larger as the States' future took up an increasing share in the consideration of future constitutional change.[69]

Birkenhead continued to stress the importance of defence, and believed that the Soviet Union as well as Afghanistan must be seen as a potential enemy.[70] Some of his colleagues even continued to believe that India could still provide support for the Empire outside its borders. In December 1926, at a critical time in China, Salisbury criticised the army for having made no arrangement with the Government of India to have troops ready for service there.[71]

Further debate on Indianisation and on the equipment of the Indian army followed. Doubts were expressed by Churchill about the desirability of allowing the Indian States to possess artillery.[72] And the possibly divided loyalties of British Indian troops led to strong opposition to their being equipped with the most modern weapons. Trenchard, by contrast, took the view that the government should abandon its 'Indian Mutiny' outlook and make India, like other parts of the Empire-Commonwealth, responsible for its own defence.[73] Connected with these questions were the objections raised by the Government of India to paying the cost of British regiments stationed in that country, on the ground that they were there for general

[68] *Royal Commission on Agriculture in India*, the Linlithgow Commission, (Cmd 3132, 1928).

[69] See Terence Creagh Coen, *The Indian Political Service* (London, 1971).

[70] Birkenhead to Irwin, 12 May and 18 August 1927: IOLR MSS.EUR.C.152/3. The Chiefs of Staff did not believe that the resources for such a war would be available: meeting of 31 May 1927, PRO CAB 53/2. Irwin doubted if British opinion would sanction a war brought about by Russia's violation of Afghan neutrality. Irwin to Salisbury, 20 May 1927, Salisbury Papers, General Correspondence, 1927.

[71] Memorandum by Salisbury, *ibid*, winter 1926 – 7. The Indian delegation to the 1926 Imperial Conference had made clear their view that the defence of India was the only task of the Indian Army.

[72] C.I.D. meeting, 6 February 1925: PRO CAB 2/4.

[73] Chiefs of Staff Subcommittee, meeting of 4 November 1929: PRO CAB 53/2. When in 1941 Indian troops arrived to take part in the defence of Malaya they had never seen a tank. S. Woodburn Kirby, *Singapore: The Chain of Disaster* (London, 1971), p. 150.

imperial purposes.[74] The need to use them outside India meant that they were trained in a more expensive fashion than would otherwise have been necessary.[75] Birkenhead was unsympathetic: 'This country is shouldering an intolerable burden of taxation and India has done nothing since the war to encourage generosity towards her.'[76]

The question of what India deserved to have done for her was a recurrent one in die-hard comment on Indian affairs. On the other hand, Indian nationalist spokesmen argued that no obligation existed: 'The Army in India is an imperial reserve for which the people of this country are made to pay. The colonies refuse to pay for it, the British taxpayers refuse to pay for it, and therefore the army in England is sent out to this country to be paid for by the people of this country for external defence.'[77] In 1929 a temporary settlement was reached between the Indian government and the War Office, but there would obviously have to be a reconsideration of the whole issue if there were to be major constitutional changes. Sir Valentine Chirol, a former *Times* correspondent with close contacts in Indian nationalist circles, pointed out to the Indian advocates of Dominion status that while the protection of the British navy would no doubt continue, the British people would not allow British troops to be employed under the orders of Indian ministers for the repression of internal conflicts, particularly if the Afghans were to intervene on behalf of the Indian Muslims.[78]

As far as the use of Indian troops outside India's borders was concerned, there were a number of attempts to get the Government of India to intervene in conflicts in the Arab world. But even though it had been agreed that the external employment of Indian forces would be paid for by the Imperial government, there were also 'internal politico-religious reasons' for India disinteresting herself from Arab politics. During the Saudi-Iraqi clashes in the winter of 1927 – 8 when the Colonial Office was supporting its Hashemite protégé, the India Office clung to its Saudi preference. Abstention seemed the safest option.[79] The Indian government was consulted about the

---

[74] Documents on this long-running controversy are in PRO T161/240/S.25234.
[75] Viceroy's telegram, 18 December 1928, C.P.1(29) in PRO CAB 24/201.
[76] Birkenhead to Irwin, 16 December 1926: IOLR MSS.EUR.C.152/2.
[77] Speech in Indian Legislative Assembly quoted in India Office memorandum, 12 November 1928, C.P.341(28) in PRO CAB 24/198.
[78] Chirol to Sir John Simon, 1 December 1927: Simon Papers.
[79] Notes by Sir Arthur Hirtzel: IOLR L/P&S/10/1104.

negotiations in 1927 for a new Anglo-Persian treaty; Birkenhead regretted that it had not intervened against the agreement reached, and deplored the tendency he detected for the Indian government to disinterest itself in Persia, despite the fact that British supremacy in the Gulf, which he thought had been imperilled, had for over a century been regarded as 'essential to the safety of India'.[80] He also objected to the idea that local officers should be given discretion to use air power to settle local Arab problems: 'A chance bomb in Nejd territory might well get Indian moslem feeling ablaze, and recreate in India the political situation of 1919 ...' It seemed to him a sufficient reason for India and the India Office not to 'disinterest themselves in Arabian policy generally'.[81] In January 1929 the India Office and the Government of India did criticise the Foreign Office for its willingness to consider Persian claims on Bahrein and the Arab side of the Gulf, so as to avoid recourse to the League of Nations.[82] In 1932 the India Office opposed arbitration on the Bahrein issue so as not to bring foreign countries in touch with the Gulf.[83] India also objected to making sacrifices to ease relations with Persia, for instance by ceding part of Baluchistan: 'it would be difficult to convince Indian opinion that Indian territory was not being bartered for Imperial objects'.[84]

The Raj and the threat from China

Apart from the growing Russian involvement in Afghanistan, the thinking of the Indian government about defence from 1925 onwards was much affected by the progress of the Chinese Revolution and the increasing role played by communists in its leadership. The Chinese left-wing press and students made British rule in India one of their principal targets for denunciation.[85] The Foreign Office were in no doubt but that the Soviet government and Comintern would try to evolve out of the Chinese Revolution a means of making trouble in India. There was evidence it believed that the Bolsheviks were gradually arranging to consolidate a position in the outlying portions

[80] Birkenhead to Irwin, 14 June 1928: IOLR MSS.EUR.C.152/4.
[81] Birkenhead to Austen Chamberlain, 14 June 1928: *ibid*.
[82] India Office minute, 24 January 1929: IOLR L/P&S/10/1252.
[83] Draft letter from India Office to Foreign Office: IOLR L/P&S/10/1255.
[84] Laithwaite, India Office, to Rendel, Foreign Office, 28 June 1932: IOLR L/P&S/10/1254.
[85] Louis, *British Strategy in the Far East*, 115. For Soviet involvement in the Chinese Revolution, see E.H.Carr, *Socialism in One Country, 1924–1926*, vol. II, pt II (London, 1964), ch. XL, 'China in Revolution'.

of the Chinese republic bordering upon India so as to 'maintain a constant direct attack' in due course.[86] In 1927 Indian delegates attended the inaugural conference at Hankow of the 'Union of Weak Races in the East'.[87] In early May the Fifth Congress of the Chinese Communist Party at Hankow was attended by the Indian, M.N. Roy, as the delegate of the Comintern.[88] There were differences of opinion between the Foreign Office, India Office and War Office as to the measures to be taken in respect of Sinkiang and Tibet, though there was agreement that the Russians were to be feared.[89] And the Foreign Office's belief that the best policy might be to seek an agreement with the more moderate wing of the Chinese nationalists was contested by the India Office,[90] while the Foreign Office disapproved of the Indian government supplying arms to the Governor of Singkiang as interference in the Chinese Civil War.[91]

Where constitutional changes were concerned, Birkenhead had entered upon office believing that nothing further should be done pending the expiry of the ten year period provided for in the 1919 reforms. In long discussions with Reading in May-June 1925 he admitted that 'dyarchy' had proved more successful than expected but claimed that the unwillingness of the nationalists to give it a fair trial made it difficult to recommend further concessions to the House of Commons.[92] Communal tensions had been increased by the inevitable propensity of the new elected members of provincial governments to favour their own people in exercising patronage.[93] In the Punjab there was endemic tension between Muslims and Sikhs, but anarchical conspiracy of a violent kind was confined to Bengal, where it had been endemic since the partition of 1905.[94] On the

[86] Minute for Secretary of State, August 1925: IOLR L/P&S/10/1152.

[87] See IOLR L/P&S/10/1197.

[88] Memorandum on Communism in China in despatch from Sir M.Lampson (Peking) to Foreign Secretary, 26 August 1927 in *ibid*.

[89] 'Northern frontiers: Soviet menace to' in IOLR L/P&S/10/1152.

[90] India Office minute of 10 December 1925 on Foreign Office telegram of 9 December: IOLR L/P&S/10/1121.

[91] IOLR L/P&S/10/1152. For Sinkiang see Max Beloff, *The Foreign Policy of Soviet Russia, 1929–1941*, vol. I, (London, 1947), Appendix D.

[92] C.P.310(25) in PRO CAB 23/50.

[93] Leslie Wilson, Governor of Bombay, to George Lloyd, his predecessor, 19 May 1924: Churchill College, Cambridge, Lloyd Papers, 10/23.

[94] See 1929 printed departmental memoranda in IOLR MSS.EUR.D.713. Birkenhead regarded some degree of communal trouble as tolerable: 'An occasional eruption can be regarded with calmness and, after all, it serves as a useful reminder of the indispensability of British control. But the disorders, if they attain to a certain degree of intensity, become alarming and reflect

other hand, fears about communism in India itself were subsiding. It was thought that much of the money sent in by the Russians was probably diverted by the agents to their personal use.[95]

In view of the country's relative quiescence it seemed possible to appoint a new Constitutional Commission to look into what should next be done. Birkenhead was keen to hasten its appointment in case Labour should win the next election, and fill it with what Birkenhead regarded as individuals with an unrealistic view of the possibilities.[96] Even so, the composition of the Commission was a crucial question. After considerable hesitation, it was decided that Indians could not be included. If it were to be small enough to be a working body it could not contain more than two or three Indian members, and even three could not represent the full variety of Indian attitudes. Nor was it thought that officials of the Indian government or Dominion ministers or ex-ministers would be considered appropriate, while an exclusively Parliamentary body might be acceptable.[97]

Such hopes turned out to be misplaced, as there was an outcry in India on the grounds that the Commission's exclusively British membership was an insult to the nationalist movement.[98] On the other hand, if the Commission's Report were to carry any conviction it must at least be all-Party, and there were fears that the Indian clamour would cause the Labour members to withdraw.[99] But this did not happen, and Major Clement Attlee was allowed to make his first though not his last mark on Indian history. The Labour Party Conference in October 1927 pledged the Party's support for Dominion Home Rule and its left-wing members continued their contacts with nationalist leaders.[100] In October 1928 Birkenhead left the India Office, which went to his Conservative predecessor Lord Peel, whose

discredit upon us as a ruling and indispensable power.' Birkenhead to Irwin, 8 July 1926: IOLR MSS.EUR.C.152/2.

[95] Note on 'unrest' by J.W.Hose, April 1925, in IOLR MSS.EUR.D.713. In an article on 'Nationalism in India', Nirad Chaudhuri argued that India was basically pro-German from the creation of the Entente till 1945. (*Survey*, (London), no. 67, (April 1968), 41 – 56.) But until the rise of Hitler, only Russia and Japan seem to have worried the Indian government.

[96] Birkenhead to Reading, 10 December 1925: Birkenhead, *F.E.*, 510 – 11.

[97] Birkenhead to Irwin, 28 April 1927: IOLR MSS.EUR.C.152/3. The Viceroy reported that two experienced governors, Hailey of the Punjab and Marris of the United Provinces, accepted these arguments. Irwin to Birkenhead, 19 May 1927, *ibid*.

[98] See Michael Brecher, *Nehru, a Political Biography* (London, 1959), 127 ff; S.Gopal, *Jawarhalal Nehru*, vol. I, (London, 1975), 116 ff.

[99] Entries of 11 and 25 November 1927 in Thomas Jones, *Whitehall Diary*, vol. 2, 115 – 7.

[100] P.S. Gupta, *Imperialism and the British Labour Movement*, 112 ff.

views were less hostile to Indian claims and closer to those of the Viceroy, who now took the lead in policy matters.[101]

The appointment of the Commission had the effect of giving pause to the fissiparous tendencies which had made themselves felt in the nationalist movement during the period of relative tranquility of the last few years. Most nationalists were agreed upon a boycott of the Commission when it arrived in India to carry out its work. But although it looked at first as though a large section of the Muslims would join in the boycott, many Muslims, like members of the other minorities worried at the prospect of a Hindu Raj, moved towards co-operation. Jinnah* however remained aloof. The boycotting parties set up a committee to draft a constitution for an independent India, and the upshot, the Nehru report of August 1928, was a highly centralist document which went nowhere near satisfying Muslim demands and threatened the Princes with a direct transfer of paramountcy which would be equivalent, as they saw it, to Congress rule in the States as well.[102]

The Round Table Conference of 1930

The advent of the Labour government in May 1929 afforded the Viceroy greater flexibility in dealing with the situation created by Congress's new and more radical stance. But the new minority government, relying as it did on the Liberals for remaining in office, and recognising the desirability of not going out too far in pursuit of a policy which the Opposition would be obliged to combat, was not likely to indulge in dramatic initiatives or to begin by repudiating the work of the Simon Commission, upon which the Labour Party had been represented.[103] It was rather the Viceroy who held the view that there should be a statement embodying a specific undertaking that Dominion status should be the ultimate goal of constitutional advance and that dyarchy in the provinces should give way to general ministerial responsibility for provincial functions. How far his thinking

---

[101] Lord Butler was to recall Irwin as saying: 'I remember so well how bloody it was serving under F.E.' Lord Butler, *The Art of the Possible* (London, Hamish Hamilton, 1971), 36.

[102] For the development of policy in respect to India in the period 1929 – 32 see R.J. Moore, *The Crisis of Indian Unity, 1917- 1940*, (Oxford, 1974). The British domestic background is dealt with in the unpublished Oxford B.Phil thesis (1972) by G.R.Peele, 'The Conservative Party and the Opposition to the Government of India Act, 1929 – 1935', and in her article, 'A Note on the Irwin Declaration', *JICH*, I (1973).

[103] MacDonald to Baldwin, 19 September 1929: Baldwin Papers, quoted by Peele, *loc cit.*

had gone when he visited England in 1929 and discussed the situation with Baldwin and Salisbury as well as ministers is unclear. The evidence is that he was, like his predecessors, convinced that Dominion status in the full sense, which would involve Indian responsibility for defence and hence the subordination of the British army in India to an Indian government, was unacceptable and that even in domestic administration British civil servants would be needed for some time to come.[104]

It therefore seems likely that Irwin hoped that he could get from the British government a statement that would be welcomed in India as a major step forward while its limitations would be fully understood in England. Baldwin had been assured that even though MacDonald contemplated consulting Indian opinion before the government fully made up its mind about the attitude to take towards the Simon Commission's recommendations, when these should become available, he hoped for a situation with which all British parties could concur. Before returning to India in October, however, Irwin found that Lloyd George, perhaps with Reading's support, might well come out against the policy he proposed, and seek an agreement with the Conservative die-hards, notably Austen Chamberlain and Churchill, as a prelude to turning out the government and forming the kind of coalition which eluded him between 1922 and 1924.[105] Other Conservative quarters were also worried lest the declaration which it was thought the Viceroy was about to make, and which would pre-empt the expected report of the Simon Commission, should take Britain well beyond the horizons set by the Montagu – Chelmsford reforms.[106] The dilemma was therefore a dual one: what could Irwin offer to rebuild some form of collaboration with at least part of the Indian political elite, and how far could this be squared with the more traditionalist view of Britain's role, so strong in the Conservative and Liberal parties and not wholly without echoes in the Labour Party itself?

Baldwin might himself have been prepared to allow Irwin's judgement to prevail but his shadow cabinet colleagues were not, and he

---

[104] Memorandum of a conversation between Salisbury and Irwin, 28 July 1929: Salisbury Papers, quoted *ibid*.
[105] Irwin to Baldwin, 8 October 1929; Baldwin Papers, quoted *ibid*.
[106] Peel to Baldwin, 14 October 1929: *ibid*. Simon himself believed that his proposals would eventually pave the way to Dominion status: see his letters to Reginald Coupland, 1 July 1930, and Geoffrey Dawson, 30 June 1930, in Simon Papers.

was asked to convey to Wedgwood Benn, the Secretary of State, and Snowden, the acting Prime Minister, (MacDonald himself being in the United States), the fact that the Conservative Party would not be able to support the proposed declaration, particularly in view of its understanding that the policy to be proposed would not have Simon's support. Irwin's knowledge of the hardening of opposition in London was inadequate, since he was falsely reassured on this score by Benn and felt able to reject Snowden's suggestion for a postponement. On 31 October the Viceroy's statement was duly made public.

The declaration embodied two main ingredients: the statement that Montagu's 1917 declaration implied that 'the natural issue of India's constitutional progress' was 'the attainment of Dominion status' and that the way forward should be through a Round Table Conference representing all interests concerned, including the Indian Princes. The former had clearly to be read within the new definition of Dominion Status agreed upon at the 1926 Imperial Conference: if and when it came about, India would have the right to secede from the Empire. The second depended upon the willingness of Congress to go back upon its claim to be the unique representative of Indian opinion and to be ready to share that role with other parties, with the Muslims and with the Princes. The vigorous debates on the Declaration in Parliament and in India itself reacted upon each other. Only general acceptance in India could assure that all-party support for the legislation which would have to be forthcoming to embark upon the path pointed to by Irwin.

The immediate outcome was more favourable in England than in India. Irwin and the Labour government survived the Parliamentary onslaught upon the Declaration, but in India, Congress after some hesitation was persuaded by Gandhi that independence rather than Dominion status should be the aim and civil disobedience rather than negotiation the means. But the readiness of other Indians of note to serve, although in an individual capacity at the Viceroy's invitation, and the willingness above all of the Princes to take an active part, meant that a conference could be held with the assent of all British parties. When it met in October 1930 the government delegation, headed by the Prime Minister, was complemented by the presence of a Conservative delegation of, on the whole, moderate opinions and led by Samuel Hoare, and a Liberal delegation headed by Reading, thus probably assuring all-Party support for whatever might come out of the meetings.

In the interim the Conservative opponents of the Dominion status goal for India had not been idle, and the Indian question became entangled with the general right-wing attack on Baldwin mounted by the two press lords, Beaverbrook and Rothermere, though the former's interest in India itself was of the slightest. Others with more specifically Indian interests formed organisations within Parliament and in the country which were to carry on a running battle against the new policies both during the lifetime of the Labour government and afterwards, until the passing of the Government of India Act in 1935. Most important of all was the assumption of the leadership of the campaign by Churchill, whose opposition, spelled out in a speech on 12 December 1930, was to any British abdication from rule over India, dangerous as he saw it to both Britain and India. In January 1931 Churchill resigned from the shadow cabinet on this issue.

At the time the Round Table Conference met, the problem of India's international status and of her Commonwealth role had not found a solution. India had of course been a founding member of the League of Nations and, as we have seen, a candidate for becoming the mandatory power in respect of Tanganyika, which some Indians believed would have enhanced its international status.[107] Subsequently the way in which India should be treated at the League and other international bodies involved two distinct issues. Should there be any conventions governing the degree to which the Secretary of State should intervene? It was necessary to avoid either giving the impression that India's international status was a mere pretence, or fostering the illusion that it was independent in the manner of the Dominions. The real results of the new status, ran an official memorandum in December 1927,

> are that the Indian public has wider opportunities of influencing imperial policy through the Government of India and the Secretary of State, of influencing the policy of the Government in international matters affecting India, of making India better known to the outside world, of participating generally in imperial and international discussions, and of bringing the experience thus gained to bear on the domestic policy of the Government of India itself.[108]

[107] Lüthy, loc cit, 57.
[108] 'Miscellaneous Notes Relative to International Status of India', (collected December 1927 for India Office use only) in IOLR L/P&S/10/1176. The memorandum goes on to quote from a circular of Montagu's of 30 December 1920: 'The status of India in International Labour

179

The Indian nationalists remained unsatisfied.[109]

The first session of the Round Table Conference which ended on 19 January 1931 was unexpectedly constructive. It was agreed that the principle of the responsibility of the Executive to the Legislature would be incorporated in a new constitution, provided that the Legislature was constituted on a federal basis. Agreement in principle was obviously dependent upon the solution of problems left unresolved. The Muslim delegates pressed for safeguards through separate electorates which the majority of British Indian delegates were unable to accept; and the question was left aside in the hope that the British government might make an award on communal safeguards acceptable to all. It was also clear that not all the Princes were convinced that this new relationship to an all-Indian governmental system would provide them with the defences they felt they needed against the more radical currents in Indian politics.

For Irwin, who could take comfort from the fact that the civil disobedience campaign launched by Gandhi had been successfully contained, it still seemed evident that unless Congress would accept some part in framing and operating the new system, federation would not provide the answer. He prepared for an attempt to secure such an outcome by releasing from gaol the leading Congressmen who had been imprisoned for their activities during the civil disobedience campaign. After a series of meetings between Irwin and Gandhi which largely dealt with local issues arising from recent events, an agreement was reached between them in March 1931 by which Congress agreed to participate in further discussions of the scheme worked out in London. But rather than Congress being represented by a delegation embodying its own different strands, Gandhi alone appeared at the new session of the Conference, which met from October to November 1931. By that time the Labour government was out of office, but the new National government excluded Churchill (and Lloyd George) and

Conferences must tend to approximate more and more to that of a Dominion – a status which the Treaty of peace implicitly confers upon her... as India has become a member of the League of Nations, labour legislation in India is bound to be influenced by this international opinion, but it would be unfair to India if she were, in addition, subject to any form of pressure from Great Britain, whose interests are in this respect not only not identical but in some respects antagonistic.'

[109] The Indian nationalists unsuccessfully appealed to the U.S. Senate to back their objections to the Kellog Peace Pact on the ground that Baldwin had committed India to an international obligation and exempted the affairs of the Empire from the operation of the Pact. G.R.Hess, *America Encounters India, 1941–1947* (Baltimore, 1971), 14.

thus seemed well-fitted to continue the effort to find a solution. On the other hand, the new strains put upon the British government by the recession made the interests of British commerce and particularly of Lancashire textiles a more important factor in the constitutional debate than hitherto.[110]

The course of the second Round Table Conference was however dominated not by imperial considerations but by the failure of Gandhi to find a solution to the problem of minority safeguards – the issue upon which not only the Muslims but the Sikhs and the Depressed Classes felt more strongly as the prospect of the transfer of power came nearer. For the same reasons the Princes also hardened their position, wishing their relations with the Indian government to be through the Viceroy rather than through the ministers of the proposed new Executive. In the face of the intransigence of all parties, British ministers were tempted to abandon the search for federation and to follow the advice of the Simon Commission by completing provincial autonomy and getting it working before proceeding with reforms at the centre.[111] And despite the advice of the new Viceroy, Willingdon, also to press on with changes at the centre, the conference ended with the British government still wedded to the earlier proposals and promising to seek through further inquiries in India for solutions to the many issues left unresolved.

[110] For Amery's caustic comments on the out-of-date views of the 'Lancashire Cotton People' see Diary entry, 29 April 1931.
[111] The Report of the Simon Commission had eventually been published in May 1930 (Cmd 3568 – 9).

PART II

THE QUICKENING PACE, 1932 – 9

Chapter 8

THE EMPIRE AND
THE WORLD DEPRESSION

The Depression and the Ottawa Conference

The world depression that set in after the collapse of the American stock market in the autumn of 1929 brought about major changes in the economic and political environment within which the statesmen of the Empire-Commonwealth had to plot their course. Efforts to deal with the problems it posed through international action directed towards tackling obstacles to trade, and in particular the instability of currencies and the burdens of international debt, revealed themselves as inadequate in the face of the pressure upon national governments to protect their own economies, and to be free to manipulate their currencies in the light of their domestic priorities. The failure of the London World Economic Conference in 1933 marked the abandonment of the international approach.[1] The advent of Hitler to power in Germany heralded not only a strengthening of the movement towards autarchy in that country and the use of its economic weapon to assist its political aims in Europe, but also the beginning of a period of massive rearmament which spread with different degrees of urgency to most other countries with any role in international politics, and this in turn reacted upon economic conditions and economic policy.

The first impact upon Britain was, as has been seen, to strengthen the case for the limitation of government expenditure, at the expense of positive measures to encourage inter-imperial trade or to develop the infrastructure of colonial economies. At the same time, the depression and the actions taken by other countries, particularly the United States, to ward off its effects by national measures gave new cogency to

[1] For a useful sketch of the economic problems of the inter-war period see Jean Halpérin, 'Les Problèmes Economiques et Financiers' in M. Beloff, P. Renouvin, F. Schnabel and F. Valsecchi (eds), *L'Europe du XIX et du XX siècle*, vol. III, pt 1 (Milan, 1964). On the impact of United States economic policy see Ch. P. Kindleberger, 'Le rôle des Etats Unis dans l'économie Europeenne', ibid., vol. III, pt 3 (Milan, 1967).

185

the old argument that the development of the Empire-Commonwealth as a whole into a single economic unit was the only way in which it could be insulated against the ups and downs of an external environment over which it had no control. The case for 'Empire Free Trade', as proclaimed by Lord Beaverbrook, and for protectionist measures in general received a new lease of life in the Conservative Party, and although Baldwin fought off precise commitments, it was clear that the Party, dominant in the 'National Government' after the general election of October 1931, would insist upon moves towards both protection and imperial preference.

One of the major aspects of the depression was its effect on agricultural prices, and here there were problems for the British government quite apart from the strong commitment of all parties not to raise the price of food. In Britain there was a feeling that the decline of British agriculture should be checked and that something should be done to produce more food at home. There were also pressures to do something on a European basis which might help continental farmers.[2] Finally, the Dominions were now finding their own position as primary producers assailed from a new quarter, in the efforts of the Soviet Union to sell more abroad so as to help finance its Five Year Plans. Canada responded by prohibiting all imports of coal, timber, wood-pulp, furs, asbestos and other commodities, and some people argued that Canada's example should be followed by Britain and the rest of the Empire.[3]

The 1930 Imperial Conference had been hesitant where economic matters were concerned, but it had been agreed that a further Conference on economic questions should be held, this time in Ottawa. It had been expected that the Conference would meet in 1931 but the upheavals of that traumatic year made postponement inevitable. In February 1932 the way was cleared for an extension of the preferential system by Britain's own adoption of a general

[2] On the advice of the Foreign Secretary, the Cabinet decided to contribute a sum to an 'International Credit Mortgage Company' set up by the Commission of Inquiry for European Union: PRO CAB 23/67, meeting of 10 June 1931. The Commission was the result of the somewhat undefined project for European union put before the League of Nations in 1930 by the French prime minister, Briand. See Paul Bastid, 'L'Idée de L'Europe et l'Organization de l'Europe' in Beloff *et al.*, loc. cit., vol. III, pt 1.

[3] 'Not for the first time, the prompt resolution of the northern Dominion has shown the way to the whole Empire ... Not for the first time the irresolution of Great Britain has halted the progress of the whole Empire.' Memorandum of the British Empire Producers Association: Grigg Papers.

protectionist tariff, from which, for the time being, Empire products were exempt. By now the dominant figure in the government was clearly the Chancellor of the Exchequer, Neville Chamberlain*, who succeeded the devoted free trader Philip Snowden, and provided a link with his father's imperial vision. By a twist of fate, Amery, who had personified the persistence of this vision, was not included when the National Government was formed in August, nor brought in in the post-election changes. Originally Thomas once again united the offices of Colonial Secretary and Dominions Secretary in his own person, but in November 1931 he surrendered the former to Cunliffe-Lister; the latter's post at the Board of Trade went to Walter Runciman* who, like Cunliffe-Lister, was disposed to seek for more positive solutions to British and Imperial trade problems.

Nevertheless, although all these ministers were to be in the seven-minister delegation to the Ottawa Conference under Baldwin's leadership, it was not the case that the government had become converted to the idea of imperial economic unity. What inspired both them and the Dominion governments, with whom there had been intensive consultations between November 1931 and the meeting of the Conference in July 1932, was a desire to meet the immediate problems posed by the depression rather than to build a new imperial system.[4] What in fact took place was a series of negotiations, primarily of a bilateral kind, through which it was hoped bargains could be driven to mutual advantage. Indeed, the British government had provided itself with an additional bargaining weapon, in that while the colonial exemptions from the tariff were to be permanent, the Dominion exemptions would expire in November unless agreements on preferences were achieved by then.[5] What the negotiations at Ottawa revealed was that if there was any element of a general imperial

[4]See K.E. Robinson, 'Le Commonwealth des Nations', in Beloff *et al.*, loc. cit., vol. III, pt 3, 300 – 1. Writing closer to the event, Hancock had been more positive: 'It would be unjust and profoundly misleading not to keep constantly in mind the crisis atmosphere in which the Ottawa Confrence met. In examining the manner in which the nations of the British Commonwealth concerted their answers to the onset of adversity, it is necessary and just to remember the brutal egotism of the Hawley-Smoot tariff and the damage done by the tariffs, quotas and exchange controls of the French, Italians, Germans and most other nations. The Ottawa Conference was the response of Great Britain and the Dominions to an unprecedented calamity. But it was something more. It was the triumph of a theory of Empire which had been for half a century the great cause for which many ardent spirits fought.' Hancock, *Survey of British Commonwealth Affairs*, vol. II, pt 1, p.229.
[5]On the Ottawa Conference, see I.M. Drummond, *British Economic Policy and the Empire*, ch. 3, and his *Imperial Economic Policy, 1917–1939*, chs 5 and 6. The *Summary of Conclusions* (Cmd 4174, 1931) is printed, together with extracts from speeches at the Conference, in N. Mansergh

outlook to be found in the British delegation, it was, at least on economic matters, scarcely visible among the Dominion representatives.[6]

The depression in Canada was to be of long duration and cause much distress: one result was Mackenzie King's replacement as Prime Minister by R.B. Bennett in 1930. Bennett's instincts were protectionist rather than imperialist. His main belief was that Canada, as a producer of raw materials, should find ways of ensuring that they were processed at home.[7] He had however been an associate of Beaverbrook's and was very put out when Beaverbrook, applauding the granting of preferences in Mackenzie King's 1930 budget, supported him in the election of that year. They were thus not in active communication during the 1930 Imperial Conference, though they were subsequently reconciled. Beaverbrook later believed the damage to his cause to have been considerable: 'If I had not lost his collaboration at the critical period of our campaign in Britain, our Empire Free Trade plan under his influence might have been forced upon the Tory Party during the autumn of 1930 while the Imperial Conference was in session.'[8]

The wholly Canadian-orientated attitude of Bennett at Ottawa, when he used his chairmanship to pursue national interests, does not make this scenario a very probable one. In fact, the main clash turned out to be with Bruce of Australia. Bruce was so concerned to get preference for Australian meat that he at one point threatened to walk out of the Conference if he did not get his own way. Baldwin, in one of his rare interventions in the Ottawa proceedings, found it necessary to appeal to him on political grounds, pointing out the possible impact of such action upon India and Ireland: 'If one of the old Dominions

(ed.) *Documents and Speeches on British Commonwealth Affairs, 1931–1952* (London, 1953), vol. I, 114 ff. The Indian delegate remarked in his speech that it was the first occasion upon which the Indian delegation to an Imperial Conference had not been led by the Secretary of State. It should be noted that Southern Rhodesia was represented at the Conference. The Irish Free State, although a member of the Conference, did not conclude any agreements.
[6]'This kind of negotiation has been a sad disillusion for Neville' , wrote Swinton in a private letter. 'He looked forward to the prospect of planning the culmination of a life's work with sympathetic and willing partners and Bennett has treated him like a trickster.' Cross, *Lord Swinton* (Oxford, Clarendon, 1982), p. 107.
[7]On distress in Canada in the 1930s see the selection of letters received by Bennett in L.M. Grayson and M. Bliss (ed.), *The Wretched of Canada* (Toronto, 1971). On Bennett, see the somewhat cursory biography by E. Watkins, *R.B. Bennett* (London, 1963).
[8]Lord Beaverbrook, *Friends: Sixty Years of Intimate Personal Relations with R.B. Bennett* (London, Heinemann, 1959), p. 64.

like Australia suddenly got up and went away, it would wreck the entire Conference if not the Empire.' Bruce's bullying of New Zealand to reduce its share of the British market for lamb also failed to contribute to the harmony of the proceedings.[9] Yet there were good reasons for the apparent intransigence of the Dominion representatives. During the period of expansion in the 1920s Australia in particular had run up considerable debts: the Dominions now had to meet them at a time when the prices for their products had fallen very heavily.

Although there was much talk of the Empire giving a lead to the revival of world trade, the effect of the bargains reached at Ottawa was to raise barriers rather than to lower them. Preferences for British exports to the Dominions were generally given by raising further duties against foreign goods rather than bringing down the duties on British goods, thus maintaining protection for domestic producers. In return, Britain agreed to impose new duties or raise existing ones on a whole range of foodstuffs, including wheat, dairy produce and fruit, with free entry for Dominion products. The free traders' election triumphs of 1906 and 1923 were thus reversed. It remained to be seen what compensation there would be for Britain in the right of audience at the Australian and Canadian tariff boards now given to British manufacturers.

The demise of the Empire Marketing Board and other results of the Ottawa Conference

In other respects the Ottawa Conference was unconstructive. The British government offered to keep the Empire Marketing Board in being if the Dominions would contribute to the cost, but while New Zealand was willing, Bruce pointed out that the British government had not fulfilled their undertakings and that there was no reason for the Dominions to contribute. Since Canada, South Africa and Ireland were already on record as unenthusiastic, it is not surprising that the British were willing to see the Board disappear. It was unfavourably reported upon by a Committee on Economic Consultation and Cooperation set up at Ottawa, and was dissolved on 30 September 1933. Some forms of collaborative action in scientific research

[9]Edwards, *Bruce of Melbourne*, 209 ff, 213 ff. Bruce had been appointed Resident Minister in London in 1932, and became High Commissioner in 1933.

continued under other auspices, but to genuine imperialists, like Amery, the blow was a considerable one.[10]

The Colonies were not directly represented at Ottawa, but Cunliffe-Lister was present to look after their interests. In a number of cases the rules governing League of Nations Mandates or other international agreements, such as the Congo Basin treaties, prevented the imposition of preferences, but for the remainder Cunliffe-Lister secured the inclusion of colonial goods in all the agreements reached, subject to the approval of the colonial governments themselves. He was to claim that these agreements had saved the sugar industry in the West Indies, Mauritius and Fiji.[11]

Despite the efforts of the voluntary societies concerned with assisted emigration and of some British parlimentarians to get the subject considered at Ottawa, emigration did not figure on the agenda. And though the Empire Settlement Act was renewed in a revised form in 1937, state-aided passages were not revived and the doors of the Dominions were not reopened.[12] A leading Australian historian has argued that the relatively low level of population achieved by Australia at the time of the First World War had been the result of a deliberate choice by the Australian electorate to limit any assistance to immigrants to compensate them for the greater expense of moving as against the journey to North America, which was the destination of most of those who left Britain. By so doing, the Australians preserved their own standard of living, buttressed by a powerful trade union movement, but stored up weaknesses for the future.[13] In general, the 1930s saw an increasing accent in Australia on its own immediate economic and defence needs, at the expense of the wider imperial view.

The expansion of Japan on the Asian mainland, beginning with the acquisition of Manchuria in 1931, provided a new challenge to the Commonwealth in the economic field as well as in respect of security. Japan was to show that with sufficient drive and ruthlessness it was possible to model an imperial economy to satisfy the needs of the home country; to the development of Taiwan as a source of foodstuffs and the investment already taking place in Korea was added

[10]Leo Amery diary, entries for 27 July 1933, 31 January 1934.
[11]Cross, Lord Swinton, p. 108.
[12]1 Edw. 8 and 1 Geo. 6, c.18, An Act to amend the Empire Settlement Act of 1922 (19 March 1937); Reese, History of the Royal Commonwealth Society, pp. 166 – 7.
[13]Geoffrey Blainey, The Tyranny of Distance (Melbourne, 1967), p. 107.

investment in Manchuria (Manchukuo as it came to be called) and subsequently in north east China.[14] For the time being attention was concentrated on the extent to which the Japanese military action was a new blow to the post-war settlement and to the primacy of international law under the League of Nations, and on the problems this posed for British naval policy. Where Japan worried the makers of economic policy was in the competitiveness of its exports; the penetration of the Indian market by Japanese textiles had already been a cause for concern. Yet when it became a question of considering the imposition of sanctions against Japan, the Secretary of State was obliged to point out that India would be the loser since her exports to Japan (including Burma's) were double the value of her imports from that country.[15] There was also worry at the loss of textile markets in the Colonies, where Japan was seeking new outlets to compensate for China's boycott. Here the government had to go warily because of treaty commitments, the unwillingness of the Foreign Office to aggravate relations with Japan, and above all the fact that the colonies themselves could not be expected to welcome measures that would raise the price of their imports. Nevertheless, in 1934 quotas were imposed in a number of colonies, and Lancashire's markets thereby extended.[16]

What is curious about the Ottawa Conference and its sequel is that while, on the face of it, the measures taken were not far-reaching, there was in fact a shift towards inter-imperial trade on a quite considerable scale. Between 1929 and 1935 the trade of British countries with each other as a percentage of their total trade increased from 40.2 per cent to 46.9 per cent.[17] Nor did the process stop there. In 1935 – 9 the Empire accounted for nearly half of Britain's exports and about 40 per cent of her imports.[18] To some extent preferences must have accounted for the shift. Only 7 per cent of U.K. imports from the Empire had enjoyed preferences in 1929: by 1937 the figure

[14]W.J. Mommsen and J. Osterhammel (eds), *Imperialism and After: continuities and discontinuities* (London, 1986), pp. 252-3.
[15]Cabinet Committee on the Far East, meeting of 8 March 1932, in PRO CAB 27/482. In 1933 India denounced the Indo-Japanese commercial convention of 1904: Drummond, *British Economic Policy and the Empire*, 132 ff.
[16]Cross, *Lord Swinton*, 114 – 5. It has been argued that the inhabitants of the West African colonies lost more through being denied cheap Japanese textiles (which took over the East African market) than they gained through imperial preference: C.C. Wrigley in *The Cambridge History of Africa*, vol. 7 (Cambridge, 1986), p. 114.
[17]Memo E(B)(37)6, in PRO CAB 32/127.
[18]B. Porter, *Britain, Europe and the World, 1850–1982* (London, 1983), pp. 94 – 5.

was between 60 and 61 per cent. In 1929 U.K. exports to the Empire enjoyed preferences in respect of between 35 and 36 per cent of the total. In 1937 this had risen to 56 per cent. Clearly, however, other elements entered into the reckoning.[19] The growth of a sterling area out of the countries in the Empire that used London as a clearing-house for their international trade was one of them. And the ending of the gold standard and the currency controls so widely introduced in the 1930s must have added to its importance. India's decision in 1931 to align the rupee with sterling is significant in this connection.

What is abundantly clear is that Ottawa was not regarded as a terminus for inter-imperial negotiations, but was at the same time not universally acceptable as pointing the right way forward.[20] The hard core of free traders in the British cabinet resigned rather than accept the decisions reached, and the Liberal Party was once more in opposition. In Canada, from the very beginning Mackenzie King denounced what had been done. It is thus not surprising that the British cabinet was wary of giving critics a forum and decided against holding another Imperial Conference in 1935, as had originally been suggested.[21] The ground had been tested by Malcolm MacDonald, the Under-Secretary in the Dominions Office, during a visit to Australia and New Zealand in 1934 – 5. He noted that Dominion producers feared that Britain was endeavouring to free herself from dependence on Dominion sources of food, and promoting only the interests of her own farmers. For political and defence reasons the stimulation of emigration was necessary, but it was difficult to make Dominions accept a policy of regulating agricultural exports while at the same time welcoming new agricultural workers.[22] A particular issue had been the failure to agree with the Australians on further meat quotas to expand their imports into the U.K. at the expense of the Argentine. Here the British ministers were at pains to stress the positive value of good trading relations with foreign countries as well as with the Dominions. British prosperity depended upon international trade, and the Empire as a

[19]The Economist Intelligence Unit, *Britain, the Commonwealth and European Free Trade* (London, 1958).
[20]One result of Ottawa was that the Dominions Office acquired an economic department. For a general survey of Ottawa and its sequels from the Dominions Office point of view, see Garner, *The Commonwealth Office*, pp. 99 – 100.
[21]Meetings, 18 and 25 April 1934, in PRO CAB 23/79.
[22]Notes by Malcolm MacDonald on 1934 – 5 trip to Australia and New Zealand, January 1935, in University of Newcastle upon Tyne, Runciman Papers, R.3/16, 1935.

whole had an interest in seeing it maintained.[23] Such was not the language of imperialism but of Adam Smith.

The aftermath of Ottawa: a tendency towards imperial disunity

The network of special arrangements for agricultural products hammered out at Ottawa were the subject of further negotiations, which did nothing to enhance imperial harmony.[24] External attempts to secure modifications of the policy of preference were also a factor in the situation. Although no further specifically economic conferences were held, the Dominion Prime Ministers did meet in London in May 1935 on the occasion of the jubliee of George V, and Robert Menzies*, the Australian minister for industry, made it known to the gathering that Japan had suggested, as a way of remedying its adverse balance with Australia, that Australia should end its Commonwealth preferences. No such suggestion had been made to Canada.[25]

By 1937 the strains upon the Ottawa system were even more visible. At a meeting of principal delegates to that year's Imperial Conference, Lyons* pointed out the continued importance to all parts of the Empire of its trade with foreign countries. Of the total trade of the Empire in 1935, 30.4 per cent had been inter-imperial and 69.6 per cent foreign. Australia had an unfavourable balance with the rest of the Empire and with the United States, but a favourable one with Japan and continental Europe. For these reasons, Australia would welcome greater freedom of trade over a considerable range, while recognising the vital importance of imperial preference to certain Australian products. The objective of an Empire trading policy should be an improvement in world trade. N.C. Havenga, speaking for South Africa, argued that the idea of imperial self-sufficiency that had been aimed for at Ottawa did not pay, and that inter-imperial trade should be seen as part of world trade, and not as an end in itself.[26]

[23]Committee on Economic Discussions with Australian Ministers, E.D.A.35, in PRO CAB 32/124.

[24]See Drummond, *Imperial Economic Policy*, chs 7 and 8.

[25]Meeting of 7 May 1935, in PRO CAB 32/125. The Ministers' meeting had been preceded by two months of unsuccessful negotiations with an Australian delegation on the still vexed issue of meat supplies, where Australia was demanding further restrictions on Argentinian imports into the U.K.: PRO CAB 32/124.

[26]Meeting of 27 May 1937, in PRO CAB 32/128. For the official summary of these proceedings, see Cmd 5482 (1937), cited in Mansergh, *Documents and Speeches*, vol. 1, pp. 133 – 4.

On the other hand, with reference to a League of Nations inquiry about raw materials and the likely demand for an open door policy in colonial territories, the President of the Board of Trade, Oliver Stanley, (who had succeeded Runciman when Chamberlain replaced Baldwin in May 1937), was worried about any British statement which might suggest the abandonment of imperial preference, and felt that there were widespread suspicions of the government's intentions in this respect, both at home and overseas. Readiness to remove preferences in the interests of world economic appeasement must be conditional upon Dominion assent. The Dominions Secretary, Thomas, was however of the opinion that the Dominion Prime Ministers might agree in principle to action along these lines.[27]

The 1935 meeting had been the last at which Bennett represented Canada. In October 1935 Mackenzie King returned to the office of Prime Minister, which he was to hold for another thirteen years. His own instincts had been against Ottawa: 'What I feel about the Conference is that it was the wrong method – the bargaining – that the aim of greater freedom of trade was achieved in very small measure and that there is a lot of humbug about the whole business, a ballyhoo for nothing with jingo emotionalism in evidence above all else.' And he gradually made his opposition an open one. In the parliamentary debate on ratifying the Treaties, he spoke of the Conference as 'a Tory conspiracy' to create a 'protectionist Zollverein'. King had not shifted from the Liberal viewpoint that Canada's economic interests were best served by agreements with the United States, and in the 1935 election campaign he had undertaken to put such an agreement at the top of his agenda. He pushed the negotiations along soon after taking office, and by 15 November the agreement was ready for signature at Washington.[28]

At the 1937 Conference, King was agreeably surprised to find Chamberlain ready to contemplate an Anglo-American trade agreement as part of world economic appeasement, even though Chamberlain's immediate purpose might be to persuade the Dominions to give up some of their preferences in the British market. By now the issue of economic appeasement and the wider issue of political appeasement in general were linked in King's mind, as they were in the minds of his British hosts.[29]

[27]Meeting of Cabinet foreign policy committee, 11 June 1937: PRO CAB 27/622.
[28]Mackenzie King diary entry, 31 August 1932, quoted in H. Blair Neatby, *William Lyon Mackenzie King*, vol. 3 (Toronto, Methuen, 1976), p. 23; ibid., p. 26.
[29]Ibid., pp. 142 – 6.

The 'New Deal' and its imperial repercussions

It was not, however, a shift in British official opinion alone that had taken place since Ottawa. Once the Roosevelt administration had got its New Deal functioning, after refusing to tie its hands by accepting the stabilisation of currencies at the 1933 World Economic Conference, it began to look outwards as well as inwards, and to seek for wider markets for American goods. Roosevelt's Secretary of State, Cordell Hull, and his Under-Secretary, Sumner Welles, began a persistent campaign against imperial preference with an attempt to make its abandonment the price of any Anglo-American economic agreement. This American attitude, which was to continue into the war and postwar years, was not merely an expression of the standard free trade doctrine; it was also given weight by the strong streak of anti-imperialism and anti-colonialism prevalent among Americans, particularly in the groups making up Roosevelt's Democratic Party.[30] In the darkening world of the late 1930s it was not something that a British government could easily ignore, especially in the light of the Canadian attitude. In a letter to President Roosevelt early in 1938, Runciman told him that when he had handed over the Board of Trade to Oliver Stanley he had urged him to pursue two objectives, a reasonable attitude to Dominion affairs and better trade relations with the United States.[31] As a private memorandum of Runciman's makes clear, one telling reason for seeking agreement with the U.S. was Germany's new pressure for economic expansion in central and southern Europe and in the Near East:

> It must be clear that if we and France do not work with the United States, the Washington Government will be forced to conclude a Trade Pact with Germany as a matter of necessity. Can we evolve a scheme that means the co-operation of Great Britain and the British Empire, the United States and France ... to help the Central, Southern European, and Near East States to develop their economic wealth, restore prosperity to their people, and act together by the abolition of trade and customs barriers, but all in collaboration with Germany, and not against her?

[30]For the impact of these policies on the imperialist wing of British politics, see Leo Amery, *My Political Life*, vol. III (London, 1955), pp. 203 – 4, 385.
[31]Runciman to Roosevelt, 18 February 1938: Runciman Papers, R3/38, 1938.

And since Germany was backing Japanese economic expansion, a settlement with Germany would help the trading interests of Britain, the United States and France in the Far East.[32] While the subject of the return of the German ex-colonies is more properly seen in the context of political appeasement, it was not unconnected with economic thinking along these lines.

Conversations looking towards an Anglo-American agreement had in fact begun in January 1938, and continued throughout the year, with accompanying consultations with the Dominions.[33] An agreement was reached on 17 November, lowering or limiting tariffs on both sides on a large number of commodities, and the White Paper announcing the agreement emphasised the readiness of the Dominions 'to facilitate the conclusion of this Agreement by consenting to such modifications of their rights under existing Trade Agreements as were necessary to enable it to be concluded.'[34] An agreement between the United States and Canada signed on the same day and one between Britain and Canada also involved the modification of some of the preferential positions enjoyed by British exporters in Canada.[35] Although the impact of these agreements was not to be fully realised in the difficult conditions prevailing as a result of the advent of war less than a year later, they can be interpreted as the beginning of a retreat from Ottawa and the preferential system, despite the fact that the system had actually been added to when the long drawn out Anglo-Irish economic conflict, which had lasted since 1932, was brought to an end by the agreement of 25 April 1938.[36]

Yet the retreat from imperial preference, and the various bilateral trading agreements which Britain entered into with foreign countries during the 1930s, did not mean either that the idea of the Empire as a meaningful economic unit had been wholly abandoned, nor that special economic relationships within it had ceased to exist. Currency questions remained one such area, and with the pressure for capital upon the London market which was the consequence of British rearmament, discrimination in favour of Dominion loans was of some importance to Dominion economies.[37]

[32]Memorandum by Runciman, 23 October 1938: ibid., R2/56, 1938.
[33]For the memorandum of conclusions of the trade discussions between the United Kingdom and Australia, see Cmd 5805 (20 July 1938), in Mansergh, op. cit., vol. 1, pp. 135 – 6.
[34]Cmd 5882 (1938).
[35]Cmd 5892 (1938).
[36]Cmd 5728 (1938).
[37]Drummond, *British Economic Policy and the Empire*, pp. 119-20.

196

The Indian experience was linked to the constitutional debates of the period and the question of the financial viability of a self-governing India. Ottawa produced a series of reciprocal preferences between Britain and India and, following discussions between the commercial interests involved on both sides, these were added to by a cotton agreement in 1933 and a steel agreement in 1934. It was not however the case that all Indian political opinion was convinced that imperial preferences were of direct benefit to India, whose autonomy in this field had been tacitly accepted by the British government early in 1932.[38] Thus although the Ottawa agreement was ratified by the Central Legislative Assembly in November 1932, the 1935 Supplementary Agreement, embodying the arrangements on iron and steel and cotton for the period of the Ottawa agreement, was rejected by the Central Legislative Assembly; and in 1936 this body also demanded that the Ottawa Agreement itself be renounced. Negotiations for a new arrangement now began, and in 1939 a new Anglo-Indian trade agreement was signed. The bill to implement this agreement was thrown out by the Assembly, but the Viceroy used his powers of certification to pass it. The British government had thus secured by negotiation favourable treatment for British exports to India, but was also constrained to see that India kept her market in Britain in order to earn the foreign currency without which she could not provide the remittances needed by the Indian government to meet its obligations, with a consequent threat to the rupee.[39]

The impact of the depression and the measures taken to meet it had different effects upon different parts of the colonial empire, and policies towards the various dependencies were affected by considerations arising from the attention being paid to sources of raw materials likely to be important as rearmament got going.[40] But in many cases it was not so much a question of providing markets for colonial produce as of finance for the development of colonial economies, and this in turn raised in an acute form the whole question of their

[38]One reason advanced against holding an Imperial Economic Conference in 1934 was the time needed to allow interests in India supporting the Ottawa Agreements to have time to grow: cabinet meetings, 18 and 25 April 1934, in PRO CAB 23/79.

[39]Tomlinson, *The Political Economy of the Raj*, pp. 131 – 5.

[40]In 1930 the cabinet were discussing the possible consequences of the recent discoveries of copper in Northern Rhodesia and the possibility of this enabling Britain to escape from the American domination of the world copper market. It was proposed that Rhodesian copper should not be exported outside the Empire. Meeting of 7 May 1930, PRO CAB 23/64.

imperial role, and of the complicated issues that this presented to the United Kingdom government.

The difficulties inherent in mobilising colonial resources were increased by the fact that the first impulse of the United Kingdom authorities had been to demand yet again even more attention to economy by the colonial administrations. Such policies not merely impeded such development and welfare projects as they might be entertaining, but also led to the shedding of personnel – a process which fell most heavily in some cases upon locally recruited officers, thus adding to the ranks of the disaffected. Changes in the structure of marketing as openings for exports became tighter could also alter the balance between local producers and traders and the main United Kingdom companies, to the benefit, it has been argued, of the latter in West Africa, since they were better able to influence government policy.[41]

[41]C.C. Dorward in *The Cambridge History of Africa*, vol. 7, pp. 443 – 4.

Chapter 9

TRUSTEESHIP, INDIRECT RULE
AND COLONIAL DEVELOPMENT

A pattern of diversity

The most obvious fact about British policy in relation to those territories for which the Colonial Office was responsible was that it could hardly be said to exist. The territories themselves – crown colonies, protectorates, mandates, and lesser islands and enclaves – were so varied in size and population and in the level of economic, social and cultural development to which they had attained, that no system that could be designed for some of them would not be wholly unsuitable for others. In this the dependencies reflected the very varied circumstances of their original acquisition and the different degrees of importance attached to them from an economic or strategic perspective. In contrast to the Indian Empire, they were not thought of in terms of future self-government, at however distant a date, nor (except temporarily in regard to the German colonial claims) was the idea of parting with any of them seriously entertained. They were territories subject to the sovereignty of the British Crown in Parliament and had to be governed in some fashion according to the constitutional precedents and available administrative machinery.

When in 1938 Lord Hailey, a former Indian governor of high repute, came to summarise the findings of his survey of sub-Saharan Africa, he wrote in terms applicable to the Asian, Caribbean and Pacific territories as well:

> The accepted policy may be said to have for its objective the creation of institutions designed to assist each unit to achieve the highest social and material advancement which its own peculiar circumstances permit. It is implicit in this policy, that the character of the political or cultural institutions to be adopted must be related to the capacity of each unit for development rather than to any

199

preconceived theory of the value of the institutions of European civilisation; it follows again that on the material side, while every effort should be made to increase the contribution which each unit can make to the commercial or military resources of the Empire, this object cannot be allowed to override the primary considerations previously mentioned. But these views constitute a philosophy rather than a policy.[1]

In such circumstances, and with an underlying philosophy of this kind, it is not surprising that the British preference for the maximum devolution of authority should have held sway. For most of the time in most of the dependencies, it was the local governor and his officials who made the decisions, taking into account local opinion through such traditional or representative institutions as might exist. It was only when something went wrong – discontent bred of economic deprivation, or political unrest on the part of settlers or indigenous groups – that London was called upon to exercise its ultimate authority, either through direct action on the part of the Secretary of State, or through the appointment of a Commission to inquire, report and advise.

In these major respects the position after 1921 did not much differ from that prevailing earlier. Despite the injection of new demands upon colonial resources and the acquisition of new experiences by some elements in the colonial populations, and the heavy lossses, mainly through disease originating from the East African campaign, the first world war played a less important part in colonial history than it did in that of the Dominions or the Indian Empire.[2] It was the philosophy discerned by Hailey as governing British administration that had already been given its expression in Lord Lugard's *The Dual Mandate in British Tropical Africa*, completed in 1921 and based on his experiences in Uganda from 1890 to 1894 and in Nigeria from 1898 to 1906 and from 1912 to 1918. It supported imperial rule as offering economic advantages to both Europe and Africa, as well as the benefit to Africans of an apprenticeship to European civilisation. It must, in his words, be 'the aim and desire of civilised administration to fulfil

---

[1] Lord Hailey, *An African Survey* (London, Royal Institute of International Affairs, 1938), p. 247.
[2] For the devastating effects of the war in East Africa upon human (and animal) life, see A. Roberts (ed.), *The Cambridge History of Africa*, vol. 7 (Cambridge, 1986), 667 ff. The war itself has been magisterially treated in fiction in William Boyd, *An Ice-Cream War* (London, 1982).

this dual mandate'.[3] In Lugard's conception this meant economic development which at the same time should protect the indigenous peoples against direct exploitation by European capital, and it was in 'indirect rule', the maximum use of local institutions and hierarchies, that he saw the best method of affording such protection. In Lugard's formulation European rulers had a duty akin to trusteeship towards the long-term interests of the peoples over whom they ruled, as distinct from the largely predatory and exploitative impulses which had often been responsible for the original contacts.[4] Since Lugard was from 1922 to 1936 a member of the Permanent Mandates Commission of the League of Nations, he had ample opportunity to develop the implementation of these views for a variety of territories.[5]

In dealing with such issues as were brought before them, the Secretaries of State in the inter-war period were subject to a number of influences. First among them was their own character and presuppositions. Only Amery can be said to have had a positive policy of development based upon the priorities of the economic needs of the Empire seen as a system. Others either accepted the ideas current in their own political milieu, or were relatively passive recipients of official advice, in an office which, particularly after its responsibilities for Dominion matters came to an end, did not rank high among the objects of political ambition and could be seen as a stepping-stone to higher things.

It was not the case that Parliament as such was an important vehicle for ideas on colonial subjects; only a crisis could stimulate concern, and then rarely in any sustained way.[6] The comparison with interest in things Indian is very marked. What was more important was what in the political science jargon of a later date would be styled 'interest groups' or 'pressure groups'.[7] One such was of course firms with a

[3] Lord Lugard, *The Dual Mandate in British Tropical Africa* (London, 1922), p. 617.
[4] On the notion of trusteeship see Kenneth Robinson, *The Dilemmas of Trusteeship* (London, 1965).
[5] Lugard's important role in retirement is dealt with all too summarily in vol. 2 of Margery Perham, *Lugard* (London, 1960). It is worth noting, for the continuity of thought in this area, that the sympathetic notice of Lugard in the *Dictionary of National Biography* is by Lord Hailey.
[6] It has been suggested that not more than fifteen or twenty M.P.s had any first-hand knowledge of any colony: Sir C. Ponsonby, *Ponsonby Remembers* (Oxford, 1965), p. 115. Ponsonby was a Conservative M.P., 1935 – 50. Speaking on the 1937 colonial estimates, Grigg pointed out that the House was very empty because it was 'Derby Day'. H.C. *Deb.*, 2 June 1937. But the colonial estimates would not have been put down for 'Derby Day' if there had been widespread interest.
[7] Where Colonial Secretaries appeared to be acting at the behest of political forces, colonial officials were apt to be impatient: 'It is dangerous that political preconceptions at home, which must frequently change, should so strongly colour central judgement of local advice and that

direct interest in colonial production and trade, and with views as to the ways in which government policy could best conduce to the profitability of their enterprises. A second element enjoying some political access, particularly to Conservative governments, were the 'white settlers' of East Africa and the Rhodesias. To them, over-sensitivity to indigenous interests or Indian susceptibilities were unwelcome obstacles to the creation of new self-governing entities inspired by the Dominion model.

Of greater significance in the upshot were those groups and organisations which espoused the cause of the indigenous peoples themselves.[8] Such groups had originally had a considerable missionary element, as exemplified in the work of J.H. Harris and the London Anti-Slavery Society. But in their approach there was an element of ambiguity, since although Harris and his associates encouraged Africans to seek higher education in England, as Indians were already doing, they did not, in accordance with the directives of cultural pluralism, see African society developing along European lines. They were therefore advocates of a degree of segregation between the races, and of trusteeship as a vehicle for the preservation of African cultures. In this respect, both Harris and E.D. Morel, whose fame derived from his exposure of the cruelties perpetrated upon the native tribes by King Leopold's agent in the Congo, were in fact segregationists. The policies of colonial governments, where such thinking was powerful, emphasised in particular practical education, giving prominence to agricultural skills on the model of the Tuskegee Institute in Alabama.

The Empire, Commonwealth and Race

By the 1920s such attitudes were having to compete with more directly anti-imperialist doctrines, whether deriving from Marxist or quasi-Marxist analysis, or from humanitarian revulsion at some aspects of colonial rule, as in the case of Leonard Woolf, who played a

they should lead to censure and over-ruling of local government even in matters where local knowledge and experience should be supreme.' Grigg to Passfield, 25 January 1930, Grigg Papers.

[8] For a discussion of groups and prominent individuals with a particular interest in Africa, see Penelope Hetherington, *British Paternalism and Africa, 1920–1940* (London, 1974).

prominent role in influencing Labour party policies in this field.[9] Such overt hostility to the idea of empire did not however exercise a major role in moulding policy in this period. The ending of indentured labour in all colonies on 1 January 1920 removed one powerful object of criticism. Instead there was some general acceptance over a wide spectrum of British politics that the healing influence of British institutions would remove the salience of racial factors in colonial politics. The Commonwealth could be interpreted as an idea transcending racial divisions. The principal theorist of the Commonwealth, Lionel Curtis, unlike thinkers of an earlier generation, saw British superiority in terms of institutions, not of race. As a recent work approaching these issues from this point of view points out,

> The nineteenth century debate on imperial race relations was thus in considerable measure perpetuated within the Commonwealth tradition of political discourse. 'The Commonwealth' as an ideal became linked with a new middle position in political debate between the advocates of global racial segregation on the one hand and the radical critics of imperialism on the other. The Commonwealth school imbibed some of the teachings of the cultural relativists and extended them on the imperial plane into a set of pragmatic policies that, as far as possible, sought mediation and brokerage between rival schools of colonial policy at the local level.[10]

Yet one must remember that in this period even liberal circles did not betray the peculiar sensitivity to colour-linked discrimination that was to become so important for a later generation. After all, Smuts was, along with Balfour, the accredited exponent of the Commonwealth ideal.[11]

The element of racial feeling embodied in British policy was not necessarily connected with extreme notions of the hierarchy of races. If it were accepted that Africans were 'different', then one could argue

[9] For the development of Labour Party attitudes to colonial questions see P.S. Gupta, *Imperialism and the British Labour Movement, 1914–1964* (London, 1975), 126 ff.
[10] P.B. Rich, *Race and Empire in British Politics* (Cambridge University Press, 1986), p. 50.
[11] Smuts' Rhodes Memorial Lectures in 1929, published in *Africa and some World Problems* (Oxford, 1930), had put the case for promoting white settlement in East and Central Africa. His views were strongly attacked by J.H. Oldham, the leading figure in that section of the missionary world concerned with colonial policy. See J.H. Oldham, *White and Black in Africa* (London, 1930). For an American view of the African scene in the 1920s, see R.L. Buell, *The Native Problem in Africa*, 2 vols (New York, 1928).

that progress towards representative government on western lines was inherently unsuitable to them, and that 'indirect rule' was a better shelter for what African culture had to offer. Because of the commitment to this belief, it could lead to the artificial creation of 'traditional authorities', even when these had not existed or had disappeared in the face of intrusions from the outside world. In West Africa it meant that fewer educated Africans were used in administration than had been used in the nineteenth century, when British rule was largely confined to the more developed coastal enclaves. Elsewhere, as in the Sudan, it meant that developments in education were looked at with suspicion, since no use could be made of educated Africans except as subordinates of British officals, a circumstance likely to lead, as it did, to political agitation.

Africa also provided a test of the assumptions of colonial rule for two other interconnected reasons. The development of Africa's resources, whether for the benefit of its own peoples, of settler communities or of foreign investors, demanded work patterns that were unfamiliar to traditional societies where men had been seen as warriors rather than wage earners. Much colonial legislation (and colonial taxation) was directed towards supplying labour, whether for public or private purposes. What was therefore being attempted was to apply traditional schemes of governance to societies undergoing economic and social change at a very rapid rate; a rate determined not by local decision-makers but by movements in world prices to which there was no easy response. In the second place, although the demand for African products in the inter-war years was less than had been assumed by protagonists of the dual mandate, mining, and in particular gold and copper, did demand and occupy an increasing labour-force, usually larger than the immediate population could supply. The same could be true of plantation crops and their seasonal needs. Africa was thus throughout the period the scene of large-scale migrations of labour, sometimes permanent, sometimes temporary as in the mining camps; migrations that took no account of the borders between colonial territories or even of those between the several imperial sovereignties. While labour migration had been and still was a feature of the colonial world in general, it was elsewhere mainly a question of movement overseas; Africa was unique in the size of the landmass involved. What it had in common with other areas was the degree of urbanisation to which such migration tended to give rise, and the problems of social and administrative organisation that faced governments whose presuppositions were basically agrarian. Labour legislation thus became a focus for colonial reformers when the depression accentuated the problems faced by the colonial administrations, with trade unions coming in some instances to act as surrogates for absent possibilities of political expression.[12]

It is worth noting that while much attention was focused on Africa, where racial conflict could be seen in terms of the rival interests of settlers and natives, over much of the colonial empire in South East Asia, in the Caribbean and in the Pacific the most important conflicts were those between different elements in their non-white population, and where the dilemma of trusteeship might be whether to protect minorities or the weaker elements in general against the more powerful local interests, and run the risk of being accused of dividing in order to rule, or alternatively to slacken the reins and let matters take their course. In both situations the opinions of the governors and even of other local officials might easily determine what was decided at the centre. Just as ambassadors notoriously identify themselves with the countries to which they are accredited, so colonial civil servants often ended up as advocates of the nationality or tribe to which they happened to be assigned.

Mindful of the difficulties of sustaining a colonial role, there were voices in the 1920s suggesting that some of the problems could be minimised and possible future conflicts avoided by giving a greater co-ordinating power to the League of Nations, which was formally confined to the problems of the mandated territories. For Amery this suggestion was anathema both when put forward in 1926 and when revived by Sir Edward Hilton Young (later Lord Kennet) in 1928. 'It is questionable', concluded a meeting of officials on 16 July 1928, 'whether the time is ripe for co-operation with other African Powers on a large scale.' Instead, 'it would be a preferable policy to concentrate on the consolidation of the British territories in Tropical Africa and the devising of satisfactory machinery for their government on as uniform lines as possible.'[13]

---

[12] These issues are explored in A.D. Roberts (ed.), *The Cambridge History of Africa*, vol. 7 (London, 1986), particularly in the editor's introduction and his own ch. 1, 'The Imperial Mind', and in ch. 2, by C.C. Wrigley, 'Aspects of Economic History'. The chapters dealing with individual territories also pay much attention to these questions.

[13] PRO CO 822/9/8, 'Memorandum on African Administration'.

Quite apart from the diversity of national commercial interests involved, there was also the fact that the other colonial empires, while obviously facing similar problems on the ground, confronted them with different philosophies. As Hailey pointed out in 1938, the French provided a clear contrast with prevailing British attitudes. France had always followed the line, which only a few British statesmen or thinkers had advocated, of treating her entire empire as a single economic unit held together by protectionist policies, except where debarred by international agreements or the provisions of the mandates. Her policy of association, which appeared to bear a resemblance to indirect rule in that it was directed to safeguarding indigenous institutions, was in fact very different, since it was based on the assimilation of selected elites through French education and their receiving a voice in government, not through locally elected bodies but through representation in the national French Parliament. Economic development was intended to be on a planned basis and to be encouraged, resources permitting, by a government-funded infrastructure as well as by protective tariffs.[14]

The view that the colonial empire must be seen in the context of the Commonwealth raised the question as to how its interests were to be represented in the counsels of the Commonwealth after the separation between the Dominions and Colonial offices. The Colonial Secretary was treated as a member of the 1930 Imperial Conference only in respect of the economic questions discussed. In 1932 the Colonial Secretary was a full member of the Ottawa Conference. The subject was discussed before the 1937 Conference, when Baldwin suggested that, to keep down the numbers of the British delegation, the Colonial Secretary should not be a member, but invited to all meetings except those dealing with constitutional questions. Chamberlain, shortly to succeed Baldwin as Prime Minister, argued that the Colonial Secretary should be a full member, pointing to the importance of the colonies to the network of preferences agreed at Ottawa, even though he agreed that 'the Colonial Empire could not be treated as a unit'. The preferences gave the Dominions an interest in the colonies which could be said to include matters of foreign policy

[14] Hailey, *An African Survey*, pp. 138 – 40. By 1928, under the influence of Woolf's Advisory Committee on International Questions, the Labour Party was advocating that the principle of trusteeship under League supervision should be applied to all British colonies in tropical Africa.

and defence. A week later the cabinet agreed to the Colonial Secretary being a full member.[15]

The financial control of the colonies

Although the Colonial Secretary was recognised as the representative of the colonial empire, the Colonial Office was not independent of other Whitehall departments. If there was trouble that could not be handled locally, it would be necessary to look to the service departments.[16] More continuous was the supervisory role of the Treasury. The degree of control varied with the financial situation of the territories. Since it was an abiding tenet of the system that colonies should normally pay for themselves, it was when a colony fell short of this desirable objective and required a 'grant-in-aid' that Treasury control was at its most rigorous. In the 1920s not many colonies required such support, but in the depression of the 1930s the number increased, rising from seven to fifteen between 1932 and 1936. In these cases Treasury control was similar to that exercised over home departments, and extended to the details of expenditure even when the bulk was financed out of the colony's own revenues and not from grants-in-aid or loans, which had largely replaced grants.[17] In 1931 advantage was taken of the financial crisis by the Permanent Secretary to the Treasury, Sir Warren Fisher, to extend a high degree of control to all colonies, whether in deficit or not, since it could not be certain otherwise that proper provision was being made to cover future contingencies when they might be asking the British taxpayer to bail them out. It is clear that recent experience had made the Treasury highly suspicious of forward-looking policies of development in the colonies.[18]

[15] Cabinet meetings, 10 and 17 March 1937, PRO CAB 23/87.

[16] When troops were required for Palestine in 1929, the private secretary to the Secretary of State for War, Tom Shaw, told General Temperley that, being a pacifist, he did not want anything to do with war or military operations. He just needed to know how many troops were being moved so as to tell the cabinet. David Carlton, *MacDonald v. Henderson* (London, 1970), 18.

[17] Types of control were spelled out in Colonial Office Misc. Paper no. 460, 8 January 1936, PRO T161/826/S.36937/1.

[18] 'I am told privately that they (the Colonial Office) would even welcome the support of the Treasury in fighting the battle of financial prudence ... against profligate Ministers such as Mr Amery and governors such as Sir Edward Grigg. They realise that an enquiry into their financial administration in the past few years would show them up badly.' Minute by Mr Waterfield, 8 April 1931, PRO T161/493/S.36290.

It was not only that the Treasury distrusted particular ministers or governors; the competence in financial matters of the Colonial Office itself was suspect.[19] And this extended to the Colonial Service. When in 1935 the Colonial Office suggested that, on the Indian model, the role of the Treasurer in the larger colonies should be enhanced so as to make him the colony's financial adviser, doubts were expressed as to whether suitable people could be found from within the Colonial Service, and it was thought that they would have to come from either India or Britain. In this case the Colonial Office got its way, and the scheme went ahead in 1937.[20] As in the case of the service departments, and on a par with what was practice in respect of the home departments, the Treasury insisted on having its say not merely in respect of the financial implications of proposals, but even in respect of the policies embodied in them. In the case of grant-aided colonies, quite minor expenditures required specific sanction.[21] It was with this background in mind that the steady opposition to projects of colonial development sustained by the Treasury throughout the period can best be understood.

Whether the poor opinion seemingly held by the Treasury of the Colonial Office could be justified by any objective test must be doubtful. It was certainly not the view of its historian.[22] And during the 1920s and 1930s, largely thanks to the impetus given by Amery, it was changing very considerably in as far as its internal organisation was concerned. In addition to the organisation on a geographical basis, there was increasing emphasis on the provision of services, and in particular of scientific research, which would be of benefit to the whole empire, or at least to large parts of it. Forestry, medicine, agriculture, veterinary services, geology and mines were studied by committees, and measures taken to train the necessary personnel.[23] Since all of this activity was based in London or other British universities, the result was a greater degree of centralisation than Amery perhaps originally intended.

[19] 'There is not a glimmer of financial sense in the place and it is the lack of it which occasions the failure to frame proposals on financially acceptable lines.' Memorandum by Mr Upcott, March 1929, PRO T161/297/S.34608.
[20] Memorandum by Sir R. Hopkins, 1935, and Colonial Office to Treasury, PRO T161/757/S.37417.
[21] During the financial year 1928 – 9 Treasury approval was required for the construction of an arts and crafts school in Trans-Jordan (£P600), and of a gallows at £P35: Treasury to Colonial Office, 16 February 1929, PRO T161/122/S.9824/06/1.
[22] See Sir Charles Jeffries, *The Colonial Office* (London, 1956).
[23] For details see C. Jeffries, *The Colonial Empire and its Civil Service* (Cambridge, 1938).

The personnel of colonial administration

More important in the eyes of those who expected the colonial system to survive into a distant future were the changes in the organisation of the Colonial Service overseas. It had been the case that the services of the separate colonies were very much their own affair, even though recruitment was done by the Colonial Office. While there was nothing comparable to the high standards of academic performance required by the administrative class of the home or Indian civil services, the physically testing conditions under which many officers had to work and their need to act on their own initiative made the accent on 'fitness of character' an intelligible one. But with the growth, however restrained by financial considerations, of more active economic and social policies, both broader experience and greater specialisation might be deemed necessary. Here again the initiative was taken by Amery, who announced on 30 April 1929 the appointment of a committee under Sir Warren Fisher 'to consider the existing system of appointment in the Colonial Office and in the public service of Dependencies not possessing responsible government, and to make such recommendations as may be considered desirable.'[24] The Committee's Report recommended the establishment of a Personnel Division at the Colonial Office and of a Colonial Service Board as part of the recruitment process.

The recommendations were accepted by Amery's successor, and in 1930 it was announced that the Colonial Service would be unified. The progress towards this goal was one of stages. In 1932 the Colonial Administrative Service was formed and in 1933 a Colonial Legal Service, in 1934 a Colonial Medical Service, in 1935 Colonial Forestry, Agricultural and Veterinary Services, and in 1938 a Colonial Police Service. In 1938 surveying and mining and geological sciences were also put on a common footing, as well as the Postal and Customs Services. The rapidity and smoothness of the transition may be credited to a single remarkable civil servant, Sir Ralph Furse, who having served as assistant private secretary or principal private secretary to a succession of seven Colonial Secretaries from Lewis Harcourt to Passfield, was appointed in 1931 Director of Recruitment to the Colonial Office, a post which he was to hold until 1948.[25]

[24] H.C. *Deb.*, vol. 227, col 1419 – 20, 30 April 1929.
[25] See on Furse and his work R.Heussler, *Yesterday's Rulers: the Making of the British Colonial Service* (Syracuse, N.Y., 1963), and Furse's own memoirs, *Aucuparius, Recollections of a Recruiting Officer* (London, 1962).

In looking at the service in 1938, Hailey found its besetting weakness the fact that the District Officers, to whose recruitment so much care had been given and who were the backbone of the administration, were too much taken up with routine work in the absence of suitable subordinates, such as were recruited at home by both the French and the Belgians. While Africans were being educated for clerical positions, they were not being prepared for greater responsibilities: 'The British have had an instinctive mistrust of the use of subordinates recruited in Europe, while African subordinates of the requisite quality and number have not yet been available.' While he agreed that the use of Africans in intermediate or higher positions was often made difficult by considerations which impeded their mobility, he was clearly unhappy about the 'preference for the uneducated over the educated native ... so much more conspicuous in British than in French territories'. Calling attention to the importance of the Indian 'provincial services', which were by now mainly Indian, he felt there should be a way for the greater use of educated Africans in the Colonial Service.[26]

At the top of the official pyramid in each dependency and the recipient of the home government's instructions stood the governor. Governors might attain this rank through promotion within the Colonial Service in which they had served continuously, as was true of fifteen of the twenty-nine governors in 1939. Of the other fourteen, four had come to the post after a regular military career and five had at some time or other been regular soldiers; another five had seen active service in the first world war.[27] Suggestions for change had come from two quarters. In the 1920s, as part of the movement for greater imperial unity, it had been suggested that suitable colonial governors might be found in the Dominions. This did not find favour.[28] In 1937 Josiah Wedgwood, now a Labour member, suggested that M.P.s would make better governors than retired military men, and claimed that such appointments had been more common in the past. Similarly, Colonial Chief Justices should be chosen from among barrister M.P.s.[29]

The problems of colonial rule and the application of the idea of trusteeship were not matters only between the British government

[26] Hailey, *An African Survey*, pp. 256 – 9.
[27] *Colonial Office and Dominions Office List*, 1939.
[28] *My Dear P.M.: R.G. Casey's letters to S.M. Bruce, 1924-1929* (Canberra, 1980), p. 98.
[29] H.C. *Deb.*, vol. 324, cols 1071 – 3, 2 June 1937.

and the indigenous populations under its rule. With one exception the Dominions did not represent a serious challenge. The Pacific imperialisms of Australia and New Zealand had been satisfied, and their activities did not bring about any further clashes with the United Kingdom. But in Africa the situation was different. The claims of the Indians in East Africa and the need to consider Indian susceptibilities complicated the problem of reconciling settler and native interests. While the condominium of Britain and Egypt over the Sudan was the formal justification for Britain's presence in that territory, actual Egyptian intervention in the Sudan's affairs was kept at arm's length. But the connection of the Islamic population of the north with Egypt accentuated the difference between that part of the country and the tropical south with its pagan and Christian tribes, for whose protection the British deemed themselves responsible.

The most important challenge to British ideas came from the Union of South Africa which, having effectively absorbed German South-West Africa, was at the beginning of the period poised to extend its influence into the Rhodesias, to demand the fulfilment of the original undertaking of Britain in respect of handing over the three High Commission territories, and which had in its own view interests to safeguard even further afield.[30] Between a British government committed to the 'dual mandate' and a South African regime in which the Boer element with its white supremacist attitudes was increasingly in charge, common ground was difficult to find.[31] The fact that there were no further territorial changes before 1939 should not lead one to forget how fluid the situation seemed to be in the early post-war years. The degree to which South Africa pursued a specifically expansionist policy has been questioned, as has the degree of difference in emphasis between Smuts and Hertzog. Smuts, it has been pointed out, had advocated the system of mandates under the League of Nations as providing a cover for the future acquisition of the Portuguese territories, but he would have preferred the direct annexation of

[30] In 1910 the three territories, Bechuanaland, Basutoland and Swaziland, as well as Southern Rhodesia, were placed in the care of the Governor-General, who was also the British High Commissioner in South Africa. In 1931 the post of High Commissioner in the Union and High Commissioner for the territories was separated from that of Governor-General.

[31] The Afrikaner community was moving in the 1920s from its previous concern with 'anti-imperialism', i.e. opposition to British influence, to a primary concern with the racial issue in the modern sense. The replacement of Dutch by Afrikaans in the Constitution in 1925 may be taken as a landmark on the path to the new self-consciousness. See L.M. Thompson, *The Political Mythology of Apartheid* (New Haven, Conn., 1985), pp. 36 – 44.

German South-West Africa. Britain itself had important interests in Mozambique. So long as Smuts retained power, the British were favourable to Southern Rhodesia entering the Union, and Churchill was in favour of this solution in the Rhodesia referendum eventually held in November 1922.[32]

Against this, it has been argued that the main issue was not one of South Africa's desire for territorial expansion conflicting with Britain's commitment to trusteeship for the Africans, but of Britain's desire to retain a say in the affairs of the whole southern part of the continent, including the Union itself. Thus it has been claimed that most Afrikaner politicians did not want to annex Rhodesia, where the majority of settlers were English-speaking, but did want to make good their claims to the territories which both represented an internal challenge to their position and might help to solve the land-pressure from their Boer supporters.[33]

Where Southern Rhodesia was concerned, the issue was settled by local opinion. The Rhodesias had not proved attractive to British immigrants, and British settlers in Southern Rhodesia (and even more so in Northern Rhodesia) were anxious lest the immigration from South Africa of Boer farmers upset their supremacy, and so they voted against incorporation. Had the Constitution of the Union been a federal rather than a unitary one, things might have gone differently. The Southern Rhodesians were also against union with the North, which the Colonial Office saw as part of Black Africa, and which it was therefore harder to see as being allowed to develop in the direction of settler rule. Northern Rhodesia was also in balance between its southward links and those with East Africa, whose future was the most contested of all the African areas.

When Hertzog attained power in 1924 he at once took up the question of the transfer of the territories, which the British government resisted on the grounds that the opposition of their peoples was supported by opinion in Parliament. In 1928 – 30 some consideration was given to the partition of Bechuanaland between Southern Rhodesia and South Africa but, when this project was abandoned,

[32] R. Hyams, *Failure of South African Expansion, 1908–1948* (London, 1972), pp. 64 – 5.

[33] See M. Chanock, *Unconsummated Union – Britain, Rhodesia and South Africa* (Manchester, 1977). This work takes a quasi-Marxist standpoint, seeing a confrontation from 1910 between the 'haves', British and Afrikaner, and the 'have nots', the Africans, in which the Imperial Government supported the former. He denies that there was a substantial difference between British and South African attitudes to the native question. This interpretation seems difficult to harmonise with the actual course of events.

there seemed no possibility of change. British public opinion was being stirred into greater awareness of the implications of trusteeship and, with the change in the constitutional position of the Union brought about by the Statute of Westminster and the South African Status of the Union Act, the conditions for the handing over of the High Commission Territories were changed, since the British government lost its powers of intervention in the affairs of the Union reserved under the 1910 Constitution. Hertzog revived his claim when in London in 1935, and interpreted Thomas' suggestion that the matter be postponed to mean that transfer could quite soon come about.[34]

The divergence in British opinion between those who, like Curtis, felt able to follow the Commonwealth route and entrust South Africa with full responsibility for the territories and those, like Margery Perham, who gave priority to the theme of trusteeship, was fully brought out in their publications at the time.[35] The issue was in fact allowed to lie dormant, and from 1938 the clouding international scene as well as the improving economic climate in South Africa brought the Hertzog-Smuts 'fusion' government closer to Britain.[36] But towards the end of the 1930s Hailey could still see South African influence in favour of segregation and of the colour-bar in skilled employment, as well as of continued white political domination, as an important factor well outside its own borders.[37]

India and Africa

Another major factor in African affairs was the Indian government, in its capacity as the would-be protector of immigrant Indians and their descendants.[38] The problems of Indians overseas had originally come to the fore in South Africa, where Gandhi's campaign for equality of treatment for Indians had helped to secure his leadership in India's subsequent campaign for self-government. But South Africa was not the only country in the Empire which had an 'Indian problem'. It proved possible to come to an arrangement with Australia whereby the existing Indian population was freed from overt discrimination, but

[34] Hyam, op. cit., pp. 104 ff, 129 – 46. For the Status of the Union Act, see Mansergh, *Documents and Speeches*, vol. 1, pp. 4 – 6.
[35] Hyam, op. cit., p. 142.
[36] Chanock, op. cit., pp. 202 – 3.
[37] Hailey, op. cit., pp. 132 – 4.
[38] The fullest treatment of the subject is by Hugh Tinker in his *Separate and Unequal: India and the Indians in the British Commonwealth, 1920–1950* (London, 1976).

Canada, where the Sikhs of British Columbia were a sizeable community, declined to admit Indians to the franchise. In Ceylon, Malaya and Burma – until 1937 part of the Indian Empire – indigenous nationalisms saw Indians as an alien and unassimilable group, and rejected attempts to give them full political equality as the progress towards representative institutions gathered pace. In the sugar colonies – Fiji, Mauritius, Guyana and the Caribbean islands – the economic hardships, especially of the depression years, were a factor in promoting friction between the Indian and non-Indian elements in their populations. Finally, in East Africa, where there had been for a brief moment the vision of an Indian overseas empire based on the proposed grant to India of the mandate for Tanganyika, the Indians contributed an extra element to the conflict over the claims of white settlers and the paramountcy intermittently ascribed by the Colonial Office to the native African peoples.[39]

In general, despite the *modus vivendi* reached in South Africa in the 'Cape Town agreement' of 1927, the efforts of the Indian government were largely unavailing, as they were also in East Africa. This was a result of the different interests espoused by the Colonial Office and of the tendency of colonial governors to seek rather to meet the wishes of the local majority.[40] This feeling of impotence had some effect in strengthening the arguments of those Indians who saw no utility in the idea of India as a future Dominion, and preferred to see its goal as independence outside the British system. Yet, even with maximum goodwill on all sides, the solution was not an easy one. The overseas Indian communities themselves were divided on lines familiar in the sub-continent. Their own political organisations, in East Africa as in South Africa, tended to divide into competing factions, which followed leaders very conscious of their personal roles and ambitions. They were divided again between moderates and radicals, between those who felt themselves part of an oppressed colonial world and those, like the Aga Khan and the Ismailis in East Africa, who prided themselves on their loyalty to the Empire.

The goals of the various movements among the Indians were not clear-cut. Did they claim equality with white settlers, that is to say to

[39] See H. Lüthy, 'India and East Africa: Imperial Partnership at the end of the First World War', *JCH*, vol. VI, no. 2 (1971), pp. 55 – 85.
[40] In the 1930s there was an attempt to find some uninhabited land which could become a colony for Indians to settle and to which the Indians of South Africa, for whom repatriation had been accepted in principle, could resort. But nothing came of it. See Tinker, op. cit., p. 130.

be able to join the privileged elements in society through arrangements for a common-roll franchise, or were they only likely to secure their position if they took part in an all-round movement towards self-government? It was one of the arguments of colonial governors opposed to their political claims that, if granted to such a minority community, it would be impossible to resist similar claims on the part of the black majority.[41] If the British overseas were prone to sentiments of racial superiority, Indians also regarded themselves as a separate and superior people; they did not easily identify with Africans, and insofar as they sought assimilation it was to elements in European, not African, culture. Ideology might impinge upon such sentiments. In 1927 Jawarhalal Nehru, in a paper for the Congress Party, declared that 'Indians should co-operate with Africans and help them as far as possible, and not claim a special position for themselves'.[42] But this was both novel and far from universally acceptable. Nor indeed were Africans ready to see the Indians, with whom in everyday life many occasions for friction arose, as natural partners.

It may be that it was this extra Indian factor which gave the India Office a say in development in East Africa that explains in part the salience of the issue in debates over colonial policy in the inter-war period, or at least up to the final rejection of plans for 'closer union' in 1931.[43] The 1923 White Paper which enunciated the doctrine of the paramountcy of the interests of the native population as against 'immigrant races' was bitterly opposed by the Indians of Kenya with the support of the Indian government. And from 1924 to 1929 the Indians boycotted the colony's legislative council. Amery's White Paper in 1927 modified the existing policy only to the extent of giving a greater prominence to the role of the European settlers as partners in the trusteeship for the native races, and in holding out the prospect of self-government for the East African territories in a much shorter

[41] At the 1923 Imperial Conference Smuts had voiced the same argument in respect of South Africa itself: ibid., p. 73. Smuts was one of the main protagonists of the settlers' cause in East Africa, with, as he believed, the potential of a new 'great White Africa along the Eastern backbone': Smuts to Amery, 25 November 1924, *Smuts Papers*, vol. V, pp. 237–9. It meant avoiding Kenya becoming 'a purely Native State with an Indian trading aristocracy in charge'.

[42] Tinker, op. cit., 93. Nehru was at this time in the grip of his Marxist phase, stimulated by his presence in February 1927 at the Communist-sponsored 'International Congress against Colonial Oppression and Imperialism' at Brussels. S. Gopal, *Jawarhalal Nehru*, vol. 1 (London, 1975), 100 ff.

[43] The subject is exhaustively dealt with in R.G. Gregory, *India and East Africa, a History of Race Relations within the British Empire, 1890–1939* (Oxford, 1971). There was also an Arab minority to take into account.

time than had previously been assumed.[44] The combination of Amery at the Colonial Office and Edward Grigg as Governor of Kenya made it look for a moment as though Smuts' idea of an East African Dominion as important as Australia had some chance of becoming a reality.

The hesitancy of the cabinet, and of other experts in the colonial field such as Amery's own under-secretary, Ormsby-Gore, was however reflected in the terms of reference of the Royal Commission (the Hilton Young Commission) set up to prepare the way forward, which allowed other possibilities of co-operation between the territories to be investigated. Two of the members of the Commission had an Indian background, and the third who made up the majority when it came to the report was the missionary Dr J.H. Oldham. The report, to which the chairman appended a dissenting opinion, did not favour federation or any other scheme likely to entrench the political position of the settlers.[45] Although Amery himself endeavoured to keep the 'closer union' idea alive by sending his Permanent Under-Secretary on another mission of investigation, the return of a Labour government in 1929 made it certain that the re-emphasis on native paramountcy in the Commission report would be upheld. Both Indian and African opinion now had an access to the government through Labour Party channels. The statement of policy by the new government seemed favourable to Indian as well as African interests.[46] But Indian concern was diverted by the magnitude of events in India itself, and the new direction was acceptable neither to the settlers nor to the South African government. The submission of the question to an all-party Parliamentary Joint Committee meant that neither the hopes of Africans and Indians for political advance nor the settlers' expectations for moves towards closer union were likely to be fulfilled. By the time the Committee finished its deliberations, Labour was out of power. A period of relative quiescence ensued, with economic issues inevitably to the fore. The Indians in Kenya continued to protest against the denial of a franchise based upon a common roll with the

[44] *Future Policy in Regard to Eastern Africa*, Cmd 2904 (1927).
[45] *Report of the Commission on Closer Union of the Dependencies in Eastern and Central Africa*, Cmd 2324, (1929). A valuable brief account of the issues faced by one of the Commission's members with an African background is in ch. VI of Sir George Schuster, *Private Work and Public Causes* (Cambridge, 1979).
[46] *Memorandum on Native policy in East Africa*, Cmd 3573 (1930); *Statement of the Conclusions of H.M.'s Government in the United Kingdom as regards Closer Union in East Africa*, Cmd 3574, (1930).

Europeans, but in 1933 their boycott of the institutions of government came to an end.[47]

'Closer union' and the destiny of East and South Africa

The objections to the proposals for 'closer union' were not confined to the Indian aspects of the East African problem. There were the legal disparities between the situation in the three territories, the colony of Kenya, the protectorate of Uganda and the mandated territory of Tanganyika; but above all there was the clash between the views of successive governors in Kenya that the European settlers were the major factor for economic progress, and work in a white-dominated economy the best apprenticeship for the Africans, and the views that tended to prevail in Tanganyika, which had a more paternalist flavour. Opinion at home, voiced in Parliament, was both susceptible to arguments from business interests and from those with links with the settlers in the Kenya 'White Highlands'.[48] On the other hand there was, as has been seen, an increasingly powerful line of argument that stressed the need to make a reality of 'paramountcy'. Oldham's role in the Hilton Young Commission was followed up by his propaganda in favour of giving priority to African advancement.[49] In this effort, Oldham was following up the long-standing interest of British missionaries in work in East Africa and their important role above all in education, which helped, even in the more secular atmosphere of the inter-war period, to provide at least some of the educated cadres which a self-sustaining African society would require.[50] It was the multiplicity of the interests involved that gave such sensitivity to what might appear minor points, such as changes in the make-up of the elective element in the Kenya legislative council;[51] in Uganda and Tanganyika, where there was no elective element, and where the accent was on indirect rule and the role of native authorities, (particularly in relation to the Ugandan kingdoms), political passions were less easily aroused.

[47] Tinker, op. cit., pp. 112 – 5.
[48] On East Africa see V. Harlow and C.M. Chilver (eds), *History of East Africa* (Oxford, 1965); recent research is summarised in A. Roberts, 'East Africa', in *The Cambridge History of Africa*, vol. 7. Some aspects of business interests in East Africa are set out in Ponsonby, op. cit.
[49] See J.H. Oldham, op. cit.
[50] See R. Oliver, *The Missionary Factor in East Africa* (London, 1952).
[51] Although the settlers did not get the degree of power at the centre which they thought themselves entitled to, they contrived to secure predominance in municipal and district government.

If one rejected the Grigg – Amery view that white settlement was the motor of economic development in East Africa, and that Africans should be encouraged to seek for betterment through reserved lands farmed on the basis of individual ownership, one was left with the awkward fact that such other models of progress depended upon some public contribution to the infrastructure, and that, in the light of the Treasury's attitude, this was not likely to be forthcoming. It seemed difficult for East Africa to attract the large-scale investment which some private companies were putting into the West African colonies.[52]

Policy towards Tanganyika was complicated by the international dimension. Under the Germans, white settlement had been encouraged, and was by East African standards fairly extensive. The Germans were expelled when the British took over, but were allowed to return, and in some cases to resume their holdings, after relations with Germany were normalised in 1925. But this in turn produced a wish to have a British counterweight and, despite the commitment to native paramountcy, some encouragement was given to British settlers. The revival of the German colonial claims in the 1930s was not an encouragement to potential settlers or investors.

The three Central African colonies of Southern Rhodesia, Northern Rhodesia and Nyasaland were linked in the British official mind both with South Africa and with the 'closer union' ideas for the future of East Africa. In fact their individual fortunes were to differ markedly.[53] After Southern Rhodesia's rejection of incorporation with South Africa, it was formally annexed by Britain in 1923. A new constitution came into effect in 1924. Its rule was now in the hands of an executive responsible to an elected legislature, though it still fell short of Dominion status, since legislation of some types and executive dealings with the native population were subject to United Kingdom control, exercised in the latter case through the High Commissioner in South Africa. In 1937 a new Constitution came into effect, giving a greater measure of independent action to the legislature and reducing United Kingdom supervision over native affairs, which would henceforth be

[52] Grigg's approach to the problem was set out in his memorandum on 'Imperial policy in East Africa', (March 1927), PRO CO 822/4/19. For a businessman's view that companies such as the United Africa Company and Shell would have as part of their function to develop West Africa economically and socially for the country's own good, see E. Henriques, *Sir Robert Waley Cohen, 1872–1952* (London, 1966), p. 313. On the United Africa Company, see C.H. Wilson, *A History of Unilever*, vol. II (London, 1954), pp. 316–30.
[53] See A.N. Wills, *An Introduction to the History of Central Africa* (London, 1964).

undertaken directly by the Secretary of State rather than through the High Commissioner in South Africa.

While a tiny number of non-whites held the franchise, the basic thrust of Southern Rhodesia policy was towards 'separate development', both in respect of landed settlement and, increasingly in the 1930s, in respect of employment, as the depression made the white population the more determined to preserve its own economic and political supremacy. On the other hand Northern Rhodesia, which became a Crown Colony in 1924 and where the settler population was too small to aspire to responsible government, was obliged to take account of the views of the home government as to the importance of the development of the indigenous population. And from 1929 onwards it moved towards indirect rule on the Lugard model.

Southern Rhodesia ranked high in the estimation of some imperially-minded people in England.[54] But its white population was not without ambitions for change. In 1927 Amery found a desire in Southern Rhodesia to amalgamate with Northern Rhodesia and perhaps Nyasaland, to create a new entity clearly separate from South Africa. Amery himself felt that ultimately Southern Rhodesia would join the Union, and that its boundaries should not extend beyond what should be the Union's northern borders; it might be possible to allow the western part of Northern Rhodesia 'with the growing demand of its settlers for every kind of expenditure' to join Southern Rhodesia (with safeguards for native administration), and link the rest of the country to Nyasaland.[55]

The Passfield White Paper of 1930 came as a shock to settler opinion in Northern Rhodesia, and gave impetus to the movement for the unification of the Rhodesias which unsuccessfully approached the British government on the subject in 1931. Nyasaland was meanwhile pursuing a path leading away from the Rhodesian pattern of settler domination. It was envisaged at one moment that there might be an area of white settlement on the model of the Kenyan 'White Highlands', but by the mid – 1930s the idea was dead. From 1933 'indirect rule' was increasingly the model, and the legislation of 1936 barred the alienation of native lands.

---

[54] 'After thirty years Southern Rhodesia was a prosperous well-organized and happy selfgoverning colony – with no questions asked in Parliament and no interference from politicians or ignorant theorists from England.' Ponsonby, op. cit., p. 123.
[55] Amery to Ormsby-Gore, Bulawayo, 21 August 1927, PRO CO 822/1/6.

The policy of the government was affected by the beginnings of copper-mining in Northern Rhodesia, believed to be of considerable importance in view of the United States' domination of the world production of copper.[56] It was felt that the Colonial Office would have to remain in a position to look after the welfare of the African mine-workers.[57] Further pressure, mainly from Southern Rhodesia, came to a head in 1936–7, but in July 1937 the Cabinet decided that amalgamation was not practical politics for the moment. It was however agreed in November that a new Royal Commission should inquire into other possibilities of co-operation between the two Rhodesias and Nyasaland.[58] The findings of the Commission (the Bledisloe Commission) included setting up a Council of Governors to look at the joint concerns of the three territories; but Southern Rhodesia opposed the idea, and it has been suggested that this impasse was the immediate reason for the setting up of the wider unofficial Hailey inquiry.[59]

Even in those parts of the colonial empire where no problem of white settlement arose, and where in principle the notion of trusteeship should have held undiluted sway, it was not sufficient to introduce impartial and efficient administration in order to avoid giving rise to the political problems, either in the short term or in the future. Administration was not and could never be wholly neutral in its impact, any more than even the minimum contacts with European institutions and ideas could leave the indigenous population unaffected in its ideas and aspirations. For instance, the fact that British missionaries in West Africa taught and preached in the vernacular helped to create and emphasise sentiments of ethnic diversity. As the southern Nigerian peoples began to stress their ethnic identity, the Hausa in the north, already united by Islam, began to seek for a wider unity in order to fend off the southern challenge.

The language policy of mission schools could have far-reaching effects. In much of Central Africa it helped to consolidate a multiplicity of local dialects into what became standard 'tribal' languages. Government policy was also important. Efforts in East

[56] Cabinet meeting, 7 May 1930: PRO CAB 23/64. See also A.D. Roberts (ed.), *The Cambridge History of Africa*, vol. 7, p. 12.

[57] Meeting, 1 July 1931, (meeting 36(31) and papers appended), PRO CAB 23/67.

[58] Meeting, 21 July 1937, PRO CAB 23/89; ibid., 17 November 1937, PRO CAB 23/90.

[59] C. Palley, *The Constitutional History and Law of Southern Rhodesia, 1888–1965* (Oxford, 1966), pp. 330–1. On developments in Southern Rhodesia in the 1930s see Robert Blake, *A History of Southern Rhodesia* (London, 1977), ch. 15, 'The Huggins Era, 1933-1939'.

Africa to make Swahili generally acceptable for public purposes succeeded only in Tanganyika and thus produced yet another obstacle to 'closer union'.[60]

In the Sudan, the murder of the Sirdar, Sir Lee Stack, in 1924 further convinced the British government that Egyptian influence must henceforth be excluded, despite the fact that the British presence there in international law depended upon the 'condominium'. The Governors of the Sudan took their instructions from the Foreign Office, nominally through the High Commissioner (later the Ambassador) in Cairo, not from the Colonial Office. The task of finding elements with which to collaborate in administering the country was made harder by the division between the Islamic north and the barely pacified Pagan south. The policy was to halt the advance of Islam on its existing line. Even in the north the Moslem political class was divided between the traditional local chiefs, the neo-Mahdists, pro-Egyptian elements, the Khatmia party, and urban radicals.

Between 1927 and 1933, under the influence of the theories of 'indirect rule', it was government policy to uphold the local chiefs against both the urban radicals and the neo-Mahdists. Faced after 1933 with a growing challenge from the neo-Mahdists, a new governor, Sir George Symes, tried to outbid them by weakening the emphasis on indirect rule in favour of seeking the support of the urban-educated through advocating the Sudanisation of the Civil Service and an expansion of opportunities for higher education. In 1940 however the organ of the educated class, the Graduates Congress, was captured by radical elements, demanding self-determination, though divided between the Khatmia and the neo-Mahdists. In 1942 another shift saw a British attempt to win the support of the neo-Mahdists and the moderates, with the Khatmia going into opposition and seeking support from the radicals.[61] This series of policy changes seems to have been the product of the reaction of those on the spot rather than of any clearly thought out policy in Whitehall.[62]

---

[60] *The Cambridge History of Africa*, vol. 7, pp. 636 – 7, 698. The French in Chad used French in their missionary work, but in the long run this does not seem to have assured political unity. See Albert Wirz, 'Imperialism and State Formation in Africa: Nigeria and Chad', in W.J. Mommsen and J. Osterhammel (eds), *Imperialism and After* (London, 1986).

[61] See R. Robinson, 'Non-European foundations of European imperialism: a sketch for a theory of collaboration', in R. Owen and B. Sutcliffe eds, *Studies in the Theory of Imperialism* (London, 1972).

[62] On the Sudan in this period see G.H.Sanderson, 'The Anglo-Egyptian Sudan', in *The Cambridge History of Africa*, vol. 7.

On the whole the British authorities took a negative attitude towards major economic development, which might render more difficult the tasks of ruling through traditional authorities. There was however one curious exception, the Gezira cotton-growing enterprise, which did create a thriving peasant farmer class in a limited area, and one which after some vicissitudes made an important contribution to the country's exports.[63] Since the Sudan did not pay for itself, and was subsidised from Egyptian revenues, (a relic of the 'condominium'), its role in the imperial galaxy must be seen as primarily a strategic one, its importance in this respect being enhanced by the Italian conquest of Abyssinia.

Indirect rule in practice in Ceylon and Malaya

In colonies outside Africa the question of racial and religious diversity was tackled in a variety of ways. In Ceylon there had been a growth of nationalist aspirations among the Sinhalese majority, and this was recognised in the 1920 Constitution, which gave the island a Legislative Council with an unofficial majority, but one which included communal as well as territorial representatives, and nominated members in addition. In 1924 a new Constitution provided for an elected majority, though with the franchise restricted to some four per cent of the population. Effective control still rested with the Governor, who retained an official majority on his executive Council. In 1927 further evidence of discontent led to the appointment of the Donoughmore Commission, which reported in 1928. It found the existing system wanting in that it separated the Executive from the Legislature, to which it was not responsible. On the other hand, the Commission argued that responsible government on the Westminster or Dominion model was impractical because of the radical diversity of the population. It therefore recommended a system of government by committees of the legislature, on the model of the League of Nations or of British local government. The chairmen of the committees would be nominated by the Governor to serve as ministers. An element of dyarchy was also introduced, in that the public service, external affairs and defence were reserved to the Governor. Communal representation was deplored as liable to harden racial divisions, but it was felt that the electorate could safely be increased to allow for universal suffrage at the age of 30.

[63] See A. Gaitskell, *Gezira: a story of development in the Sudan* (London, 1959).

The Constitution of 1931, which was based upon the Donoughmore Report, was never reckoned a great success. The absence of political parties made coherent policy difficult, and there was no administrative co-ordination between the separate departments under ministerial control. The Tamils, the most important minority, boycotted the first election in 1931, but entered the legislature in 1935 when another election was held. Between 1931 and 1935 there was both an Indian and a Muslim minister, but in 1935 an all-Sinhalese ministry was formed, this being thought more likely to lead to further constitutional progress.[64]

The experience of the British in Malaya provides the best example of how indirect rule could be used to diminish the need for a full colonial bureaucracy in a country in which the original inhabitants were challenged by the reinforcement of the long-standing Chinese community through immigration, and an Indian community attracted by the economic development taking place under colonial rule though at private hands.[65] It is perhaps a testimony to the degree to which the system depended upon prestige that during the period the average total of Malayan Civil Service officers in any one year was about 200. Most of these were British expatriates, chosen on Furse's principles for likely adaptability, rather than as for the I.C.S. on intellectual attainment. A policy of bringing Malays forward was latterly in force, but in 1939, out of a total of 184 officers, only 22 were Malays. It was clear enough that the perpetration of the Malay Sultanates alongside the directly ruled Straits Settlements was designed for convenience rather than out of sensitivity to national feeling, and that in major matters it was the Sultans' British advisers whose word had to be heeded. The situation further differed from that of many other parts of the colonial empire in the importance attached to economic development, both in respect of plantation crops, principally rubber, and of tin-mining. The international connections which Malaya's importance engendered, as well as the large non-Malay elements in the population, explains the decision arrived at in 1903 that English would have to be the official language of the federation.[66]

The actual extent of devolution to the Malay authorities depended upon the commitment to it of successive governors. Some were

[64] Sir Ivor Jennings and H.W. Tambiah, *The Dominion of Ceylon: the Development of its Laws and Constitution* (London, 1952), pp. 20 – 3.
[65] The subject is dealt with at length in R. Heussler, *British Rule in Malaya* (Oxford, 1981).
[66] Ibid., pp. 18, 266.

primarily concerned with development, others with what they saw as the protection of the Malays from too destabilising a contact with the modern world. On the other hand, as so often, those in the service who were concerned with the minorities tended to become powerful advocates of their cause and of the protection they were believed to require against exploitation, including, in the case of immigrants, exploitation by their fellow-nationals. Yet what was done was not enough to give the Chinese a feeling of identification with their British rulers. Instead, like Chinese elsewhere in the colonial world, they tended to look for protection to their home country, and this meant their involvement in the continuous internal Chinese struggles of these years. In particular, this involvement created a base for a strong Communist Party in Malaya, based in the Chinese community.[67]

Colonial development in the depression and after

If one takes the inter-war period as a whole, one can see a very gradual move away from the limitation of colonial administration to law and order and the basic administrative services, as well as the taxation designed to pay for them, to a more positive assumption of responsibility for economic development and the provision of welfare services.[68] Changing public opinion at home and the resultant pressures on the Colonial Office was one reason for the change, and in the 1930s additional stimulus was provided by the impact of the depression upon primary producers, notably in the sugar colonies, and the political disturbances to which these gave rise.[69] Yet the idea of the colonial empire as a unity providing with the metropolis a single self-sustaining economic system never captured the British

[67] For the point of view of one 'Protector of the Chinese', see Victor Purcell, *Memoirs of a Malayan Official* (London, 1965).

[68] The subject is treated in detail in S.Constantine, *The Making of British Colonial Development Policy, 1914–1940*, (London, 1984), and more broadly in the early chapters of vol. 1 of *The Official History of Colonial Development: The Origins of British Aid Policy, 1924–1945*, by D.J. Morgan (London, 1980).

[69] Thinking on the British Left was affected by the belief that the colonial regimes were needed to protect the indigenous population against capitalist exploitation and uncertainty as to how, without external capital investment, development could proceed. Most people in Labour Party circles were in favour of transferring power to the local peoples in the Caribbean, but doubted that Africans could as yet run their own affairs. The preference for peasant holdings was challenged on the basis of West Indian experience, with collective or communal farming seen as an alternative, together with a publicly provided infrastructure. Little thought was given to the future of populations detached from agriculture and beginning to form indigenous urban proletariats. See Rich, *Race and Empire in British Politics*, 77 ff.

imagination except in the most restricted circles. The contrast with the French, both in the general approach and in the extent of invest-ment in the colonial territories, is a striking one.[70] Furthermore, tariff policy, which was also affected by Dominion interests, was never a very important means of assuring either outlets for colonial produce in the United Kingdom or a guaranteed place for United Kingdom exports in colonial territories. When in 1936 – 7 there was serious pressure on the colonial powers to consider the 'open door' principle as an alter-native to the cession of colonial territories to Germany, it was pointed out that British policy had always been more liberal than that of other powers, indeed, that only the United Kingdom and Holland had a creditable record in this respect. It was France's 'acute selfishness' that had given rise to such dissatisfaction among powers not possess-ing tropical colonies.[71]

In the earlier part of the period, the only arguments that could sway politicians were those related not to the interests of the colonies themselves but to unemployment at home. The three Trade Facilities Acts of 1924, 1925 and 1926, which gave some relief on interest payments for loans raised for development in the colonies as well as the Dominions, proved to be in respect of stimulating British exports 'singularly useless'.[72] Their only value was as a precedent for some slight interference with the normal course of credit operations. Indeed, they were not the product of Colonial Office thinking, which was, as already noted, much concerned with prospects in West Africa, and was prepared to argue with the Treasury in favour of developing railways in Kenya and Uganda, facilitated by a loan for this purpose in 1924. Further financial assistance for East African development was urged upon the government by the East Africa Commission set up in 1924 and, once again, by interests at home. But the East Africa Loans Act of 1926 was drawn up on terms so strict, in order to meet Treasury misgivings, and in amounts so small, that its impact was not considerable.

The first Colonial Development Act of 1929 was preceded by even

[70] The level of investment in the French colonial empire increased fourfold between the two world wars, bringing its share in France's external portfolio from 10 per cent in 1914 to nearly 45 per cent in 1939. Indo-China, which attracted most private capital, was responsible for about 40 per cent throughout. More government investment was put into West Africa. See Dieter Brotel, 'Imperialist Domination in Vietnam and Cambodia: A Long Term View', in Mommsen and Osterhammel, op. cit.

[71] Meeting of Cabinet Foreign Policy Committee on 11 June 1937, PRO CAB 27/622.

[72] Constantine, op. cit., p. 112.

more marked differences as between Amery at the Colonial Office and Churchill at the Treasury, and became law only under the Labour government. It was important rather for the degree to which all colonial territories could benefit and for the lack of any restriction as to the type of expenditure for which loans could be raised, than for the extent of the resources provided, and was yet again primarily a response to pressures for action to deal with unemployment in Britain itself.[73] But it did leave as a permanent addition to the government's economic armoury a Colonial Development Fund, and money from this source was made available to a number of territories during the subsequent decade. The consideration of such applications was entrusted to what was styled the Colonial Development Advisory Committee, but which was in effect an executive body outside the direct machinery of the Colonial Office, and the membership of which was largely drawn from the business community, though with some former officials among its number. The Colonial Office was of course involved on behalf of the territories under its care, and pressed for the sums made available to be grants rather than loans, in order to avoid burdening colonial governments with interest payments they might find it hard to meet. The Committee itself also fought off the pressures to tie development grants and loans directly to the purchase of British goods, thus accepting the argument that the development of healthy economies in the Empire would in the end work through to Britain's benefit.

In other respects the depression years were inevitably damaging to the prospects of the colonial territories, not simply in terms of the declining prices obtainable for their products, but also as a result of the Colonial Office being forced to cut its expenditure. Thus while the Colonial Office was now suitably organised to provide specialist services, appointments of medical, veterinary, educational and agricultural specialists fell sharply in 1931 and 1932, as did general recruitment to the colonial service. It was however economic troubles that through their impact upon the political situation in the colonies themselves made the biggest impact upon government thinking and action. The disturbances in the West Indies were the most serious, but there were also riots, strikes and boycotts of markets in territories as

---

[73] 'The Colonial Development Act of 1929 may be a landmark in the history of British Colonial policy but its impact was barely perceptible.' C.C. Wrigley in *The Cambridge History of Africa*, vol. 7, p. 134.

far apart as Mauritius, Northern Rhodesia and West Africa. These troubles had the effect of stimulating a number of official inquiries and investigations, of which the most significant was the Royal Commission on the West Indies under Lord Moyne, which reported in December 1939. The attention of Parliament was also aroused by these events and the international context, with the German colonial claims setting the pace, likewise contributed to the perceptible shift towards a more positive policy of colonial development. Trusteeship as the mere safeguarding of local institutions and cultures was now widely seen as insufficient. In this atmosphere a review of the existing machinery for development was inevitable, and was in fact taken in hand in 1938. The outcome, the Colonial Development and Welfare Act of 1940, can in part be seen as a reaction to the coming of the war and the need to make the best use of colonial resources, and present the best possible image to the world of Britain as a colonial power; but it was also the culmination of a shift towards a more positive view of the potential of government action which had been growing over the past two decades, and which was of course equally relevant to Britain's domestic affairs.

The defence of the colonies

One issue where Britain's practice was largely distinct from that of other empires past and present was in respect of the military use of subject peoples. Vital in the case of India, the use of colonial manpower for military purposes did not figure very largely in the discussions of the period. This was not because conflicts over the future of colonial territories were not expected to arise. 'Given the gulf – a gulf which no bridge will span – between Anglo-Saxon and French mentality, there will continue, probably for ever, to be differences of opinion and friction in almost every question that arises'; so declared a Foreign Office memorandum in 1926.[74] And in 1929 Walter Elliot, a future minister, gave public expression to his view that the future conflict in West Africa would be, not between white and black or even black and black, but between white man and white man, that is to say, between the British and the French. Unless there

[74] 'Memorandum on the Foreign Policy of His Majesty's Government with a list of British Commitments in their Relative Order of Importance', 10 April 1926, *DBFP*, Series IA, vol. I (London, H.M.S.O., 1966), pp. 846 – 81. An instance of difficulty referred to is the New Hebrides, where Australian ambitions were a complicating factor.

was give and take and confidence between the two sides, 'the eleven unguarded paper frontiers with five battalions on the British side and twenty on the French' would be a soldier's nightmare.[75] Yet the French troops recruited in France's African colonies were clearly not thought of in local terms, as so much as one way in which France's deficiencies in manpower as against Germany might to some extent be made up.[76]

British colonial forces were primarily for local defence. A War Office list of 1930 gave particulars of twenty-nine local forces: almost all were part time, though the King's African Rifles and the West African Frontier Force offered a full-time career to native recruits. Only in the Sudan and Trans-Jordan were there non-European officers. Most contingents were quite small. The discussions on the military forces in the colonies were largely concerned with finance, arising from the British government's insistence that they should be paid for from local taxation. In addition it was held that where a garrison of British regular troops was maintained, the colony should pay a contribution towards the cost of its defence. As the calls upon British resources mounted in the 1930s, both British and colonial forces were subjected to cuts. What was however an axiom of policy was that the government should never be in a position where troops might have to be used to enforce government policy against Europeans. The case was put by the Duke of Devonshire when the cabinet discussed the settler protests in Kenya in 1923; if native troops were used against Europeans, he said, 'it would be disastrous to the discipline of the troops; it would be fatal to British prestige throughout Africa; and it would mean that in the whole of the continent the life of a European would not be safe in any area of native population'.[77]

The issues involved were considered anew when Hankey visited South Africa in 1934 as part of his review of the Empire's defence requirements. He was fearful lest South Africa's suggestions of cooperation in the defence of East and Central Africa should create suspicions at a time when there appeared to be a generally stable situation.[78] In 1938, when the international situation looked more

[75] *The Times*, 7 May 1929.
[76] *Notes on the Land and Air Forces of the British Overseas Dominions, Colonies, Protectorates and Mandated Territories*, (London, H.M.S.O., 1930). In British Africa military establishments were smaller in relation to population than in the French, Belgian and Portuguese Colonies: *The Cambridge History of Africa*, vol. 7, p. 49.
[77] C.P. 99(23), PRO CAB 24/158.
[78] Hankey to U.K. High Commissioner in South Africa, 5 July 1934, PRO CAB 63/69.

threatening, it became clear that Southern Rhodesia shared South Africa's unwillingness to see the black population armed, and it was suggested that its best contribution would be to supply white officers for Northern Rhodesian levies.[79] The Overseas Defence Committee of the C.I.D. held that the South Africans and Rhodesians were right and that it was preferable 'in the interests of the natives themselves' that they should not be armed.[80] The War Office itself laid it down in September 1938 that the African colonial forces in time of war would be transferred to War Office control from that of the colonial governments and would be deployed anywhere that might be necessary, subject to enough troops being left for local defence.[81] The situation differed from that in 1914 in that there were no German colonies in Africa, so that the Italian possessions were the only targets south of the Sahara. In the rest of the Empire, it was the possibility of conflict with Japan that was the issue for the military planners, and here the forces likely to be involved and the naval aspect of any such conflict made the locally raised forces of little more than symbolic significance.

[79] Evidence of Major-General Giffard to Commission on Closer Association between Southern Rhodesia, Northern Rhodesia and Nyasaland, 21 April 1938, PRO CAB 21/466.
[80] Paper prepared by the Overseas Defence Committee for the Commission, 17 October 1938, ibid.
[81] War Office memorandum, 'Control of African local military forces in War', 28 September 1938, PRO CAB 5/9.

Chapter 10

THE EMPIRE AND REARMAMENT

Imperial disunity and foreign policy

The history of British imperial policy from 1931 to 1939 was largely coloured by the darkening international situation. As the ambitions of Japan, Italy and Germany were successively revealed, British policy-makers were forced to explore three lines of approach to what might well seem an insoluble problem, should these potential enemies combine in an assault upon Britain and her continental and overseas interests. The first was rearmament, the creation of sufficient forces to deter aggression or make victory likely should deterrence fail. The second was to attempt to lessen the potential burden upon Britain's own forces by reducing overseas commitments arising from imperial responsibilities. The third was to seek through diplomacy to reduce the number of potential foes, and at the same time convince domestic and foreign opinion that it was not British obstinacy in the face of well-founded grievances that was at the root of a potential conflict. In actual fact, all three options were pursued simultaneously, and decisions in one area had inevitable repercussions on the others. All three were affected by the extent to which lessons drawn from the past might be held to be relevant, and by speculation as to the extent to which these might have been overtaken by the new developments in the weapons of war. Finally, all were affected by the differences of opinion as to the aims of the potential enemies and as to how these should be assessed. Since such assessments were not agreed upon by British policy-makers with the greatest access to information, public and clandestine, it is not surprising that Dominion governments with fewer such resources might differ from Britain and from each other. In these circumstances the changes in military priorities which were so marked a feature of the period are not too hard to understand.[1]

[1] For the shifts in British thinking see the classic analysis in Michael Howard, *The Continental Commitment* (London, 1972).

230

While a full-scale narrative would have to follow the unfolding of events and the emergence of problems as they presented themselves, for purposes of analysis there is an argument for treating the three facets of policy separately, and to begin with rearmament itself. The successive stages of the expansion of Britain's forces and the machinery through which they were directed has been fully explored in works rightly focussing on the United Kingdom, which bore the brunt of the effort.[2] What requires answering in the present context is the question of the light thrown on the assumed unity of the Empire-Commonwealth system by the process of rearmament and the extent of the imperial contributions to its achievement.

The attempt to formulate a single Empire foreign policy had been abandoned at the time of the 1923 Imperial Conference, but this had not had the consequence of making the Dominions autonomous in the field of defence; on the contrary, 'by 1932, despite the defeat of the Admiralty's schemes for a single Imperial Navy, the Commonwealth amounted for defence purposes virtually to a permanent alliance'.[3] Between the armed forces of the Dominions and those of the United Kingdom there was a large measure of implicit integration. While it had been made clear that the Dominions were responsible for their own local defence, it seemed, according to the Chiefs of Staff, that it was taken for granted that in a major war the United Kingdom would take responsibility for their defence. The way in which the Singapore issue had been handled confirmed this view, and while it was admitted that the Dominions must in the last resort have the right to decide the extent of their participation in a conflict, this should not, in their view, rule out joint planning beforehand. Hankey agreed with the Chiefs of Staff in regretting the failure of the 1930 Imperial Conference to discuss defence matters adequately.[4] A meeting of the Committee of Imperial Defence at which Dominion representatives were present revealed little more than general anxiety about the situation and the wish on the part of most of the Dominions to be better informed.[5]

---

[2] The story can be followed in N.H. Gibbs, *Rearmament Policy*, (London, 1976), which is the first volume of the official series, *Grand Strategy*.

[3] D.C. Watt, 'Imperial Defence Policy and Imperial Foreign Policy, 1911–1939', *JCPS*, vol. I, (1963), pp. 266–81 (quotation on p. 275).

[4] Chiefs of Staff to Prime Minister, 29 October 1930, and Hankey to C.I.G.S. (Milne), 14 November 1930, in PRO CAB 21/336. Bennett had prevented the circulation of a paper by Hankey on strengthening defence consultation: Roskill, *Hankey*, vol. II, pp. 528–9.

[5] C.I.D. meeting, 28 November 1930, PRO CAB 2/5.

It remained true that the United Kingdom government, while wishing to see the defence burden more equitably shared, was unwilling to see its views brought out into the open, and was in particular wary of the tendency of Dominion governments to share their defence thinking with their Parliaments, as MacDonald pointed out to the New Zealand Prime Minister, Forbes. Such inhibitions did not prevent contact at the professional level. In response to an inquiry from Forbes in November 1930, the Chiefs of Staff prepared a paper setting out their views as to what New Zealand should expect to contribute to imperial defence in the event of war. In August 1932 a similar paper was prepared for the Australians, giving particular importance to its naval contributions.[6]

The period between 1930 and 1933 or even 1934 is curious in that the public commitment of the British and other governments was to disarmament, while the developing threats were pushing the service chiefs and their political masters towards making up for Britain's own weaknesses in defence. The main issues in the search for disarmament were related to the situation in Europe and the balancing of German claims for 'equality' with the French demand for 'security'. Here Britain to some extent saw itself as a mediator. But there were questions that directly involved Britain's imperial position. One was the issue of naval quotas. The Washington and London naval treaties had handled the Empire-Commonwealth as a single unit, leaving to its own decision the distribution of naval vessels between Britain and the Dominions. Since the treaties were not League instruments, the Dominions had found it possible to accept this arrangement without raising constitutional objections. Now it was suggested that to limits on tonnage and the number of vessels permitted in each class should be added budgetary limitation on the same lines. This was felt to be technically difficult, but the Admiralty wanted a single quota so as not to prevent any one part of the Commonwealth increasing its proportionate contribution to defence.[7]

[6] 'Imperial Defence as affecting New Zealand', Report by Chiefs of Staff, 11 March 1931, paper 358-C, and 'The Defence of Australia', 30 August 1932, paper 372-C, in PRO CAB 5/7. For the development of Australian thinking on defence matters in this period see John McCarthy, *Australia and Imperial Defence, 1918-1939* (St Lucia, Queensland, 1976), and P.G. Edwards, *Prime Ministers and Diplomats, The Making of Australian Foreign Policy, 1901-1949* (Melbourne, 1983).
[7] Draft report of the Cabinet Committee on the Disarmament Conference, sent to Cecil by its chairman, Simon, on 28 December 1931: Cecil of Chelwood Papers, BL Add MSS 51082. The Chief of the Canadian Naval Staff, pleading for maintaining a Canadian naval force, pointed out that Canada's destroyers were counted as part of the Commonwealth's forces in the naval treaties, and that if they were not kept in an efficient state, the Commonwealth as a whole would be weakened. Eayrs, *In defence of Canada*, vol. I (Toronto, 1964), p. 282.

Discussion of disarmament in the air raised further problems. When it was proposed at Geneva that the five major military powers should each have 500 front-line aircraft, the Dominions came forward with the wish to have their own air forces. But if this was accepted, the Empire's total air strength would be three times that of any other power. One could argue the constitutional point that Britain did not control the Dominion air forces or even have military agreements with the Dominion governments, but as Eden* privately pointed out, it was hard to deny that their forces would be available in time of war: 'And if we did, with the record of the Dominions in the last war fresh in the memory of other nations, no-one would believe us.'[8]

A possible agreement on the abolition of all bomber aircraft raised further questions. The use of aircraft for certain purposes of imperial defence in outlying areas had become a part of defence doctrine in the 1920s. To abandon it now was strongly opposed by the Government of India and also by the Dominions. To go over to the use of ground forces would be more expensive. Lord Londonderry, the Secretary of State for Air, argued that Britain's giving way on this point would not affect the real issues which the Disarmament Conference had to confront. In reply to a letter from him, Austen Chamberlain pointed out that although a good case would be made for the use of air bombing in Iraq, the Sudan and on the North-West frontier, since it made it possible to deal with trouble immediately and prevent it developing, France and Italy would claim the same exemption and be able to use their aircraft based in Africa to reinforce their strength in Europe.[9]

In fact all these arguments were becoming academic. Smuts could argue as late as April 1933 that the moment was right for pressing forward with disarmament, since Germany's domestic revolution would for some years incapacitate her from action abroad. But the movement was all in the other direction. In November the cabinet tacitly admitted that the ten-year rule was no longer binding and that rearmament would have to proceed.[10]

While the Dominions had been consulted about disarmament proposals, it seems that in respect of the vital steps in rearmament the

[8] Eden to Simon, 1 May 1933: Simon Papers.
[9] Cabinet meeting, 7 June 1932, PRO CAB 23/71; Londonderry to Chamberlain 24 June, Chamberlain to Londonderry 26 June 1933, Austen Chamberlain Papers, A.C. 40/122.
[10] Gilbert Murray to Robert Cecil, 24 August 1933, Gilbert Murray Papers, Cecil correspondence. On the somewhat confused circumstances in which the ten-year rule was allowed to lapse see Roskill, *Hankey*, vol. II (London, 1972), 536 ff.

preference for keeping things quiet now reasserted itself. The Secretary of State for War urged upon the cabinet that it was for it to choose what policy to adopt and then decide how much should be communicated to the Dominions and the Opposition. In July the cabinet went ahead with a major reinforcement of the R.A.F.[11] Failure to consult the Dominions did not mean that the imperial element was absent from government thinking. It was for its sake that the insurance of larger armaments was required: 'The insurance premiums must bear a higher ratio to the property insured – namely the incalculable estate known as the British Empire.'[12]

The reticence of the British government where informing the Dominions was concerned is amply illustrated in the proceedings of the cabinet, its committees and the C.I.D. One reason may have been the possibility that one or more of the Dominions might declare its neutrality in the event of war, and that possibility and its consequences was investigated by the Dominions Office from 1937, as well as the effect of a declaration of war being postponed by one or more Dominions to allow for the parliamentary process to take effect.[13] A more important reason was that policies forced upon the United Kingdom by the stretching of its resources would not satisfy the Dominions.

The Japanese invasion of Manchuria in 1931 brought about an almost immediate decision of the British government to accelerate the Singapore project. And by early 1933 a programme of expansion was agreed upon. The Australian government shared the British anxiety about the possibility of war with Japan, but pointed to its people's feeling of security and reluctance to spend money on defence. It was evident that the Dominions felt they could rely upon Britain, but this feeling was based in the Admiralty's view upon a false view of the situation. As the newly appointed First Sea Lord, Chatfield, informed his colleagues in February 1933, it was not true that Singapore, 'the gateway to the Indian Ocean', was secure. The British public was unaware of the defenceless state of Britain's Far Eastern possessions: 'a strong Singapore did not exist ... the whole bases of our war policy were, in fact, built on sand'. At a C.I.D. meeting in April Bruce, representing Australia, declared that if Britain were not prepared to complete the defences of Singapore, Australia would have to divert its

[11] Cabinet meetings, 25 April and 18 July 1934, PRO CAB 23/79.

[12] Report of the Defence Requirements Subcommittee, 28 February 1932, PRO CAB 16/109.

[13] J. Garner, *The Commonwealth Office, 1925–1968* (London, 1978), 91 ff.

resources from the navy to the army and air force, so as to provide for her own defence.[14]

The anxieties of the Pacific dominions about Britain's intentions continued to be expressed; nor were their anxieties without foundation, since the policy now being recommended gave priority to the defence of the United Kingdom in the air over naval requirements. The Admiralty however claimed that while Germany might be the major threat in the future, as the Chancellor of the Exchequer suggested, it was Japan that presented the more immediate menace. It was these uncertainties at home that made it difficult to be open with the Dominions, and led to the decision to send Hankey on a mission to the Dominions to give a personal explanation to their Prime Ministers of the issues involved.[15]

Hankey's tour of the Empire, 1934–5

Hankey himself was committed to the principle of the previous reports on Imperial Defence. It is not clear whether the Australians were aware that powerful influences on the British scene were opposed to Hankey's position. Warren Fisher in particular believed that Japan was being unneccessarily estranged by British naval policy and that this was being done in order to please the United States. He took the view that the real threat was from Germany and that it was not too late to find an accommodation with Japan. Meanwhile the Japanese were trying to persuade the British government that their own naval programme was solely directed against the United States, and that they would accept Britain's right to a larger navy than they possessed; to following that line, however, there was the obstacle that Britain had agreed with the United States on parity between their two fleets.[16]

Hankey's interpretation of British policy was that there would be 'a naval base at Singapore sufficiently strongly defended to hold out until the arrival of the Main Fleet of capital ships, which thereafter [would

---

[14] Remarks by J.G. Latham at Chiefs of Staff subcommittee meeting, 2 June 1932, and subcommittee meeting, 28 February 1933, PRO CAB 53/4; C.I.D. meeting, 6 April 1933, PRO CAB 2/5. Australian thinking on the Singapore issue was largely limited to the possibility of a war against Japan alone. The difficulties that would arise if Britain was meanwhile having to deal with threats from hostile European navies tended to be ignored. McCarthy, op. cit., pp. 129 – 31.

[15] Ministerial Committee on Disarmament Conference, 24 July 1934, PRO CAB 53/5. The mission is discussed in Roskill, *Hankey*, III (London, 1974), ch. 3.

[16] Middlemas and Barnes, *Baldwin*, pp. 780 – 1; Cabinet meeting, 29 October 1934, PRO CAB 23/80.

provide] the shield to cover the whole of our interests in the South Pacific and Indian Ocean'.[17] Such a policy implied completing the base by 1938. But Hankey did not propose to show the document containing this definition of policy to the Australians. And indeed when he got to Australia he avoided a direct pledge: 'I have made it clear that our Government has taken no commitment to send the fleet to Singapore - any more than [the] Australian government will take commitments to help us. (They can't though they will come alright on the day as far as their resources permit.)'[18] Hankey was of course well aware of the reiterated unwillingness of the Chiefs of Staff to give such an undertaking – an unwillingness which was to be increased as Italy's stance in the Mediterranean became more hostile.[19]

The priorities in South Africa, Hankey's first stop, were peculiar to its own situation. Its defence forces were believed in London to have been neglected, though some additional expense had been approved at the end of 1933. But the object was to help prevent the return to Germany of South West Africa and Tanganyika, and the defence minister, Pirow, had made it clear at a meeting of the C.I.D. on 24 July 1933 that under no circumstances would South African forces be available for service outside the continent. More recently he had publicly declared that South Africa would neither contribute to the British navy nor create a fleet of her own.[20] What was felt in London to be unacceptable was the suggestion that South Africa should co-operate in the defence of the colonial and mandated territories of East and Central Africa. Pirow was not in South Africa when Hankey's visit took place, and he was warned by Smuts about the defence minister's German sympathies. Hertzog too, while not directly criticising British rearmament, was dubious about what seemed to be the increasing British alignment with France and its willingness to consider a continental role.[21]

[17] Hankey to Baldwin, 30 July 1934, PRO CAB 63/66.

[18] Hankey to MacDonald, 3 August 1934, PRO CAB 21/434; Hankey (from Australia) to Baldwin, 17 November 1934, Baldwin Papers, vol. I, pp. 52 – 8.

[19] See e.g. Chiefs of Staff subcommittee meeting, 5 February 1937, PRO CAB 53/6.

[20] Memorandum, 'The Military Defence Situation of South Africa', July 1934, prepared for Hankey's tour. Hankey preceded his visit by letters to Hertzog and Smuts: Hankey to MacDonald, 7 September 1934. Smuts in reply had expressed fears about Japanese ambitions in Mozambique and Abyssinia, and agreed that if Singapore fell, South Africa would be 'in the front line'. Hankey to Chatfield, 11 September 1934, PRO CAB 63/69.

[21] Hankey to High Commissioner in South Africa, (Sir Herbert Stanley), 5 July 1934, ibid.; Roskill, *Hankey*, vol. III, pp. 124 – 7. From the imperial point of view, the key question in relation to South Africa was the naval base at Simonstown, which the Union had taken charge of in 1922.

In Australia, the most important thing was to find some way of dealing with the argument that Britain could not be relied upon to send the Fleet to the Far East and that Australia should therefore give priority to defence forces intended to guard itself against invasion. Hankey himself believed that the motive to do so would be very strong and even though it would stretch British resources if there was trouble in Europe at the time, they should be sufficient. What was required was enough strength in Australia to prevent public opinion from demanding the retention of Australia's forces at home since it was clear that in the event of war Australian forces would be needed overseas, for instance to defend the Suez Canal. Here he felt himself able to make quite precise recommendations about both the scale and the composition of Australia's forces.[22]

The New Zealand defence plans were also based upon the assumption of the British fleet going to Singapore. It was both strengthening coastal defences and preparing a small expeditionary force. The meetings Hankey held in New Zealand were attended by the Australian External Affairs Minister, Sir George Pearce, who put in a plea for close co-operation in defence matters between the two Dominions.[23]

From the discussions Hankey had in the Pacific Dominions, the key importance of Singapore was more than ever made evident.[24] But the actual construction and defence of the base continued to bedevilled by the old question of guns against aircraft. In the end some ground was given to the Treasury, the main supporter of the case for guns, and

The nationalists in opposition had been concerned to see how South Africa's neutrality could be preserved in a British war and had considered ceding Simonstown to the United Kingdom as a possible safeguard. Hailey, *African Survey*, pp. 146 – 7.

[22] Hankey's report on 'Certain Aspects of Australian Defence', 15 November 1934, PRO CAB 63/74. Hankey's discussion on the creation of an Australian Council of Defence had begun in London with an Australian air force representative in April 1934. In May 1935 the Dominions Office was informed that Hankey's suggestions had been accepted: E.T. Crutchley (Canberra) to Dominions Office, 2 April 1935, PRO CAB 63/70. For the development of the Australian defence programme see Paul Hasluck, *The Government and the People, 1939–1941*, Canberra, 1952), 30 ff.
[23] Hankey's report to the Prime Minister on 'Discussions on Defence in New Zealand', 14 January 1935, PRO CAB 63/78. New Zealand revived a proposal made by Britain in 1931 that it should send a battalion to Singapore. Hankey felt that this might have an effect on discussions about defence in Central Africa, as supporting the settlers' view that only white forces should be maintained there. Hankey to the D.M.O., (Major-General John Dill), 2 December 1934, ibid. For New Zealand's considerable defence effort between 1935 and 1937 see F.L.W. Wood, *The New Zealand People at War: Political and External Affairs* (Wellington, 1958) pp. 62 – 76. See also B.K. Gordon, *New Zealand becomes a Pacific Power* (Chicago, 1960), pp. 77 – 97, and R.M. Burdon, *The New Dominion: New Zealand, 1918–1939* (London, 1965), pp. 269 – 70.
[24] See Hamill, *The Strategic Illusion*, ch. XI.

237

although a second aerodrome was sanctioned, it was still the case that the main reliance was placed upon guns; by the time of Hankey's tour this decision could no longer be challenged.

For Canadians, the growing uncertainties of the international situation increased the desire to remain aloof from the quarrels in Europe even if, like the influential editor John Dafoe, they believed that, constitutionally speaking, Canadian belligerence would be automatic if Britain went to war: 'The Dominions have feelings of loathing and fear for Europe and her hopeless insanities, and when Great Britain gets pulled into a European massacre of the nations the desire of large elements of the population of those Dominions will be to keep away from the explosions and the falling walls.'[25] The Prime Minister, Bennett, was well aware of these feelings and also cognisant of British apprehensions made plain to him during a visit to Britain earlier in the year. But he took no action to overcome Canada's lack of a serious military capacity, and showed the same sensitivity as Mackenzie King to any suggestion of being involved in policies of Empire defence.[26] In this he was not unrepresentative of much Canadian opinion.[27] It was not surprising that Hankey's visit produced a pessimistic report, finding little preparedness for an overseas force even if Canada should decide to co-operate in a future war. Canada's chief concern was to be able to defend its neutrality in the event of a war between the United States and Japan, and for this it would rely chiefly upon its air force. Naval questions were regarded with almost total apathy.[28]

When Hankey reported to the cabinet in January 1935 he claimed that all the Dominion Prime Ministers had expressed 'their understanding and their acquiesence in the policy of the cabinet'. But the

[25] Dafoe to Lothian, 10 October 1934, in R. Cook, *The Politics of John W. Dafoe and the Free Press* (Toronto, 1963), p. 237. The views of many important figures in the Canadian civil service ran along the same lines. See J.L. Granatstein, *The Ottawa Men: The Civil Service Mandarins, 1935–1957* (Toronto, 1982).

[26] Eayrs, *In Defence of Canada*, vol. I, p. 316. Bennett had attended a meeting of the Committee of Imperial Defence, but then wrote to Hankey asking to have his name deleted from the list of its members, since he regarded it as wholly a United Kingdom body. E. Watkins, *R.B. Bennett*, (London, 1963), p. 149.

[27] In a report of 1934 a study group of the Canadian Institute of International Affairs expressed concern about Canadian servicemen being sent for training in England and the co- ordination with the British army of Canadian army regulations and equipment: 'At critical moments on the eve of war, the advice of the military authorities is apt to become only too influential, and in Canada this advice would be imperialist in sympathies.' Eayrs, op. cit., pp. 89 – 90.

[28] Hankey, 'Impressions of Canada, December 1934', memorandum of 1 January 1935, PRO CAB 63/81. In 1937 a distinguished Canadian intellectual, Professor Frank Scott, was arguing that installing a couple of coastal batteries at Esquimault and Vancouver diminished Canada's security. Eayrs, op. cit., p. 121.

cabinet held that the secret nature of his report was such as to preclude its immediate communication to the Dominion Prime Ministers, and that it should be held over until they arrived in London for George V's silver jubilee. Three such meetings were held at the beginning of May, and were notable for New Zealand's again expressing anxieties over progress at Singapore. Menzies for Australia pointed to his country's general lack of interest in foreign affairs, but admitted to its special interest in the defence problems of the Far East.[29] In other respects the presence of the Dominion Prime Ministers seems to have made little difference to imperial relations in the field of defence. Indeed, one has the feeling that for British ministers and officials the succession of crises in Europe in 1935 and 1936 and the acceleration of the rearmament programme which they produced took precedence over considerations of the Empire's role in defence, and that it was on the diplomatic side if anywhere that we should trace the influence of Commonwealth governments.[30]

For those intimately concerned with such matters there was indeed an appreciation of the increasing gulf between the informed sections of British opinion and opinion in the Dominions. When Bruce urged the Committee of Imperial Defence in July 1936 to find a way of stimulating Dominions interest in defence matters, Hankey's reply was relatively optimistic, except in respect of Canada, which had made least progress and was rarely represented at C.I.D. meetings.[31]

The Imperial Conference of 1937 and its aftermath

The prospect of the next Imperial Conference, due to meet in May 1937, found British ministers in the same dilemma where the Far East was concerned. The Chiefs of Staff were very reluctant to give a pledge to send the Fleet to Singapore should war break out. At the same time, ministers had been urged to draw the attention of the Dominions to

---

[29] Meeting 16 January 1935, PRO CAB 23/81; PRO CAB 32/125.

[30] During the Prime Ministers' meetings Hertzog and, to a lesser extent, Lyons had disagreed with what was now the British interpretation of the origins of the German threat. See the account of the meetings in H. Duncan Hall, *Commonwealth*, (London, 1971), pp. 729 – 37.

[31] C.I.D. meeting, 30 July 1936, PRO CAB 2/6. When a correspondent of Grigg's wrote to say what a falling off in defence organisation he had found in Australia and New Zealand compared with 1909, Grigg replied: 'What you tell me about Australia causes me no surprise. All the Dominions have been looking inwards for many years past and have seemed to become absolutely unconscious of their external relations in a very dangerous world.' Sir Frank Fox to Grigg 19 September, and Grigg to Fox, 9 October 1935: Grigg Papers, 1931 – 8.

the measures taken in the United Kingdom and to urge them to help reduce the burden by doing more themselves.[32]

What was now needed was something very difficult to achieve, namely to make the position sound serious enough to persuade the Dominions, even South Africa, to increase their defence expenditure without making it seem as though Britain could not carry out its own proclaimed intentions. For this might lead them to abandon the idea of imperial co-operation, and content themselves with local defence measures only. Our policy, said Samuel Hoare, the First Lord of the Admiralty, 'should be to some extent to leave them guessing.' Swinton, the Secretary of State for Air, suggested that the Australians should be given a fright, while Inskip, the Minister for the Co-ordination of Defence, 'thought that it would only be necessary to tell the truth'.[33] The private discussion of the correct tactics to be adopted towards the Dominion Prime Ministers seems a far cry from the reiterated public declaration of constant and intimate cooperation between the members of the British Commonwealth; but it illustrates the true position.

British policy was seriously questioned at the Conference itself, particularly by the New Zealand Prime Minister. Savage wished to know why, if it was Britain's intention in time of war to send a sufficient force to Singapore, it was not possible to keep one there in peacetime for deterrent purposes. In reply the British government could only reiterate its policy, and admit that there would be a period from the spring of 1938 to the summer of 1939 when Britain would have to rely on French assistance in home waters, and when the fleet that could be sent to the Far East would be 'slightly inferior to the full Japanese naval strength'. No answer was given in the full conference to Savage's inquiries, but a meeting was held between the Australian and New Zealand delegations and the Chiefs of Staff, where the more serious discussions of the defence situation took place.[34]

---

[32] Notes for discussion in cabinet, March or April 1937, Cambridge University Library, Templewood Papers, IX.2; Chiefs of Staff Subcommittee meeting, 5 February 1937, PRO CAB 53/6; Report of Defence Policy and Requirements Committee, 12 February 1936, PRO CAB 16/123.

[33] Defence Plans (Policy) Committee of the C.I.D., meeting of 11 May 1937, PRO CAB 16/181.

[34] Hamill, op. cit., 278 ff; Gordon, op. cit., 76 ff; Hall, op. cit., 744 – 6; meetings of Chiefs of Staff Subcommittee, 7 and 21 June 1937, PRO CAB 53/7.

The 1937 Imperial Conference clearly revealed that the Commonwealth was in fact split on the defence issue.[35] Whatever their disagreements in detail, Australia and New Zealand agreed about the seriousness of the situation and the need for common action to meet it. But South Africa and, to an even greater extent, Canada were opposed to any general plans being made: 'Centralization', declared Mackenzie King, 'inevitably meant disunity. A system of separate national defence policies might be unwieldy and costly, but the alternative would be more costly still. The best contributions Canadians could make either to Canada or to the Commonwealth would be to keep Canada united.' Canadian public opinion supported a national defence policy only.[36]

The question of the role of the Dominions in defence did not disappear from the British government's agenda. On 16 February 1938 the cabinet discussed a gloomy report on the defence outlook by the Minister for the Co-ordination of Defence, who saw it as the plain fact 'that it was beyond the resources of this country to make proper provision in peace for the defence of the Empire against three major powers in three different theatres of war'. It was decided that a version of the report should be produced for the Dominions in such a way as not to leak secrets and to avoid 'alarming some of the Dominions unduly'. In July, faced with the financial obstacles to attaining the desired fleet levels, attention was again focused on persuading the Dominions to take their proper share in defence. The First Lord of the Admiralty pointed out that the Dominions had been left in the dark since they had been assured at the 1937 Imperial Conference that Britain could send a fleet to the Far East, with no mention of lack of money as a possible obstacle. In March, indeed, Chamberlain had assured Lyons that it was untrue that in the event of war Britain would be unable to defend her overseas possessions: 'As a result of our progress in rearmament including Singapore, we are in fact in a better position in this respect than we were three years ago.'[37]

[35] The official report naturally stressed such areas of cooperation as existed. *Imperial Conference 1937: Summary of Proceedings*, (Cmd 5482, 1937).

[36] Meeting of Principal Delegates to 1937 Imperial Conference, 24 May 1937, PRO CAB 32/128. For Mackenzie King's role at the Conference see Neatby, *William Lyon Mackenzie King*, vol. III, ch. 12. Mackenzie King was much more concerned with the foreign policy aspects of the discussions.

[37] Cabinet meeting, 16 February 1938, to discuss C.P.24(38), 'Most Secret further Report by the Minister for the Co-ordination of Defence on Defence Expenditure in Future Years', in PRO CAB 23/92; cabinet meeting, 20 July 1938, PRO CAB 23/94; Chamberlain to Lyons, PRO PREM 1/309.

Meanwhile the United States had begun from December 1937 to show more interest in naval co-operation with Britain after a long period of distancing itself, following the disagreements over the reaction to Japan's invasion of Manchuria in 1931. And the British were heartened by the visit of three American cruisers at the opening ceremony of the Singapore graving dock in February 1938. But it is clear that the United States had no intention of basing its own naval action, or even part of it, on the British base.[38] What mattered more immediately was what could be done to strengthen the base's defences, and here there were many impediments.[39] One was the reluctance of the civil authorities under the governor Sir Shenton Thomas to take any responsibility for the defence of the civilian population. Another was the insistence of the Treasury on keeping to the principle of a colony paying for its own local forces and budgeting for such expenditure for a number of years ahead. It was only gradually accepted during 1937 that there was a possibility that the base would be attacked overland through Malaya.[40] The British Chiefs of Staff could only reiterate their view that in time of war Singapore would have to be reinforced from India. But it was recognised that India's forces were not suitably trained or equipped for such a role. A commission of inquiry under Chatfield was sent out to investigate the position but its report did not come before the cabinet until June 1939.[41]

One might add that Hong Kong's position also came up for discussion at this time, with even less hope of finding a solution for the problem of its defence. Again, much was seen to depend upon India, and India was thought unlikely to act. The hope of interesting the Americans in its defence was unrealistic. Japan having given notice in 1934 of her intention to terminate her adherence to the Washington Treaty from December 1936, the Chiefs of Staff were able to discuss whether the limitations on Hong Kong's defence imposed by the Four Power Pact, signed at Washington on 21 December 1921,[42] could now be reviewed. But policy-makers disagreed about the value of

[38] Hamill, op. cit., pp. 302 – 3. For the naval conversations with the Americans see Roskill, *Naval Policy between the Wars*, vol. II, pp. 366 – 8.

[39] See S.W. Kirby, *Singapore, the chain of disaster* (London, 1971), 31 ff.

[40] Material on these points is to be found in the papers of General A.E. Percival in the Imperial War Museum.

[41] Chiefs of Staff subcommittee, 14 December 1938, PRO CAB 53/10. For the composition of India's armed forces at the time see *Official History of the Indian Armed Forces in the Second World War*, vol. 1 (Delhi, 1956).

[42] Text in Cmd 2037, (1924).

strengthening its defences. Chatfield felt that this could have a deterrent effect on Japan, while Chamberlain argued that the longer the colony held out, the greater the blow to prestige when it fell.[43]

The limitations of imperial defence co-operation

In other respects, all that the United Kingdom could do as far as the Dominions were concerned was to seek assistance on particular points concerned with its own preparations for war, not always with success. In 1935 South Africa refused to follow the remaining Dominions and Southern Rhodesia in agreeing that all its civil and military airfields would be available to the R.A.F., on the grounds that this would be attacked by the Opposition as 'truckling to imperialism'. Hertzog himself tried to soften the blow by referring to the cordial relations that had always existed between the R.A.F. and the forces of the Union, and saying that the R.A.F. would always be welcome in South Africa. Following the 1937 Imperial Conference there were also discussions in London about the defence of Simonstown and Cape Town. Late in 1938 there were further talks on defence with Pirow in London, which included giving the South Africans informal indications of what the United Kingdom would like the Union to do both in regard to preparations in peacetime and in war, should it come.[44] It is clear, however, that there was still suspicion in London that South Africa's own plans involved a more active role outside its borders than the United Kingdom wished to see.

The much expanded air force which was at the heart of Britain's rearmament programme raised the question of the supply and training of air crews. As early as December 1934 the Air Ministry had suggested that Southern Rhodesia should concentrate on the training of pilots for the R.A.F. A system was also devised for granting short-service commissions in the R.A.F. to candidates from the Dominions, and both Canada and Australia took part, though Australia withdrew in 1938 because of the conflict with its own expansion plans.[45]

[43] Chiefs of Staff subcommittee meetings, 24 July 1934 and 4 October 1935, PRO CAB 53/5; C.I.D. meetings, 22 November 1934 and 10 July 1936, PRO CAB 2/6.
[44] PRO DO 114/57; Chiefs of Staff subcommittee meetings, 6 and 28 July and 4 November 1937, PRO CAB 53/8; Report from Dominions Office to High Commissioner in South Africa on talks with Pirow 1 – 16 November 1938, in PRO DO 114/85. On Southern Rhodesia see C.I.D. meeting, 18 December 1934, PRO CAB 2/6.
[45] C.I.D. meeting, 18 December 1934, PRO CAB 2/6; PRO DO 114/84.

Difficulties arose in 1938 when it was suggested that the R.A.F. itself might set up training schools in Canada for both British and Canadian candidates. Mackenzie King objected as it meant being drawn into a commitment; the Dominion must not lose its freedom of action. The proposal was therefore withdrawn, but Mackenzie King pointed out that British pilots could still be trained in Canadian establishments, and a scheme along those lines was announced in May 1939.[46]

The question of additional help in providing the aircraft for the air crews to fly had also preoccupied the government from an early stage of the rearmament programme. It was reported to the cabinet in July 1936 that assistance had been offered by private firms in Australia and Canada, though Lord Weir, the Air Ministry's adviser on aircraft production from May 1935 to May 1938, objected to creating new facilities in Canada while the U.K.'s own capacity was not fully utilised, but the Defence Requirements Subcommittee expressed a welcome for the possibility of thus expanding supply. As far as Australia was concerned, there was a setback in the failure of the government to persuade the Australians to bar all American investment in their major aeronautical company, and to build exclusively British-type machines. In December 1938 it was agreed to investigate a scheme by which aircraft would be built in Australia for both the Australian and British governments.[47]

The importance of Canadian co-operation was regarded as even greater. In October 1936 Hankey urged the Prime Minister to put in a word with Mackenzie King, shortly to be his guest, about securing the assistance of Canadian industry. Baldwin did indeed press upon him the need for more help from the Dominions now that United States neutrality legislation had made it impossible to place orders there.[48] Despite the fact that Canadian costs were estimated as 25 per cent above those in the United Kingdom, a definite interest in a scheme for manufacturing aircraft in Canada developed in 1938, and

[46] Ibid. For the announcement of the agreed scheme see H.C. *Deb.*, vol. 360, cols 1507 – 8, 1 May 1939. By the time the first British trainees were due to arrive in September war had broken out, and the scheme was cancelled. Neatby, op. cit., pp. 281 – 3.

[47] C.I.D. Subcommittee on Defence Policy and Requirements, meeting of 23 July 1936, PRO CAB 16/136; PRO DO 114/57; meeting of 21 December 1938, PRO CAB 23/96.

[48] Hankey to Baldwin, 22 October 1936, PRO CAB 21/440; Middlemas and Barnes, *Baldwin*, 968.

it was agreed to place 'educational orders' with Canadian industry, without involving the Canadian government.[49]

Any proposals for co-operation in the supply of arms ran a political risk. An agreement had been reached in March 1938 for the manufacture in Canada of Bren guns for both the British and the Canadian forces – a project which had been discussed at the Imperial Conference. When this agreement was leaked in Canada it caused a minor political crisis, largely because Canada shared in the storm of suspicion directed towards the private manufacturers of armaments then raging in North America. The opposition failed however to bring home the point that Mackenzie King's procrastination, which had delayed the scheme for almost two years, had weakened Canada's own defence capacities.[50] Mackenzie King's suspicions would have been strengthened had he known that, in commending the aircraft proposal to the cabinet, Chamberlain had said: 'If Canada could become interested in the provision of aircraft to this country, the aloofness of that Dominion from Imperial defence and its dissociation from the problems of the United Kingdom might be reduced.'[51]

Even with New Zealand, where there were no such inhibitions against imperial collaboration, difficulties could arise. A paper outlining suggestions for New Zealand's defence policy was prepared by the Chiefs of Staff early in 1938, but was delayed so as to await a favourable opportunity for its presentation. In fact New Zealand had already worked out its own programme, in which a key element had been the establishment in 1937 of its own Air Force. In October 1938 it submitted plans for increasing co-operation in air defence, but the Chiefs of Staff held that the priority given to the air did not fit in with their own views, and again raised the question of how New Zealand might best be made aware of them.[52] By the end of 1938, with 'Munich' having proved to be no more than a temporary lightening of British anxieties in Europe, and with Japan fully embarked upon its China campaign, it appeared inevitable that the whole question of imperial defence in the Far East would once again require examination.

---

[49] Cabinet meetings, 13 April and 18 and 25 May 1938, PRO CAB 23/93; ibid., 29 June 1938, PRO CAB 23/94; Ian Colvin, *The Chamberlain Cabinet* (London, Gollancz, 1971), p. 136.
[50] Neatby, op. cit., pp. 279 – 81.
[51] PRO CAB 21/495.
[52] Burdon, op. cit., pp. 269 – 70; Chiefs of Staff subcommittee meeting, 19 October 1938, PRO CAB 53/9.

Chapter 11

CLEARING THE DECKS: IRELAND, INDIA, THE MIDDLE EAST

Reducing the commitments

An imperial system threatened by major enemies is bound to try to rid itself of peripheral responsibilities in defence that may detract from its principal concerns; if the legions can be recalled, it is safer to recall them. If political means can be found for reducing the call upon military resources, then the search for such means becomes an acceptable object of policy. Neither the overt arguments in favour of the particular policies adopted nor the arguments against them may be framed in precisely this fashion; arguments over relations with the Irish Free State, over the constitutional evolution of India and over Britain's interests in and policies towards Egypt, Iraq and Palestine had their own content and momentum. Links between them have always been accepted: the interplay of the Irish and Indian national movements; the Middle East as the point at which British and Indian interests were linked; the asserted concern of Arab and Moslem countries with the Arab-Jewish conflict in Palestine. Historians, in treating them independently of each other, only mirror the facts that the issues normally concerned different sectors of the United Kingdom bureaucracy and excited different elements in the Parliamentary and political worlds. Perhaps only Churchill among leading political figures, with his instinct to see the external world in terms of global strategy, showed a lively interest in all the problems involved. But in the routine work of the Committee of Imperial Defence and the Chiefs of Staff and in the deliberations of cabinet, matters affecting one or other area required constant attention.[1]

The defence dimension of these problems was accentuated by the increasing realisation that Britain might after all be drawn back into

[1] See e.g. 'Review of Imperial Defence by the Chiefs of Staff Sub-Committee of the Committee of Imperial Defence', 22 February 1937, *DBFP*, 2nd Series, vol. XVIII (London, 1980), Appendix 1.

direct participation in a European war, since the advent of the air arm gave rather more than less importance to the historic concern with the Low Countries and north-eastern France. At a discussion between the Prime Minister and a deputation of members of both Houses of Parliament with particular concern for defence, held in July 1936, Edward Grigg compared the existing situation with that in 1914: 'In 1914 the danger of trouble in the Empire when we were engaged in war was really very slight, but I do not think we can take risks in India or the Middle East.'[2] For Grigg and those who thought like him the important thing was to make it clear to the French that Britain had no automatic commitment to send an expeditionary force to the continent in the event of war, and to continue to give priority to the training of a reserve to defend the overseas Empire. But the alternative was to reduce the commitments to which Grigg referred.

Ireland

The dissatisfaction of the Irish even with the revised status of Commonwealth countries agreed upon at the 1926 Imperial Conference was recognised and at the 1930 Conference Irish insistence on pushing their point of view was enhanced by the proximity of a general election at which de Valera would be campaigning for a still further loosening of the surviving ties with the United Kingdom.[3] In 1927 de Valera had made it clear that, in his view, neutrality was the proper policy for Ireland to adopt and that England represented the obvious threat of aggression.[4] In these circumstances, the unwillingness of the British government to contemplate the kind of close relations between the armed forces of the two countries such as existed with the other Dominions is readily understandable. Furthermore there were two areas of possible direct conflict. The unity of Ireland, by which de Valera meant the incorporation of Ulster in the Free State, was and remained the ultimate objective of his policy. Partition made agreement on foreign or defence issues with Britain out of the question.[5] Secondly there were the

---

[2] Two such meetings were held on 28 and 29 July 1936. Baldwin was accompanied by Inskip on both occasions and by Lord Halifax, now Lord Privy Seal and leader of the House of Lords, on the first. There is a record in the Simon Papers.

[3] For the 1930 Imperial Conference, see Hall, *Commonwealth*, pp. 690 – 5.

[4] Patrick Keatinge, *A Singular Stance: Irish Neutrality in the 1980s* (Dublin, 1984), p. 14.

[5] See John Bowman, *De Valera and the Ulster Question 1917–1973* (Oxford, 1982).

British rights in the southern Irish ports, safeguarded in the Treaty of 1921, which could both be seen as an encroachment on the Free State's sovereignty and as likely to impede acceptance for its neutral standing in a British war. This issue was dormant in the 1920s, but with the worsening of the international situation and the possibility that Britain might once again have to face a submarine campaign against her shipping, the importance of the ports was likely to be enhanced in the eyes of naval strategists, even though it could be and was argued that they would be difficult to utilise in the face of a hostile Irish people and government.[6]

In the February 1932 election the return of de Valera for what was to prove a sixteen-year term of office brought the Anglo-Irish question once more to the fore.[7] Although there was no immediate repudiation of the Commonwealth ties, and although Ireland did take part in the Ottawa Conference, that was to be her last formal appearance as part of the Commonwealth family.

The priorities of de Valera's policy were to remove the oath of allegiance, in conformity with his Republican views, and to cease paying the land annuities which had been part of the general settlement of Anglo-Irish issues. The British government was mindful of de Valera's narrow majority and hopeful that the Irish electorate might reverse its decision, but were impelled by Churchill's insistence that the Treaty must stand to express their commitment to the retention of the oath. The rest of the Commonwealth was hostile to any preciptate action, and Smuts in particular wrote to urge that the Empire be not allowed to break up on account of a 'lunatic' who was a mere transient apparition.[8] After the failure of the first round of talks, the government announced that if the land annuities were withheld the money would be recouped by duties on imports from Ireland. Neither talks during the Ottawa Conference nor a visit by de Valera to London could bridge the gap.

Before acting, the British government had to take into account the stirring up of hostile feeling in the United States, and further talks

[6] The military considerations are analysed in Roskill, *Naval Policy between the Wars*, vol. II pp. 446 – 7.

[7] Developments in the 1930s are discussed in Paul Canning, *British Policy towards Ireland 1921–1941* (Oxford, 1985), pt II, and Irish policy in Deirdre McMahon, *Republicans and Imperialists: Anglo-Irish Relations in the 1930s* (New Haven and London, 1984).

[8] Canning, op. cit., p. 132. On the attitude of the Commonwealth governments and on the efforts of the officials of the Dominions Office to play a mediating role, see Holland, *Britain and the Commonwealth Alliance*, pp. 155 – 7.

were held, only to reveal de Valera's intransigence on both the issues at stake. A second Irish election in January 1933 gave de Valera the overall majority he had hitherto lacked. Amendments to the Irish constitution reduced the powers of the Governor-General and ended the right of appeal to the Privy Council. Legislation was passed purporting to deprive Irish citizens of the status of British subjects, and describing British subjects in the Free State as aliens. They were in fact exempted from its consequences.[9] De Valera's victory also enabled him to terminate payment of the annuities, with the expected response by the British government. For the next two years there was in effect a trade war between Britain and the Free State. During this period, the attention of the British government was so absorbed by other pressing matters that Irish questions were neglected, but the damage being done to the economy of both sides produced further negotiations late in 1934, and in January 1935 a partial agreement, the so-called 'coal-cattle pact', was concluded.

The political issues were unaffected by this deal, and early in 1935 it would seem that a tentative approach was made on de Valera's behalf, suggesting a sovereign federal Irish Commonwealth, to be composed of two Dominions, north and south, linked to the Commonwealth by an external association. Consideration of this idea in London, which concluded that the proposals did not take one very far, noted that, apart from constitutional questions, the scheme envisaged the Treaty Ports being garrisoned by Irish forces. Nor, in the end, was such a scheme acceptable either to Ulster or to Irish nationalists.[10]

After the British general election of 1935 the new Dominions Secretary, Malcolm MacDonald, saw it as his mission to restore harmony to relations with Ireland,[11] and he was supported by most ministers, though Zetland, the Secretary of State for India, expressed some worry over the possibility that constitutional concessions to the Irish might have an impact on the Indian scene. MacDonald's belief that de Valera shared his keenness for a settlement proved overoptimistic; the only argument that could be advanced to him against going ahead with his plans was that leaving the Commonwealth would make more difficult any future reunification of Ireland.[12]

[9] David Harkness, 'Mr De Valera's Dominion', *JCPS*, vol. VIII (1970), pp. 206 – 28.
[10] Bowman, op. cit., pp. 118 – 23.
[11] Harkness, loc. cit.
[12] Canning, op. cit., 164 ff.

The British government was somewhat more open to suggestions from de Valera, such as were put forward during the Abyssinian crisis in October 1935, because it was believed in the Dominions Office that unless de Valera got his way on the constitutional issues, he might be replaced by even more hard-line Republicans.[13] But the other major factor, the deterioration of the international outlook, was clearly the decisive one; the next round of talks, in which further concessions were made to de Valera's point of view, were held in London in April 1936 when the Rhineland crisis was still unresolved.[14]

Irish determination on the issue of the Crown could not be doubted. When George V died on 20 January 1936, de Valera refused to allow the Irish High Commissioner to sign the proclamation of accession or attend the coronation council, though he continued to attend the meetings of High Commissioners on foreign affairs. Further complications were created by the Abdication Act ending the reign of Edward VIII. The consideration of the External Relations Bill was hastily completed, and the sole function assigned by it to the King was to act in external affairs so long as the Free State continued to be associated with Britain and the other Commonwealth countries who recognised him as a symbol of their association and so long as he continued to act on their behalf.[15]

According to all the principles that had guided the creators of the new-style Commonwealth of the Balfour formula and the Statute of Westminster, the Irish Free State had ceased to be a member of the Commonwealth, and the new Constitution adopted in 1937 and approved by referendum emphasised the country's remoteness from the Commonwealth model. Yet the British government itself and the Dominions who were consulted at length proved reluctant to make any move which could be interpreted as a final severance of the tie.[16] If it could be shown that the Commonwealth was sympathetic to Ireland's national aspirations and could accommodate them, it was hoped that some kind of arrangement could be arrived at in respect of defence, which was by now the overriding concern of ministers and officials alike.

In July 1936 the Chiefs of Staff had submitted a report on relations

[13] Holland, op. cit., 161 ff.
[14] On the Anglo-Irish discussions during this period see McMahon, op. cit., ch. 9.
[15] On account of legalistic complications, the office of Governor-General was not abolished until the passage of the Consequential Provisions Act of June 1937: ibid., p. 200.
[16] On the consultations with the Dominions see ibid., ch. 10.

with the Free State in time of war, and had emphasised the need not only to deny Irish ports and airfields to the enemy, but to have their use for Britain's own forces. Since Britain's purchase or leasing of the bases was unlikely to appeal to the Irish, it was desirable that their upkeep should be the responsibility of the Irish government but this, in the view of the Chiefs of Staff, involved the two countries entering into a formal treaty of alliance. It might be better to regard the Commonwealth chapter as closed and to treat Ireland as a friendly foreign country. Given both Ireland's disillusion with international action after the failure of the League sanctions against Italy, of which de Valera had been a strong supporter, and above all the Ulster impediment, it does not seem likely that much hope was placed in such ideas.[17]

In fact the issue of defence was only part of a continued search for an agreement, and the talks were conducted on the British side on the assumption that in the last resort Commonwealth members would decide on their own policies in a time of crisis irrespective of their formal constitutional status. Canada could hardly have been clearer on that point.[18]

Irish neutrality would have to be taken as a strong possibility, and the future of the Treaty Ports was now reassessed in the light of that fact.[19] It was clear that the Admiralty did not attach the same degree of importance to the ports now that Germany was the probable enemy as it had when France had been seen in this light.[20] What would have been acceptable would have been to turn over the ports to the Free State with a guarantee that they would be handed back if war came; meanwhile money might be saved – an important consideration for Chamberlain – if the costs of maintenance were taken up wholly or in part by the Irish government. Since it was unlikely that the Irish would be forthcoming on any of these points and since it was the view of Chamberlain, who became Prime Minister while these matters were under consideration, that the important thing was to assure a friendly Ireland, negotiations for a general settlement, including cession of the ports, was the only option left. These negotiations began in January 1938.

[17] Ibid., pp. 188 – 91.
[18] Holland, op. cit., pp. 163 – 6.
[19] The Irish ports issue is put in its context in Canning, op. cit., ch. 9.
[20] This assessment was to some extent supported by General Marshall when the Americans made an assessment of the ports in August 1943, since he argued that they would be of little use so long as the *French* coast was under German control. McMahon, op. cit., 234 fn.

The difficulties that then arose were due to the attempt by de Valera to use the British government's willingness to settle the financial question and to cede the ports, to press also for some movement towards the ending of partition, and the difficulties that this represented for the British government both in Ulster itself and in Parliament. For Ulster also an agreement on trade without financial compensation was itself unacceptable, and, even after the decision had been made to give up the ports, this issue delayed completion of the agreement. The eventual Treaty, signed on 25 April, settled a variety of financial and trade matters, but in respect of defence all Britain could achieve in return for the cession of the ports was an undertaking to keep them up to British standards with no promise as to their future use. By then the ports were in fact far from being on a war footing.[21]

Neither the press nor Parliament showed much apprehension about the defence implications of the agreement. Only Churchill, in the debate on 5 May, expressed serious misgivings, and he was criticised as an alarmist.

It can be argued that the case for cession was unanswerable, and that the naval history of the war when it came does not invalidate it. But what is even more clear is that the hope that the concessions would not matter because of the goodwill that would flow from an agreement was incorrect. The issue of partition had not been allowed to impede the agreement but it had not disappeared, and de Valera's concern about the alleged oppression of Catholics in the North was taken up by sections of the British press and by the Labour Party. The Dominions Office also tended to see the justice of the Irish government's case, and there was some movement in Whitehall towards examining the question of whether the ending of partition might not be to Britain's advantage.[22] The international situation again proved a factor in suggesting the desirability of being on good terms with Ireland, and de Valera's support for Chamberlain over Munich gave rise to the view that even a technically neutral Ireland might turn out to be willing to offer some co-operation in the event of war.[23] The service departments certainly assumed as much in their planning. On

[21] Letter to the author from David Harkness, 12 February 1973.
[22] Canning, op. cit., ch. 11.
[23] On 8 September 1938 Inskip* lunched with de Valera, whom he found worried about the possibility of war, and asking for advice as to the best use of his resources. His idea was 'a few planes'. This was discouraged by Inskip, who suggested that he take measures for the defence of the ports. Churchill College, Cambridge, Caldecote Papers, Inskip Diary, vol. 1, p. 4.

the other hand, an Irish Republican Army (I.R.A.) terror campaign on the mainland which began in January 1939 had the effect of making Ulster's case more acceptable to British opinion. Nevertheless, Britain made one more concession. Fearful that de Valera might use the Ulster question to stir up American opinion, Chamberlain agreed to exclude Ulster from Britain's first peace-time measure of conscription, the Military Training Act of 26 May 1939.[24]

India

If the Irish problem was a nagging one because of the element of propinquity and the influence of the Irish in the Dominions and in the United States, the Indian situation was of far greater importance to British policy-makers and the British Parliament, since it was widely assumed that the cardinal axis of the Empire was that between London and New Delhi. After the collapse of the Round Table Conference at the end of 1932 and the defeat of 'Civil Disobedience' in India, the way was clear for another attempt through a British government initiative to seek for a new constitutional settlement according a greater measure of Indian self-government, while not unduly relaxing the ties that bound India into the imperial structure as a whole.[25] A White Paper issued on 18 March 1933 substantially embodied what the Government had offered at the final session of the Round Table Conference: a federation in which princely India would take its place alongside the provinces of 'British India'. The proposals were considered by a Joint Committee of the two Houses of Parliament, which was in session from April 1933 to October 1934 and was the foundation of the Government of India Act of 1935. In 1937 the first elections for the new Provincial Councils took place, but the failure to persuade the Princes to take part in the new structure meant that the federal part of the Act did not come into play before the advent of war brought about a new crisis in India's affairs.

The issues raised by these constitutional proposals and their partial introduction were what principally attracted the attention of British politicians, since they provided the opportunity for the expression of continued dissent on the part of Churchill and others which at one

[24] Bowman, op. cit., pp. 203 – 4.
[25] See R.J. Moore, *The Crisis of Indian Unity, 1917–1940* (Oxford, 1974), and J.A. Cross, *Sir Samuel Hoare*, (London, 1977), ch. 4.

moment threatened to split the Conservative party and perhaps endanger the government.[26] But this is to look at the Indian scene at only one level. Other developments were longer term: the progressive Indianisation of the Indian Civil Service and, more haltingly, of the armed services. In this way the ground was being prepared for at least the 'Dominion status' which British liberal opinion saw as the desirable outcome of the constitutional changes.[27] At the same time the Indian Congress, increasingly under the sway of Jawaharlal Nehru, was working towards independence on quite different lines, not those of a federal system, but of a State in which power would be held by a Congress Party organised on centralised lines and accepting national leadership.[28]

It has been pointed out that by comparison with other movements against imperial rule in this period, the Indian experience was unique, particularly in the tactics employed by Congress and by Gandhi personally. 'Civil Disobedience' was a difficult weapon to counter for those professing British liberal views and bound by India's commitment to British legal norms. It enabled Gandhi to take the high moral ground even when the immediate objective was not attained.[29] On the other hand, the strongly Hindu aspects of these tactics did nothing to reassure Muslims as to their future in a Congress Raj. Inevitably, as had been the case in the early 1920s, civil disobedience did not preclude a high degree of violence. By August 1932 seven battalions of troops were required to aid the civil power. Thereafter there was a gradual decline in violence until 1936.[30]

From the point of view of the Empire as a whole, the role of India's armed forces in this period of growing international tension was the most important thing of all. How far was it possible to get India to pay for the larger and better equipped forces which were increasingly thought desirable? What prospect was there for such an improvement to be the occasion of releasing British forces for duties closer to home?

[26] See G.R. Peele, 'The Conservative Party and the Opposition to the Government of India Act, 1929–1935' (unpublished Oxford B.Phil. thesis, 1972).
[27] The problems of this curious phase of transition where Indian members of the I.C.S. were concerned are well illustrated in N.B. Bonarjee, *Under Two Masters* (London, 1970).
[28] For the development of Congress politics in this period see B.R. Tomlinson, *The Indian National Congress and the Raj 1929-1942* (London, 1976).
[29] See the unpublished paper by D.A. Low, 'The Imprint of Ambiguity: Britain and India in the 1930s', kindly communicated to me by the author.
[30] C. Townshend, *Britain's Civil Wars: Counter-Insurgency in the Twentieth Century* (London, 1986), 146 ff.

How far were the familiar defence problems of the North-West frontier and of Russian pressure through Afghanistan to be seen as secondary to the Japanese threat?[31] What contribution could India continue to make to those parts of the Middle East for which she had historically been responsible? And finally though less tangibly, how did the nature of the forthcoming conflict as seen by India's British rulers correspond to the world view of Nehru and his colleagues, and also to that of the 'martial races' upon whom the Indian army had hitherto relied for most of its recruitment?[32]

A principal source of British concern during the constitutional negotiations was precisely the unwillingness of the British government to see ministers responsible to an Indian electorate control the armed forces. A correspondent of Simon's in 1930 suggested that the British Army in India should be stationed in an enclave in the North West Frontier Province and Baluchistan, which should be separated from the rest of India and not controlled by the Indian government. From there it could carry out its task of imperial defence and assist with internal security. In his reply Simon pointed out that the size of India and the difficulty of communications made it necessary for the army to be distributed throughout the country, so as to be at hand when needed. And he recognised that the moment was in any event a difficult one for a federal solution to India's problems:

> Speaking in philosophic terms there is really at present a centrifugal movement going on in India, as a result of which states and provinces will ultimately develop their full individual life. Until that centrifugal movement is completed, the centripetal impulse towards federal union cannot really begin. And one of the greatest difficulties of this problem is to make tentative arrangements for the subsequent process while the former process is still only begun.[33]

---

[31] The threat of Soviet aggression against India was still recognised as a real one by the Chiefs of Staff, but given a lower priority than the threats from Germany, Japan and Italy. Memorandum of 22 February 1937, *DBFP*, 2nd Series, vol. XVIII, p. 984.

[32] The persistence in the belief that only certain elements in the Indian population were suitable for military service died hard. It was held in the 1930s that these amounted to only 10 per cent of the population, all from the north of India. By 1939 there was still no regiment recruited from central or southern India. *The Economist*, (London), 24 October 1987. Changes came during the war on Auchinleck's initiative: see Sir N. Prasad, *Expansion of the Armed Forces and Defence Organization* (Calcutta, 1965), pp. 84 – 9, in the series edited by B. Prasad, *Official History of the Indian Armed Forces in the Second World War*.

[33] C.M. King to Sir John Simon, 2 July 1930, and Simon to King, 7 July 1930: Simon Papers.

Worries about paying for defence were among the reasons which also led to hesitation about a constitutional settlement in which responsibility for finance would be in Indian hands: 'The impression prevails that both on principles and on practice, whether the question be currency or private debts or army expenditure or taxation, we cannot rely on an Indian legislature supporting sound finance.' Was there not a risk that, in order to maintain financial stability, it would either be necessary to suspend the new constitution or for the British taxpayer to assume the whole burden of Indian finance?[34] And such fears by a financial expert expressed in private were echoed publicly by the die-hard opponents of the India Bill, who were encouraged in their resistance both by some of those in official positions and by part of the British business community.

Simon's view of the strength of centrifugal tendencies was confirmed when, after the coming into force of the India Act in its provincial aspects, Congress governments, and other governments based upon an Indian electorate, took over in the Provinces. If they were to prove stable it was essential that they be allowed to retain the revenues they raised, and that meant that the central government would not be in a position to pay for the strengthening of the armed forces which the British military increasingly thought to be essential for imperial defence.[35]

In fact, it was recommended by a tribunal in 1933 that the British government should make some contribution towards Indian military expenditure, mainly on the ground that the Indian army could serve outside India in an emergency; and though this was accepted in principle, the Treasury fought a successful action to reduce the sum asked for. In 1937 India and Burma accounted for the disposition of almost a third of the British regular army, and after a further inquiry in 1938 it was accepted that more money would be required, though it was shortage of industrial resources rather than cash that was by the eve of war the main reason for India's manifest deficiencies in defence.[36]

An additional difficulty was the changing perspective as to the direction in which India's defence effort should be directed. In 1934

[34] Sir Frederick Leith-Ross to Reading, 29 September 1931, PRO FO 800/226.
[35] The unpreparedness of India was emphasised by Sir Ivo Vesey, Chief of the Indian General Staff, at a meeting of the Chiefs of Staff Sub-committee on 21 June 1938, PRO CAB 53/9.
[36] Peden, *British Rearmament and the Treasury*, pp. 138–44. Lord Zetland told his fellow delegates to the 1937 Imperial Conference that 41 per cent of India's central revenues were spent on defence. Meeting of principal delegates to the Imperial Conference, 25 May 1937, PRO CAB 32/128.

the Defence Requirements Subcommittee reported that it was unnecessary to examine the defence of India separately, since if the deficiencies in relation to Germany were met, its needs could also be met. But when this was discussed in the relevant cabinet committee, it was pointed out that the Defence of India plan contemplated an expeditionary force from the United Kingdom to assist in a war with Russia on the north-west frontier.[37] Linlithgow, on arriving in India in 1935 as the new Viceroy, found his anxieties about Japan as being the major threat and Burma as the weak point were not shared by the Commander-in-Chief, who with his experts believed that naval cover was all that was needed, and would prove adequate. Differences with the War Office also arose over the Viceroy's opposition to proposed increases in pay for British forces serving overseas which would fall on the Indian taxpayer. Linlithgow urged instead that money was needed to bring the Indian Army up to date.[38] At the same time, Indianisation was being blamed in Britain for instances of administrative muddle and financial waste.[39] Only after exhaustive discussion in a cabinet committee on the defence of India was the distinction between India's local defence and the needs of the Empire expunged from the official vocabulary and joint responsibility agreed to by the Secretary of State and the Viceroy, at a meeting on 22 May 1939.[40]

It had also proved difficult to reduce India's own overseas commitments. Indeed, these were added to when the decision was taken in 1933 that the India Office should take over from the Colonial Office responsibility for the affairs of the Persian Gulf, now increasingly important with the development of an air route to India. On the other hand Aden, hitherto attached to the Bombay Presidency, became a Crown Colony in 1937. In 1935, during the Abyssinian crisis, India had sent troops to Aden and Port Sudan and had agreed if an emergency arose to send troops to Somaliland, Iraq and Egypt.[41] On

[37] Report dated 28 February 1934, PRO CAB 16/109; meeting of cabinet committee on disarmament, 3 May 1934, PRO CAB 16/110.
[38] See John Glendevon, *The Viceroy at Bay* (London, 1971), pp. 26 – 8, 44 and 93 – 102. On Linlithgow's viceroyalty see also G.Rizvi, *Linlithgow and India: a study of British Policy and the Impasse in India, 1936–1943* (London, 1978).
[39] See the letters from Field-Marshal Birdwood to Major-General R.D. Inskip. Birdwood had carried the Viceroy's Council against Irwin in defeating the proposal for an Indian military college, but this had come into being as soon as he left India in 1930. Papers of Major-General R.D. Inskip, Imperial War Museum. On the progress of Indianisation see S.P. Cohen, *The Indian Army,* (Berkeley & London, 1978) 108 – 36.
[40] PRO CAB 27/653.
[41] Meetings, 26 July 1933, PRO CAB 23/76, and 3 March 1936, PRO CAB 16/136.

India's own borders neither Afghanistan nor Tibet seemed likely to provoke trouble in the 1930s, though vigilance about German activities in Afghanistan surfaced from time to time.

In view of the salience of the defence issue in the attention given to India in official circles, it is not suprising that there was an overlap between those in British politics opposing the constitutional changes and those who were increasingly aware of the new menaces to British security and worried about the slowness of rearmament. After the India Act's passage, Parliamentary opposition had ceased to be so directly relevant, though there was some fear that the Orders in Council which would be necessary to implement federation would be opposed by Lord Salisbury and his friends. But before federation could be brought in the consent of the Indian Princes would be required, and this proved hard to obtain.[42] Historians sympathetic to the Indian nationalist movement as represented by Congress have regarded the inclusion of the Princes in the political equation at the centre as peculiar.[43] Much importance has been attached to the alleged encouragement of their resistance to the terms on offer by the die-hards in Britain. But any examination of their position in the light of the actual situation in which they found themselves can hardly disagree with an authority on this period who writes: 'In order to explain the princes' failure to accede to the all-India federation it is unnecessary to look beyond the policies that the Congress developed towards the states.'[44] What the die-hard contribution amounted to was some obstacle to the Viceroy bringing the pressure against the Princes which he might otherwise have done.[45] They did not need to tell the Princes that the unitary conception that Congress had formed of its own role and of the kind of India it hoped to achieve gave them no place and no prospects: in this they were perfectly correct.

Congress's self-image was equally significant in respect of the Indian Muslims. Although nominally a secular nationalist movement, its Hindu roots were always evident and were even more visible after Congress governments assumed power in the provinces. It became

[42] Glendevon, op. cit., p. 43. On the Indian Princes and their relations with the Indian government see T.C. Coen, *The Indian Political Service* (London, 1971) and R. Jeffrey, (ed.), *People, Princes and Paramount Power: Society and Politics in the Indian Princely States* (Delhi, 1978).
[43] Anil Seal, *Imperialism and Nationalism in India*, p. 19.
[44] R.J. Moore, *The Crisis of Indian Unity*, (Oxford, Clarendon, 1974), p. 305.
[45] Coen, op. cit., p. 103. For criticism of the Viceroy's handling of the Princes and for an expression of the belief that more skilful diplomacy might have brought them round, see Conrad Corfield, *The Princely India I Knew: from Reading to Mountbatten* (Madras, n.d.), pp. 93 – 5.

clear that while Muslims would rule in provinces where they were a majority, where they were not they would be perpetually subordinate. Increasingly therefore they looked across provincial boundaries to a new territorial entity that could ensure their separate survival: 'As the Congress began to undermine the foundations of the Raj, the Muslims began to leave by the back door.'[46] Nehru could speak to the hearts of the British Left; but the Muslims with their fighting men had the bargaining power when it came to government. By 1939 all hopes of clearing the decks where India was concerned had been abandoned.

Reflecting on Britain's predicament in May 1939, a long-term and sympathetic observer of the Indian scene wrote of the impossibility for Britain of dissociating herself from India: 'Whether we wish it or not we are tied to India; we are as much India's prisoners as she is ours. While Great Britain remains a Great Power we cannot see India lapse into disorder.' Discrimination and the racial feelings on which it was based had proved to be Britain's weakness and prevented Indians from identifying themselves with the Empire: 'The capital need for us is to recapture the Indian imagination ... India sees Englishmen chiefly as officials, businessmen or missionaries; it is out of the intellectual swim of the Empire.' And this was clearly of great consequence, since 'with India finally estranged the commanding world position of the Empire is lost forever; and the units which remain will be face to face with Asiatic and world problems which are likely to complete its dissolution'.[47]

The Middle East

Between 1932 and 1939 Britain also made a conscious though largely unsuccessful effort to minimise its commitments to the Middle East in the light of the threats posed in Europe and the Far East to which her defence chiefs gave priority. If there had to be retraction it was to be in the Mediterranean, and the role of the Middle East was to be that of providing an alternative route between India and the Suez Canal. It was presumed that, as relations with the French drew closer, the defence of the western Mediterranean could be treated as a matter for them, but the co-operation in planning developed in respect of

[46] David Page, *Prelude to Partition: The Indian Muslims and the Imperial System of Control* (Delhi, Oxford University Press, 1982), p. 262.
[47] Guy Wint, 'Some Reflections on India', memorandum of May 1939: Lothian Papers, Box 208.

Europe was not extended to the Middle East, where each country took individual action. The French were in fact following a parallel effort at partial disengagement from Syria and Lebanon, culminating in the signature on 9 September 1936 of a Treaty intended to form the basis of Syrian independence which, however, remained unratified at the beginning of the war.[48] But the French regarded the British as rivals for Arab goodwill and were not disposed to sacrifice the latter in order to be in Britain's good books. Thus when in the autumn of 1937, during the Arab rebellion in Palestine, the Mufti of Jerusalem who was at its heart sought refuge in Lebanon, he was allowed to remain there in freedom and to pursue his plotting against the British authorities until October 1939 when, fearful of the French at last bringing in restrictive measures, he betook himself to Iraq and the more attractive prospects of collaboration with the Axis powers.[49]

For it was of course not rivalry with France but the new aggressiveness of Italy and Germany and their attempts to cultivate Arab opinion, as well as the military threat posed by the Italians in Libya to the security of Egypt, that made disengagement so difficult, and made it seem essential that the independent governments of the Middle Eastern countries should favour the British cause. But as in the previous decade, such efforts came up against the totally different aims and aspirations of the conflicting dynasties and indigenous political movements.

It had been hoped that relations with Iraq after that country's independence was confirmed by the League of Nations would provide a model of what disengagement could produce: the necessary degree of influence without a military commitment. But the experience did not prove an altogether happy one. The Treaty had provided for British assistance to Iraq against external aggression; but the Iraqi government still required assistance internally, and in 1935 asked that the R.A.F. should make demonstration flights to subdue a tribal revolt. The request was supported by the British minister in Baghdad, who feared that otherwise the government might fall, and argued that there was no suitable replacement. But the cabinet decided against helping

[48] In 1937 the French had made their task harder by ceding to Turkey the Sanjaq of Alexandretta, thus affronting the Syrians for the sake of good relations with the Turks. See S.Longrigg, *Syria and Lebanon under French Mandate* (London, 1958), chs VI and VII.
[49] On the French attitudes and actions during the Palestine Rebellion see Michael J. Cohen, *Palestine, Retreat from the Mandate – The making of British policy 1936–1945*, (London, Elek, 1978), ch. 4.

out, because the Iraqi government was anti-British while the tribes were pro-British.[50] The Iraqi government was in fact primarily concerned with its own role and ambitions in the Arab world, and in pursuit of these sent armed bands to join in the Palestine rebellion of 1936.

When the British government accepted the Peel Report on Palestine recommending partition, the Iraqi government, far from giving it support, not only advised the Palestine Arabs to reject it, but also spoke out against it in the League of Nations Mandates Commission. To achieve the British objective it was then thought necessary to associate Iraq as well as other Arab governments with the search for a solution in Palestine, since the possibilities of disengagement and a reduction of military burdens were held to depend upon their goodwill. Such indeed was the view of the Foreign Office, which in the 1930s reversed the decisions of the Cairo Conference that had made the Colonial Office the lead department in Britain's Middle East policies, and itself claimed to take the lead as against both the Colonial Office and the service departments.[51]

Egypt

The wish to find a solution to the problem of retaining the essentials of Britain's position on the Suez Canal with the assent of the Egyptian government and Parliament was given greater urgency by the darkening international situation.[52] The failure to achieve agreement in 1930 was followed by political and constitutional upheavals in Egypt, which for a time seemed to give political power into the hands of the monarch, King Fuad, who succeeded in securing the abrogation of the 1923 Constitution. But the combination of internal political pressure from the Wafd and of British influence secured the restoration of the Constitution in December 1935. A Wafd government under Nahas was returned in May 1936, and a treaty of alliance with Britain rapidly concluded and signed in August. It was followed in May 1937 by the abolition of the Capitulations, the most obvious sign of Egypt's subordination to external interests. In May 1937 Egypt entered the League of Nations.

[50] Cabinet meeting, 17 May 1935, PRO CAB 23/81.
[51] This process is full documented in Cohen, op. cit.
[52] For a brief summary of Anglo-Egyptian relations between the wars see M.W. Daly, 'Egypt', in *The Cambridge History of Africa*, vol. 7.

The importance of the Suez Canal to imperial communications was signaled by the consultations with Australia and South Africa about the proposed Treaty. There was a discussion as to whether on the expiration of the Treaty the British position in Egypt should be subject to review by the League of Nations or some other third party. Dr Earle Page argued that the matter was much too vital to be left to any outside body to determine. The Australians wanted communications through Egypt to be 'assured in perpetuity'. Otherwise they would feel that their war effort had been thrown away. The South African High Commissioner, who was speaking without instructions, supported the Australians.[53]

No change was made in the position in the Sudan, where British troops in some numbers had been committed in minor operations.[54] But where Egypt itself was concerned the only British troops were to be in the Canal Zone and were to be limited to a maximum of 10,000 men. (Actual withdrawal to the Canal Zone was however delayed.) Under the Treaty Egypt now had the possibility of pursuing her own foreign policy and managing her own armed forces. But in the light of Mussolini's conquest of Ethiopia and of his other Mediterranean ambitions, it was not possible for Britain to abandon interest in what went on in Cairo. The hostility between the monarch and the Wafd continued under Fuad's successor Faroq, who came to the throne while still a minor in April 1936, and posed to the British ambassador problems not dissimilar to those faced by himself and his High Commissioner predecessors before the signature of the Treaty.[55] Lampson's renewed appointment has been criticised:

[53] C.I.D. meeting, 27 April 1936, PRO CAB 2/6. At a meeting on 29 April the cabinet accepted the Australian argument: PRO CAB 23/84. It has been suggested that this is not to be seen as an example of Dominion influence on foreign policy, since the whole thing had been contrived by Hankey. New Zealand was not represented on this occasion, but in 1930 it had appointed a representative to the British negotiators on the subject. The representative Thomas Wilford asked the New Zealand government to cable its concern for the maintenance of communications through the Canal, and this was done. F.L.W. Wood, *The New Zealand People at War* (Wellington, 1958), pp. 19 – 20.

[54] A. Clayton, *The British Empire as a Super-Power, 1919–1939* (London, 1986), 216 ff. For an account of the handling of the administration of the Sudan under British Foreign Office control see K.D.D. Henderson, *Set under Authority: being a portrait of the life of a British District Officer in the Sudan under the Anglo-Egyptian Condominium* (Castle Cary, 1987).

[55] Sir Miles Lampson (from 1943 Lord Killearn) had become high Commissioner in December 1933 and remained as the first ambassador. His period in office is recorded in Trefor E. Evans (ed.), *The Killearn Diaries, 1934–1946* (London, 1972).

It seems in retrospect to have been a strange thing that after the Anglo-Egyptian treaty of 1936, when we gave independence to Egypt, we should have kept on as Ambassador the same man who had been High Commissioner (i.e. Governor) under the previous dispensation. There he was, behaving in much the same way as before the Treaty, with his special train and all, flying his flag in the same conspicuous Residence, associated in every Egyptian mind with British rule since Cromer. There were British troops in Cairo as well as on the canal and Russell Pasha commanded the police.[56]

Yet such criticism presupposes that Egypt's interests would be seen by its rulers to be identical with those of Britain, and that they would not seek to use other countries to free themselves from what was still seen as British tutelage. By the end of 1937 it was clear that this was not the case. The young King was making difficulties for Nahas who, it was feared, might be overthrown, and there were suspicions that he was intriguing with Italy.[57] Since the ability to send the main fleet to the Far East depended upon control of the Canal, it is not surprising that such reports should have been received with some alarm. Nor were the Egyptians any more helpful than the Iraquis where Palestine was concerned, though it is fair to add that their opposition to any concessions to the Zionist point of view was encouraged by Lampson, who was described by the Colonial Secretary, Malcolm MacDonald, as 'out-Arabing the Arabs'.[58]

The third pillar of British policy, and increasingly the one regarded as most important, was Saudi Arabia, where the monarchy of Ibn Saud appeared to be more stable than either the Iraqi or the Egyptian regimes. His support was consequently cultivated assiduously.

Palestine

I confess [wrote the Zionist leader Weizmann from Jerusalem on 22 October 1935] that British policy at the moment is beyond my comprehension. It looks as though England is prepared almost anywhere to put a premium on violence: here are Hoare's peace

---

[56] Evelyn Shuckburgh, *Descent into Suez: Diaries 1951–1956* (London, Weidenfeld & Nicolson, 1986), p. 6. Shuckburgh had served on Lampson's staff.

[57] Cabinet meeting, 1 December 1937, PRO CAB 23/90A.

[58] Cohen, op. cit., p. 68. On the other hand, the Foreign Secretary was prepared to report to the cabinet on 19 October 1938 that the Egyptian government 'had responded admirably in every way to the Czech crisis': PRO CAB 23/96.

proposals; here is Egypt suddenly granted a constitution as a reward for continuous disaffection, and now we have in Palestine to face the problem of the Legislative Council, which after the recent outbreaks of terrorism in the North must look like yet another instance of yielding to pressure.[59]

Weizmann was in fact correct in suspecting that there were afoot changes in British policy in Palestine, which had seemingly reverted to upholding the mandate after a political outcry had caused the abandonment of the Passfield White Paper of 1930. He was also correct in tracing a connection between the Hoare – Laval attempt to bring about a settlement of the Abyssinian conflict and British policy in the Middle East, for the establishment of Italy's new East African Empire presented a new threat to the British position, diminishing her prestige in the Arab world, and giving Italy new opportunities for propaganda and mischief-making throughout the Middle East.[60]

For Weizmann, as for some of the defenders of the British commitment under the Balfour Declaration such as Churchill and Amery, the new threat could have been met by a vigorous policy of building up the Jewish National Home, perhaps as a Dominion but in any event as an instrument of British policy and, if necessary, of British strength in the area. Such a policy would have treated the additional immigration of the early 1930s, largely of German Jews with economic skills and some capital, as a positive development. It would have insisted on the same enforcement measures for the preservation of law and order as were undertaken in other parts of the Empire where British rule was challenged by violent means. It was compatible with 'partition'.

The protagonists of such policies were however eventually outnumbered in cabinet and unable to prevent the triumph of precisely the opposite policy, of which the Foreign Office, now taking the lead in policy-making with, on the whole, the support of the service departments, became the principal exponent. In the Foreign Office perspective the new international situation demanded that an attempt be made to secure the friendship and collaboration of the Arab world and a settlement of the Palestine question acceptable to

[59] Weizmann to Lord Lugard, 22 October 1935, in *The Letters and Papers of Chaim Weizmann*, Series A, vol. XVII (Rutgers University Press and Hebrew University of Jerusalem, 1979).
[60] The Italian danger was stated at a cabinet meeting on 13 May 1936: PRO CAB 23/84. The Italians also tried to enlist Zionist support, but without success: Weizmann to Ormsby-Gore, 19 July 1936, ibid., p. 314.

the Arab rulers as well as to the Arab notables who claimed to represent the Arab population of Palestine itself.[61]

Since to do this was incompatible with maintaining Britain's commitment under the Mandate to the building-up of the Jewish National Home, it was necessary to liquidate the commitment, or argue that it had already been fulfilled. If a choice had to be made between Arabs and Jews, as now appeared essential if Britain's burdens were to be lightened, *realpolitik* indicated that it was the Jews who should be sacrificed, since while they might oppose the new policies they had, unlike the Arabs, no alternative protectors. The rise of Hitler guaranteed their acquiescence in British rule come what may.[62]

Even within the government, support for the Foreign Office line was not unanimous. The Colonial Office had reservations about abandoning a commitment on which much effort had been spent. But it was unable to do more than exercise a delaying role. Neither Malcolm MacDonald during his brief tenure of the Colonial Office in 1935 nor his successor J.H. Thomas carried much weight. Ormsby-Gore, who became Colonial Secretary in May 1936, while himself a long-time Zionist sympathiser, was obliged to follow the government's general line, and retired two years later largely discredited. Malcolm MacDonald, returning to office, showed none of the sympathies for the Zionists of his earlier years in politics, and proved a resolute defender of the new line, which culminated in the White Paper of 17 May 1939. This finally buried the Mandate by providing for the establishment of an independent Palestinian State within ten years, for limited Jewish immigration for five years from 1939, and with an Arab veto on its further extension.[63] As might have been expected, the India Office, with its concern about Muslim opinion, was a supporter of the Foreign Office line, though there were reports that in 1936 the ex-Viceroy, Willingdon, took the opposite view, feeling that concessions to the Arabs would encourage the Indian nationalists.[64]

[61] See Foreign Office paper, 'Palestine', of 20 June 1936, CP 178(36) in PRO CAB 24/263.

[62] The making of British policy and the interaction between the administration in Palestine and Whitehall are the theme of Cohen, *Palestine: Retreat from the Mandate*. See also G. Sheffer, 'Policy-making and British Policies towards Palestine, 1929-1939', (unpublished Oxford D.Phil thesis, 1971).

[63] *Palestine: A Statement of Policy*, (Cmd 6019, May 1939).

[64] Weizmann to M. Shertok, 15 June 1935, Weizmann, op. cit., p. 271. Communication between the Zionists themselves and the leaders of the Indian Congress was in fact established through the efforts of a South African Jewish disciple of Gandhi, but in 1939 Gandhi published a letter condemning Zionism. Ibid., vol. XVIII, pp. 182, 237.

The issue of Palestine's future was raised more acutely than before by the Arab general strike in May 1936 and the willingness of the British administration to encourage the rulers of Iraq and Saudi Arabia as potential mediators. But, before the end of the strike, it had been decided to try once more the time-honoured device of a Royal Commission. It was during the period when the Commission was engaged on its task that the novel expedient was floated of dividing most of the country into separate Arab and Jewish states, with Britain retaining only a strategic enclave from Jerusalem to the sea. Convinced by what they saw and heard that the conflict was one of two mutually contradictory claims which could not be reconciled, the Commission did indeed end by recommending partition. And for the moment the government was prepared to grasp this possibility.[65]

The government may have been encouraged by the fact that General Dill's arrival in Palestine as Commander of the British troops there had been a signal for the ending of the general strike.[66] The replacement of the endlessly pacific Sir Arthur Wauchope as High Commissioner in the autumn of 1937, following the murder of the acting District Commissioner for Galilee and the dissolution of the Arab Higher Committee, was also the prelude to firmer military action which contained the Arab rebellion, without however eradicating Arab terrorism. But it became evident, with the announcement of a further Commission of Enquiry and with the adoption of restrictions on immigration, that the Government's commitment to partition was less than wholehearted.

It has been argued that, had the Zionists and their friends shown themselves wholly enthusiastic about partition, the Government might have found it difficult to go back on a scheme to which both the Permanent Mandates Commission and the League Council had given their rather reluctant blessing. In fact, the Zionists themselves were divided, as shown by the vote of only 299 to 160 in the Zionist Congress of August 1937. Outside their official ranks, others opposed the scheme on the grounds that the National Home must include the whole country, including, in the Revisionists' opinion, Trans-Jordan as well. On the other wing stood some leaders of American Jewry and a few in Britain, who thought an agreement with the Arabs on a united

[65] *Report of Palestine Royal Commission: Peel Report* (Cmd 5479, July 1937); *Palestine: A Statement of Policy,* (Cmd 5513, July 1937).
[66] The cabinet's decision at a meeting on 2 September 1936 to take firm action is described in the diary of Sir John Simon, who presided in Baldwin's absence: Simon Papers.

country still obtainable. Furthermore, many of the Zionists' friends in Parliament, including Churchill and Lloyd George, were opposed to the partition as being a retreat from the spirit of the mandate. General Smuts also felt that the Jews were being given too precarious a toe-hold and that they should use their proximity to the Suez Canal and their potential as defenders of the Empire to get better terms.[67]

At a cabinet meeting in December 1937 Chamberlain outlined the dangers of Axis propaganda in the Middle East and the need to retain 'old friends' like Ibn Saud. Both the Colonial and Dominion Secretaries still believed that partition would be the only feasible solution in the long run, but agreed that for the time being there must be caution. It is in fact clear that by now partition was not seen as something on the immediate horizon, and that it was expected that the second Commission (the Woodhead Commission) would supply arguments to prove its unviability. This indeed proved to be the case when the Commission reported in September 1938.[68] But well before that date the government was exploring what had come to be its preferred option, of coming to an agreement with the Arab rulers. They could then be used to overcome the objections of the Palestinian Arabs, whose demands for the total elimination of the British presence were unacceptable. The Jews could be given the minimum acceptable to political opinion at home and in the United States, though American interest in the problem was not at a very high level.[69] The Conference in London in February 1937, the St James's Palace Conference, was a stage towards the completion of the new policy. Even before it ended, the British acceptance of the Arab position was manifest; the Arabs and Jews were clearly too far apart for any mediation to be more than a face-saving device. Further concessions were made to the Arab rulers after the Conference met and before the publication of the White Paper. They were not enough to satisfy the Mufti and his followers, and those more moderate Arab leaders who might have found them acceptable were too much under the threat of terror for their views to have much chance of being heard.

---

[67] Weizmann to Smuts, 29 September 1937, Weizmann, op. cit., pp. 214 – 22.
[68] Cabinet meeting, 8 December 1937, PRO CAB 23/90A; *The Palestine Partition Report*, (Woodhead), (Cmd 5854, October 1938).
[69] In 1936 Cordell Hull, the American Secretary of State, had warned the British government of possible serious repercussions in the United States if concessions were made to the Arabs at the Jews' expense: cabinet meeting, 2 September 1936, PRO CAB 23/85.

The move away from the obligations of the Mandate produced in some Zionist circles in England a revival of the idea of the incorporation of Palestine within the British Empire, first as a Crown Colony and ultimately as a Dominion. Given the British interest in the potentialities of Haifa as a naval base, this seemed not implausible but, apart perhaps from Ormsby-Gore, no minister was sympathetic to this departure from the policy now the official line. By October 1938 the movement had once again petered out.[70]

Even if critical voices in Britain had not made themselves heard, as well as the doubts of the Dominions,[71] it would have remained the fact that, given opposition to any scheme of partition in the Arab countries, whose right to have a say in Palestine's affairs had been accepted, it is highly improbable that the British government would have followed a different course.[72] It was after all the failure to carry out the Mandate's provisions that had plunged the country into the troubles which had persuaded the Peel Commission that the Mandate was inoperable. The Permanent Mandates Commission and the League Council had been obliged to conclude that there was no way of making the British enforce the Mandate if they did not wish to, and hence to accept the drastic option of partition. But if the task of going through with the Mandate had proved too difficult, how, at a time of strained resources, could the complex operations needed to implement the Peel Report be undertaken?

The pressure on resources was undoubted. After a year or so of relative peace, the Arab rebellion was renewed in the summer of 1938, just at the time of the Czech crisis, and was not subdued until the autumn.[73] In July two battalions were dispatched from Egypt, and in August a division was requested from Britain. Since this would

---

[70] See N. Rose, 'The Seventh Dominion', *HJ*, vol. XIV, (1971), 397 – 416; N. Rose, *The Gentile Zionists* (London, 1973), 75 ff.

[71] At the Imperial Conference in 1937 the Dominions pressed for a more pro-Arab line and expressed their doubts about partition: Hamill, *The Strategic Illusion*, 288 – 9. At a meeting of the League Council in September 1937 de Valera denounced any plan for partition. McMahon, *Republicans and Imperialists*, p. 222.

[72] The only Arab leader sympathetic to the Peel proposals was the Emir Abdullah, whose territory would have received the addition of 'Arab Palestine'. But this possibility increased the hostility to the partition scheme of Ibn Saud, who had no wish to see a Hashemite ruler in possession of Akaba. Giving evidence to the Woodhead Commission, Lt. Col. Peake, the Commander of the Trans-Jordan Frontier Force, expressed himself favourable to partition, but argued that the Force should remain under British control. Papers of Lt. Col. F.G. Peake, Imperial War Museum, DS/Misc/16, FGP 5.

[73] On the Arab rebellion see A.M. Lesch, *Arab Politics in Palestine, 1917–1939* (Ithaca and London, 1979).

interfere with the possible need to dispatch the field force to France, the request was refused, but an undertaking was given to produce the equivalent of a division by sending units from India. Only at the end of September was the situation thought to be sufficiently in hand to return two battalions and a cavalry regiment to Egypt.[74] Even so, it was necessary in March 1939 to assure the Australians that British forces in both Egypt and Palestine and in posts east of Suez were being strengthened.[75]

British policy directed towards limiting the Palestine commitment had not been successful. All that could be hoped for was that, in the war now seen on the horizon, Palestine might prove relatively secure and the Arab world resistant to Axis blandishments. It is not suprising that during this period personal tensions should have developed between British policy-makers and their Zionist interlocutors, or that there should have been resentment in Whitehall at the access the Jews enjoyed to a segment of Parliamentary opinion. British officials on their side failed, in their natural preoccupation with the wider strategic scene, to allow for the pressure exercised on the Zionist leadership by the increasingly desperate situation of European Jewry. What is curious is not the amply documented British impatience with the Jews but the fact that so many British public servants, civil and military, should have placed their confidence in the Arabs to be 'loyal' to an Empire towards which they exhibited no attraction. For this confidence they were to pay heavily in Egypt and Iraq as well as in Palestine in the years that followed.

---

[74] M.J. Cohen, 'British Strategy and the Palestine Question, 1936 – 1939', *JCH*, vol. VII, nos 3 & 4, (1972), pp. 157 – 83. Palestine, writes a student of the disposition of British forces in this period, 'was a summation of the Empire's dilemmas': Clayton, op. cit., p. 487. General Ironside was unusual in challenging reliance upon the Arabs, arguing that the British objective could be attained by supporting the Jews. *The Diplomatic Diaries of Oliver Harvey* (London, 1970), p. 330. The War Office had indeed supported the Foreign Office against some Colonial Office doubts as to the wisdom of the 1939 White Paper: see J.R. Colville, *Man of Valour: the Life of Field Marshal Viscount Gort* (London, 1972), pp. 107 – 8.
[75] Chamberlain to Lyons, 10 March 1939, PRO PREM 1/309.

Chapter 12

THE EMPIRE AND APPEASEMENT

The role of the Dominions

Pressures on British resources for defence and attempts to bring about a greater measure of burden-sharing with the Dominions do not exhaust the importance of the imperial factor in the attempt by Britain to ward off the dangers of war by trying to find areas of agreement with potential enemies even at the price of concessions, the policy that has gone down to history under the name of appeasement.[1] Two questions demand further examination. What was the actual influence of the Dominions themselves, and how was it brought to bear on British decision-makers?[2] And second, what part did concern for the Empire-Commonwealth as a whole have in their minds? Among what might loosely be called British imperialists, there were on this issue two divergent schools of thought. To those who attached the greatest importance to making a reality of the new system of a British Commonwealth consisting of autonomous countries, (or of those likely in due course to attain that status), British ties to Europe were a threat to the process and should be avoided as far as possible. Of this group, the most typical and perhaps the most influential was Lord Lothian.[3] On the other hand, to those to whom the Empire in the sense of British control in India and of colonial territories was what

[1] For an earlier version of the present chapter see 'The Imperial Factor in Appeasement' in *Culture, Science et Développement: Mélanges en l'honneur de Charles Morazé* (Toulouse, Privat, 1979).

[2] The main lines of the historiography of British foreign policy in the 1930s were established during and immediately after the war in a manner which gave little attention to the imperial factor. The balance was first redressed by Nicholas Mansergh in *Survey of British Commonwealth Affairs: Problems of External Policy, 1931–1939* (London, 1952). Subsequent documentation, largely from Commonwealth archives, has broadly confirmed his analysis.

[3] Lothian's view was that Britain's entry upon the European scene from 1914 on had helped to create the revisionist stance of Germany, and that trouble would continue distracting Britain from her true imperial role until Germany became a sated power. In talking with Hitler, Lothian expressed his agreement with Cecil Rhodes' view that together the United States, the British Empire and Germany could uphold the peace of the world. Lothian to Simon, 30 January 1936: Baldwin Papers, vol. 3.F(2) (B), p. 11.

mattered most, appeasement could be seen as part of a general process of imperial retreat. Of this strand of opinion Churchill came to be the accepted leader, though his evolution towards this stance was a complicated one. The typical figure is perhaps Lord Lloyd, who in the autumn of 1937, after that year's Imperial Conference where all these issues were for the first time confronted by the leaders of the Empire-Commonwealth in conclave, stated his view trenchantly enough in a private letter:

The dissolution of what we fought to save and consolidate in 1914, goes rapidly on. Just think back. In 1919, the Dominions were encouraged to vote as separate nations; in 1926 Great Britain and the Dominions were wonderfully declared to be 'Autonomous communities within the Empire, equal in status, in no way subordinate to one another *in any aspect of their domestic or external affairs*'; and in 1931, the Statute of Westminster gave legal form to this disastrous declaration – protested against by both New Zealand and Australia and disliked by Canada but sponsored and achieved by Baldwin. Look at the further results. Canada is economically a satrapy of the U.S.A. for she is financially dependent upon her however much she dislikes her. Ireland is a Republic in all but name. Australia and New Zealand hold to us – New Zealand entirely from love, Australia partly through fear. The Irak mandate has been given up; Egypt has been given her independence and India promised Dominion status which is the same thing in the end. The tragedies of the war were great enough; but the tragedy of the peace which follows it has been to me infinitely more terrible.[4]

Yet the precise conclusions to be drawn from such premises were not always obvious. Lloyd himself was against alienating Italy over Abyssinia, though hostile to concessions to Hitler. Other right-wing imperialists followed the Chamberlain line in seeking agreement with the 'dictators'.[5] Chamberlain himself, the driving force in British policy for most of the period, was not particularly aware of or concerned with imperial issues or the views of Commonwealth

[4] Lloyd to Colin Forbes Adam, 29 August 1937: Lloyd Papers, 19/5.6. Lord Lloyd's role is well set out in John Charmley, *Lord Lloyd and the Decline of the British Empire* (London, 1987).
[5] See Neville Thomson, *The Anti-Appeasers* (Oxford, 1971), pp. 137 – 8. A rather exceptional figure is that of Sir Arnold Wilson, who supported appeasement because he thought Nazi Germany embodied the imperial virtues he admired. See J. Marlowe, *Late Victorian: the life of Sir Arnold Wilson* (London, 1960), p. 352.

leaders; it was Britain's own balance sheet that determined his approach.[6]

One problem in trying to assess the Empire's contribution to appeasement is the difficulty of distinguishing between those views expressed by Dominion statesmen that were clearly their own and based upon an independent view of the evolving situation, and those which merely echoed what they had heard, either from the British government itself or from their own particular network of correspondents in London. For despite the autonomy now enjoyed in external affairs by the Dominions, it remained very largely a fiction so long as they did not possess alternative sources of information to those provided by the circulation to them of such papers as the Foreign Office or other departments thought suitable via the Dominions Office, by meetings between the Dominions Secretary and the High Commissioners in London, or occasional contacts between the British High Commissioners in the Dominion capitals and the Dominion Ministers.[7]

The British government still thought in terms of unity of action. When in 1936 the Cabinet approved of Australian counsellors being attached to the embassies at Washington and Tokyo, it was with the proviso that they should be subject to the authority of the British Ambassador, and that he should see all their communications to their own government. It does not appear that the Australians demurred to this proviso.[8] It would also seem to have been the case that only selected material was passed on to the Dominions and that their governments were not admitted to the full confidence of British ministers. It may be that to some extent the Dominions took advantage of their membership of the League of Nations to balance what they got from Geneva for the London view but, apart from New Zealand, the League approach does not seem to have interested them a great deal.[9] And there were a few foreign capitals in which South Africa and, towards the end of the 1930s, Canada were represented. Ireland's

[6] It remains to be seen if the promised second volume of the biography by Professor David Dilks leads to any modification of this view.

[7] Ch. 7 of J. Garner, *The Commonwealth Office*, dealing with these matters, is very sketchy. The best description of the machinery is in the introduction to vol. I of R.G. Neale (ed.), *Documents on Australian Foreign Policy, 1937–1939 (DAFP)* (Canberra, Australian Government Publishing Service, 1975).

[8] *DAFP*, vol. I, p. 5.

[9] For New Zealand's role see B.K. Gordon, *New Zealand becomes a Pacific Power* (University of Chicago Press, 1950), and F.L.W. Wood, *The New Zealand People at War* (Wellington, 1958).

representation did not figure in the Commonwealth machinery; but it could hardly be said that this gave them the necessary basis for a foreign policy of their own.[10]

Canada was to some extent an exception to this dependence on British sources of information. Mackenzie King was suspicious of too close an entanglement with the London-based machinery of consultation as well as of the League of Nations. Where the German threat was concerned, he was determined to see for himself, and in consequence made a much publicised visit to Hitler in June 1937. The initiative was clearly welcome to the Germans. In May 1937 Ribbentrop, the German ambassador in London, sent Berlin a list of various eminent Britons who should be invited to visit Germany. The list includes 'the Canadian Prime Minister, Mackenzie King who is very friendly towards Germany and whose visit I consider particularly important in view of the significance of the Dominions for British Foreign Policy.'[11] It would seem doubtful that King made much impression upon Hitler by explaining that, although the Commonwealth governments had freedom to choose their own policies, they would rally to the defence of any one of them which had become the victim of aggression.[12] According to a close colleague, King brought three main impressions away from Berlin: that there would have to be some satisfaction of Germany's national aspirations or there would be war, that Hitler did not really want to fight Britain, and that therefore there was room for accommodation, and that Germany's military strength was already so great that Britain and France combined would not be able to match it. On his way home he made a speech in Paris, saying that Canada would go to war if world freedom were threatened, but avoided making any direct commitments, partly because these might provoke Hitler and damage the chances of a peaceful settlement, and partly because such commitments would not secure the support of all Canadians. But neither then nor later did Mackenzie King seriously contemplate the possibility that Canada could remain neutral in a major war in which Britain was engaged.[13]

[10] There is a useful survey of the literature in an unpublished paper by Dr Reinhard Meyers of the Political Science Seminar of Bonn University, 'The Young Children: the role of the Dominions in British Foreign Policy-making in the interwar years' (1979).
[11] Ribbentrop to Foreign Ministry, 18 May 1937, *Documents on German Foreign Policy* (*DGFP*) Series C, vol. VII (London, H.M.S.O., 1956), pp. 759 – 60.
[12] W. Blair Neatby, *William Lyon Mackenzie King*, vol. III (Toronto, 1976), pp. 222 – 4.
[13] J.W. Pickersgill, *The Mackenzie King Record*, vol. I (Toronto, 1960), pp. 10 – 13.

Mackenzie King returned to Canada impressed with Hitler's apparent desire for peace but worried that the German dictator seemed to think of Canada entirely in the North American context; Canada's wider interests arising from Commonwealth membership had escaped him.[14] It is of course correct that Canada was inevitably influenced by the United States, upon whose strength her own security in the last resort depended.[15]

It was of course important for both Britain as well as her potential enemies to assess the importance of the Commonwealth factor in the making of her foreign policy. Thus, according to the French, the reports reaching Berlin from the 1937 Imperial Conference had convinced the Germans that Commonwealth opposition would prevent Britain from intervening in central or eastern Europe.[16] On the French side, the ties of Britain to the Dominions had been pointed to by Laval, when arguing against sanctions over the Abyssinian war, as helping to make Britain too weak to be a useful substitute for Italy in building up resistance against Germany.[17] And at the time of the 1937 Imperial Conference, France's ambassador in London noted how ill-informed about European matters were the Dominion delegates arriving in London, pointing out that since for most of them it was the Mediterranean that was the most immediate concern, they would be likely to act as a brake on British action in central Europe.[18]

It may be argued that both the French and the Germans overestimated the extent to which Dominion influence was an independent factor, but they were clearly right in supposing that what influence there was would be in support of a policy of 'appeasement'. Their views may also have been coloured by the knowledge that, quite apart from the calculations of the Dominion governments themselves, their London High Commissioners, who were responsible for most of the time for conveying their governments' views to the British authorities, were in the case of the three most important countries

---

[14] So reported by the French Minister at Ottawa on 20 July 1937: *Documents Diplomatiques Français (DDF)*, 1932 – 9, Second Series, vol. VI, pp. 430 – 1.

[15] The Dominions and the United States are dealt with together in Ritchie Ovendale, *Appeasement and the English-Speaking World: Britain, the Dominions, the United States and the policy of 'Appeasement', 1937–1939* (Cardiff, 1975), which is the fullest treatment of the period between the 1937 Imperial Conference and the outbreak of war.

[16] Francois-Ponçet to Delbos, 3 June 1937: ibid., p. 18.

[17] Sir George Clerk to Samuel Hoare, 28 August 1935, *DBFP*, 2nd Series, vol. XIV (London, 1976), p. 550.

[18] Corbin to Delbos, 4 June 1937, *DDF*, 2nd Series, vol. VI, p. 36.

strong personal supporters of the appeasement line. This was true of Te Water of South Africa and of Vincent Massey of Canada.[19] Most influential of them was Bruce of Australia, who as an ex-Prime Minister occupied a special place on the British scene, and was closely associated with Geoffrey Dawson, the editor of the *Times*.[20] Dawson, it has been said, 'knew that the Dominions were passionately pacifist, and the ruling passion of his life was to keep the Commonwealth together'.[21]

Just as the Commonwealth leaders were not much respected by their British counterparts, so the High Commissioners were not regarded as very helpful by British officials. 'I think', wrote the Permanent Under-Secretary at the Foreign Office, 'they are the most undependable busybodies. Bruce is bad; I suppose they really haven't enough work to do.'[22] Most of the substance of the 'appeasement' issue was not something about which the Dominions or their representatives could be expected to have special knowledge. In the case of Japan, what was immediately at issue from 1931 onwards was her conduct on the mainland of Asia; the possible threats to British possessions and imperial routes in which Australia and New Zealand were vitally interested were a later development. In the case of Italy, the issues were the attitude to be taken up towards her conquest of Abyssinia and subsequently the Spanish Civil War. On aspects of the Abyssinian question, South Africa had its own decided views; but the Dominion interest in free passage through the Mediterranean, and consequently in favour of mending relations with Italy should this be proved possible, was an obvious and uncomplicated one, except for the weakening of the League system which this would entail. The German question was increasingly one of the extent to which German claims for hegemony in central and eastern Europe and territorial expansion there could be reconciled with Britain's security; and this in turn depended upon the appreciation made of Hitler's ultimate objectives

[19] Massey's influence was restricted through Mackenzie King's unwillingness to enter into any form of discussion of foreign policy issues. See V. Massey, *What's Past is Prologue* (London, 1963), p. viii.

[20] E.M. Andrews, 'The Australian Government and Appeasement', in *AJPH*, vol. XIII (1967), pp. 34 – 46.

[21] Colin R. Coote, *Editorial* (London, Eyre & Spottiswoode, 1965), p. 167. Members of the Round Table Group like Dawson tended to take this view, though not unanimously. Some, for instance R.H. Brand, were more reluctant to accept Hitler's declarations of peaceful intent.

[22] Sir Alexander Cadogan, diary entry, 13 September 1939: David Dilks (ed.), *The Diaries of Sir Alexander Cadogan, 1938-1945* (London, Cassell, 1971), p. 216.

on which, as the Mackenzie King visit showed, Dominion governments would not be able to shed much light.

The question of the German ex-colonies

The exception was the revival of the German claim to the recovery of
her colonies, originally a Nationalist demand but adopted by Hitler
after he came to power, though always in a fashion subordinate to his
main goals.[23] Could this demand be made a bargaining instrument,
had Britain the opportunity to use possible colonial concessions as a
part of a wider agreement with Germany? To these questions, decided
opinions could not be voiced by the two Dominions most concerned,
Australia in respect of New Guinea and Nauru, and South Africa in
respect first and foremost of her own mandate in South West Africa
and more generally in respect of Tanganyika and, by extension, of the
remainder of tropical Africa which might be affected in any general
settlement.

It had been assumed in British government circles as early as 1934
that a demand for the return of the German colonies might well be
made. By June 1934 Simon, the Foreign Secretary, was sure this would
be the case.[24] And in 1935 Hitler made it clear that Germany would
not accept that she was being treated as an equal unless some, and
perhaps all, of her colonies were returned.[25] Most British opinion was

[23] The possibility of Germany asking for a colonial mandate when she became a member of the
League had been looked at in the Foreign Office in 1926. 'German writers', it was noted, 'have
constantly pointed out that the greatest benefit which this country derives from the government
of India and the colonies is that it has given to the educated upper and middle classes opportunities for work of the highest interest, with adequate remuneration, and that these men
become in time an essential element in the constitution of the social fabric.' The memorandum
concluded by referring to the fact that some people favoured giving back colonies to Germany
because they would be a hostage to sea-power. But it was because of the colonies that Germany
had built a powerful fleet before the war, and that it was this challenge to the Royal Navy that
made war with Britain inevitable. Memorandum by Mr J. Troutbeck, 14 September 1926: DBFP,
Series IA, vol. II (London, H.M.S.O., 1968), pp. 371 – 81; quotation is on p. 379. This view of the
origin of Wilhelmine Germany's naval policy would not command general acceptance.
[24] Defence Requirements Subcommittee, meetings of 30 January and 16 February 1934, PRO
CAB 16/109; conversation between Simon and Lord Cecil of Chelwood, 14 June 1934, Cecil of
Chelwood Papers, BL Add MSS 51082.
[25] Minutes of meeting between Simon and Hitler, 25 March 1935, DBFP, Series 2, vol. XII
(London, 1972), pp. 726 – 7. On Hitler's adoption of the colonial demands see K. Hildebrand,
Vom Reich zum Weltreich; Hitler, N.S.D.A.P. und koloniale Frage, 1919–1945 (Munich, 1969). The
Germans had intermittently pressed the case for revision of the colonial settlement in the peace
treaties in the 1920s, partly as a matter of honour and partly on economic grounds. It had
surfaced particularly at the time of the proposals for 'closer union' in East Africa, which would
have closed the door on the recovery of Tanganyika. See W.W. Schmokel, The Dream of Empire:
German Colonialism, 1919–1945 (New Haven, 1964).

hostile to this demand, but some advocates of appeasement held that it would be absurd to allow a question of little substantial importance to stand in the way of a settlement that might avert a European war.[26] Against this, it was argued that it was impossible to consider such concessions in isolation and any discussion of the question should wait until Germany had defined more clearly her general aims in foreign policy:

> There is obviously no way of dealing with the colonial question so far as Germany is concerned until she has come to an understanding with us on her position and our's in the world. The real point is this — that a state of competition, however veiled, between Germany and ourselves must ultimately lead some day to another war and that we have to do our utmost to see that she finds it possible to pursue a policy of legitimate developments without hardening once again to a conviction that her development necessitates a challenge to the Empire and all its works.[27]

It was clear that any public airing of the German demand would set against it both the old-style imperialists who could not tolerate any diminution of the imperial position, and people on the left holding to the philosophy of colonial trusteeship, who thought it impossible to hand over non-white peoples to the rule of holders of Nazi racial doctrines. 'Such a suggestion', wrote Lord Cecil, 'will frighten every Tory in the kingdom out of his senses, and indeed in present circumstances I could not myself contemplate handing back to Nazi Germany populations which are at present governed by ourselves or even France.'[28]

South Africa, the Dominion most directly interested in the revival of German claims, was somewhat ambivalent about them, since its primary concern was to uphold white supremacy, which figured in the Nazis' own propaganda. Thus a public speech by the South African Defence Minister, Pirow, in January 1935 expressed the hope that Germany would soon become a colonial power again.[29] On the other hand, it became clear that Tanganyika would be among the territories

---

[26] See e.g. the letter from J.A. Hobson to Lord Allen of Hurtwood, 10 January 1937, in M. Gilbert, *Plough My Own Furrow* (London, 1965), p. 380.
[27] E. Grigg to F.S. Joelson, 12 December 1935, Grigg Papers, 1931–1938.
[28] Cecil to Allen of Hurtwood, copy in letter from Cecil to Gilbert Murray, 17 November 1936: Gilbert Murray Papers, (Bodleian Library), Cecil Correspondence.
[29] Speech by Oswald Pirow, 4 January 1935, quoted by Schmokel, op. cit., p. 71.

claimed by Germany, and South African politicians were not prepared to accept the idea. They wished among other things to be able to look forward to an imperial air route to South Africa, in which Tanganyika would be an essential link.[30] They also considered that the reappearance of the Germans in East Africa might lead to unrest among the native population that might spread to South Africa. For strategic reasons the return of South West Africa was also ruled out, a point on which Smuts also agreed with the position taken by Hertzog. Australia indicated from the beginning its hostility to surrendering New Guinea or Nauru.[31]

While these views had to be taken into account, the possibility of some colonial concessions to Germany being part of a general settlement with that country – which itself corresponded to the wishes of the Dominions – could not be excluded from British diplomacy. The difficulty was that such an idea did not figure in Germany's own thinking. In 1936 there were informal discussions at the Foreign Office in which both Bruce and Lester Pearson, then on the staff of the Canadian High Commission, took part. One idea was a customs union between Britain and Germany, taking in British colonies and the former German colonies, over which Germany would receive a mandate. But it was clear to the participants that Germany's interests lay in central and south-eastern Europe and that she was not to be diverted from them.[32]

Nevertheless, the possibility of a colonial settlement as a method of limiting the deterioration of relations with Germany did occupy the attention of the cabinet early in 1937. Conversations on the subject between Dr Schacht, the chief German enthusiast for the retrocession of the colonies, with French ministers in August 1936 and with Sir Frederick Leith-Ross, representing the British Treasury, on 2 February were reported in a memorandum by Eden, the Colonial Secretary, on 15 March. Eden argued that the duties of Britain to her colonial subjects precluded such concessions, and that the cession of some colonies would only increase Germany's appetite.[33]

[30] Swinton's report on talk with Pirow, cabinet meeting, 23 June 1936: PRO CAB 23/84. The Aga Khan objected to the idea of returning Tanganyika to Germany as detrimental to Indian interests. H. Tinker, *Separate and Unequal: India and Indians in the British Commonwealth, 1920–1950* (London, 1976), p. 148.
[31] M. Chanock, *Unconsummated Union – Britain, Rhodesia and South Africa* (Manchester, 1977), 206 – 9; Hancock, *Smuts*, vol. II, pp. 275 – 7; Edwards, *Prime Ministers and Diplomats*, p. 99.
[32] *Memoirs of Lord Gladwyn* (London, 1972), 56 ff.
[33] *DBFP*, Series 2, vol. XVIII, pp. 418 – 28; memorandum by Ormsby-Gore, 16 March 1937, ibid.,

The discussions at the Imperial Conference in 1937 found South Africa arguing for limited colonial concessions to Germany in West Africa, perhaps involving the territories of other colonial powers in that region. But the issue was subordinate to the general consideration of the international scene.[34] The contacts with Schacht were reported to the Dominion ministers, but they were told that the information from Germany was that the government had not authorised Schacht to deal with other than economic matters, and that it was prepared for the time being to let the matter stand over. In June Schacht, in a conversation with Sir Frederick Leith-Ross, again suggested that concessions on colonial matters which would help the Germans in respect of their raw materials needs would be an obstacle to those in Germany pressing for expansion in Europe.[35]

The matter was taken up by Lord Halifax during his visit to Germany in November 1937, when he reported on the basis of his conversation with Hitler:

> It seems to boil down to whether or not we should feel it possible ... to explore a colonial settlement *on broad lines*, with the idea, if such seemed feasible, of using it as a lever on which to pursue a policy of real reassurance in Europe: in other words, instead of trying to do a bargain on the line of getting him to drop colonies as a return for a free hand in Europe, to try for the more difficult but possibly sounder bargain of a colonial settlement as the price of being a good European.

A possible scheme for West Africa, perhaps including Belgian and Portuguese territories, was adumbrated by Schacht.[36] These conversations were reported to the French at a ministerial meeting in London; but it was clear that there would be opposition in both countries to any colonial concessions which did not form part of a wider settlement. The ground was gone over again at a meeting of the cabinet committee on foreign policy on 24 January 1938, when

---

pp. 433 – 7; Cabinet Committee on Foreign Policy, meeting on 18 March 1937, ibid., pp. 449 – 59.
[34] See Ovendale, op. cit., ch. II; R. Tamchina, 'In Search of Common Causes: The Imperial Conference of 1937', *JICH*, vol. I (1972), pp. 79 – 105.
[35] Meeting of Principal Delegates to the Imperial Conference, 4 June 1937, *DBFP*, 2nd Series, vol. XVIII, pp. 847 – 51; note of conversation with Dr Schacht, 29 June 1937, ibid., pp. 960 – 4.
[36] Account by Lord Halifax of his visit to Germany, 17 – 21 November 1937, *DBFP*, 2nd Series, vol. XIX (London, H.M.S.O., 1982), pp. 540 – 54 (quotation on 548); conversations between British and French ministers, 29 and 30 November 1937, ibid., pp. 590 – 621.

Chamberlain advanced his own ideas, by which the question should be subsumed in 'an entirely new chapter in the history of African development', based on the creation of a zone covering most of tropical Africa, where all the administering powers (which would include Germany) would be subject to the same restrictions covering native rights, demilitarisation, and freedom of trade and communications.[37]

The Germans were worried about the reports that were appearing in the press to the effect that they would be willing to compromise on a demand for less than their full demands. They were also disturbed at the movement of South African opinion, particularly among the nationalists, against the retrocession of South West Africa, which seemed to lessen the chances that, in a war against Germany, South Africa would retain its neutrality.[38] The British proposals, based on the ideas adumbrated by Chamberlain, were actually presented to Hitler by the British ambassador on 3 March 1938.[39] By that time the crisis leading up to the Anschluss with Austria was reaching its climax, and Henderson's reception was far from cordial, though he concluded that on the matter of Germany's colonial claims a solution was not regarded by the Germans as a matter of urgency.[40] The Anschluss itself precluded further British proposals, though the idea of seeking a colonial settlement as part of a general settlement was never wholly abandoned on the British side before the outbreak of war. And the South Africans continued to press for this to be done. Pirow suggested in November 1938 that Germany should be given Togoland, the Cameroons and French Equatorial Africa, for which the British should compensate the French elsewhere, an idea which was now regarded by the Foreign Office as possible only to someone 'living in a fool's paradise'.[41]

The consideration of Germany's colonial claims was carried out mainly through confidential soundings, and in public the attitude of

[37] Meeting of cabinet committee on foreign policy, 24 January 1938, ibid., pp. 777 – 91.

[38] Ribbentrop to Foreign Ministry, 2 December 1937, DGFP, Series D, vol. I, (Washington, 1949), p. 91; German Minister in South Africa to Foreign Ministry, 16 December 1937, ibid., pp. 128 – 9.

[39] The German record of the conversation is printed ibid., pp. 240 – 9. The British documentation of Henderson's approach is in DBFP, 2nd Series, vol. XIX, pp. 985 – 7.

[40] Ibid., p. 988.

[41] Minute by Mr Roberts on talks between Malcolm MacDonald and Pirow, PRO FO 371/21682, paper C.13874/184/18. The French Ambassador in London reported early in 1938 on the growing intransigence of South Africa and Australia on the colonial issue. Corbin to Delbos, 1 February 1938, DDF, 2nd Series, vol. VIII, pp. 176 – 7.

the Government was firmly against any handing over of the mandates. It was under pressure from the East African territories and in particular from Tanganyika itself against any possible deal involving that country. The anxiety was increased because of the level of German economic penetration. In 1938 the Germans held more agricultural estates than British settlers, although a smaller acreage, and in 1939 there were 3,205 Germans in Tanganyika as against 4,054 British residents.[42] Yet there was on both sides an element of shadow-boxing on this issue. Germany had no incentive to acquire colonies from which in time of war she would be cut off by superior naval forces, and the British were frequently reminded that historically the fate of colonial territories had been decided by the outcome of conflicts in Europe, not the reverse.[43]

The Dominions and Europe

It was the influence of the individual Dominions on Britain's European and Far Eastern policies in general that was more significant. And here South Africa's attitude was the most active and most individual. Smuts believed, and Hertzog even more firmly, that Germany had not been treated well since the war and that Britain was wrong to make so much of its policy depend upon France. In a conversation with a member of the Dominions Office in March 1935, the South African High Commissioner Te Water said that he understood that the policy of the U.K. government was to steer an independent course between France and Germany. If this was the case, the U.K. would get the support of all the Dominions. The same point was made by Hertzog during the ministerial meetings in 1935. After Hitler's occupation of the Rhineland, Hertzog noted: 'Today and the following days Great Britain must choose between hegemony with France and the leadership of the British Commonwealth of Nations.'[44] Smuts argued that it would be folly to ignore Hitler's peace plan of 1 April 1936, and when it became clear that no progress was being made

[42] *Cambridge History of Africa*, vol. VII (Cambridge, 1986), 687 ff.
[43] For a recent summary of the German position on colonies see Hartmut Pogge von Strandmann, 'Imperialism and Revisionism in Interwar Germany', in W.J. Mommsen and Jurgen Osterhammel (eds), *Imperialism and After: Continuities and Discontinuities* (London, 1986).
[44] Batterbee to Sir George Mounsey, 26 March 1935, PRO CAB 21/493; Meeting of British Commonwealth Prime Ministers, 7 May 1935, PRO CAB 32/125; C.M.Van den Heever, *General J.B.M. Hertzog* (Johannesburg, 1946), p. 267.

towards a settlement, Hertzog noted on 24 May, 'If the future policy of Great Britain is to be that there shall be no strong power in Europe except France and Italy, South Africa will be obliged to reconsider the basis of her co-operation with the British Commonwealth.'[45] At the Imperial Conference in 1937 he strongly urged the case for not following any policy in Eastern or Central Europe that might threaten German interests, and he argued that the British opposition to the proposed Anschluss with Austria was a legitimate cause for German complaint.[46] Indeed, South Africa went further than merely attempting to influence Britain, and sought actively to mediate between Britain and Germany.[47]

Canada

The Canadian scene was as complicated as the South African, and as dominated by internal politics.[48] The 1930s were a period of unique depression in Canada's internal affairs, with a net loss by emigration in a country whose ethos had been based upon continuous westward expansion.[49] It was not an encouraging time for those who felt that Canada could play a wider role in world affairs. And this reluctance was fortified by the division between English- and French-speaking Canadians: Bennett when Prime Minister had written to remind Sir John Simon, then Foreign Secretary, that the French-speaking element was 28 per cent of the whole.[50] On foreign affairs it was apt to take a different line. During the Abyssinian crisis, while opinion among English Canadians, like that in Britain, was hostile to Mussolini, the French Canadians sympathised with the Italians, their co-religionists. As one French Canadian intellectual put it, 'Why should Canadians fight to rescue a certain tribe of negroes from the clutch of an imperial power'? The same division was apparent during

---

[45] Middlemas and Barnes, *Baldwin*, 949; quotation is from Van den Heever, *loc. cit.*

[46] Minutes of Twelfth Meeting of Delegates to Imperial Conference, 3 June 1937, *DAFP*, vol. I, 127 ff.

[47] D.C. Watt, 'South African attempts to mediate between Britain and Germany', in K. Bourne and D.C. Watt (eds), *Studies in International History* (London, 1967).

[48] See M. Beloff, 'Britain and Canada between two World Wars: A British View', in Peter Lyon (ed.), *Britain and Canada: Survey of a Changing Relationship* (London, 1976). Since that essay appeared there has been a major work on the subject: C.P. Stacey, *Canada and the Age of Conflict*, vol. 2, 1921 – 48, (Toronto, 1977). See also ch. 15, 'Canada on the Road to War', in J.H. Thompson and Allen Seager, *Canada 1922–1939: Decades of Discord* (Toronto, 1985).

[49] Donald Creighton, *The Forked Road. Canada 1939–1957* (Toronto, 1976).

[50] Bennett to Simon, 23 April 1932, PRO FO 800/286.

the Spanish Civil War. Among English-speaking Canadians opinion was divided as it was in Britain. But French Canadians on both religious and political grounds strongly sympathised with Franco.[51] Above all, it was clear that French Canadians would be averse to incurring the danger of having to enter upon a war which could be seen as being for the sake of the British Empire. And this in turn heightened the imperial sympathies of many members of the other community.

In the circumstances, Mackenzie King's priorities were perhaps inevitable: 'I believe that Canada's first duty to the League and to the British Empire with respect to all the great issues that come up is to keep the country united.'[52] And this depended, as he frequently reminded British statesmen, on keeping Canada out of war.

King himself did not, as has been noted, believe that Canadian neutrality in a general war could be maintained; what he was concerned to make clear was that whatever Canada did should be the responsibility of its own Parliament, and not following a lead from London. When the limited measure of rearmament was adopted in the late 1930s, it was argued for in terms of improving Canada's home defences, and attacked on the Left as implying a commitment to backing Britain in Europe.[53] It was not spoken of in terms of Commonwealth co-operation, of which Mackenzie King persistently fought shy despite his ultimate personal commitment to the Empire.[54] His professional advisers did not dissent from his main line of conduct, though some were sceptical about the possibility of Canada following a completely independent line, pointing out that, despite objections in Canada, the government had in fact gone along with League sanctions against Italy.[55] But his principal adviser, O.D. Skelton, was ever on the watch against British influence.

All this acted as a powerful impetus in favour of appeasing the dictators, and Germany in particular. Mackenzie King was influenced in 1937 by the admiration he conceived for both Chamberlain and Hitler and was supported by Canada's representatives in London, Geneva and Paris, who were ready to believe in Germany's peaceful intentions and in 1938 that the Czechs had brought their troubles

[51] Neatby, *Mackenzie King*, vol. III, 139, p. 233.
[52] Speech in Canadian House of Commons, 23 March 1936, ibid., 139.
[53] See J. Eayrs, *In Defence of Canada*: vol. II, *Appeasement and Rearmament* (Toronto, 1965).
[54] On Mackenzie King's position in this respect see Stacey, op. cit., pp. 178 and 234.
[55] See J.A. Munro, 'Loring Christie and Canadian External Relations, 1935 – 1939', *Journal of Canadian Studies*, vol. VII (1972).

upon themselves.[56] It has been argued that had Canada had its own man in Berlin and not relied upon British despatches, different conclusions might have been come to in Canada.[57] But this does not seem very plausible. Nor, as the crisis worsened, could Canada's representatives in London fail to be drawn into the almost daily network of consultation, even though Massey appears to have acted without express authorisation.[58]

While the Munich agreement was welcomed in Canada, it did not dispel fears that Canada might be sucked into a conflict not of direct concern to her.[59] 'The plain fact is', wrote Skelton on 2 March 1939, 'that if we go into any European war it will be simply and solely on the grounds of racial sympathy with the United Kingdom. Why obscure this fact or try to dress it up with talk about saving democracy or our League obligations?'[60]

The idea of Canada as a totally independent and self-sustaining entity was however belied by circumstance. In fact, what was happening in the late 1930s was a process set in motion by the U.S.-Canadian Trade Agreement of 1938; for this, as a Canadian historian has pointed out, 'marked the beginning of a *rapprochement* which was to go on for many years, and to effect a dramatic alteration in Canada's traditional international position. To put it briefly and bluntly, from 1935 onwards Canada's relationship to Britain became less important and her relationship to the United States more important in her scheme of things.'[61] It was inevitable that Canada's attitude towards appeasement should to some extent mirror the attitude of the United States. And although it is true that it was the imperial tie that brought Canada

[56] See e.g. Canadian Minister in Paris to Ottawa, 9 September 1938, *Documents on Canadian External Relations (DCER)* vol. VI (Ottawa, 1972), p. 1089.
[57] J.Eayrs in H.Keenleyside (ed), *Growth of Canadian Policies in External Relations* (Durham, N.C., 1960), p. 70.
[58] Hall, *Commonwealth*, p. 600.
[59] 'Clearly if the European situation has been cleared up, however unsatisfactorily, the Commonwealth situation has not ... one thing is certain, the generation of young Canadians now developing a political interest, irrespective of race, will not stand permanently for their destinies being determined by irresponsible bodies in London.' Memorandum by Skelton, *DCER*, vol. VI, 1103. According to the historian of Canada's war effort, the Canadian isolationists 'realized after Munich that their battle was lost'. C.P. Stacey, *A Date with History* (Ottawa, 1983), p. 58.
[60] Skelton to Hume Wrong, 2 March 1939, *DCER*, vol. VI, p. 1131.
[61] Stacey, op. cit., p. 117. Some observers had noted the Canadian slant towards the United States earlier than this. A former New Zealand minister who had attended the (unofficial) British Commonwealth Relations Conference at Toronto noted the extreme nationalist and isolationist views of many Canadians and their refusal of any policy unacceptable to the United States. Downie Stewart to Grigg, 30 September 1933, Grigg Papers.

into war in the end, it was only after the hardening of Roosevelt's attitude towards the Axis had made it unlikely that this decision could have adverse repercussions on Canada's relations with the United States.[62] It must be added that it was possible to see the moves by Canada towards greater understanding with the United States as something which could be exploited to bring about a general *rapprochement* in foreign policy between the Empire-Commonwealth and the United States. Lord Tweedsmuir (John Buchan), the Governor-General from 1935 to 1940, made himself an instrument of this policy.[63]

Australia

The Australian situation was somewhat different, since the degree of dependence on Britain in a variety of ways was much more pronounced. It has already been noted that Australia attached a high degree of importance to its representation in London. And although, as has been seen, direct contacts with Washington were established in 1937, it was not until the approach of war that Australia felt the need, as a Pacific Power, to have its own sources of information on developments in that area.[64] The first Australian High Commissioner in Ottawa was appointed in March 1940, and a legation in Tokyo was opened in October 1940. In October 1941 the first Minister to China arrived at his post.[65]

---

[62] The Canadians had also been aware that Britain herself was in a measure dependent upon the United States. In a Memorandum of 20 May 1936 on proposed changes in the League Covenant, the Department of External Affairs had made the point directly: 'From the point of view of defence of the oceanic and world position, not only must harmony with the United States always have the most exceptional importance for Great Britain, but she must so contrive that action by the United States shall be *pari passu* with her own, or failing that ideal, that her own action shall not be too far in advance of the United States' action or too exhausting.' DCER, vol. VI, p. 909. On the role of the United States in general see C.A. MacDonald, *The United States, Britain and Appeasement, 1936–1939* (London, 1981).

[63] See Janet Adam Smith, *John Buchan* (London, 1979), ch. 15. In October 1937 Cordell Hull, Roosevelt's Secretary of State, stayed with Tweedsmuir in Ottawa and explored the world scene, political and economic. Copy of letter from Tweedsmuir to Neville Chamberlain, 25 October 1937, Simon Papers.

[64] In a broadcast on 26 April 1939 Menzies, who had that day become Prime Minister, said: 'Little given as I am to encouraging the exaggerated ideas of Dominion independence and separation which exist in some minds, I have become convinced that in the Pacific, Australia must regard herself as a principal, providing herself with her own information, and maintaining her own diplomatic contacts with foreign powers.' DAFP, vol. II, (Canberra, 1976), pp. 97–8.

[65] Edwards, op. cit., pp. 123–5. The impetus to an exchange of High Commissioners with Canada seems to have come from Ottawa: ibid., pp. 230–7.

In respect of Europe, Australian dependence on British sources of information was even more pronounced. Nor was this only true of government. It was also true of the general Australian public who were, in the words of a distinguished Australian, characterised by a 'marvellous nonchalance' about their own future:

Roughly 85% of the overseas news published in our papers comes through London, 12% through New York and the remaining 2 to 3% direct from the rest of the world ... It is not only a British view, but on balance the official British view, that dominates the Australian newspapers' account of world affairs.[66]

The Australians may have believed too readily that they were fully in the confidence of the British government. In 1938 Casey could write: 'I may say without exaggeration that the Prime Minister of Australia today receives as much information on the foreign affairs of the United Kingdom as most members of the British cabinet.'[67] He was careful not to say all members. The inner circle kept its secrets. Thus there is no indication that Australia, indeed any other Dominion was informed of the Roosevelt offer of January 1938 or its rejection and the debates preceding it.

Although there was a growth in the official machinery for conducting external relations in the 1930s, in particular through the establishment of External Affairs as a separate department in November 1935, in reaction in part to what were held to have been inadequacies in handling the Abyssinian crisis, domestic considerations mirrored in party divisions were in part at least responsible for the strong appeasement line taken by the Australian government during the Lyons administration from 1932 to 1939. The high proportion of anglophobe Catholics of Irish descent in the opposition Labour Party did play something of the same role as the French-Canadians in Canada. They also supported the Italians over Abyssinia and were in general close to the Vatican line of giving first place to the communist danger and of being moderately pro-Mussolini and not very

[66] W. Macmahon Ball, preface to W.G.K. Duncan (ed.), *Australia's Foreign Policy* (Sydney, Angus & Robertson, 1938). The Duncan symposium gives the whole range of Australian opinion, from those who believed that imperial solidarity was the only guarantee of Australia's security to those who demanded a great measure of independence. The 'nonchalance' extended to defence matters as well. When Ben Chifley was defence minister for ten months in 1931 he was asked no more that eight questions in Parliament on general issues of defence policy and preparedness. L.F. Crisp, *Ben Chifley* (London, 1961).
[67] Duncan, op. cit., p. 55.

emphatically anti-Hitler. In general, the Australian reaction to the Hoare – Laval Pact was favourable, though the original reaction altered when the British popular outcry became known. Over the Rhineland, opinion generally favoured the German case. The Spanish Civil War produced a split in opinion, with the Catholic element supporting Franco and communist-influenced Labour circles the Republic. Although the Anschluss worried some Catholics, Australian opinion in general remained unmoved.[68]

In 1936 Menzies, a rising figure in the governing coalition, visited England, and on his return published a series of articles, praising Baldwin's efforts for peace and denouncing French intransigence.[69] At the 1937 Imperial Conference Australia's voice was strongly in favour of appeasement, though much of Lyons' energy was taken up with launching a somewhat vague idea for a Pacific Pact which, taking no account of Japan's threat on the mainland of Asia, was thought to be peripheral to the real issues.[70] From the end of April 1938 until August Menzies was again in England, as a member of a trade delegation and, although maintaining contacts with Churchill and Amery, fully identified himself with the appeasement policies of Chamberlain, which he strongly defended after his return to Australia. Like Mackenzie King, he had sought to assess the German situation for himself, and in July 1938 paid a four-day visit to Berlin, where he met various officials as well as Schacht and Sir Nevile Henderson.[71] He came away believing that the annexation of the Sudetenland was not on the Germans' immediate programme and that they might be satisfied with a loose federal system for Czechoslovakia. It was the Czechs he saw as the threat to peace: 'I am more than ever impressed with the view that this problem requires a very firm hand at Prague; otherwise Benes will continue to bluff at the expense of more important nations including our own.'[72]

Despite the wide acceptance of the view that in the last resort,

[68] E.M. Andrews, *Isolation and Appeasement in Australia: Reactions to the European Crisis, 1935–1939* (Canberra, 1970).
[69] E.M. Andrews, 'The Australian Government and Appeasement', *AJPH*, vol. XIII (1967), pp. 34 – 46.
[70] See comments at the Conference on 22 May, *DAFP*, vol. I, pp. 78 – 83. Lyons believed that his proposals had received more international backing than was to prove the case: see Lyons to Sir George Pearce, (Minister for External Affairs), 10 June 1937, ibid., pp. 158 – 9.
[71] Stirling, External Affairs Officer in London, to Secretary of Department of External Affairs, ibid., pp. 398 – 400.
[72] Menzies to Lyons, 6 August 1938, ibid., pp. 400 – 1.

whatever might be the constitutional position, Australia's fate was too closely tied to that of Britain for neutrality to be a conceivable option in a major war, there were obvious differences between the two countries' perspectives and priorities. One was the increasing importance attached to Asia and the Pacific, exemplified in the growing Australian awareness of a Japanese threat. As Robert Menzies was to say in his first broadcast as Prime Minister, on 26 April 1939, while in Europe Australia would continue to be guided by Britain, the problems of the Pacific were different: 'What Great Britain calls the Far East is to us the near North....in the Pacific Australia must regard herself as a principal, providing herself with her own information and maintaining her own diplomatic contacts with foreign powers.'[73]

The second difference in perspective was that in relations with the United States. The primacy attached to questions of overseas trade was signaled by the fact that Sir Henry Gullett, the minister in charge of trade treaties, advised by the Customs Department rather than External Affairs, was allowed to push his own policy of diverting trade from Japan and the United States to Britain from 1936 until his resignation in March 1937 owing to his failure to get cabinet backing for limiting Canadian imports.[74]

Australia's need to maintain a trade surplus in order to meet its immediate obligations was not an argument that told with the Americans, and a good deal of friction was engendered by this trade dispute. An American observer found the Australians given to anti-American feeling. 'Various explanations are given', he wrote early in 1937,

> our late entry into the war, our failure to join the League of Nations; our attitude towards war debts and our ungenerous tariff policy. To these I would add two which are not generally given: first a conscious desire on the part of British organs of public opinion to diminish our influence (both commercial and cultural) and second a form of inferiority complex which makes the Australian most resent in others the accomplishments he most craves for himself.

He also found in Australia the widespread belief 'that the world would be best served by a British-American alliance in which America would

[73] Quoted by P.G. Edwards in *Prime Ministers and Diplomats* (Melbourne, Oxford University Press, 1983), p. 120.
[74] Ibid., p. 100. See also T.B. Millar, *Australia in Peace and War: External Relations 1788–1977* (London, 1978), 112 ff.

be expected to limit herself to the role of a brilliant second'. He noted also the bitterness felt by Australia on the U.S. attitude to the Empire's need for cruisers at the London Naval Conference of 1930, and her fear that the independence promised to the Phillipines in March 1934 signaled an abandonment by the U.S. of its interests in the Pacific. By 1937 Australia was more conscious of the Japanese threat, but had none of the American tenderness for China. Indeed, Australians observed with equanimity the increasing embroilment of Japan in Manchuria and North China as rendering any southward push by it less likely.[75]

In the end Australians were bound to conclude that they would need the Americans if their worst fears were realised. The trade dispute was ended by the fading-out of discrimination on either side in 1938. But the Australians did not want the Americans to feel that they expected their active participation in defensive measures, and when in 1937 Lyons announced his project for a Pacific Non-Aggression Pact, he had made it clear to the U.S. ambassador in London that he was not expecting U.S. participation, only general approval of the idea.[76]

New Zealand

Without representation in foreign capitals, and relying for communications with the imperial government on the Governor-General until the arrival of the first British High Commissioner in 1939, (and formally-speaking for two years after that), New Zealand was of all the Dominions the one in which foreign policy figured least in public debate. Although New Zealand had supported Australia over the abrogation of the Anglo-Japanese alliance, its own perception of the Japanese danger became fainter, and the country showed little active concern over the Manchurian crisis in 1931 – 2.[77]

The New Zealand Labour Party, which was in opposition until 1935, was deeply committed to a theory of international relations which held that wars were always the consequence of economic rivalries and could be averted by sane economic policies, while at the same time

[75] From an essay written towards the end of his tour of duty by J.P. Moffat, U.S. Consul-General in Sydney from September 1935 to March 1937. N.H. Hooker (ed.) *The Moffat Papers: selections from the diplomatic papers of Jay Pierrepont Moffat, 1919–1943*, (Cambridge, Mass., Harvard University Press, 1956), pp. 124 – 5, 129 – 30.
[76] Millar, op. cit., p. 116.
[77] B.K. Gordon, *New Zealand becomes a Pacific Power* (Chicago, 1960), pp. 64 – 5.

relying upon the League of Nations to be a guarantor of security. In 1927 the Labour Party opposed the New Zealand contribution to the Singapore base on the ground that the project itself was contrary to the spirit of the League, and in 1933 unsuccessfully tried to get the country's Parliament to go on record as approving the League's condemnation of aggression.[78]

In 1935 the two New Zealand parties kept in touch over the Abyssinian crisis and deliberately kept the issue out of the election campaign of that year, which was won by the Labour Party on domestic issues. The new Prime Minister, M.J. Savage, was now in a position to express the party's views both at Geneva and in the Commonwealth forum. The New Zealand government deplored, though in private, the Hoare – Laval proposals, and consented to go along with the abandonment of sanctions against Italy only on condition that the League machinery should be reviewed, and itself put up suggestions for tightening its coercive powers, thus urging a policy exactly opposite to that favoured by the other Dominions.[79]

The paradox in New Zealand's position was that while it alone differed from Britain on the principles of foreign policy, it was the most firmly committed of the Dominions to taking part in any war in which Britain was engaged; this was made clear at the time of the Abyssinian crisis and again in the course of the 1937 Imperial Conference.[80] Reporting on the Conference, Savage said: 'We did not agree on everything, far from it; but the objective was about the same and if Britain were in difficulties tomorrow, I think about the same would happen as last time.'[81] During the Spanish Civil War, New Zealand made it plain at Geneva that its sympathies lay more with the Spanish Republican government than did Britain's, and urged League arbitration or some other external attempt to bring about peace. On the other hand, little concern was shown about the worsening of the situation in central Europe.[82] It was however the case that New Zealand was kept more closely in touch with events by the British government in this period, and since the High Commissioner in London, W.M. Jordan,

---

[78] F.L.W. Wood, *The New Zealand People at War* (Wellington, 1958), p. 29.
[79] Gordon, op. cit., pp. 69 – 73. On New Zealand party politics see L. Lipson, *The Politics of Equality* (Chicago, 1948).
[80] Note by Malcolm MacDonald on the views of the New Zealand delegation, 28 May 1937, PRO CAB 32/127.
[81] Wood, op. cit., 44 ff.
[82] Gordon, op. cit., pp. 93 – 4.

was on close personal terms with his Prime Minister, he could effectively represent his views.[83] New Zealand's own worries were of course related to Japanese expansionism, and again, unlike the other Dominions, her advice was on the side of those who favoured sanctions.[84] Her anxieties here also led her to press British claims to certain Pacific islands which, although within the area allotted to the New Zealand navy for patrol, were claimed by the United States. The motive here was not only one of building up imperial defences, but also of securing the future needs of civil aviation.[85]

India and the Japanese threat

India, although not self-governing, was recognised as having a voice in the making of imperial foreign policy both at Imperial Conferences and in the British cabinet. Its voice was also on the side of appeasement in Europe, partly because of its greater concern with the threats from Soviet Russia and Japan and partly because Indian opinion, like the opinion of the Left in Britain, had turned against the Versailles settlement.[86] The Aga Khan was reported by the Dominions Secretary in February 1932 to be pro-Japanese, though it had been expected that he would be pro-Chinese. Ramsay MacDonald pointed out that the reason was that the Japanese victory over Russia in 1905 had given the first impetus to Indian nationalism. Later in the year the Aga Khan warned the British government against taking up a stance at the League which might totally alienate Japan without strengthening the Empire's position in regard to Europe through a League policy.[87]

If one looks at the way in which Dominion influence was exercised in the successive decisions made in the field of British foreign policy in the 1930s, it must be admitted that for the most part it did not conflict with the views that British ministers themselves had arrived at. What it did was to give those who advocated appeasement an additional argument against their more sceptical colleagues. Even in respect of the Far East, where Dominion interests were most directly

---

[83] Wood, op. cit., 44 ff.
[84] B.A. Lee, *Britain and the Sino-Japanese War, 1937–9*, (Stanford and London, 1973), p. 19.
[85] Wood, op. cit., pp. 74 – 9.
[86] D.C. Watt, 'Der Einfluss der Dominionen auf die Britische Aussenpolitik vor München 1938', *Vierteljahrschrift fur Zeitgeschichte* (Stuttgart), vol. VIII (1960), pp. 64 – 74.
[87] Meeting of Cabinet Committee on the Far East, 15 February 1932, PRO CAB 27/482; Aga Khan to Sir Samuel Hoare, 6 September 1932, PRO 800/287.

engaged and where the question of the Singapore base and the redeployment of British naval power was so urgent a matter of concern, the preference for going as far as possible to avoid antagonising Japan was felt throughout the Commonwealth. And this was true from the time of the Japanese invasion of Manchuria.[88] Indeed, some New Zealanders at that time took the view that Japan should be supported against China, as being the strongest power in the Far East, a menace to Australia and New Zealand but also a bulwark against communism, the greater danger to the world. Only South Africa and Ireland, and later New Zealand, took a pro-League view.[89]

The Indian government was also in a vulnerable position if the European powers could be seen to be acting in concert against an Asian power, Japan. When in 1933 it was announced that the Indian government intended to abrogate the 1904 commercial convention with Japan, it was thought by the general public in Japan to be part of bringing pressure to bear on behalf of the League, and placards appeared in Tokyo calling upon Japanese, Chinese and Indians to rise together to 'emancipate India from British bondage'.[90]

In trying to avert a final breach with Japan the Dominions were in accord with an important body of opinion, in Britain itself represented notably by Neville Chamberlain and Warren Fisher, who did not believe they could rely upon the United States if trouble came. On the other hand, the Dominions themselves, as Hankey found during his journey in 1934, were keen on the maximum degree of co-operation with the United States which, the Australians believed, would never allow Australia to be overwhelmed.[91] But the U.S.A. of the mid-1930s was also appeasement-minded.

---

[88] 'While the Dominions were kept informed of Britain's general policy, they contributed almost nothing in the way of advice or even demands for discussion at government level. They *existed* as a defence responsibility, that was all.' C. Thorne, *The limits of Foreign Policy: The West, the League and the Far Eastern Crisis of 1931–1933* (London, Hamish Hamilton, 1972), 141, n. 2. For Australia's policy see John McCarthy, *Australia and Imperial Defence 1918–1939* (St Lucia, Queensland, 1976).

[89] Thorne, op. cit., p. 299.

[90] M.D. Kennedy, *The Estrangement of Britain and Japan, 1917-1935* (Manchester, 1969), pp. 272 – 3. However, Thorne points out that there is very little evidence that the cabinet made any connection between the Far Eastern problem and that of India's defence: op. cit., p. 295.

[91] Ibid., p. 398. For the general framework of British policy in this area see William Roger Louis, *British Strategy in the Far East, 1919–1939* (Oxford, 1971).

The Dominions and the challenge from Italy

In relation to the challenge from Italy in the Abyssinian crisis, the Dominions acted differently.[92] Australia, as has been noted, supported British policy but was relieved when the issue was not pressed. New Zealand protested against the recognition of the Italian conquest but kept its reservations private, being unwilling to display Commonwealth disunity.[93] The Aga Khan wrote to Eden, who as minister for League of Nations affairs had been keeping the Dominions in touch with the development of the crisis, that extreme measures should be taken to prevent Italy establishing itself in Abyssinia, which would mean a menace to India, Ceylon and the British position in the Middle East.[94] The South Africans also took a strong anti-Italian line, and indeed Smuts urged that sanctions be continued even after it was clear they had failed in their purpose.[95] Canada reluctantly went along with the League's decision to brand Italy as the aggressor, and was a member of the Committee of Eighteen which imposed sanctions against her. But it was clear that military sanctions, which would seriously divide the country, would be unacceptable. From the episode Mackenzie King drew the conclusion that the League could be a menace to the national unity which it was his primary political purpose to maintain.[96] Thereafter the main Dominion concern was that of Australia and New Zealand lest the new threat from Italy in the Mediterranean and the Red Sea should divert British naval power from what they saw as its prime task in Far Eastern waters. Their fears were not in fact misplaced; in February 1938 the

[92] See David Carlton, 'The Dominions and British Policy in the Abyssinian Crisis', *JICH*, vol. I (1972), pp. 59 – 77.

[93] Telegram from government of New Zealand, 5 April 1938, PRO CAB 21/493.

[94] Letter from Eden to Hoare, 25 September 1935, quoted in the Earl of Avon, *Facing the Dictators* (London, Cassell, 1962), pp. 269 – 70.

[95] This demand by Smuts infuriated Neville Chamberlain: 'I differ entirely from Smuts as to the effect their continuation would have, and the dangers in Europe seem so near in point of time that it would be madness for us to involve ourselves in what would certainly be a bloody struggle in the Mediterranean. Is it not rather odd that with such a passionate feeling as to what *we* ought to do, Smuts countenances the continuation of the subsidy paid to Italian shipping by the government of South Africa. He seems to have the faculty of combining advice to other people to take a very high stand, but accommodating his principles to the convenience of South Africa.' Chamberlain to Gilbert Murray, 6 May 1936: Gilbert Murray Papers, LNU correspondence.

[96] Neatby, *Mackenzie King*, vol. III, pp. 136 – 42. Canada's hesitations were aggravated by the fact that the question came up at the time of a general election and that the Prime Minister, Bennett, was unwilling to commit his successor. E. Watkins, *R.B. Bennett*, pp. 195 – 6. For documents dealing with the imposition of sanctions see W.A. Riddell, *Documents on Canadian Foreign Policy, 1917–1939* (Toronto, 1962), pp. 533 – 588.

Chiefs of Staff reiterated their view expressed in 1937 that war against Germany, Italy and Japan, even if in alliance with France and Russia, would 'place a dangerous strain on the resources of the British Empire, but if it did come they would give priority to the defence of the United Kingdom and Singapore over the Mediterranean'.[97]

The Dominions, the German threat, and the Roosevelt initiative

In respect to the German threat in Europe there were no direct Dominion interests involved, and little direct Dominion input into the policy-making machine. What concerned the British cabinet was the extent to which the Dominions should be consulted, in the light of the need not to make commitments which they would not wish to see Britain honour. The question was argued at length in respect of the Belgian demand for a unilateral British guarantee of Belgian independence in May 1934.[98] It was decided that the issue should be resolved without consultation with the Dominions, whose concerns were strongly voiced by some ministers, but that they should be informed before any communication was made to the Belgian government.[99] In the end the matter was not proceeded with, but the Belgian request had perhaps served to alert ministers to this relatively new aspect of British policy-making.

The question of reforming the League Covenant also presented problems because of the differences of opinion between the Dominions. Eden argued that there would be a benefit from ensuring that any war in which Britain was engaged was a League war since then the Dominions could not be neutral. On the other hand, the ventilation of the issue of reform was to be avoided if possible, so as not to reveal the extent of the divergences within the Commonwealth.[100] The issue was closely related to the revelation at the time of the Rhineland crisis of the depth of Dominion hostility to Locarno.[101] In Canada's case in particular, Mackenzie King was determined to ensure that Canada,

[97] N.H. Gibbs, *Grand Strategy*, vol. I, 419.
[98] Ministerial Committee on Defence Requirements, meetings of 11 and 21 June 1934, PRO CAB 16/110.
[99] Cabinet meeting, 27 June 1934, PRO CAB 23/79.
[100] Cabinet Foreign Policy Committee, meetings of 30 April and 25 August 1936, PRO CAB 27/622.
[101] Cabinet meeting, 16 March 1936, PRO CAB 23/83.

not a signatory of the Treaty, should avoid making any statement on the situation now created.[102]

It must be assumed that Neville Chamberlain's understanding of Dominion attitudes had an effect on his own determination to use his premiership for a more definite attempt at 'appeasement' in Europe. In February 1937 the American Secretary of the Treasury had sent Chamberlain a message, saying that he wished to know whether there was any way in which the United States and Britain could co-operate to bring down the level of armaments, which was dragging down the credit of the major countries. In replying, Chamberlain said that the main cause of the armament programmes was the conduct of Germany, which was trying to make herself strong enough to prevent anyone from withstanding her claims to territory in Europe and in the colonies. The greatest contribution the United States could make to the preservation of world peace was to amend the neutrality legislation, which was of assistance to Germany. The British government would also welcome an opportunity to put relations between Britain, the United States and Japan on a better footing.[103] Morgenthau's reply, to the effect that there was little chance of Congress agreeing to an amendment of the neutrality legislation, may have helped to make up Chamberlain's mind to seek for a solution to Europe's problems through his own diplomacy, and thus would in part explain the rejection of Roosevelt's initiative in January 1938 towards some kind of international gathering to discuss both the possibilities of the reduction of armaments and access to raw materials. Such an initiative, which had been long brewing in various guises in American administration circles and which has been described as the 'brainchild' of Tweedsmuir, was seen by Chamberlain as a diversion from the real problems of Europe which he was trying to tackle.[104] In particular, Roosevelt's approach specifically ruled out any American involvement in the settlement of territorial issues. Chamberlain's temporising reply was part of the reason for Eden's resignation from his cabinet, and was subsequently strongly denounced by writers from Churchill downwards as the missing of a golden opportunity.

It would be possible to defend Chamberlain's position by pointing

[102] Vincent Massey, *What's Past is Prologue: Memoirs* (London, 1963), 229 ff.

[103] John Blum, *From the Morgenthau Diaries*, vol. I (Boston, 1959), 458 ff.

[104] For the ascription to Tweedsmuir see the reference to a communication from Tweedsmuir to Roosevelt of April 1937 in the Hyde Park archives, referred to by F.H. Hinsley in his review of Eden's memoirs in *Times Literary Supplement*, 23 November 1962.

out that for Hitler and Mussolini it was the political aspect that mattered most, and that Roosevelt was in effect evading the issue. What is of greater relevance to the theme of the present inquiry is that there seems no evidence that Chamberlain sought the advice of any of the Dominion governments on a matter of such vital interest to them.[105] It may be that Chamberlain was well aware of their reluctance to face the full realities of the situation and the possible appeal to them of what could seem a way around it. Nor does it appear that any other member of the cabinet involved – Eden was away, of course – pressed for this consultation to take place, despite the fact that the Foreign Policy Committee devoted detailed attention to the Roosevelt message and the reply to be made.[106]

When one comes to the events leading from the Anschluss to Munich, Dominion attitudes show little sign of change. The French ambassador, after discussions with the Dominions representatives in London, expressed the belief that a more positive policy of collective security would rally Dominion opinion, and that the Dominions would fight if England were menaced or parts of the Empire attacked.[107] The latter part of the analysis would seem to have been more firmly based than the former.

Throughout the period between the Anschluss and Munich, Dominion pressure on the British government not to make commitments to Czechoslovakia and not to tie itself too closely to French policy was unremitting. British advocates of appeasement could point to the Dominion attitudes as justification for their stand.[108] Consultations with the Dominions during the September crisis saw no departure from their known positions. At each stage in the revelation of Hitler's demands, the voice of the High Commissioners was in favour of Britain

---

[105] The U.S. documents relating to the offer and its antecedents insofar as they are in the files of the State Department are in *FRUS* 1938, vol. I, pp. 115 – 32. The fuller British record is in *DBFP*, Series 2, vol. XIX, pp. 725 – 830.

[106] 'The Foreign Policy Committee of the Cabinet has been busy all week with a very secret message from Roosevelt as to a message he contemplates on world affairs and with its bearing on our conciliatory plans to improve our relations with Italy.' Simon Diary entry, 23 January 1938, Simon Papers.

[107] Corbin to Paul Boncour, *DDF*, Series 2, vol. IX, pp. 33 – 6.

[108] In a letter to Wickham Steed, published in the *News Chronicle* (London) on 16 August 1938, Lord Rothermere wrote: 'The day Great Britain goes to war in pursuit of some aim or design in Central Europe, two or three of our most important Dominions will declare their neutrality and by so doing will bring an end to the British Empire.' Cited by F.R. Gannon, *The British Press and Germany, 1936–1939* (Oxford, 1971), pp. 18 – 19.

insisting upon their acceptance by the Czechs.[109] The most pressing were the Australians.[110] On 28 September 1938 a cable was received in London from Lyons suggesting an appeal to Mussolini to intervene and offering Bruce's services to go to Rome to deliver the message.[111] But Chamberlain himself had by then approached Mussolini, with the Munich meeting as its outcome.[112]

Evidence that the Dominions' reservations weighed with the cabinet is abundant;[113] nor in retrospect was their influence minimised. Dealing in his memoirs with the critics of Munich, Halifax wrote: 'They either did not know or greatly care that there was great doubt whether the Commonwealth would be at one in supporting the United Kingdom in a policy of active intervention on behalf of Czechoslovakia in 1938.'[114]

By the end of 1938 the difficulties of reaching a lasting settlement with Nazi Germany were all too apparent. Australians were perhaps typical of all the peoples of the Dominions in rejecting the alternative of 'diverting and braking German expansion' whenever it seemed possible to do so. For this would not merely put Anglo-German relations back in 'the uneasy and sterile state which led to the conflict of 1914'; such an argument, it was claimed, 'overlooked a fundamental difference between that period and the present':

> Whereas then British policy turned on the doctrine of the European balance of power, it has now to take into account the views of the Dominions, which are quite ready to accept the fact of German

[109] See e.g. the record in PRO DO 114/94 of discussions at Geneva between Lord De La Warr and Dominion representatives, 12 September 1938, and between Malcolm MacDonald and High Commissioners, 23, 26 and 27 September 1938. There were other similar meetings at both Geneva and London, as well as meetings between Malcolm MacDonald and individual High Commissioners. The suggestion made by Keith Middlemas that on 27 September Bruce and the other High Commissioners were arguing for a tougher line does not seem to be borne out by the record. K. Middlemas, *Diplomacy of Illusion* (London, 1972), p. 391.

[110] It was not, however, as far from British thinking as the South African government. When there was a question at one stage of a British guarantee for a truncated Czechoslovakia, Bruce argued that the Dominions should be associated with it. The South African High Commissioner, Te Water, said that there was no question of South Africa participating, and was reminded by MacDonald that South Africa might one day want assistance from European countries in the event of aggression against South West Africa. *DAFP*, vol. I, pp. 442 – 6.

[111] Ibid., pp. 470 – 2.

[112] Andrews, *Isolation and Appeasement in Australia*, p. 130. Bruce, in his narrative account of the crisis sent to Lyons on 7 October, states that it was Lyon's suggestion that had prompted Chamberlain.

[113] See e.g. cabinet meetings on 12, 14, 19 and 25 September 1938, PRO CAB 23/95.

[114] The Earl of Halifax, *Fullness of Days* (London, 1957), pp. 197 – 8.

domination of the Continent east of the Rhine. This acknowledgement is not in itself of course enough to avert eventual war, but it does offer a condition on which the Third Reich and the British Commonwealth can live together, *provided always* that specific differences as they arise are handled from the British side resolutely enough to discourage Nazi opportunism.[115]

The Dominions felt themselves, if the writer's views are to be taken as typical, well placed to insist that British policy took account of their perceptions of where the interests of the Commonwealth as a whole could be discerned. But the hope that there was some middle way which could prevent a reaction against the fruits of appeasement from being jettisoned in favour of a combination of powers against Germany was to prove a vain one. One is tempted to echo the opinions of two historians of an earlier phase of imperial retreat: 'Appeasement is nearly always marked by self-deceptions. To believe that it is undertaken for reasons other than fear and a sense of impotence is part of its pathology. For the appeaser, the will to believe is substituted for the will to act.'[116]

[115] Memorandum by J.D.L. Hood, External Affairs Office, London, 1 November 1938, *DAFP*, vol. I, pp. 529 – 33.
[116] R.W. Tucker and D.C. Hendrickson, *The Fall of the First British Empire* (Baltimore and London, John Hopkins University Press, 1982), p. 231.

PART III

THE ACCOUNTING

Chapter 13

THE EMPIRE GOES TO WAR

Appeasement abandoned

The first half of the year 1939 saw a major reversal of British foreign policy, given added momentum by Hitler's occupation of the remainder of Czechoslovakia in March, which convinced most British opinion that agreements reached with him were of no value, and that the ambitions which drove him on went far beyond the unification of Europe's German-speaking peoples. While it was generally recognised that at some point he would seek expansion in the East, there was no guarantee that he would not first try to secure his rear by an onslaught on his western neighbours; in the light of this apprehension, British military policy had to take greater heed of the likely requirement for a continental expeditionary force. Furthermore, while it was hoped that self-interest would keep Italy neutral, there was no certainty that she would not seek further to extend her power in the Mediterranean and her influence in the Middle East. And fears for the Eastern Mediterranean called into question the allocation of British naval forces in wartime, as set out to the Dominions at the Imperial Conference of 1937. In the case of Japan, appeasement was still being attempted, but the fundamental likelihood that Japan would seize upon any opportunity created in Europe to pursue her imperial ambitions was ever present in British minds.

The importance attached at the time of Munich to not becoming involved in a conflict in which the Empire-Commonwealth might not act together did not prevent the British government from acting largely independently in the rapidly changing situation that developed in the following year. The diplomatic initiatives in Eastern Europe, culminating in the guarantees to Poland and Rumania, the search, ultimately frustrated, for the association of the Soviet Union with a European security system headed by Britain and France, the decision to treat Hitler's invasion of Poland as the *casus belli*: all these were actions taken by the British Government, and did not commit any other autonomous member of the Commonwealth. The Commonwealth countries were kept informed largely through the activities of their High Commissioners in London; their views were sometimes made known to the British Government, but they were not partners in the full sense in the series of decisions that ultimately led to war. Nor indeed did either the British government or their own governments see how they could be.[1]

What was revealed in the exchanges of view that took place and is indeed confirmed by all other evidence is that the changed perceptions of the British public and of many British political leaders were not mirrored in the Dominions. Their general adherence to appeasement, their reluctance to see Britain following the lead of France in making commitments in Eastern Europe, the priority they attached to their own domestic concerns and in military matters to local defence – all these were largely unaffected by events in Europe which were to them remote. And although in the end all of them (except Eire) went to war and fell in to a greater or lesser extent with the military priorities worked out by Britain, this did not seem to mark an irrevocable shift in attitudes. The Dominion governments remained more hopeful than the British government of some possible formula that would permit peace to be restored. While appeasement in Britain had been expelled to the political fringes, its appeal to the Dominions remained largely unimpaired. It was only after the rapid collapse of western Europe under Hitler's onslaughts in the spring and early summer of 1940 that the reality of the situation was finally accepted. June 1940, not September 1939, is the crucial month for the Empire-Commonwealth.

The prospects for co-operation with the Dominions

The problem of how the Dominions might be represented in the higher direction of the war when it came was canvassed by the Dominions Office in the winter of 1938 – 9, but Sir Edward Bridges, who had succeeded Hankey as secretary to the cabinet and of the C.I.D. in July 1938, discouraged the Minister for the Co-ordination of Defence

---

[1] For a preliminary sketch from public sources see N.Mansergh, *A Survey of British Commonwealth Affairs: Problems of External Policy, 1931–1939*, (London, 1952), ch. X. See also J.C. Doherty, 'Die Dominions und die Britsichen Aussenpolitik von München bis zum Kreigsausbruch 1939', *Vierteljahrshefte fur Zeitgeschichte* (Stuttgart), 20 (1972), pp. 209 – 34.

from making arrangements in advance.[2] The question of giving the Dominions more information about the intelligence on which the British government was basing its policy was raised in the Foreign Office. But Cadogan, the permanent secretary, was doubtful whether this could be done without danger. It would be necessary to make a selection, and the different High Commissioners might make different assessments and thus produce different reactions from the different Dominions. Lord Halifax was opposed to showing the Dominions secret reports, and he added: 'Mr Jordan [the New Zealand High Commissioner] would still think whatever his natural instinct suggests.'[3]

The problem of Irish neutrality

One reason for the reticence of the British ministers where the Dominions were concerned was the fact of the differences between them as to the extent to which their support could expected in the case of a general war. The position of Eire was obviously the most suspect. The Anglo-Irish treaty had not created the improvement in relations for which Chamberlain had hoped, and by the autumn of 1938 it was already clear that de Valera, having attained his other objectives, would now use Britain's difficulties to press the question of partition; and unease was increased with the inception of a terrorist campaign in mainland Britain by the I.R.A. in January 1939.[4] It was hoped that Eire would be able and willing to defend its neutrality, but in November 1938, when it was believed that de Valera intended to appoint a French consultant on the defence of the ports, the Chiefs of Staff were reluctant to provide Eire with secret information. In May 1939 the cabinet learned that in the light of the frank staff conversations that had taken place with the French it was thought that more information could now be supplied to Eire and that, with limits on access to material still not freely communicated, Irish servicemen could attend courses of instruction in the United Kingdom.[5]

[2] Memorandum by Harding, Dominions Office, 2 November 1938; reply by Bridges, 6 February 1939; Bridges to Chatfield, 1 March 1939: PRO CAB 21/488.
[3] Minutes by Hadow, Foreign Office, 9 February 1939, Cadogan, 11 February 1939, and Halifax, 11 February 1939: PRO FO 372/3315, folios 167 ff.
[4] P.Canning, British Policy towards Ireland, 1921–1941 (Oxford, 1985), 235 ff.
[5] Chiefs of Staff meeting, 1 November 1938, PRO CAB 53/9; C.I.D. paper 493-C, 13 May 1939, PRO CAB 5/9.

Eire was thus not a participant in the meetings of ministers with the High Commissioners through which the stages in Britain's diplomatic revolution in 1939 were communicated to the Dominions and through which Dominion opinion was made known to the British government, nor did the two governments directly correspond on matters of foreign policy and defence. When war came in 1939, de Valera declared Ireland's intention to maintain and defend her neutrality, and the hopes of obtaining naval facilities, to which Churchill attached importance from the moment of his return to the Admiralty, proved ill-founded. His suggestions that Irish neutrality should be challenged on legal grounds and the harbours then seized, were rejected by his colleagues as likely to arouse hostility on constitutional grounds in South Africa and Canada and have unfortunate repercussions in India and the United States. By the end of the year, Irish neutrality was perforce accepted as tolerable, and there were some slight if secret derogations from it in Britain's favour, though I.R.A. activity remained a source of worry.[6]

The Dominions, the guarantees and the Nazi-Soviet Pact

The governments of Australia, New Zealand, Canada and South Africa were kept informed both of the gathering storm and to a limited extent of Britain's ideas for dealing with it when it came. At every crucial juncture it is possible to note their opinions, as did British ministers at the time, but not to estimate the weight which these opinions may have carried.[7] It has been stated by the official historian that the Dominions were hardly mentioned in relation to Britain's guarantee to Poland announced on 3 April 1939, but that the evidence suggests they were on the whole favourable.[8] Other historians have attached more importance to the Dominions' dislike of it.[9] The negotiations with the Russians were never favourably looked upon by the Dominions,

[6] Canning, op. cit., 241 ff.

[7] Their role is dealt with fully in Ritchie Ovendale, 'Appeasement' and the English-Speaking World (Cardiff, 1975), 206 ff. The statement by his first biographer that Neville Chamberlain's speech at Birmingham on 17 March 1939, which heralded the new course, was affected by 'strong representations as to opinion in the House, the public and the Dominions' seems hard to substantiate where the Dominions are concerned. Keith Feiling, The Life of Neville Chamberlain (London, Macmillan, 1946), p. 400. The general situation in 1939 is most usefully set out (in the light of the documents by then available) in the volume of the Survey of International Affairs entitled The Eve of War, 1939, by A. and V.M. Toynbee (London, 1958).

[8] See N.H.Gibbs, Grand Strategy, vol. I, p. 699.

[9] See Sidney Aster, 1939. The Making of the Second World War (London, 1973), p. 228.

though they reluctantly accepted the necessity for perseverance in pursuit of an agreement.[10] Throughout the period up to the declaration of war their preference remained one of seeking agreement with Hitler to the extent of accepting as valid his case over Danzig and Poland.

The Pacific Dominions were mainly concerned to make certain that the British government would remain able to carry out its pledges of support, and the Defence Conference held at Wellington in April 1939, while directed to improving co-operation in defence and liaison between the Dominions themselves, was an occasion for trying to reassure them.[11]

When the Nazi-Soviet Pact was concluded around midnight on 23 August the fact that war was now almost unavoidable became evident to all concerned, though at a meeting with the High Commissioners attended by Halifax as well as the Dominions Secretary, Inskip, the South African High Commissioner still urged that the powers in the 'Peace Front' should state their continued willingness to discuss all outstanding problems, including economic and colonial issues.[12]

At a cabinet meeting on 26 August it was reported that the four High Commissioners all said that their governments favoured a discussion with Germany, but the cabinet rejected a suggestion from the Canadian Prime Minister that George VI should be invited to send a letter to Hitler, asking him to find a peaceful solution.[13] When Inskip met the High Commissioners on the same day, he also had messages from the British High Commissioners in the Dominions: Canada would fight if war came, though only after its Parliament had met to approve of the policy, while Smuts had said that he would press Hertzog to make up his mind between neutrality and belligerency and was hopeful of the latter. On 27 August there was a message from Menzies suggesting an appropriate answer to Hitler's latest message. Curiously enough, when the High Commissioners met Inskip again on 28 August, only the Irish High Commissioner, less neutral in spirit than de Valera, asked who had been the intermediary with Goering in the

[10] See Ian Colvin, *The Chamberlain Cabinet* (London, Gollancz, 1971); Gibbs, op. cit., p. 732. Those who urged caution – the Canadians and South Africans – emphasised the need to prevent German public opinion turning against Britain. Meeting at Dominions Office, 6 April 1939, PRO FO 372/3317, folios 179 ff.
[11] Report on Pacific Defence Conference, 25 April 1939; Sir H. Batterbee to Inskip, 26 April 1939: PRO ADM 116/3803.
[12] Meeting of High Commissioners, 24 August 1939, PRO FO 371/23962.
[13] Colvin, op. cit., p. 241.

latest effort to avoid war. On 30 August Inskip met the High Commissioners again to present them with the draft agreed upon by the cabinet for a reply to Hitler's Polish proposals. They wanted to have it toned down; but Halifax, after being at first inclined to accept their criticisms, decided against it, pointing out that they did not know the whole picture, including the fact of the Prime Minister's latest private letter to Hitler; they could be told about that in confidence, not for the information of their governments.[14]

To the end therefore there remained the same unwillingness to take the Dominion governments fully into confidence. Just after midnight on 3 September the British cabinet decided that the German foreign minister should be informed that the United Kingdom would be at war with Germany at 11 a.m., and Inskip was told to send the Dominions a telegram to this effect at 9 a.m. Believing it impossible to leave them in the dark until only two hours were left, Inskip disobeyed instructions and sent the message at 1.30 a.m.[15]

Australia: the last appeasers

The entry of the Dominions into the war took place according to their own conceptions of the imperial relationship at the time. About Australia's stand there could be little doubt. While the Australian government had been a supporter of the Munich policy, it also shared in the disillusion that followed and was more aware of the need to improve its defences. The German colonial claims were a particular source of concern, and it was made clear in November 1938 that there was no question of giving up New Guinea, and that in this respect the government was supported by the Labour opposition. The Australian government and public opinion followed Chamberlain's lead after his Birmingham speech and accepted the need for guarantees to Eastern

[14] Inskip Diary, vol. II. Mackenzie King had himself appealed to both Germany and Poland on 25 August. It is difficult to see why his biographer holds that 'King made no effort to influence events in Europe': Neatby, *William Lyon Mackenzie King*, vol. III, p. 316. Menzies' telegram of 27 August is in *DAFP*, vol. II, pp. 191 – 2. The intermediary referred to was the Swede Dahlerus: see L.B. Namier, 'An Interloper in Diplomacy' in *Diplomatic Prelude* (London, 1948).

[15] Inskip Diary, vol. II. That is Inskip's own account. The telegram printed in *DAFP*, vol. II (Canberra: Australian Goverment Publishing Service, 1977), 221 was dated 3 September, 2.10 a.m. Aster, op. cit., 357 ff, also makes use of the Inskip diary, but he is wrong in suggesting that Lyons had suggested a 'Munich type' conference three days earlier. Lyons had died in April. The reference must be to Menzies' telegram to Chamberlain on 18 August, expressing the hope that every advantage would be taken of moves towards a peaceful settlement. It does not however suggest a conference. *DAFP*, vol. II, p. 171.

Europe and for seeking to bring the Soviet Union into the anti-Hitler front, though worried that an agreement with the Soviet Union might contribute to Japan's hostility.[16]

What was different was that those at the centre of Australian affairs were much less ready to assume at any time before the actual outbreak of war (or indeed later on) that there was no hope of finding an accommodation with Germany. In January 1939 Bruce came back from London to do a tour of the Australian states and to give his support to the line the government had been following; nor was his optimism destroyed by Hitler's move into Prague in March. Menzies, on becoming Prime Minister in April 1939, showed a new willingness to assert Australia's own particular interests and to seek overseas representation in order to assist in promoting them:

> Little given as I am to encouraging the exaggerated ideas of Dominion independence and separatism which exist in some minds, I have become convinced that, in the Pacific, Australia must regard herself as a principal, providing herself with her own information and maintaining her own diplomatic contacts with foreign powers.[17]

But in Europe he was still prepared to follow the British government's line, though placing on it his own interpretation. He believed that Chamberlain's new policy of guarantees in eastern Europe was no change of course, but merely a detour on the road to an agreement with Germany. As late as August 1939, while Hughes was predicting an imminent war, Menzies was still asserting publicly that the problems of Europe could be settled peacefully.[18] At the same time he was telling Chamberlain that there should not be too much pressure upon Poland to make concessions in case this was thought to invalidate the Anglo-French guarantee and thus make war more likely. Bruce went further than Menzies in upholding appeasement, believing that, even after the announcement of the Nazi-Soviet Pact, the important thing was not to encourage Polish intransigence.[19]

[16] E.M. Andrews, *Isolationism and Appeasement in Australia, 1935–1939* (Canberra, 1970), pp. 155–72.
[17] Menzies, broadcast, 26 April 1939, quoted in P.G. Edwards, *Prime Ministers and Diplomats* (Melbourne, Oxford University Press, 1983), p. 120.
[18] E.M. Andrews, 'The Australian Government and Appeasement', *AJPH*, vol. XIII, (1967), pp. 39–42. For an attempt to interpret Menzies' policies during his first premiership see David Day, *Menzies and Churchill at War* (London, 1986).
[19] Menzies to Chamberlain, 18 August 1939; Bruce to Menzies, 23 August 1939: *DAFP*, vol. II, pp. 173–4, 180–1.

In Canberra the dangers of the situation were fully appreciated, and after a cabinet meeting Menzies stated publicly that if war came it would be because Germany insisted upon a military solution, and in that case Australia would stand where it had stood twenty-five years earlier. Constitutional developments in the British Empire should not be interpreted by foreign countries; the independence of the Dominions did not indicate separatism. There would be full co-operation with Britain by Australia and, he believed, by the other Dominions as well. Bruce was urging Menzies to support his efforts to persuade the British government to keep the door open to negotiation.[20] The unity of Australia seemed to be weakened by the statement from the Labour leader, Curtin, that the safety of the Australian people impelled them to recognise the impossibility of sending 'Australians overseas to participate in a European war'. Menzies however continued to make preparations for war if it should come, and while urging generosity in dealings with Germany warned Chamberlain against conniving at a Polish settlement likely to make her future history resemble that of Czechoslovakia. But by now there was no turning Hitler from his course. And when the news of his invasion of Poland and of Britain's consequent actions reached Australia, Menzies went on the air to tell the Australian people that Britain had declared war on Germany and that 'as a result' Australia was also at war: 'There can be no doubt that where Britain stands there stand the people of the entire British world.'[21] Yet as Curtin's warning had indicated, Australia's position was not as clear cut as the Prime Minister's statements appeared to suggest; not only was the country now more conscious of its separate individuality and its remoteness from European issues, but it had to contend, as it had not had to in 1914, with the potential Japanese menace to its own security. And the fact that Britain and France proved unable to follow up their declaration of war with any action to prevent the new partition of Poland, was bound to be a discouraging one. The official historian of the Australian civilian war effort (and a later Governor-General) put the situation that now developed in the starkest fashion: 'The Australian people entered the war with a united will to resist Hitlerite aggression. A month later there were clear signs

[20] Statement by Menzies, 23 August 1939; Bruce to Menzies, 23, 26 and 27 August 1939, ibid., pp. 182, 184, 189 – 90.
[21] Statement by John Curtin, 25 August 1939; Menzies to Chamberlain, 27 August 1939: ibid., p. 187 n.4, 191.

of flagging interest.'[22] The view expressed here seems to overlook the internal tensions that would require resolution. As a more recent historian has written,

> The Labor Party had resisted defence preparations during most of the 1930's, had stood firmly against involvement in European 'imperialist' wars and was totally opposed to expeditionary forces or to compulsion for military service. These attitudes broke down during the first years of the war as Labor leaders realised that they did not fit in with the mood of the people or the obligations undertaken by the nation.[23]

There was however no opposition expressed to Menzies' announcement on 3 September 1939 that, since Great Britain had declared war on Germany, 'as a result, Australia is also at war', though the Labour Party leader Curtin emphasised the points upon which Labour would stand fast in relation to the actual policies to be pursued. It was the war itself that brought about a change in the constitutional perceptions of Australia's international role, since, with Labour now in power, the declaration of war upon Finland, Rumania and Hungary in December 1941 was made on the King's behalf by the Governor-General on the advice of the Australian cabinet.[24] It was no longer automatic that Australia was committed by British action.

Australia and the co-ordination of the Imperial war effort

Problems were also created by the difficulties of organising the machinery for conducting the imperial war effort, a subject in which Australia in particular was interested. To recreate an imperial war cabinet on the 1917–18 model was politically no longer possible.[25]

[22] Broadcast by Menzies, 3 September 1939, ibid., pp. 221–6; P. Hasluck, *The Government and the People, 1939–1941*, (vol. 1 of the Civil Series of *Australia and the War of 1939–1945*: Canberra, Australian War Memorial, 1952).

[23] T.B. Millar, *Australia in Peace and War: External Relations, 1788–1977* (London, C. Hurst, 1978), p. 136.

[24] N. Mansergh (ed.), *Documents and Speeches on British Commonwealth Affairs, 1931–1952* (London, 1953), vol. I, pp. 479 ff, 484 ff. For relations between the Australian and British governments in respect of the conduct of the war and the deployment of Australian troops, see David Horner, *High Command: Australia and Allied Strategy, 1939–1945* (London, 1982), ch. 2, 'Paying the premium on imperial defence: September 1939–January 1941'.

[25] On the problems created by Dominion sensitivity on this issue see the Earl of Avon, *The Reckoning* (London, 1966), p. 76. Avon (Sir Anthony Eden) re-entered the cabinet as Dominions Secretary on the outbreak of war and remained in that office until succeeded by Lord Caldecote in the Churchill government in May 1940.

Conferences with Dominion ministers such as were planned for the autumn of 1939 involved such large numbers as likely to be consuming of time rather than productive of results.[26] The main burden of co-ordination would fall as in peace time, on the daily meetings between the Dominions Secretary and the High Commissioners. But these meetings were more a matter of conveying information to the Dominions than of seeking their views, since the British government held that decision-making was a matter for itself. Thus Chamberlain over-ruled the Dominions' objections to the leaflet campaign carried out by the R.A.F. over Germany in the early weeks of the war.[27] In the matter of the Dominions' own contribution to the struggle, the initiative in suggestions also came from London, and in some detail.[28] Even on the nature of the contributions that could be made to the general war effort in the form of supplies, there was in Australia (as in the other Dominions) much attention paid to what would be the effect of any trade diversions upon post-war economic conditions.

The difficulties for the Australian government in complying with the desire of the United Kingdom that Australia should prepare an expeditionary force, either to serve in the main theatre of war or to relieve British troops in Singapore, Burma and India, were largely political. With Russia hostile to the war effort of the western allies, the Communist parties everywhere were mobilised for anti-war activities. While this was not of great significance in the United Kingdom or the other Dominions, the Communists had an important hold in the Australian trade unions and used it to press for a negotiated peace. The Labour Party was more guarded in this respect, but did not rule out such a policy if it seemed at all feasible.[29] When Hitler launched his 'peace offensive' in October, the Australian reaction was not wholly negative.

The Australian government did not regard Hitler's speech of 6 October as providing any basis for negotiation, and was unimpressed by Mackenzie King's suggestions for a counter-offer or an appeal to the United States, the Kings of Italy and Belgium and the Queen of

[26] Bridges to the Minister for the Co-Ordination of Defence, (Chatfield), 29 October 1939, PRO CAB 26/491.
[27] Inskip Diary, vol. I, 15 September 1939. (Inskip had ceased being Minister for the Co-ordination of Defence and became Lord Chancellor as Viscount Caldecote on the outbreak of war, when he was suceeded by Chatfield.)
[28] Eden to Sir Geoffrey Whiskard, the High Commissioner in Australia, 8 September 1939: *DAFP*, vol. II, 249 – 52.
[29] Hasluck, op. cit., p. 194.

Holland to put forward a basis for a European settlement. It may have been strengthened in this attitude by the report of the Australian Counsellor at the British Embassy in Washington about the unfriendly reaction to Hitler's proposal in American opinion.[30] On the other hand, when sent a draft of the proposed speech by Chamberlain in reply, Menzies argued that it should contain 'some simple presentation' of war aims in order to make Britain's position clear to the rest of the world. Changes were made, but Bruce when shown them still considered that the statement could have been more 'constructive', and protested that no time had been allowed for further consultation with the Dominions.[31]

In arguing for his continued presence in London, Bruce made it plain that he still thought it desirable to be in a position to counter, in respect of any peace settlement, the influence of 'intransigent elements' in Britain and above all in France. And he advocated consultation between the four Dominion Prime Ministers to counter the influence of the French and of that element in Britain headed by Churchill which would be likely to support their idea of a peace settlement based on holding down Germany.[32]

The offer by the King of the Belgians and the Queen of Holland on 7 November to act as intermediaries in seeking out possible terms of an agreement was made at a time when German troops were being massed upon their frontiers. Bruce was anxious that the British reply should not give the Germans any ground for propaganda to the effect that the continuance of the war was due to allied intransigence. The reply to the two sovereigns by the King was made, it was stated, on the advice of the Dominion as well as the United Kingdom governments, and took account of a suggested revision by Canada. The Australians were critical of the British draft reply to French proposals for a new statement of war aims. Once again, while deploring any 'patched up compromise', the Australians asserted the need to disclaim any intention of dismembering Germany. The criticisms were repeated at a meeting between British ministers and Australian and New Zealand

---

[30] F.K. Officer (Washington) to Department of External Affairs, 9 October 1939: *DAFP*, vol. II, p. 317. Hitler's peace offer is briefly discussed in Llewellyn Woodward, *British Foreign Policy in the Second World War* (London, H.M.S.O., 1970), vol. I, pp. 12-13.
[31] Menzies to Eden, 11 October 1939; Bruce to Menzies, 12 October 1939: *DAFP*, vol. II, pp. 328 – 9, 332.
[32] Bruce to Menzies, 18, 26 October 1939: ibid., pp. 346 – 8, 353 – 5.

representatives on 16 November. No agreement on a war aims statement had been reached by the end of the year.[33]

Eden meanwhile was arguing that the despatch to Europe of the first Canadian contingent, due in December, should be followed by the arrival of Australian and New Zealand troops, which would have a profound effect upon the psychology of allies and enemies alike. But it was argued that the Labour Party opposition in Australia to the sending of a force overseas would disappear if there were a flare-up of fighting on the western front and that it was better to wait. Meanwhile the Australians were placed in an embarrassing position by the announcement that the New Zealand government was going ahead on its own. In the end the Australians came round in order to help release British troops from the Middle East, but according to Menzies there had been in this matter, in his cabinet's opinion, 'a quite perceptible disposition to treat Australia as a colony'.[34]

Australia, Japan, the Middle East and defeat in Europe

Interventions in European diplomacy must be seen as a facet of Australia's continuing worries over the course of Japan's policy and the importance of trying to find some way for Japan to get out of her predicament in China that would prevent an agreement between Japan and Soviet Russia, which would be full of danger, though it was realised how difficult this would be in the light of the United States' commitment to China.[35]

The likelihood of Australians seeing active service in the Middle East may have encouraged Bruce to intervene in policy in that area. At a meeting of the High Commissioner with Eden on 2 January, he expressed his worry about the suggestion that Lothian's instructions as Ambassador to the United States might be varied to assist in allaying Zionist apprehensions: 'if it meant any yielding to Jewish pressure to

[33] Bruce to Menzies, 8 November 1939; Eden to Menzies, 11 November 1939; Commonwealth Government to Eden, 14 November 1939; note by Bruce of meeting on 16 November 1939: ibid., pp. 380, 398 – 9, 403 – 4, 409 – 10. The diplomacy of the November crisis is dealt with in Woodward, op. cit., pp. 14 – 19.

[34] Eden to Chamberlain, 3 November 1939; Whiskard to Dominions Office, 24 November 1939; Menzies to Casey, 1 December 1939: DAFP, vol. II, pp. 368 – 9, 431 – 4, 441 – 2. R.G. Casey, Minister for Supply and Development in the Menzies government, arrived in London for consultations in October and remained there until March 1940, when he became the first Australian Minister to the United States.

[35] Menzies to Bruce, 7 December 1939, DAFP, vol. II, pp. 451 – 2.

the detriment of the Arabs there would be the strongest objections from Australia'.[36] But for the most part Bruce's interventions, whether in formal meetings or in private conversations, were still directed to exploring the possibilities of some new form of appeasement.[37] The British reservations regarding the visit of the American Under-Secretary of State, Sumner Welles, to Europe, which it was feared might contribute to allied disunity, were seen by Bruce as showing 'the marked influence of the pro-French school in the Foreign Office'.[38] Meanwhile, however, Menzies was finding that his cabinet was showing an increasing inclination to fall in with the 'realist' school and to criticise him for not giving voice to their views. Menzies believed that his own views were in accord with those of Chamberlain and Halifax and that it was Churchill whose stirring up of hatreds was the real menace. The Soviet attack upon Finland at the end of November 1939 and differences between Britain and France as to the possibility of some intervention to assist the Finns does not appear to have directly involved the Dominions in consultation; nor was the Finnish decision to conclude an armistice on 12 March seen as of direct concern. The important meeting of the Supreme War Council on 28 March, which looked again at possibilities for offensive action and at what was to be done if the Low Countries were invaded, also issued a communiqué pledging the British and French governments not to sign or seek a separate peace, and to insist on positive guarantees against a defeated Germany as the basis of dealing with any proposals which might reach them.[39] It did not prove possible to reach unanimity with the Dominions on this document, but Menzies accepted it as the best obtainable in the circumstances.[40]

The series of events that began with the invasion of Norway in April and the defeats there (which cost Chamberlain the premiership), continuing with the over-running of the Low Countries, the British

---

[36] Note by Bruce of High Commissioners meeting, 2 January 1940, *DAFP*, vol. III (Canberra, Australian Government Publishing Service, 1979), pp. 4 – 5. The Government did in fact decide to stand by the White Paper policy and to implement its land regulations; but Lothian and other ambassadors were instructed to avoid calling attention to the policy and to try to avoid controversy. Michael J. Cohen, *Palestine: Retreat from the Mandate* (London, 1978), p. 90.

[37] Day, op. cit., pp. 13 – 17.

[38] Menzies to Bruce, 22 February 1940, *DAFP*, vol. III, 99 – 103. Menzies foresaw that Bolshevism would be the beneficiary in eastern and south-eastern Europe of a prolonged war, and that there would come to pass a 'new alignment of nations' in which Germany and Italy would combine with Britain and France to resist it.

[39] V. and M. Toynbee (eds), *The Initial Triumph of the Axis*, (London, 1958), p. 188.

[40] Menzies to Eden, 15 March 1940, *DAFP*, vol. III, p. 146.

retreat to Dunkirk, and the conclusion of an armistice by France, moved at too rapid a pace for detailed consultations with the Dominions. They could only hope that Churchill's obstinacy in clinging to the remote prospect of victory would prove more credible than it seemed to Menzies and Bruce. The more immediate concerns of the Pacific Dominions were focused on Japan, and still more so when the German conquest of the Netherlands seemed to call into question the future of the Dutch East Indies. They were both indisposed to take any action in respect of Japanese traffic with the Soviet Union (still supplying Germany) that might precipitate matters.[41]

After the early catastrophes in France, Menzies and Bruce agreed that the possibility of an invasion of Britain itself should be tackled by engaging Mussolini and Roosevelt as mediators, an idea put by Bruce to Chamberlain in a conversation on 27 May.[42] Meanwhile Menzies had been in touch with Smuts and Mackenzie King and the New Zealand Prime Minister, Fraser, about a possible appeal to Roosevelt for assistance to the allies.[43] But the reports from Casey in Washington were discouraging; the United States was a country where public opinion ruled and the President could not afford to get ahead of it. After the fall of France, the Australians were clearly warned of the effects of the changed situation on British naval strategy and consequently on the balance in the Far East. It was no longer possible for Britain to contemplate withdrawal from the Eastern Mediterranean.[44] The situation which Australian pressure for appeasement had been intended to avert had come to pass, as was made clear in an exchange of messages between the Australian and British governments on 12 and 13 June, when the latter made it clear that Britain would have to rely on the United States to defend its interests in the Far East. On 16 June the Australian government decided to train and equip a militia for home defence.[45]

[41] Commonwealth Government to Eden, 16, 17 April 1940; Fraser to Menzies, 20 April 1940: ibid., pp. 201, 205, 215 – 16.

[42] Martin Gilbert, *Winston S. Churchill*, vol. VI (London, 1983), pp. 410 – 11, 435 – 6; Day, op. cit., p. 24. Day criticises Gilbert for detecting a difference of approach between Menzies and Bruce, in that Menzies was at the same time offering Australian troops to be used in defence of Britain if need be. But it does not seem that Menzies at any time denied the necessity of Australia contributing to the struggle against Hitler or that his views were misrepresented by Bruce. Clearly Bruce was more open in London to the views of those who were sceptical about the possibility of victory, for instance Lloyd George.

[43] Australia had had a High Commissioner in Ottawa since March 1940: Edwards, op. cit., p. 123.

[44] Casey to Department of External Affairs, 29 May 1939; Caldecote to Commonwealth Government, 28 June 1940: *DAFP*, vol. III, pp. 354 – 5, 517 – 18. For a review of the new naval situation at the time see J.R.M.Butler, *Grand Strategy*, vol. II (London, 1957), ch. XIV.

[45] Horner, op. cit., pp. 35 – 6.

The Anglo-French Union proposal

One episode in the attempt to keep France in the war which would in more normal circumstances have been the subject of much inter-Commonwealth discussion was the project for an 'indissoluble union' between Britain and France, put to the French cabinet on 16 June 1940.[46] At the meeting of the war cabinet which discussed the proposal it had been stated that 'It seemed likely that the Dominions would assent to any decision taken by the Government of the United Kingdom.'[47] The objections which might arise in Britain itself were thought to be more cogent, though in the current situation even so revolutionary a proposal was thought worth trying.

The Dominions were in fact informed about this development, and Bruce gave his reaction to the document in a telegram to Menzies:

> Wiith regard to the Dominions, my first reaction is – I only saw the document two hours ago – that provided position of King is safeguarded and as citizenship of Frenchmen is limited to that of United Kingdom, we notwithstanding our great interest and concern in everything affecting Great Britain, can hardly, in face of deadly and imminent peril with which she is now faced, object to United Kingdom Government pursuing course which they believe vital.[48]

In his message to the British High Commissioner in Australia, Caldecote (Inskip) assured him that the failure to consult was because events had left the United Kingdom government no option.[49] By the time Menzies came to give his reaction to Churchill, which was one of entire approval for the course taken, the rumours of the resignation of the French government which reached him suggested that the proposed union would not be achieved, but he still called attention to Australia's particular problems in respect of citizenship, the 'White Australia' policy which would affect her attitude to non-European French citizens.[50]

---

[46] On the background to the Union proposal, see my essay 'The Anglo-French Union Project of June 1940', originally published in *Mélanges Pierre Renovin* (Paris, 1966), and reprinted in Max Beloff, *The Intellectual in Politics* (London, 1970), and David Thomson, *The Proposal for Anglo-French Unity in 1940* (Oxford, 1966).
[47] Woodward, op. cit., vol. I, p. 279.
[48] Bruce to Menzies, 16 June 1940, *DAFP*, vol. III, pp. 442 – 4.
[49] Caldecote to Whiskard, 16 June 1940, ibid., pp. 444 – 5.
[50] Menzies to Bruce, 17 June 1940, ibid., pp. 446 – 7.

Mackenzie King, who had himself appealed to the French premier to continue the struggle, does not appear to have reacted to the union proposals.[51] Smuts' reaction was a fleeting one: 'I am most dubious about that Anglo-French Union, except as a tonic to a very sick patient.'[52] His main energies at this time were concentrated upon resisting the suggestion that the war was hopelessly lost and that in consequence South Africa should withdraw from it.[53]

The pressure from London to get Australian troops into the Middle East theatre in pursuit of Churchill's major strategy was not diminished by the growing peril in the Far East. Australia also became involved in the attempt to ensure that the French Empire remained an allied asset. The Australian flagship, H.M.A.S. *Australia*, was involved in the ill-fated Dakar expedition, and in the Pacific an Australian warship took part in the ousting of the Vichy authorities from New Caledonia.[54]

Although agreement had been reached in April about keeping Australia's forces together and about the political responsibility of their General Officer Commanding to his own government, this position was challenged in October and November by the developments in the Mediterranean and Middle East, with Wavell anxious to have a free hand with the disposition of all the troops under his command. Although immediate problems were ironed out, they must be taken into account in assessing the disillusion with Britain's handling of overall strategy that seems to have begun in Australia towards the end of the year.[55]

New Zealand: an antipodean contrast

The presence of a Labour government and the somewhat idiosyncratic attitude of the High Commissioner in London had, as has been seen, made some difference to the attitude of New Zealand to the international scene in the 1930s. But after Munich, public opinion in New Zealand hardened, and although there was some hostile press

---

[51] J.W. Pickersgill, *The Mackenzie King Record*, vol. I (Toronto, 1960), p. 123.
[52] Smuts to Amery, 19 June 1940: J. van der Poel (ed.), *Selections from the Smuts Papers*, vol. VI (Cambridge University Press, 1973), pp. 236 – 7. Amery was in fact a leading figure among the British progenitors of the scheme: memorandum, 'Anglo-French Unity', by Amery, 14 June 1940, Amery Papers.
[53] Smuts to Hertzog, 20 June 1940, loc. cit., pp. 237 – 9.
[54] Horner, op. cit., p. 40.
[55] Ibid., pp. 23, 45 – 50.

comment after Prague on the idea of a British guarantee to Poland, it was supported when announced by both the government and public opinion.[56] Opinion in New Zealand seems also to have been more outraged by Japan's aggression in China in 1937 than was opinion in Australia, and while the Australians were fearful that Britain might go too far in opposing Japan, New Zealand was more worried that it might be tempted too far along the road of appeasement. While New Zealand was kept informed of the negotiations with the Soviet Union, its government intervened on only one occasion, to stress the advantages of coming to an arrangement. Britain's decision to inform Germany that the Nazi-Soviet Pact would not prevent the fulfilment of the guarantee to Poland was approved.

When it was learned that Britain had declared war, the New Zealand cabinet took the decision to declare war independently, thus interpreting the new relations within the Commonwealth in a different way from Australia. New Zealand was also concerned with what the wartime relationships would be between her own forces and those of the United Kingdom: a problem which had not received full attention in peacetime. Where the navy and air force were concerned, it was impossible to avoid virtual incorporation in British forces, but an agreement providing for the New Zealand expeditionary force and its commander to retain direct relations with their own government was arrived at on 5 January 1940, three months before a similar agreement between Australia and the United Kingdom.[57]

The other principal subject of concern was the difficulty for New Zealand in equipping from her own industrial resources the larger armed forces she was now recruiting; nor had the United Kingdom spare capacity from which to assist her. It was obvious that closer ties with the Americans would be needed, though the New Zealand government was less sceptical than the Australians about the renewed promises from London that, if the crunch came with Japan, the promised fleet would be sent. The claims that had been pressed against the United States in respect of the islands between Hawaii and Samoa were consequently dropped in November 1939.[58]

[56] The following paragraphs are based on F.L.W. Wood, *The New Zealand People at War* (Wellington, 1958). See also *Documents Relating to New Zealand's participation in the Second World War* (Wellington, 1959).

[57] On the general contribution of Commonwealth forces to the allied cause in the early part of the war, see Butler, op. cit., pp. 42 – 5.

[58] A. David McIntyre, *The Commonwealth of Nations – origins and impact, 1869 – 1971* (New York, 1977), 205 – 7.

The internal political situation in New Zealand was something the government had to take into account. The only outright opposition to participation in the war came from the Communist Party, but many in the Labour Party were worried about the lack of clear war aims, and expressed the fear that the war would become one of old-fashioned imperial rivalries, and might even find the allies turning against the Soviet Union. It is therefore understandable that in the autumn of 1939 New Zealand should have, like Australia, pressed for generosity in expressing the allied war aims, and even for a general conference including neutral powers, to see if a peaceful settlement were possible. Dissent over war aims was combined with left-wing criticism of government policy in economic matters as being insufficiently socialist; but at the Labour Party Conference on 25 March 1940 the Left was defeated. When two days later the Prime Minister, Savage, died, he was succeeded by Peter Fraser, who had visited England to deal with supply matters early in the war, and was to remain at the helm for the remainder of the conflict.

During the critical summer months of 1940 the New Zealand government kept closely in touch with the Australians, and suffered the same anxieties as the magnitude of Britain's defeat became apparent. When the New Zealand government received the Secretary of State's telegram of 13 June 1940 to the effect that, if Japan moved, Britain would not have any force left over from having to deal with the combined German and Italian Navies, and would have to rely on the United States to look after its interests in the Far East, Fraser pointed out in a telegram to Churchill that this was a departure from the Singapore strategy on which New Zealand's entire defence policy had been based, but could only express the hope that the undertaking to send a fleet would be renewed when circumstances permitted.[59]

South Africa: the lukewarm belligerent

South Africa continued to be the most forceful advocate of appeasement among Commonwealth governments, and was the only Commonwealth country (apart from Eire) which presented the possibility that it would remain neutral. Smuts himself continued to

[59] Dominions Secretary to British High Commissioner in Wellington, 13 June 1940; New Zealand Prime Minister to Prime Minister of United Kingdom, 15 June 1940: W.D. McIntyre and W.J. Gardner, *Speeches and Documents on New Zealand History* (Oxford, 1971), pp. 367 – 8.

hold to the view that while the Dominions would all probably fight in Britain's cause, they could not be expected to follow her in seeking to maintain a European settlement which he regarded as unjust. 'Chamberlain's Polish guarantee has simply made us gasp – from the Commonwealth point of view', he wrote to a British friend. 'I cannot see the Dominions following Great Britain in this sort of imperial policy, the dangers of which to the Commonwealth are obvious.'[60] Hertzog's position was even less favourable to participation in a war, since he argued that, in view of the widespread objections to it among Afrikaners, it would militate against the continued fusion of the two streams of the white population and give strength to the extreme nationalists who wished to leave the Commonwealth altogether and set up an independent republic. He felt that South Africa could meanwhile fulfil its Commonwealth obligations by allowing Britain the continued use of the Simonstown naval base and South Africa's other port facilities. If South Africa were to be drawn into the war later, it would be on the side of the allies.[61]

Smuts however by now was convinced of the case for war and insisted upon an immediate decision. On 4 September Hertzog was defeated in Parliament, which by 80 to 67 votes decided upon an immediate declaration of war, and rejected Hertzog's proposed declaration of neutrality. Hertzog, refused a dissolution by the governor-general, Sir Patrick Duncan – a former member of the Milner kindergarten – resigned and was succeeded by Smuts, who remained in office throughout the war. But South Africa's contribution to the war was necessarily a restricted one compared with that of the other Dominions, and basically confined to the struggle in Africa.[62] Smuts himself was favourable to the attempts by Menzies to see that the doors were not closed against the possibility of a negotiated peace in the autumn of 1939, and supported him in his efforts to secure a clarification of British war aims. For the most part he was concerned in the early years of the war with raising and arming troops and with countering nationalist efforts to reverse the decision made in September 1939. When France was on the verge of falling and Italy

[60] Smuts to Gillett, 6 April 1939, *Smuts Papers*, vol. VI, p. 159.
[61] M. Wilson and L. Thompson, *Oxford History of South Africa*, vol. II (Oxford, 1971), pp. 382 – 3.
[62] Smuts to Menzies, 14 October 1939, *DAFP*, vol. II, pp. 140 – 1. For Smuts' wartime role see W.K. Hancock, *Smuts*, vol. II, pt. IV. For the 'Milner kindergarten' see *Imperial Sunset*, Vol. I, p. 123.

entered the war, Smuts both secured a declaration of war against Italy and assumed the office of Commander-in-Chief of South Africa's forces. As his biographer points out, this was no empty gesture:

> As Commander-in-Chief (as well as Prime Minister, Minister of External Affairs and Minister of Defence) he was able in the years ahead to answer with an immediate Yes or No all proposals put to him by Churchill or by local commanders for the employment of South African forces in the field, and he was able with the same freedom to make proposals of his own. No comparable concentration of political power in the hands of one man existed anywhere else in the Commonwealth.[63]

It also remained the case that, alone among the Dominion Prime Ministers, Smuts retained a high degree of personal prestige in London, dating from his involvement in British affairs in the first world war, and that his views on matters affecting the war, and in particular the arrangements for co-ordinating the efforts of the Commonwealth, were more readily accepted by Churchill and other British figures than those of the leaders of countries whose contribution to the war was more considerable.

Canada: the American pull

Of such countries, Canada was the most important but after March 1939, as previously, Mackenzie King's intentions and activities were shrouded in a mist of ambiguity.[64] He remained anxious that no actions by the Canadian government should be seen as preempting Canada's decision as to making war, and instructed the High Commissioner in London not to participate in the frequent meetings with the Dominions Secretary attended by the other High Commissioners. Massey felt himself at liberty to disobey this instruction when he felt attendance to be vital.[65] However, he, like his Prime Minister, was in

---

[63] Ibid., p. 350.

[64] As late as May 1939 the Department of External Affairs was still suggesting to the Americans that Canada would remain neutral. C.P. Stacey, *A Date with History* (Ottawa, 1983), p. 52. Herbert Marler, the Canadian Minister at Washington, was described as an ardent nationalist and isolationist, who kept telling his government that the U.S.A. had no intention of becoming involved in Europe's troubles. Grant Dexter to Lothian, 13 May 1939: Lothian Papers, Box 208.

[65] Vincent Massey, *What's Past is Prologue* (London, 1963), p. 297. On Massey's period as High Commissioner see Claude Bissell, *The Imperial Canadian: Vincent Massey in Office* (Toronto, 1986).

favour of trying to appease Germany for as long as possible. When the Nazi-Soviet Pact was announced, Massey did take part in the High Commissioners' meeting with British Ministers, where it was stated that the British government proposed to announce its intention of standing by the guarantee to Poland, against which Bruce protested. The Canadian High Commissioner, according to a member of his staff, was at a loss as to what should be done:

> Poor Mr Massey – he has a cold and no role to play and no idea what he would do if he had such a role. He is as undecided as I am what is the proper line for the Canadian government to take. He put the pros and cons to me without any idea of interpreting them and said 'Of course, Bruce' – the Australian High Commissioner – 'has a fine mind.'[66]

At the same time, Mackenzie King had not doubted that if war did come Canada would have to be involved, and on 23 August it was announced that the Canadian Parliament would be summoned at once if efforts to prevent a war should be unsuccessful. It met in fact on 7 September and by a vote on 9 September approving the address was taken to have given its assent to a declaration of war, which was made by the Prime Minister on the next day.[67] For a week therefore Canada, while taking precautionary measures in its own defence, had been neutral while Britain was at war. The new relationship between Commonwealth countries could not have found a clearer expression. An historian of a different political complexion has argued that Mackenzie King never intended to play a full part in the war, but only to participate to the extent necessary to keep Canada politically quiescent and the Liberal Party in power.[68] And on the basis of the early concentration on home defence and on the air force and navy rather than on an expeditionary force this judgement can be justified. It would however be proper to add that Britain for its part had shown no great interest in probing the Canadians as to what contribution they might make should war come.

[66] Diary entry, 22 August 1939: Charles Ritchie, *The Siren Years: Undiplomatic Diaries, 1937–1945* (London, Macmillan, 1974), p. 40.
[67] J.W.Pickersgill, *The Mackenzie King Record*, vol. I, ch. 2.
[68] Donald Creighton, *The Forked Road: Canada, 1939–1957* (Toronto, 1976), p. 2. Creighton himself had not been an advocate of a greater war effort, deploring the nationalism that the war had brought to the fore. Stacey, *A Date with History*, p. 84. It is worth noting that, in the eyes of the same author, 'Mackenzie King had always hated the army, and he didn't like the other fighting services much better'. Ibid., p. 193.

The sending overseas of Canadian troops was suggested by the British government in reply to Mackenzie King's inquiry as to possible modes of contribution to the war effort, and in spite of the stringent financial limitations upon Canada's armed services, the first Canadian division reached Britain in December. Much energy was also taken up in the negotiation of what became the British Commonwealth Air Training Plan, suggested by the British government on 26 September 1939. King was annoyed that the special mission sent from the United Kingdom seemed to take Canada's assent to the idea for granted, seeing the fulfilment of the plan as a duty rather than as a gift. He also felt that Canada's financial contribution was too large unless reached as part of a general settlement in which Britain would give an under-taking about the purchase of Canadian wheat. Despite these and other difficulties raised by the ever suspicious Prime Minister, the agree-ment, to which the Australian and New Zealand governments were also signatories, was signed on 17 December 1939.[69]

Questions that seemed academic to British participants in the discussions, who were concerned only to find means of checking the ascendancy of the *Luftwaffe*, were not so to Mackenzie King. 'It will never be known', he wrote in his diary,

> what we have saved this country by making clear that Canada has gone into this war of her own volition to co-operate; also what has been saved for the British Empire of possible dismemberment as a consequence of this attitude. We would get nowhere if it were for a moment assumed that as part of the Empire, it was for the central part to tell the outlying parts what they were to do.[70]

It is certainly the case that Canada's conduct after war came can only be understood in the light of Mackenzie King's long-established sense of national and party priorities.[71]

The same long-term considerations also affected Canadian attitudes to the potential the country possessed for producing and delivering war supplies, the more important because of the inhibitions for the

---

[69] On Canada's war effort in general see C.P. Stacey, *Arms, Men and Governments: The War Policies of Canada, 1939–1945* (Ottawa, 1970). On the negotiations about air training see ibid., pp. 81 – 9, and Appendix D, (text of agreement), and Pickersgill, op. cit., ch. 3.
[70] Quoted in Pickersgill, op. cit., p. 43.
[71] For this aspect see J.L. Granatstein, *Canada's War: The Policies of the Mackenzie King Govern-ment, 1939–1945* (Toronto, 1975).

United States of its existing neutrality legislation.[72] But Canada was not only a competitor with the United States, it was also a country whose own industrial development was interlocked with that of her more powerful neighbour; nor should one underestimate the importance from Britain's point of view of the fact that Canada was not part of the sterling block at a time when, with the experience of the first world war in mind, the conservation of dollars was already an important factor in its policies.[73] Once war was upon him, King felt less inhibited about Canada's views being expressed, and Massey was allowed to join the High Commissioners at their almost daily meetings with ministers. His comment on Chamberlain's reply to Hitler's peace proposals of October 1939 has already been referred to.[74] His principal adviser, Skelton, did not let up in his francophobia, which came out in relation to the French demand that any peace settlement must include guarantees against future German aggression. 'Those now in authority in France', he minuted, 'have learned nothing and forgotten everything.' They did not seem worried about the Russians, only the Germans.[75]

In a memorandum on war aims in November, Mackenzie King wrote that Canada's entry into the war had been the result of the threat by the Dictators to British liberties. What was needed for the future was a new 'non-coercive' League of Nations based on public opinion.[76] The unwillingness of Canada to be associated with discussions leading to the declaration against a separate peace agreed upon by Britain and France on 28 March was partly influenced by Mackenzie King's unwillingness to be seen as politically involved in Europe on the eve of a general election in Canada. Canada, although claiming to be acting as a sovereign state, had placed its forces in France under the British command and did not claim direct access to the French Commander-in-Chief, nor did it cultivate direct relations with the Anglo-French Supreme War Council. Its air squadrons were largely

---

[72] The issue of supply was raised by the Canadian minister of Mines and Resources during a visit to London in October 1939: Stacey, op. cit., pp. 11 – 12. Documents concerning the negotiations at this time are in *Documents on Canadian External Relations*, vol. VII (Ottawa, 1974), 375 ff.

[73] At this time Amery unsuccessfully urged upon the Treasury the desirability of using the new situation to bring Canada onto a sterling basis. Amery, *My Political Life*, vol. III, p. 349.

[74] Mackenzie King to Chamberlain, 8 October 1939, DCER, VII, 170 – 1.

[75] Ibid., pp. 184 – 5.

[76] Memorandum of 2 November 1939, ibid., 187 ff.

incorporated in the R.A.F.[77] The sweeping victory won by Mackenzie King in the election on 26 March does not seem to have altered his fundamentally cautious approach, nor before the German invasions of Denmark and Norway, followed by the attack along the western front, had any progress been made with what was to be a serious concern of Canada's almost to the end of the war, its inability to find the proper means through which to convey its strategic concerns to the British government without a greater degree of involvement than was considered politically desirable. In particular, Mackenzie King was at pains to deny reports that some kind of imperial war cabinet might be revived, although in early November 1939 there were enough senior Dominion representatives in London, including his Minister of Mines and Resources, T.A. Crerar, for some fairly broad-ranging discussions on the war situation.[78] In April 1940 the Canadian Minister of National Defence visited London for discussions of a largely technical nature, and was instructed to inform the British government of Mackenzie King's inability to agree to a proposal for a Conference of Dominion Prime Ministers which it had been suggested might be called for that summer. Apart from the belief of Mackenzie King that his presence was necessary in Canada in order to maintain national unity behind the war effort, he called attention to the importance of his presence at home in case he was needed to maintain 'the most friendly relations between Britain and the United States'.[79] Once again, the vision of Canada as the bridge between the Empire and the United States was an element of profound importance in his self-assessment.

America, Canada and a new world order

The idea of a new world order, upheld by a partnership between the

[77] Stacey, *Arms, Men and Governments*, 142 ff. The problem of the status of Canadian troops and their commanders' responsibilities is further explored in Stacey, *A Date with History*, pp. 74 – 5, 235 – 7.

[78] 'The matters of high policy which in the Imperial War Cabinet in the last war were considered in conference around the council table by the heads of the several governments of the British Empire, are today discussed in cable communications conducted under cypher code.' Mackenzie King memorandum, 3 November 1940, *DCER*, vol. VII, p. 434. '... to summon an Imperial War Cabinet now would only emphasise the lack of unity which exists in the Commonwealth in regard to the prosecution of the war, the Free State being neutral, South African participation being only nominal and India using Britain's extremity to press for wider autonomy.' Memorandum by J.S. Macdonald, November 1940, ibid., p. 437.

[79] The proposal had been launched in a British note of 22 April 1940: ibid., pp. 410 – 16.

English-speaking peoples under the leadership of the United States, had taken hold of the imagination of some individuals in Britain, disillusioned with the workings of the League of Nations in the absence of U.S. membership. 'I am more than ever convinced', wrote Lothian to Smuts on 1 December 1938, 'that the only foundation from which you can begin to rebuild the world is an English-speaking foundation. The United States will eventually see the point and as Rhodes foresaw, take the lead.' But he was well aware that to preach this idea openly would be taken as a plea 'that the United States should underwrite the British Empire or follow Great Britain into war'. Canada might more safely be used as a channel for ventilating these ideas in the United States, and on 9 March 1939 Lothian wrote to Mackenzie King on the 'possibility of stabilising the world through the oceanic co-operation of the English-speaking democracies', which they had discussed when Lothian visited Ottawa in January.[80]

Such ideas were however not easily reconciled with Mackenzie King's own vision of a wholly non-coercive world organisation, since he did not share Lothian's view of the lessons to be drawn from the history of sea-power.[81] Nor, with his concern for Canada's unity, was the description 'English-speaking' likely to appeal to him.

Another obstacle to pursuing this approach was the strongly pro-appeasement line taken both before the outbreak of war and afterwards by Joseph Kennedy, the U.S. Ambassador in London. In late 1938 Lothian wrote to Sir Ronald Lindsay, whom he was to succeed as Ambassador in Washington in August 1939, that Kennedy had asked him to collect material on the possibilities facing the United States if the British Empire disappeared or was destroyed.[82] While Roosevelt was fully aware of his ambassador's tendencies – 'Joe Kennedy has been an appeaser and always will be an appeaser'[83] – he retained him at his post. And in May 1940 Kennedy told Churchill that he was fearful of the U.S. giving help which 'would leave the United States holding the bag for a war in which the Allies expected to be beaten...If

[80] Lothian to Smuts, 1 December 1938; Lothian to F.Milner (New Zealand), 1 June 1939: Lothian Papers, Box 208; Lothian to Mackenzie King, 9 March 1939: ibid., Box 206.
[81] Lothian wrote to Smuts on 6 June 1939 of 'the great Pax of the nineteenth century which was created by the British Navy': ibid., Box 208.
[82] Lothian to Lindsay, 31 March 1939: ibid., Box 207.
[83] Morgenthau Diary entry, probably early October 1939: J.M. Blum, *From the Morgenthau Diaries: Years of Urgency, 1938-1941* (Boston, Houghton Mifflin, 1965), p. 102.

we had to fight to protect our lives we would do better fighting in our own backyard.'[84]

India: confrontation, collaboration and stalemate

Mackenzie King's view that the war was being seen in India as a chance to bring pressure on Britain for concessions going beyond the 1935 Act was undoubtably correct. Some of the leaders of the independence movement had indeed expected a situation of this kind.[85] Nehru, so Lothian noted in the summer of 1939, was so deeply saturated with the Marxist interpretation of history that war and revolution were inescapable consequences of the capitalist order: 'he expected world war to break out in Europe in the next year or two and that as a result India will be able to establish complete independence from Downing Street control'.[86] To the British government, still hoping that the obstacles to federation would be overcome, the maintenance of Britain's position in India was taken for granted, though in some quarters the demands of Indian defence were thought to be putting too great a strain on Britain's resources.[87] Some of those acquainted with the Indian scene thought that the danger to India itself might be overestimated: 'the idea that Japan can attack India through Burma is to my mind quite absurd'.[88] The Viceroy, with his immediate responsibilities, was less sanguine, and feared the consequences if lending India's anti-aircraft battery for the defence of Britain, as requested by the Chiefs of Staff in July 1939, was to leave her unprotected in the event of an emergency.[89] In August Congress showed its opposition to any Indian participation in a war now increasingly likely, by criticising the dispatch of Indian troops to Aden, Egypt and Singapore.[90] What the British saw as India's need of Britain to

[84] Kennedy to Secretary of State, *FRUS*, 1940, vol. III, pp. 29-30. For a provocative if somewhat disjointed exploration of the whole theme see D. Cameron Watt, *Succeeding John Bull: America in Britain's Place 1900–1975* (Cambridge, 1984).

[85] Subhas Bose had been the principal advocate of calculating upon Britain's problems in Europe to bring pressure on the British government to accede to the nationalist demands for independence. See Nirad C.Chaudhuri, *Thy Hand, Great Anarch: India, 1921–1952* (London, 1987), Book VI.

[86] Lothian to General Ironside, 8 July 1938: Lothian Papers, Box 205.

[87] Secretary of State for War to Prime Minister, 1 November 1939: R.J. Minney (ed.) *The Private Papers of Hore-Belisha*, (London, Collins, 1960), p. 66.

[88] Lothian to Sir Shafa'at Ahmad Khan, 6 December 1938: Lothian Papers, Box 206.

[89] John Glendevon, *The Viceroy at Bay* (London, 1971), p. 133.

[90] Gowher Rizvi, *Linlithgow and India: A Study of British Policy and the Political Impasse in India, 1936–1943* (London, 1978), p. 131.

defend her against external threat was seen by Congress as imaginary; it was Britain which would need India's resources to make possible her own war effort.[91] Indian Liberals, worried about Britain's ability to defend India with so many other commitments, might urge more rapid Indianisation of the forces as a means of making Indians take a more direct interest in defence, but this argument did not take account of the fundamental Congress position.[92]

The possibility that the provincial governments controlled by Congress would not be willing to play their part in a war effort was foreseen by the Viceroy, and the Government of India Amendment Act of April 1939 authorised powers of direction by central government in an emergency. When war did come on 3 September, Linlithgow took the constitutionally correct position that since Britain was at war, India was so automatically. It was however argued that the Viceroy should have involved the Central Legislative Assembly in the decision, or in some way consulted spokesmen of nationalist opinion, and the failure to do what would have been obligatory had the federal portions of the 1935 Act been in place made the political situation more difficult than it need have been. Against this it can be argued that whatever the views of those consulted had been, it would still have been the Viceroy's duty to declare that India was at war.[93] Indeed, the criticism came later; at the time neither Gandhi nor any other responsible leader raised his voice against the Viceroy's action.[94] Nehru, while opposed to co-operation under existing circumstances, indicated his willingness to see India as a participant in the struggle against fascism, provided it did so as a fully independent country.[95] A minority in Congress led by Subhas Bose rejected the idea of a political bargain implicit in the actions of Congress, and wished to see Britain's difficulties exploited more aggressively. One problem was that the Indian leadership demanded not merely a commitment in respect of India's constitutional future, but also a statement on allied war aims in general – the very issue that was troubling the British

[91] B.R. Tomlinson, *The Indian National Congress and the Raj* (London, 1976), p. 141. In September 1939 an unofficial attempt was made to get Nehru's terms for Congress to cooperate in the war effort so as to separate him from Gandhi's total repudiation of armed defence. But it came to nothing. Desmond Young, *Try Anything Twice* (London, 1963), pp. 245 – 6.
[92] Sir Tej Bahadur Sapru to Lothian, 4 November 1938: Lothian Papers, Box 206.
[93] Rizvi, op. cit., 129 ff.
[94] Glendevon, op. cit., p. 135.
[95] The complexities in Nehru's position and the interplay of ideology and personality among the Indian leaders are fully set out in S. Gopal, *Jawarhalal Nehru*, vol. 1, ch. 16, 'The War Crisis'.

cabinet, and the subject of such difficult exploration with France and the Dominions.

The situation was as always complicated by the parallel demands of the Muslims, who welcomed the inevitable decision not to proceed with the federal scheme, and through the Muslim League declared that the support of their community could only be obtained through a new political settlement which took full account of their claims. An attempt to bring Congress and the Muslim League together in a joint policy towards the war broke down on their differences.

The belief that India could play its part in the war without the support of Congress was exemplified in the Viceroy's statement of 17 October offering consultations on constitutional revision at the end of the war, with the only immediate change being the proposed setting up of a consultative group of selected Indians to advise on the war effort. Congress thereupon decided that it could not support the government in its prosecution of the war and called upon the Congress ministries to resign, which they did by 10 November in all the eight provinces they controlled; their rule was in consequence a matter for their governors, and was to remain so until the end of the war. To account for his unwillingness to go further, Linlithgow could point to the inability of Congress and the Muslim League to agree. But he was under pressure from the Secretary of State to try a more specific offer on the constitutional side, and in a speech on 10 January 1940 held out the prospect both of full Dominion status after the war and, immediately, of establishing an Executive Council expanded to include representatives of the political parties, as well as the appointment of a consultative committee on defence matters.

While in India this was seen as a possible basis for negotiation, at least by Gandhi, the reaction in some quarters in Britain was that the Viceroy had gone too far in appeasing Congress; in any event, the conditions put forward by Jinnah would, if accepted, have nullified what Congress was willing to agree to. In Britain, this intransigence was not regretted by everyone; Churchill, back in government, had not swerved from the position that had led to his long battle against the 1935 Act, and argued that the Viceroy should not be instructed to promote a settlement of the communal rivalry, since it was what made the continuation of British rule possible.[96] In the early part of the war

[96] War Cabinet meeting, 2 February 1940, PRO CAB 65/5; Inskip Diary, vol. II, 103, entry for 5 February 1940.

the political negotiations were however largely peripheral to the main task, in which the Viceroy appeared to be succeeding: recruiting to the armed forces, preventing the communal feud from affecting their performance, and finding for them the necessary arms.

Financial as well as industrial limitations had to be taken into account. The agreement reached in 1939 was that the Indian government should meet the cost of Indian and other troops stationed in India and of all supplies required for India's own defence, while the British government assumed responsibility for expenses above this level and for the cost of Indian troops and equipment used outside India itself. Defence expenditure chargeable to India rose from 49.54 crores in 1939 – 40 to 73.61 crores in 1940 – 41, while the British government added in 1940 – 41 an extra 53 crores, figures which would of course come to be dwarfed in both categories in the later years of the war.[97]

The most striking feature of the war years was to prove to be the way in which the by now largely and increasingly Indianised services continued to play their role as upholders of law and order and in making the ordinary as well as the expanded machinery of government function. Whatever the private feelings of Indian civil servants may have been, there was no reason to doubt their loyalty in action to their immediate employer, the Government of India – not even during the 'Quit India' crisis of the summer of 1942. The steel framework of the I.C.S. and of the provincial services held firm. Nevertheless the situation was more complex than the official records suggest. The Indian intelligensia identified with the nationalist movement did not relax their hostility to Britain or refrain from rejoicing at the setbacks to both Britain and her allies. In the early part of the war, while Germany and the Soviet Union were working together, pro-Germans like Subhas Bose and those sympathetic to the Soviet Union like Nehru could equally enjoy satisfaction at the course of events. On the other hand, as with other belligerents, the demands of the war gave many new opportunities for civilian employment, and this was particularly true of the expansion of the government machine, which provided jobs for many of the graduates whose personal frustrations had helped fuel their nationalist enthusiasm. It is thus not suprising that, despite the resignation of the Congress ministries, there was not a great deal of

[97] B.R. Tomlinson, *The Political Economy of the Raj*, p. 93.

329

political trouble in India until it faced the very different situation created in 1942 by the Japanese advance towards its borders.[98]

The crisis of May 1940 brought Churchill, the old antagonist of Indian nationalism, into power, but his choice of Leo Amery as Secretary of State for India gave day to day responsibility for Indian affairs to someone whose imperialism found room for the idea of a self-governing India as part of the Commonwealth partnership, and who was keen to see a new offer made to the Indian leaders. At the same time, the Congress leadership was facing the problem of what to do if India itself came under attack, and was in its majority opposed to Gandhi's prescription of total non-violence. The fall of France seemed to make imperative yet another attempt at a political agreement.[99]

Colonial Development and Welfare and the 1940 Act

By 1939 the new impetus towards a more active policy for colonial development had gained further ground; there was now wide acceptance for 'a more positive paternalist view, which represented a reaffirmation of Britain's civilising mission, purged of its evangelical overtones'.[100] And this point of view had gained ground in the Colonial Office, where a review of the existing legislative framework was already in progress. The coming of the war made the proclamation and implementation of a major new policy something which the government was bound for the moment to set aside. Indeed, the first effect was to make the Treasury suggest that a curb should be put on all existing expenditure unless it directly contributed to the war effort.[101] On the other hand, the war was also an argument for going ahead with new schemes. It was essential that colonial resources should be mobilised and that the colonies should remain peaceful and make no demands on military manpower for maintaining order. It was also argued that to proclaim a large and generous scheme of development would have an effect upon opinion at home and in neutral countries, particularly the United States.[102] And while the Report of the West India Royal Commission (received in December 1939) was

[98] See Chaudhuri, op. cit., Book VII, 'India Enjoys the War', for a vivid description of this period.
[99] Tomlinson, *The Indian National Congress and the Raj, 1929-1942*, pp. 148 – 50.
[100] P.Hetherington, *British Paternalism and Africa, 1920–1940* (London, Cass, 1978), p. 104.
[101] D.J. Morgan, *The Official History of Colonial Development*, vol. 1, chs 7 and 8.
[102] S.Constantine, *The Making of British Colonial Development Policy, 1914–1940* (London, 1984), 246 ff.

not published because of the damaging impact its picture of conditions in the Caribbean might have on opinion if the more negative portions were seized upon by enemy propaganda, its reception in government circles did provide an additional impetus towards a new policy.[103] The autumn and winter of 1939 – 40 were largely occupied with inter-departmental discussions on proposed new legislation, with the Treasury objecting in particular to the inclusion of social services as well as matters of direct economic benefit in what could be financed by the British government.[104] By 20 February the Colonial Secretary had got his way sufficiently for the publication, together with the *Recommendations of the West India Royal Commission*, of a *Statement of Policy.*[105]

The bill, which became the Colonial Development and Welfare Act, 1940, included not only a widening of the scope of direct assistance for development, but also provision for the cancellation of the debts owed by some colonial governments, which had been a burden on their budgets. It was presented to the House of Commons by Malcolm MacDonald on 2 May 1940, and received its second reading on 20 May. By this time its importance was eclipsed by the grave military events in Europe. Indeed, in the cabinet changes brought about by Churchill's accession to the premiership, MacDonald himself had now been moved to the Ministry of Health and replaced at the Colonial Office by Lord Lloyd, who piloted the bill through to Royal Assent, which it received on 17 July 1940. Its full implementation was difficult under war conditions, but enough energies were found among individuals not directly involved with the war effort for a beginning to be made, particularly in the fields of research and education.[106]

---

[103] Morgan, op. cit., ch. 9. The Report was published in October 1945 as Cmd 6607.
[104] Sir John Simon, the Chancellor of the Exchequer, would seem to have been more convinced of the merits of putting money into the Colonial Empire than his civil servants, and was thanked by Malcolm MacDonald for his support. Malcolm MacDonald to Simon, 15 February 1940, Simon Papers.
[105] Cmd 6174 and Cmd 6175.
[106] Morgan, op. cit., 89 ff; J.M. Lee, *Colonial Development and Good Government* (London, 1967), 111 ff.

Chapter 14

DEFEAT AND THE
SHADOW OF DISSOLUTION

Britain a junior partner: the price of avoiding defeat

The entry of Italy into the war, 'Dunkirk', and the acceptance by
France of the German terms for an armistice marked the bankruptcy
of Britain's European policy.[1] Neither appeasement up to March 1939
nor the subsequent policy of guarantees had prevented all western and
central Europe coming under German domination, with a patent
threat to the Iberian Peninsula and the Balkan states. Britain, in the
phrase of the time, stood alone. It was paying for miscalculating both
the strength of its enemies and the strength and determination of its
allies. That Stalin had made the same over-estimate of French military
might was little consolation.

The war had now become not one for victory, which it was clearly
beyond Britain's power to achieve, but one for survival, first in the
home islands – the Battle of Britain – and then in the pivotal area of
North Africa and the Middle East. The first glimmerings of a possible
defeat for the Nazis came with the prolongation of Russian defence
after Hitler's attack upon the Soviet Union in June 1941. The most
substantial guarantee of success came in December that year, when
Japan finally took up the challenge to her expanding East Asian
hegemony by the simultaneous attack upon the United States Pacific
fleet and the Asian Empires of the British and the Dutch. Despite
initial losses in territory and prestige, in which the fall of Singapore
counted for most, the British could now hope to be part of a victorious
coalition in what had become to a much greater extent than had been
true of the war of 1914 – 18, a world war.

It was however increasingly a coalition in which Britain was at best

---

[1] On the military consequences of the French collapse from June 1940 to June 1941 see J.R.M.
Butler, *Grand Strategy*, vol. II (London, 1957), chs IX-end. For the period from June 1941 to the
fall of Singapore see J.M.A. Gwyer, *Grand Strategy*, vol. III, pt. I (London, 1964), chs I-XVI.

a junior partner, even though admitted on apparently equal terms to a war-making partnership with the United States and, in so far as co-operation was practised by the Russians at all, also by the Soviet Union. It was only gradually that the relevance of contrasting strengths and in particular of the weight of American human and material resources made themselves felt in the decisions taken first in respect of the war itself, and then in the tentative provisions for a new world settlement.

In these developments the existence of the Empire-Commonwealth played a vital though ambiguous part.[2] The British when they spoke of themselves 'standing alone' meant of course that it was the Empire-Commonwealth, not the United Kingdom, that was engaged. And Commonwealth leaders, not to mention subsequent Commonwealth historians, were at pains not to allow the British to forget that fact. Clearly the air-defence of Britain, on which so much else rested, would not have been possible without the contribution of many British Dominion airmen and the constant reinforcements available through the Commonwealth Air Training Plan. Commonwealth soldiers took an important, sometimes a predominant, part in the early campaigns in the Middle East, North Africa and Greece. And while Canadian forces largely awaited the reentry into Europe, Canadian industry was an increasingly important element in providing the weapons of war.

On the other hand, the preservation of the British imperial system was never a war aim of either the Soviet Union or the United States. Both governments, from their different vantage points, rejected 'imperialism' and 'colonialism'. Yet to sustain and deepen the relationship with the United States appeared to Churchill and to his military, industrial and financial advisers the most important objective of the British government, and one to which if necessary imperial positions and Commonwealth interests might have to be sacrificed.

Sometimes the sacrifices were more in the realms of language than of reality. The provisions of the 'Atlantic Charter', the agreement reached by Churchill and Roosevelt on 14 August 1941, included respecting the right of all peoples to choose the form of government under which they would live. But Churchill did not intend this to apply to countries except where a transference of sovereignty arose. It was

---

[2] For a preliminary survey see N.Mansergh, *Survey of British Commonwealth Affairs, 1939–1952* (London, 1958).

not to apply, that is, to the existing non-self-governing territories of the British Empire.[3]

In other cases the action taken was in line with previous policies over a much longer period. The exchange of bases in Newfoundland and the Caribbean for fifty American destroyers, negotiated in the late summer of 1940, may be said to have done no more than recognise the fact that Britain's positions in the western hemisphere, once defended by her own sea-power, were now wholly dependent upon the United States.[4] To seek U.S. assistance in persuading the Irish to forego a neutrality which was to be so costly in terms of British lives lost at sea was not surprising in the light of the previous interest shown in the United States in the Irish question. Yet on cardinal issues such as the future status of India, Britain's responsibility would not willingly be shared. Nothing Churchill did, even at the time of Britain's maximum weakness, invalidated his later claim that he had not become 'the King's first minister in order to preside over the liquidation of the British Empire'.[5] On paper, all the British objectives were ultimately realised. In point of fact the war had helped to swing the balance of power to a point where they could not long be maintained.

The general attitude of the British government towards the European dictators was by and large shared by the Dominions; there was no serious suggestion that a compromise peace was possible, and when Russia was attacked in June 1941 they showed no disposition to reject her as an ally. But there were differences of opinion of varying degrees of importance about the attitudes to be taken towards occupied Europe and the peripheral areas to which the war had not yet come. The French-Canadians found much to sympathise with in the Vichy regime, and were notably less enthusiastic for the war once France was no longer a belligerent.[6] They shared with the Americans some suspicion of the Free French movement and of General de Gaulle. The Australians, having to handle the direct repercussions of the changes

[3] Martin Gilbert, *Winston S.Churchill*, vol. VI (London, 1983), pp. 1161 – 3. For an American historian's view of these proceedings see W.R. Louis, *Imperialism at Bay, 1941–1945: The United States and the Decolonization of the British Empire* (Oxford, 1977), 121 ff. The text of the Atlantic Charter is in *FRUS*, 1941, vol. I, pp. 367 – 8; a facsimile of the original draft with Churchill's emendations is in W.S. Churchill, *The Second World War*, vol. III (London, 1950), p. 305.

[4] The course of the negotiations is outlined in Churchill, *The Second World War*, vol. II (London, 1949), ch. XX, 'United States Destroyers and West Indian Bases'. See also *DCER*, vol. VIII, pp. 65 – 276.

[5] Speech of 11 November 1942, quoted in Louis, op. cit., p. 200.

[6] See the message from Bruce in London to Menzies, 22 August 1941, *DAFP*, vol. V (Canberra, Australian Government Publishing Service, 1982), pp. 82 – 3.

in status of the French Pacific islands, were originally also somewhat prone to think Vichy the better bet,[7] but this attitude changed after Japan, by occupying French Indo-China with Vichy's consent, brought the Japanese threat to Singapore that much closer.[8] However, Australia's main focus of concern in 1940 – 41 was the Middle East and the Balkans, where the changing fortunes of the war directly involved its own forces.

The gradual development of the largely secret co-operation between the United States and Britain after Roosevelt's re-election in November 1940, while welcome to all the Dominions in as far as they were informed, affected them in different ways, as did the Lend-Lease Act of 11 March 1941 which was its principal overt manifestation. In particular, there were doubts about the pressure brought upon Japan to try to avert its entry into the war, an event which became more likely after Japan's adherence to the Axis pact on 27 September 1940. Accepting the view that the defeat of Japan could only be brought about by American intervention and that the constitutional impediments to action by the U.S. administration made advance guarantees to the British, Australians or Dutch apparently impossible, it is understandable that the Australians felt that, rather than a policy of economic pin-pricks, it would be better to try to find some more positive policy leading either to an understanding, or to a war fought by a grand alliance distributing its resources in the most effective manner.

Obstacles to imperial co-operation

The prerequisite appeared to them to be that here and elsewhere there should be a greater degree of cohesion in imperial policy making.[9] It meant either the advocacy of some kind of Imperial war cabinet or of a Standing War Council for the Empire, or at least of more frequent consultation between British and Dominion Ministers.[10] Alternatively, since Prime Ministers could not be absent for long from their own countries, there was the idea put forward by Menzies in August 1941 that other Ministers from the Dominions

[7] See e.g. Caldecote to Whiskard, 30 August 1940, and Memorandum by Department of External Affairs, 13 January 1941, ibid., vol. IV, (Canberra, Australian Government Publishing Service, 1980), pp. 125 – 6, 334 – 5.
[8] The Japanese began to move into Indo-China on 28 July 1941.
[9] Gwyer, op. cit., pt. I, ch. IX.ii, 'Commonwealth Problems'.
[10] See e.g. Menzies to Cranborne, 8 November 1940, DAFP, vol. IV, p. 263.

might sit with the war cabinet in London, but this idea was unacceptable to the other Prime Ministers, and strongly rejected by Churchill himself. In reply, the new Australian Prime Minister, Fadden, pointed out that he was not surprised to find that Canada and South Africa had different views; their attitudes had been well known since the Imperial Conference of 1926, but, he added, 'We too have a special viewpoint, based on the closest possible degree of Empire co-operation which, speaking with the frankness permitted within the family circle, is evident by comparison of our all-round war effort on land, sea and in the air.'[11]

Churchill's resistance to the closer involvement of Dominion ministers in the making of grand strategy was put down by Australians to his 'lack of appreciation of importance of Dominions'.[12] Menzies himself believed that Churchill had 'no conception of the British Dominions as independent entities' and was anyhow not used to his views being questioned, even by his British colleagues.[13]

What was left was the existing provision for information to be given by the Dominions Secretary (not a member of the War Cabinet) to the High Commissioners, and for him to act as a channel for their observations. For Bruce at any rate this was unsatisfactory, especially since he had a low opinion of Caldecote. When Caldecote quitted the office to become Lord Chief Justice, Bruce somewhat incautiously went to see Churchill to suggest that his successor should be 'an absolutely first-class man and that he should attend all cabinet meetings'. Churchill's indignation at what he said was an attempt to dictate the composition of his cabinet and to ensure that the British cabinet should never meet without the Dominions being represented was understandable, and perhaps indicative of his general attitude. Bruce nevertheless returned

[11] Menzies to Bruce and Bruce to Menzies, 13 August 1941; Churchill to Fadden in Cranborne to Fadden, 29 August 1941; Fadden to Cranborne (for Prime Minister), 5 September 1941: DAFP, vol. V, p. 71 – 2, 73 – 5, 90 – 2, 99 – 101. Fadden had succeeded Menzies as Prime Minister on 29 August and was succeeded by the Labour leader John Curtin on 3 October. For Mackenzie King's view on this and similar Australian suggestions for greater participation in decision-making in London, see J.W. Pickersgill, The Mackenzie King Record, vol. I, pp. 213 – 5, 250, and Vincent Massey, What's Past is Prologue, 313.

[12] Bruce to Menzies, 26 September 1940, DAFP, vol. IV, 183. Bruce was indignant over the failure to give advance information to the Australians about the attempt to seize Dakar. On this abortive expedition see Butler, op. cit., pp. 313 – 9.

[13] See Menzies' report on his overseas visit in Advisory War Council Minute, 28 May 1941, DAFP, vol. IV, pp. 681 – 6. These sentiments were fuelled by the views of Australian military men that they were not treated as equals by British officers and were denied their proper share of major posts. See D.M. Horner, High Command: Australia and Allied Strategy, 1939–1945 (London, 1982), chs 4 – 8.

to the question in a meeting with Churchill on 19 December 1940, though professing himself satisfied with Cranborne, who had been appointed to succeed Caldecote. The Dominions Secretary, so Bruce argued, should be the 'best man in the Cabinet after the Prime Minister'. Churchill, he wrote, 'was inclined to dissent from this and said that after all the Dominions Office was only a Post Office, and that the Dominions would not tolerate any dictation from the Dominions Secretary'.[14] What Churchill seems to have had in mind was more relevant to an earlier period – the Dominions would not wish to be ordered about from London; but that they might have something to contribute to the general policy of the Empire or that the British government needed to be kept in touch with Dominion opinion was something rather remote from his way of looking at things.

In any event, consultation between the British and the Dominion governments remained on the same level of improvisation, dependent upon the energy and assiduity of their High Commissioners and the visits to London of varying duration of Premiers and other ministers.[15] It is true that Dominion sources of information had been extended by their separate representation at Washington; here Canada had the edge given by proximity, but Australia had in R.G. Casey someone who contrived to get close to the workings of the American government. Furthermore, from December 1940 Australia had an independent insight into Japanese affairs through the presence in Tokyo of Sir John Latham as ambassador, and from September 1941 of a *charge d'affaires*, F.K.Officer, and at Chungking from October 1940 of Sir Frederic Eggleston as Minister to China. There was also increasing participation, notably by Australians, in military conferences, beginning with that at Singapore in September 1940. Yet the crucial element in Anglo-American planning, the decision reached between Roosevelt and Churchill in December 1941 to give priority to the defeat of Hitler, a decision implicit in the earlier activities of the U.S. navy in the Atlantic and its reinforcement from the Pacific, remained secret even from the Australians. It was only made patent to Curtin's

[14] Notes by Bruce on conversations with Churchill, 2 October and 19 December 1940, *DAFP*, vol. IV, pp. 198 – 200, 309 – 11. Churchill's handling of this question showed some uncertainty. In February 1942 Cranborne was replaced by the Deputy Prime Minister, Clement Attlee, but in September 1943 the office reverted to Cranborne.

[15] Sir Earle Page, the Australian Minister of Commerce, went on a mission to London in September 1941, and after he left office remained there until March 1942 as the government's Special Representative. His presence occasionally complicated communications between the two governments. See Horner, op. cit., chs 6 and 7.

Minister for External Affairs, the strongly anti-British and nationalist H.V. Evatt, during the course of his mission to London in May 1942.[16]

Although there were disagreements on some issues, what was common to Britain and the Dominions throughout was an understanding of the vital importance of the security of Britain itself: upon that, as all their leaders admitted, all the rest of the imperial war effort depended. The Battle of Britain made the prospect of an actual invasion remote, and pressure was further lightened when the Germans opened the eastern front. But, as in the first world war, there were still the questions of the safety of supply upon which the British industrial effort depended, and of the transit of troops to and from British ports. It was in this respect that the Irish anomaly still made itself felt.

Irish neutrality and the war

The danger to Ireland of developments on the western front was pressed upon the Irish government by the British from the beginning of the German offensive, and after Dunkirk the anxieties in London inevitably grew, though Churchill did not share the apprehensions of Chamberlain and Halifax.[17] The Irish themselves did not believe that Germany would attack them and were unwilling to make defence preparations in advance. There was also anxiety that German agents might repeat their attempts during the first world war to exploit the I.R.A. for their purposes. In these circumstances, de Valera saw the possibility of another bid to end partition: the North should join a United Ireland whose neutrality would be guaranteed by all sides, including the Germans. There were indeed people in England who believed that the situation was so dangerous that the idea was worth exploring. The principal such figure was Ernest Bevin, soon to become a member of Churchill's war cabinet, who involved Lionel Curtis in the talks. But the discussions between de Valera and Malcolm MacDonald on 17 and 20 June 1940 showed how far apart the two governments were. The importance of the southern Irish made it possible to argue for another attempt, and further proposals were taken to Dublin by MacDonald on 26 June. The British could offer arms, of which de Valera realised Eire stood in need, and would

[16] Evatt to Curtin, 28 May 1942, *DAFP*, vol. V, pp. 795 – 7.
[17] The following paragraphs summarise the accounts given in John Bowman, *De Valera and the Ulster Question, 1917–1973* (Oxford, 1982), 208 ff, and P. Canning, *British Policy Towards Ireland*, 262 ff.

be willing in principle to concede the need to work out a scheme for the unification of Ireland; but for that Eire would have to enter the war at once, and become part of the general allied effort. To achieve this aim, the British were prepared to try to get Craigavon's consent. In fact, before a revised offer, on which the Americans had been consulted, was made on 29 June Craigavon had indignantly repudiated the whole idea. Meanwhile the Irish were using the British approaches to try to get undertakings from Germany not to collaborate with the I.R.A., and not use Eire as a base from which to attack Britain. Given the parlous state of Britain's own defences, it is not surprising that by 4 July the British overtures had been rejected.

It was clear that nothing short of a guaranteed and neutral Ireland would have any serious appeal to the Irish government, and with Chamberlain, who had taken the lead in pressing for an accommodation, a sick man and shortly to leave the cabinet, the doubts all along expressed by Churchill became the basis of official British policy. Instead, Churchill sought some measure of coercion which could bring Eire into the war. But the only instrument available was the denial of arms, and this was a double-edged weapon if it was believed that the Irish would in fact defend themselves if actually attacked. By the end of July, arms shipments were authorised.

After the Battle of Britain, during which the Irish question was allowed to be dormant, attention was once again focused on the Irish ports, the unavailability of which was contributing to Britain's growing losses at sea. It was hoped that the Americans, themselves now alarmed at the naval situation, might collaborate in bringing pressure upon de Valera. But it became clear that this hope was for the moment misplaced. Once again, the possibility of economic pressure was investigated, and once again without a way being found through the practical difficulties involved. On 29 December 1940 economic sanctions were authorised, but on so limited a scale as to lack any coercive force. More and more, the question of how United States opinion might react to British policies was dominant in the cabinet's considerations, and this aspect of affairs played its part in the decision in May 1941 not to extend conscription to Ulster.

In October 1941 there were soundings by the Canadian High Commissioner in Dublin, who seemed to believe that a bargain to end partition in return for entering the war was still possible. But de Valera's attitude had not altered. Nor was Menzies any more successful when he visited Dublin early in March 1941.[18] The entry of the United States into the war seemed to provide another opportunity, but a visit to Dublin by the Dominions Secretary on 17 December produced no result. Indeed de Valera, who had been annoyed by the presence of American technicians in Ulster to assist in preparing its defences, was outraged by the arrival in the province of American troops in January 1942. Despite the darkness of the hour, the likelihood of Eire having to deal with a German-dominated Europe, including Britain, had receded for good. To all intents and purposes Eire was a foreign country, while Ulster had become a province with an especial claim on British gratitude.[19]

Securing Egyptian co-operation

Egypt was as important in relation to Britain's position in the Middle East as was Ireland in relation to the western approaches. The Treaty of 1936 had seemed to be a way of reconciling Egyptian nationalism with the requirement of imperial defence. With the collapse of France and the entry of Italy into the war, Egypt had become vulnerable to overland attack. Hitherto all that Britain required in the way of facilities had been obtainable without the need to call for an Egyptian declaration of war, but when Italian belligerence became probable it was decided by the war cabinet that this was now required. Subsequently it was decided that a declaration of war would not be necessary, provided the Egyptian government broke off diplomatic relations with Italy as it had with Germany, prohibited trade with the enemy, and maintained internal security. The Prime Minister, Ali Maher, after some hesitation agreed to break off diplomatic relations with Italy and told his Parliament that Egypt would declare war if attacked. The British ambassador, Lampson, and the Commander-in-Chief, Wavell, were however worried by the apparent slowness of the Egyptians in carrying out their undertakings, and at the freedom

[18] David Day, *Menzies and Churchill at War* (London, 1986), pp. 112–13. A new factor was the need for air bases which could give fighter cover for shipping off the west of Ireland. Menzies to Fadden, 5 March 1941, *DAFP*, vol. IV, 470–1. Menzies' intervention was not welcomed by Churchill.
[19] On the establishment of neutrality as a national policy and the Irish claim that it represented a higher morality, see Patrick Keatinge, *A Singular Stance* (Dublin, 1984) pp. 17–19. Menzies, whose journey took in Belfast as well as Dublin, found some discontent in Ulster with its treatment by the United Kingdom government. See his memorandum written between 5 and 10 April 1941, *DAFP*, vol. IV, pp. 549–54.

allowed to German and Italian nationals. They came to the conclusion that the Prime Minister and behind him the King were trying to rein-sure against the possibility of an Italian victory. Lampson persuaded the King to dismiss Ali Maher. His resignation was announced on 23 June, and the Italian Ambassador and his staff left the country the same day. A new Prime Minister, Hassan Sabry, was appointed, and on his death on 14 November he was succeeded by Hussein Sirry Pasha. Under both Premiers co-operation with the British military authorities appears to have been satisfactory.[20]

The crossing of the Egyptian frontier by Italian troops on 13 September 1940 and the bombing of Alexandria raised the question of Egyptian belligerency, but during the subsequent vicissitudes of the desert war Egypt remained outside the conflict. Some political trou-ble was injected into the Egyptian scene by the Iraqi putsch in April 1941, and the economic difficulties consequent upon the war with the interruptions to supply helped to produce a mood unfavourable to the British, who were seen as being responsible for them. The news of the early Japanese victories after Pearl Harbour and a German advance in Cyrenaica also encouraged opposition elements and, following street demonstrations, the Prime Minister resigned on 2 February. On the following day Lampson intervened with the King to point out that Axis intrigues were being given too much scope and that the security of the country was in danger. The King was told that he could only deal with the situation by calling to the Premiership the leader of the Wafd party, Nahas Pasha. Upon the King's demurral, a display of force was mounted and the King gave way; Nahas formed a government on the understanding that Egypt as an independent country would co-operate in the fulfilment of the 1936 Treaty.[21] Britain had prevented the Axis from exploiting Egyptian nationalism, but at the expense of adding to the powerful myths that were to sustain it in the future.[22]

---

[20] Woodward, *British Policy in the Second World War*, vol. I, pp. 247 – 50. For a general account of the Middle East during the war years from mainly public sources see George Kirk, *The Middle East in the War* (London, 1952). It should perhaps be pointed out that Kirk shared to the full the pro-Arab bias and sympathy with Arab national movements common to the publications on the Middle East which came from the Royal Institute of International Affairs under the influence of Arnold Toynbee. See ch. 12 in E. Kedourie, *The Chatham House Version and other Middle Eastern Studies* (London, 1970).

[21] The incident is vividly described in Lampson's own diary: see Trefor E. Evans (ed.), *The Killearn Diaries, 1934–1946* (London, 1972), pp. 213 – 5.

[22] The incident is placed in historical perspective in W.R. Louis, *The British Empire in the Middle East, 1945–1951* (Oxford, 1984), pp. 226 – 31.

Syria and Lebanon: the French connection once again

The fall of France was of direct consequence to the British position in the Middle East, since it raised the question of the attitude which would be taken by the French authorities in Syria and Lebanon.[23] They decided after some hesitation to throw in their lot with Vichy, but the British government at first decided to avoid a direct clash which might reanimate Anglo-French rivalries in the area. The attitude of the French High Commissioner became increasingly hostile, and an investigation of the situation by de Gaulle's emissary, General Catroux, showed that there were scant hopes of a successful coup by Gaullist sympathisers. The failure of the Dakar expedition on 23 September contributed to their doubts.

Early in 1941 the situation was discussed in the light of suggestions of joint Free French and British action combined with an attempt to win Arab support by promising the eventual independence of the two territories. The British were however reluctant to engage themselves in Syria if it could be avoided, and still hoped that the new High Commissioner, General Dentz, would resist Axis infiltration. The situation changed in April 1941 when the German advances in the Balkans threatened a descent on the Middle East via Turkey, and when the Rashid Ali coup in Iraq temporarily removed Britain's most reliable Arab client. It was the reported presence of German airplanes on Syrian airfields and the news that French supplies were being sent to the Iraqi regime that brought about the decision to intervene. Action began with the bombing of Syrian airfields in mid-May. Smuts added his voice to those in Britain supporting an actual invasion of Syria, despite Wavell's hesitation about the commitment involved. On 8 June British and Free French forces crossed the border and a declaration was issued that the peoples of Syria and Lebanon would be 'sovereign and independent peoples'.

The campaign, in which Australian and Indian as well as British and Free French forces participated, was a difficult one, and it was only on 14 July that the whole area came under allied control.[24] Not surprisingly, the political handling of the situation produced much friction between the British and the Free French authorities, the former suspecting that the French did not intend to give proper effect to their promises to the Arabs, while the latter subscribed to the traditional

[23] Woodward, op. cit., pp. 560 – 70.
[24] For the campaign itself see Butler, op. cit., pp. 516 – 23.

view that the objective of British policy was to supplant France in the Middle East and rule alone over the Arab peoples.

Iraq: coup and counter-coup

Iraq had been looked upon as an example of a successful discharge of a British imperial responsibility. Now an independent country, but with a strong British connection, it was hoped that its facilities would play a useful part in resistance to Axis aggression. In fact the army, which was the most important organised element in Iraqi society, was jealous of its British mentors, and an obvious focus for both local nationalist agitation and the determined efforts of Axis propaganda.[25] Hostility to British and French policy in Palestine and Syria afforded extra ammunition to the propagandists, especially when, after the outbreak of war, Baghdad gave hospitality to the exiled Mufti of Jerusalem, originally but mistakenly in the hope that he would decide that his cause would best be served by supporting the Allies. Rashid Ali, the Premier appointed by the regent in March 1940, was soon engaged in intrigues with the Axis powers, and when Italy entered the war refused to break off diplomatic relations with her. The anxieties of the British government were added to by the inability of the hard pressed Middle East command to spare any reinforcements. British victories in the western desert had their effect on Iraqi opinion, and on 31 January 1941 Rashid Ali was forced out of office, though his successor did not show any more eagerness to fulfil the country's Treaty obligations, in particular the breaking off of relations with Italy. On 31 March Rashid Ali carried out a coup with the support of pro-Axis army officers and the Mufti.[26] The British government refused to recognise his regime, but were hesitant about being able to spare the forces necessary to remove it. Troops were sent for from India, but the new Premier gained time by proclaiming Iraq's intention to honour the Treaty. The landing of troops at Basra and the objections to their presence raised by Rashid cast doubt on his good faith, and on 29 – 30 April Iraqi troops surrounded the air base at Habbaniya and declared that they would shell aircraft attempting to leave. It was now a matter of open hostilities. Mediation was offered both by Egypt and by

[25] See Kirk, op. cit., pp. 56 – 68; Woodward, op. cit., pp. 571 – 81.
[26] The Regent sought refuge in the American legation 'in native woman's dress covering dressing gown and pyjamas', and later made his way to a British cruiser in the Gulf. Minister Resident in Iraq to Secretary of State, 2 and 3 April 1941, *FRUS*, 1941, vol. III, pp. 491 – 2.

Turkey, but was rejected on the ground that Britain could not abandon its Treaty rights. It was in fact clear that Rashid Ali had been intending to await Axis troops before moving against the British and that he had been forestalled.

In the event, the Germans, occupied with the battle for Crete, found themselves unable to assist Rashid Ali, and in the course of the next month military operations by the British put an end to the new regime and restored the Regent, making certain that for the rest of the war Iraq would fulfil its role in imperial strategy. Nuri Pasha returned to the premiership, and was for years to come to be relied upon as a bulwark of 'moderation' and of British influence; the British seem to have been unaware of his own discreet flirtation with the Axis powers. Preoccupied with the wider war, the British could afford to dismiss the Rashid Ali affair as a mere revolt; only later was its connection with the wider Pan-Arab movement fully understood.[27]

What linked Arab leaders, even moderates, was aversion to western penetration of the Arab world; sympathies for the Axis did not mean that German or Italian domination would have been preferred to British or French control, but only that it was hoped the Axis powers could be exploited for Arab ends. Among these objectives, the ending of the Palestine mandate and with it of the Jewish National Home was paramount. It is not surprising that the Mufti should have become an enthusiastic camp-follower of Hitler's.

Palestine: an unhappy balancing act

The entry of Italy into the war and the threat to Egypt, the German push through the Balkans and the menace this presented to Turkey and to Syria and Iraq had made Palestine more than ever the hinge of the British Empire's Middle East defence. Its security was thus a matter of prime importance to the military. In the earlier debates over British policy towards the land, its inhabitants and would-be inhabitants, the military had on the whole accepted the pro-Arab view dominant in the Foreign Office.[28] The essential thing had been to retain the confidence not just of the Arabs of Palestine itself but of the surrounding countries; and this belief was even more powerfully held

[27] For a reassessment of the politics of wartime Iraq see Louis, op. cit., pp. 307 – 13.
[28] For developments in Palestine after the outbreak of war as seen through foreign eyes, see Woodward, op. cit., vol. I, pp. 552 – 60.

after the war came closer.[29] Nor, as has been noted, was this a matter upon which American pressure in the opposite direction was likely to be effective.

The reaffirmation of the 'White Paper' policy by the publication of the Land Sale Regulations on 28 February 1940 and the government victory in the subsequent division by 292 votes to 129 set the pattern for the paradoxical situation that prevailed for the rest of the war.[30] The Arabs, too mistrusted to be armed, were courted politically; the Jews, who of all the inhabitants of the Middle East had the most cause to resist the advance of the Nazis, were largely denied the opportunities to display their military zeal by the fear that any recognition of them as belligerents would increase their pressure for a return to the spirit of the Mandate. At the same time, every effort was made by the Colonial Office to placate the Arabs by preventing the refugees from Hitler's Europe from reaching the only haven which could guarantee their safety. The objections of Churchill at the Admiralty to using the navy in this abhorrent task led the Colonial Office to produce a new reason for keeping out the refugees: the possible presence among them of Nazi agents, for which, not surprisingly, no evidence could be found.[31]

While the High Commissioner, MacMichael, though scarely pro-Zionist was susceptible to humanitarian appeals, the Colonial Secretary in Churchill's government, Lord Lloyd, was deeply committed to the pro-Arab line and to the deportation of any 'illegal' immigrants who managed to reach the shores of Palestine. In taking this stand he was supported by the Australians. He approached Bruce to get the support of his government to back him with the war cabinet, 'of whose attitude he was a little apprehensive owing to pro-Jew tendencies of some of its Members'. Menzies responded in a telegram to Lord Cranborne, in which he called attention to the 'attempts being made under the instigation of Axis Powers to resume illicit entry of

---

[29] An exception was Field-Marshall Lord Ironside, who took a rather pro-Zionist view. See *The Diplomatic Diaries of Oliver Harvey* (London, 1970), p. 330, entry of 17 November 1938.

[30] These paragraphs are based upon Michael J. Cohen, *Palestine: Retreat from the Mandate* (London, 1978), ch. 6, and R.W. Zweig, *Britain and Palestine during the Second World War* (Boydell, Woodbridge, and Royal Historical Society, London, 1986). The background to the Palestine policy can be studied in B. Wasserstein, *Britain and the Jews of Europe, 1939–1945* (Oxford, 1979).

[31] R.T.E. Latham of the Foreign Office commented that he believed that 'the whole idea is a C[olonial] O[ffice] canard, begotten of their desire to fortify themselves in pursuing a policy which, however necessary on political grounds is unavoidably inhumane to a degree'. Quoted by Zweig, op. cit., p. 79. Inter-departmental friction over Palestine clearly continued into the war years; the memoranda that passed make grim reading.

Jewish immigrants into Palestine'. Any relaxation of controls would, he believed, 'arouse the Arab world' against the British in an area where Australian troops were concentrated.[32]

The military situation and Churchill's own long-standing sympathy for the Zionist cause did bring about some pressure to look more closely at the use that could be made of Jewish manpower, and on 29 July 1940 Lloyd agreed that Jews outside as well as inside Palestine could be recruited through the Jewish Agency, but would have to be incorporated in British army units for service in any theatre of war. Three weeks later the government accepted in principle the raising of a Palestinian force on condition that numerical equality should be maintained between Jews and Arabs. But neither project made practical headway. The unwillingness of the Arabs to serve meant that the Jews could not be recruited. Differences among the Zionist leaders themselves, between those who felt that Jews should fight in any theatre, and those who felt that, for Jews recruited in Palestine, it should be for its defence only, further protracted the negotiations. Even more crucial was the reiterated British fear, now coming in particular from the Ministry of Information, that the prospect of a 'Jewish Army' would have disastrous effects upon the standing of Britain in the Middle East. With Wavell himself taking the same line as well as the Foreign Office and the Colonial Office, implementation again was postponed, with shortage of equipment given as the public explanation for the delay.

The critical position in the Middle East in May 1941 produced a waiving of the parity rule, but Jewish mobilisation in Palestine was confined to that required for the defence of the Jewish settlements themselves. Auchinleck's desire to recruit Jews to form companies to guard British installations and relieve regular British troops for active duty in the Western Desert produced the usual warnings of the need to avoid irritating the Arabs, particularly from Lampson at Cairo, and the objections were allowed to prevail. With the military situation improving, Auchinleck dropped his proposal. It was only in November 1941, when Weizmann accepted the failure of his long struggle, that the demand for a Jewish Army was revived, but this time in New York. Shortly after the launching of this new movement the United States entered the war and the whole question of Palestine, like so much else,

---

[32] Bruce to Menzies, 20 November 1940; Menzies to Cranborne, 6 December 1940: *DAFP*, vol. IV, pp. 274 – 6, 292.

was subsumed in the general context of Anglo-American relations.

While the 'White Paper' policy provided what could be seen as a breathing space, some more generally acceptable solution to the whole Palestine problem had retained its attraction for British policy-makers. Malcolm MacDonald's inclinations towards a 'cantonal' solution ceased to be relevant after he left the Colonial Office when Churchill became Prime Minister.[33] And this made room for consideration of a solution in which a Jewish entity could by agreement form part of a wider Arab federation. Such a scheme was peddled by the Arabist St John Philby, with the proviso that Ibn Saud, whom he had served, would preside over the federation. Although Weizmann was initially attracted, it soon became clear that Philby had no authority to negotiate such a scheme, and by early 1940 it was obviously dead. The Foreign Office had itself also been interested for some time in the idea of a federal solution, but had concluded that there was no prospect that Britain, by embracing such an idea, would reconcile the Arabs to Jewish immigration. Encouraged however by a reference by Lord Lloyd to the federal idea, Weizmann took it up with Halifax on 28 August 1940. And the matter was explored by Lloyd with the High Commissioner. Neither the Foreign Office nor the Colonial Office was receptive to the idea, and after Lloyd's death in February 1941 his successor, Lord Moyne, was faced with a memorandum from the Middle Eastern department deploring any new discussion of the Palestine question as likely to create new doubts among the Arabs as to the British commitment to the White Paper policy, and also to worry the French.

It was events elsewhere in the Middle East that once again raised the general issue of British policy in Palestine. The Rashid Ali coup in Iraq in April 1941 and the decision to intervene against the Vichy authorities in Syria led Churchill to propose a new version of the federation scheme, in which Syrian independence would be offered, while Iraq and Trans-Jordan with an autonomous Jewish state in western Palestine would come under a federation headed by Ibn Saud. The idea was no more favourably received now by the Foreign Office than it had been earlier; in particular, there were objections to any

[33] It is for the biographer of Churchill to explain why he chose as Secretary of State for India a man whose fundamental approach to the Indian problem was so different as was Amery's, and for the Colonial Office a man like Lloyd who differed so strongly from him on Palestine, one of the few colonial issues in which Churchill himself had shown a personal interest. Amery recorded his surprise at his own appointment: Leo Amery, *My Political Life*, vol. III, p. 109.

tampering with the position in Palestine. The same fate befell Amery's alternative version of the same basic notion, by which the Emir Abdullah of Trans-Jordan, rather than Ibn Saud, would receive the throne of Syria. The High Commissioner was prepared to concede a 'token' Jewish State, but if this were found unacceptable would have preferred to see the Mandate abandoned, together with the constitutional promises of the White Paper, and Palestine to become a crown colony until its people could 'manage to live together in amity'.

Further discussion ensued because of Amery's interest in the matter and alternative ideas were canvassed, but the divisions among officials and ministers remained alive, with Churchill once again, on 1 October 1941, placing on record his commitment to the idea of a 'great Jewish state' as an inevitable consequence of an Allied victory. Whatever Churchill's view – and his own enthusiasm for Zionism was to be shattered by Lord Moyne's assassination at the hands of Jewish extremists in November 1944 - British policy had by now congealed into the belief that it was possible so to guide and influence the Arab national movement as to make it an enduring bastion of Britain's position in the Middle East: a classic case, as it was to prove, of 'backing the wrong horse'.

South Africa: a dignified distance

An occasional intervention by a Dominion government or individual Dominion statesman in the British conduct of the war was less important than the cumulative experience that tended to enhance the separate status of the Dominions and to detach them from the Empire as their main external point of reference. Each responded in a different way according to its own circumstances.

South Africa was the least affected. It was of course vitally concerned with the possible impact upon the African continent and race relations in the broadest sense by the Italian entry into the war. In July the Italians overran British Somaliland and made incursions into the Sudan and Kenya. Thereafter came a pause, following which in January 1941 counter-attack began. In the subsequent fighting British Somaliland was retaken and Italian Somalia occupied, and the Italians forced out of Ethiopia and Eritrea. By midsummer the main objectives were secured, and although fighting continued until November 1941 it was possible to redeploy to the struggle in the western desert the South African (and Indian) troops who had been the main elements in the campaign.[34]

These successes rendered otiose the advice that Smuts had given to Churchill in June 1940, to face the necessity of giving up Egypt and to form a bastion further south to defend the Cape route, which he saw as essential to the survival of the Commonwealth. He had indeed found it impossible to move South African troops direct to Egypt, as Churchill would have wished, as being too far to come under the formula 'the defence of the Union'. In October 1940 he had taken part in a conference at Khartoum with Eden and Wavell in which the future course of the war in Africa was worked out. In March 1941 he was in Cairo where, as noted, he was in favour of risking the Greek enterprise. And in August, after the redeployment of the first South African division to Egypt and the preparations made for a second to follow, he again went north to confer with Auchinleck, Wavell's successor.[35] His role as the elder statesman of the Empire seemed confirmed, and South Africa's role in the Commonwealth undiminished.

Mackenzie King fights the Canadian corner

Mackenzie King possessed neither Smut's self-confidence as a strategist nor his international standing. But as the senior Dominion, removed from direct danger and with great industrial potential, Canada was bound to play an important part after the crisis of 1940. It had already made its point about the need for adequate consultation when it complained that the Canadian government, as well as General McNaughton, the commander of the Canadian troops in England, should have been consulted before their troops were assigned to the proposed attack on Trondheim.[36] After the withdrawal from Dunkirk, Canadians – apart from the airmen in the Battle of Britain – did not take part in the fighting until the Dieppe raid in August 1942. The issues that faced the Canadian government were industrial, financial, constitutional, diplomatic and above all, as was inevitable with Mackenzie King, political.

When defeat already loomed in France, Mackenzie King was asked

[34] Butler, op. cit., vol. II, pp. 379 – 80, 449 – 50.
[35] Hancock, *Smuts*, vol. II, pp. 354 – 6, 359 – 61.
[36] Butler, op. cit., p. 559.

to send all available Canadian destroyers across the Atlantic to help with the defence of Britain. The Prime Minister concurred, and acquainted Roosevelt with the Canadian decision. On 26 May he received a message from Roosevelt asking him to persuade the Dominions to bring pressure on Britain not to make a 'soft peace' but to send her fleet across the Atlantic and fight on from the Empire. Mackenzie King had no inclination to try to influence Australia or South Africa, and was indeed doubtful about how Roosevelt wanted his message handled; not for the last time, different voices in Washington uttered different thoughts. By 30 May he did indeed pass on Roosevelt's hopes, with the gloss that the Americans thought that if British and French resistance were prolonged, they might themselves come to their assistance.

Despite the fact that American promises of help were hedged with conditions which the Neutrality Acts imposed and that no response was forthcoming to the most immediate need, that for planes, the British determination to fight on embodied in Churchill's speech of 4 June was to be made good; though, as Churchill warned Mackenzie King, no-one could say what a future British administration might do if Britain were overpowered while America remained neutral. On 14 June, at Churchill's suggestion, Mackenzie King addressed a last appeal to France to remain in the war, speaking of the throwing of the resources of the whole North American continent into the struggle against Nazism.[37] The complex triangular discussions needed to elucidate British and American intentions towards each other continued until the end of the month. At the same time, Mackenzie King began efforts to bring together the Canadian and U.S. military authorities to discuss joint defence.

Mackenzie King thus found his role both as an intermediary between the United States and Britain – one that became less necessary as Churchill and Roosevelt built up their own relationship and extended it to their military and civilian advisers – and as the advocate of a defence arrangement in North America which would place Canada more firmly under the U.S. umbrella. At the same time, it is clear that Ottawa was galvanised into a sense of urgency by the French collapse, of which the first fruit was the National Defence Resources Act of 21 June 1940.[38] In the view of a Canadian historian,

[37] Pickersgill, op. cit., vol. I, pp. 116 – 26.
[38] Stacey, *Arms, Men and Governments*, 31 ff.

what had until the summer of 1940 been Britain's war became for Canadians from now on a national war.[39]

On the diplomacy of the conflict, Canada clearly wished to be consulted. Indeed, on 3 July 1940 Vincent Massey wrote to Churchill to protest that the newly appointed Dominions secretary, Caldecote, was not to attend meetings of the war cabinet and was thus unable fully to inform the High Commissioners. The question of the reply to be given to Hitler's probable peace offensive, raised by Smuts in July 1940, was commented on by the Canadians, and there was further consultation about the Swedish peace initiative of 2 August. Since it was clear that no acceptable peace with the Nazis was possible, the means for continuing the war bulked larger, and in August 1940 Mackenzie King achieved what he considered an important coup in the Ogdensburg agreement setting up a joint U.S.-Canadian defence board.[40] Churchill, more concerned with the final terms of the destroyer-bases deal which was then under discussion, was unenthusiastic about the Ogdensburg agreement. Its importance was also discounted by Arthur Meighen, the former Prime Minister. The achievement was in any event somewhat overshadowed by the shortfall in recruitment to the Canadian armed forces, and the emergence of the conscription question was one that Mackenzie King, with memories of the first world war, was determined to avoid if possible.[41]

On issues of general policy, Mackenzie King took his own line where a particular Canadian interest seemed to be involved. He remained until well into 1941 convinced of the desirability of not taking a hostile line towards the Vichy government, objected to the Dakar enterprise and, coming nearer home, to assisting the Free French to take over the islands of St Pierre and Miquelon.[42] When the tripartite pact between Germany, Italy and Japan was announced on 27 September 1940, Mackenzie King took the view that no advance announcement should be made of Canada's intention to stand by the United States if

[39] See the evidence in J.L. Granatstein, *Canada's War – the Politics of the Mackenzie King Government, 1939–1945* (Toronto, 1975).
[40] Massey, op. cit., p. 299; Stacey, op. cit., 337 ff. For an American appreciation of Mackenzie King's motives in seeking the Agreement, see the U.S. Minister in Canada to the acting Secretary of State, Sumner Welles, 14 August 1940, *FRUS*, 1940, vol. III, pp. 144 – 5. The text of the communiqué of 18 August is printed ibid., p. 146.
[41] Pickersgill, op. cit., vol. I, pp. 130 – 7; Stacey, op. cit., pp. 397 – 9; Granatstein, op. cit., 201 ff.
[42] Pickersgill, op. cit., vol. I, p. 147. When the coup by the Free French Admiral Muselier took place in December 1941, Mackenzie King, like Churchill, was willing to accept it in spite of the indignation expressed by the American Secretary of State. Ibid., pp. 318 – 9.

Japan attacked, since this would imply a North American rather than a Commonwealth policy for Canada. The balance between them had to be maintained. On the other hand, he resisted a suggestion from his own army chiefs that Canadian troops should be sent to fight against the Italians in Libya, 'our position being that we were at the side of Britain, and not to begin to play the role of those who want Empire war'.[43]

In relations with the United States economic and financial issues continued to bulk large, and were the main subject of conversation with Roosevelt when Mackenzie King went to the United States in April 1941.[44] The 'Hyde Park Agreement' was concluded on 21 April. Its essence was that each country should produce the war supplies most needed by both and that the United States would help to finance British purchases of Canadian goods. In June a joint economic committee was agreed upon, a precursor of the much closer arrangements to be reached in 1942.[45] On the other hand, both the United States and Britain resisted the suggestion of a Canadian joint staff mission to Washington. The United States was more ready, once lend-lease was through, to look at the global struggle as a unity and not to restrict itself to hemispheric defence.[46] Canada was itself conscious of the need to assist the United Kingdom in respect of the drain on her dollar resources, and after long negotiations developed the solution of a 'billion dollar gift', which became effective in January 1942.[47]

On the economic side, it is obvious that Canada (like Australia) was fearful lest the ultimate effect of lend-lease would be to put the United States in a too advantageous trading position in the post-war world.[48] Equally, if, as seemed increasingly likely during 1941, Japan did come into the war, it was clear that the United States would be the

[43] Ibid., pp. 150, 156.
[44] Ibid., 189 ff; Granatstein, op. cit., p. 143.
[45] Ibid., p. 146. For the negotiations for the Hyde Park Agreement see DCER, VIII, pp. 277 – 351.
[46] Granatstein, op. cit., pp. 147 – 8; FRUS, 1941, vol. III, pp. 129 – 36.
[47] Granatstein, op. cit., 186 ff.
[48] Ibid., p. 195. It is notable that, even during the crisis after Pearl Harbour, the United States kept up its pressure for its own views of the post-war trading world, including of course the elimination of imperial preference. Lease-Lend was a weapon in the struggle to get these views accepted. Australian War Cabinet Submission, 10 February 1942; Commonwealth Government to Cranborne, 11 February 1942: DAFP, vol. V, pp. 504 – 9, 515 – 16. For the objections to this pressure of a long-time advocate of imperial preference see N. Mansergh (ed.), The Transfer of Power, vol. I, pp. 7 – 13.

predominant partner in the defence of North America. 'Just what may result from this line it is difficult to say', reflected Mackenzie King. 'I, personally, would be strongly opposed to anything like a political union. I would keep the British Commonwealth of Nations as intact as possible. Canada, in time, and sooner than we expected perhaps, would become its centre.'[49]

Domestic politics made Mackenzie King reluctant to accede to Churchill's suggestion that he come to London in the early summer of 1941. Nor, as has been seen, was he sympathetic to Menzies' attempt to secure his support for the establishment of an imperial war cabinet. The unwillingness of New Zealand to go along with the idea, reported to Ottawa by the Canadian High Commissioner in Wellington, strengthened his hand. But he did visit the United Kingdom in August-September that year and, as already noted, found himself opposed to Menzies by deprecating the notion that any Dominion statesman, other than a Prime Minister, should be able to attend the war cabinet.[50]

The entry of Russia into the war presented something of a problem for Canada where anti-communist feeling was powerful, but it does not appear that any attempt was made to influence Britain against Churchill's policy of giving maximum assistance. But when in December the Russians asked for declarations of war against the satellite governments of Hungary, Romania and Finland, there were objections from Canada on the ground that this might adversely affect United States opinion.[51] But in the end Canada went along with the declaration, as being recognition of the fact of their belligerency; on this occasion, there was no waiting for Parliamentary approval.[52] On the day after the decision was taken, Mackenzie King received the news of Pearl Harbor.

---

[49] Pickersgill, *The Mackenzie King Record*, vol. I, p. 203.

[50] Ibid., pp. 236 – 50; *DCER*, vol. VII, pp. 424 – 50.

[51] Australia had agreed, if that was what Russia wanted; Smuts, while believing that in the end the decision should rest with the British government in consultation with the United States, would have preferred to temporise, arguing that if these countries were declared to be enemies, Russia might use this as a reason for their annexation after the war, and the allies might have to revive Germany as a counterweight. In a note of 27 November 1941 the British government disputed the view that a declaration of war against the satellites would make it necessary to declare war against Japan if she were to strike against Russia, as seemed very possible at that time. *DCER*, vol. VII, pp. 349 – 59.

[52] Pickersgill, op. cit., pp. 296 – 7.

Australia: Menzies' ambitions and setbacks

The worries in Australia about the direction of British policy and the competence shown in its exercise have already been noted. They now became more acute. The development of Australia's anxieties caused it to travel further from its earlier role in the Empire-Commonwealth than any other Dominion. Despite the fact that of its three chiefs of staff two were serving British officers at the time of appointment, its armed forces were regarded both by the Australian military and the Australian government as those of an independent ally of the United Kingdom's, not as integral components of an imperial army. Much energy was spent on upholding their status as such, and on attempts to prevent them from being used in separate detachments to suit the convenience of British military planners. It also became necessary to insist that only those forces voluntarily enlisted for overseas action were available for use in the Middle East or Malaya and that the rest of Australia's manpower could only be used for home defence. The tendency of Churchill and of commanders such as Wavell to ignore such national susceptibilities was increasingly resented. The Labour Party in particular, although partially discarding its earlier pacifism, was a vehicle for such sentiments both as representing the Opposition in the War Advisory Council and after October 1941 when in government.

In making the transition to such national independence, the Australians remained handicapped by their lack of a fully separate apparatus for following developments abroad, and during the campaigns themselves from the inability of their commanders to get complete access to the military intelligence available to the British; intelligence some of whose nature and importance has only been revealed quite recently.[53]

The detail of Australia's relations with Britain and the other Dominions in 1940 – 41 was also directly affected by the volatile opinions, dynamic personality and personal ambition of Robert Menzies. Perhaps because there was something Churchillian about Menzies, he and Churchill found it hard to agree.

The fall of France and Italy's entry into the war not only strengthened Australia's concern for the Middle East, but made Menzies determined that his country should seek an independent role

[53] See F.H. Hinsley *et al.*, *British Intelligence in the Second World War* (London): vols I, (1979), II, (1981), III, pt. 1, (1984), III, pt. 2, (1988).

in the making of the Empire's strategy, insist upon institutions that would embody this approach and give Menzies himself the kind of role that Smuts had filled in the first world war.[54] Like Mackenzie King, he criticised the Dakar operation, though on the grounds of non-consultation, since an Australian cruiser had been used, and for military rather than political reasons. More important was the insistence on the need to find ways of dissuading Japan from entering the war. Menzies objected to Britain's (temporary) closure of the Burma road in 1940 at the behest of the United States and suggested that economic concessions to Japan and perhaps some territorial adjustments would be preferable.[55]

By the time Menzies left Australia for London at the end of January 1941 his confidence in Churchill's strategic judgement was much shaken.[56] He travelled via Singapore, where he was critical both of the preparations for defence and of the mood of complacency that he saw prevailing, and then via Cairo, where he saw Wavell on 3 February after the first victories over the Italians. Once again, he was unimpressed. Although the question of intervention in Greece was much on people's minds in Cairo, it does not appear that Menzies discussed the issue.

Menzies arrived in London on 20 February. While there he attended the war cabinet though, as he discovered, this was not where the vital decisions were taken. Nevertheless it remains true that he was present when the war cabinet decided on 7 March to send troops to Greece. He may well have underestimated the extent to which this was understood to be a forlorn hope undertaken for political reasons which seemed compelling to Eden and Dill on the spot. But he did feel that Australia should not have been asked to send its troops to fight as the result of an agreement made by the British with the Greeks to which no Australian representative had been party. The acting Prime Minister in Australia was later disconcerted to find out that General Blamey, commanding the Australian troops, had not been asked for his advice on the enterprise and had regarded the decision as constituting an order which he had to obey: 'This not only deeply affects the

[54] The most useful account is that in Day, op. cit., though the writer possibly gives too much weight to the idea that in 1941–2 Menzies was actually seeking to supplant Churchill as the *British* war leader.

[55] Ibid., pp. 25–7; Menzies to Bruce, 29 September 1940, *DAFP*, vol. IV.

[56] Menzies was not in a strong position at home, since his party had lost ground in the Australian General Election of September 1940: Menzies to Churchill, 4 October 1940, *DAFP*, vol. IV, pp. 204–5.

Empire relationship, but also places us in an embarrassing situation with the Advisory War Council and with Parliament.'[57]

The defeats in the western desert at the hands of the Germans in late March and early April 1941, leaving a garrison mainly of Australians isolated in Tobruk, fortified Menzies' criticisms of the way in which the war was being handled. Nor was this all. In early April the German offensive began in Greece, leading to the decision to evacuate the British forces, including General Blamey's Anzacs, which was taken on 21 April. By the end of May Crete also had had to be evacuated, with further Anzac losses. Even before this final blow, Menzies would appear to have taken a pessimistic view of the situation in the Middle East as a whole, speaking at the war cabinet in favour of the need to plan a withdrawal from Egypt itself.[58]

Menzies now urged the calling of an Imperial Conference which, according to one version, might force on Churchill the creation of a new war cabinet which would endeavour to find a formula for a compromise peace.[59] Yet another source of anxiety was the signature in Moscow on 13 April of a neutrality pact between Japan and the Soviet Union, which revived fears of a Japanese push southwards.[60] Since this followed a visit by the Japanese foreign minister to Berlin, it looked as though the Germans, Japanese and Russians were working on agreed lines.

Menzies' efforts to mobilise the rest of the Commonwealth in support of his plans for an Imperial Conference were checked by Mackenzie King, who proved unreceptive to the idea when Menzies visited Ottawa in May. Menzies went on from Canada to Australia,

[57] Menzies to Fadden, 8 March 1941; Fadden to Menzies, 27 March 1941: ibid., pp. 484 – 6, 523 – 5. The complicated question of the relations between Wavell, the Australian and New Zealand Commanders, Blamey and Freyberg, and between the British and Dominion governments over the intervention in Greece and the attempt to hold Crete are dealt with at length in Horner, op. cit., chs 4 and 5.

[58] John Connell, *Wavell: Scholar and Soldier* (London, 1964), p. 422. It has been argued that Menzies was remote from the preoccupations of the Australian government and its military advisers, and allowed the British to believe that agreement from a Dominion Prime Minister to a course of action was equivalent to agreement with his government as a whole. Edwards, *Prime Ministers and Diplomats*, p. 138.

[59] 'Under the guise of improving communications and according to the Dominions fair representation, an Imperial Conference would bring overwhelming pressure on Churchill to establish a small War Cabinet in which Churchill's supporters would be replaced by those of Menzies. They would include Beaverbrook and Lloyd George. This would allow Churchill's formula of total victory to be moderated and a formula found to usher in a compromise peace.' David Day, *Menzies and Churchill at War*, (London, Angus & Robertson, 1986), p. 145.

[60] Latham (Tokyo) to Department of External Affairs, 15 April 1941, *DAFP*, vol. IV, pp. 584 – 5.

where he gave his own Advisory War Council a pessimistic view of British fortunes under Churchill.[61]

Hitler's invasion of Russia in June 1941, foreshadowed for some time previously by western observers who also discounted the Soviet Union's capacity for prolonged resistance, turned out to be the major turning point in the war and, together with the increasing help given by the United States to Britain, reanimated Churchill's leadership. When on 21 August Mackenzie King finally arrived in London, it was, as has been seen, to reject Menzies' idea of an imperial war cabinet. In this position he found support from the Prime Minister of New Zealand, then also in London.[62]

In other respects as well, Menzies had not been fortunate in getting acceptance for his ideas. The British war cabinet had not endorsed his proposals for shifting war industries to Australia. His own aversion to dependence on Indian supplies had not affected the general planning for the far eastern sector of the imperial war effort, and his criticisms of India's supply organisation did not lead to major changes. Late in August the weakness in his own position in Australia became apparent and, having got his cabinet to agree to send a minister other than the Prime Minister to London, he resigned, presumably in the expectation that he would be asked to go to London. His successor, Fadden, who took office on 28 August, preferred to keep Menzies in his cabinet and chose Earle Page as his envoy. This appointment was confirmed by Fadden's successor John Curtin, the Labour leader, who took over on 3 October.[63]

The claim of the Australian government to act as the voice of Commonwealth opinion was somewhat weakened by the fact that it still had no direct relations with South Africa, and even in New Zealand only a trade commissioner, who was not thought a proper intermediary for discussions on matters arising from the war. Curtin was however more prepared than his predecessor for Australian ministers to criticise the U.K. government's conduct of affairs, and to do so in public. Churchill protested against ill-informed criticism by the Australian foreign minister, Evatt, about the delay in declaring war upon Finland, Hungary and Romania, pointing out that the British government had never publicly criticised the Australians for insisting

[61] Pickersgill, op. cit., pp. 213 – 17; Day, op. cit., pp. 176 – 7; Advisory War Council Minute, 28 May 1941, *DAFP,* vol. IV, pp. 681-6.
[62] Day, op. cit., pp. 224 – 6.
[63] Ibid., p.95, 228 ff; *DAFP,* vol. IV, pp. 204, 588.

on the withdrawal of Australian troops from Tobruk, which had been costly in itself and added to Auchinleck's difficulties in preparing his projected offensive. Curtin's reply, while agreeing not to give public expression of any divergence of views, stressed the importance of the Australian government taking an independent stance on foreign policy issues, rather than being wholly dependent upon the United Kingdom.[64]

By this time, however, differences with the United Kingdom were already taking second place. What absorbed Australia's attention was the working out of American policy towards Japan, and the need to make sure that no action was taken by Commonwealth countries that could risk them having to fight the Japanese without American assistance. Casey in Washington believed as late as 24 November that some formula might be found that would strengthen the hands of the moderates in Tokyo while admitting that Japan as well as the allies might prefer to delay a trial of strength. Evatt was even keener on not bringing matters to a head.[65]

As the possibilities of appeasing Japan were seen to be exhausted, it was reported from London that the war cabinet was discussing what the Commonwealth countries should do if Japan attacked Thailand, the Dutch East Indies, Russia or Kunming and the Burma Road. Churchill took the view that their decision should wait upon American action unless British territory such as Hong Kong was attacked. And this view was supported by Canada. Other ministers felt that the United States was more likely to come in if the British Empire were seen to be resisting; and in this they were supported by South Africa and New Zealand.[66] Less than a week later the Japanese made such efforts to define a common policy otiose by attacking the United States and the Empire at the same time, leaving Russia for the moment as a neutral in the Far Eastern war.

New Zealand: still the antipodean contrast

In New Zealand, the course of action continued to be dissimilar to what was the case in Australia. The crisis of May 1940 led to calls for

[64] Churchill to Curtin, 28 November 1941; Curtin to Churchill, 29 November 1941: *DAFP*, vol. V, pp. 232 – 3, 237 – 8.
[65] Casey to Curtin and Evatt, 23 November 1941; Evatt to Casey, 25 November 1941: ibid., pp. 220 – 3.
[66] Bruce to Curtin, 1 December 1941, ibid., pp. 254 – 5.

a more determined handling of the economy and for a national government, and/or conscription. The government took new emergency powers but resisted the idea of a National Government, though setting up a War Council which included the Opposition leaders as well as representatives of the employers and trade unions. But on 16 July a war cabinet was in fact created, including the Opposition leaders, with the existing Labour cabinet being retained for matters not directly related to the war. In practice the war inevitably affected larger and larger areas of government activity, and by early in 1942 the war cabinet was dealing with ninety per cent of government business.[67]

Despite the introduction of conscription in July 1940 the war remained a remote affair, and the not negligible Communist Party continued to argue against New Zealand participation. The propaganda was not without effect: 'the suspicion that the British government might not be unwilling to turn the fight against Russia died hard, and was a thread in New Zealand thinking about foreign relations.'[68]

The Greek venture was not an element in the party political conflict which had survived the creation of the war cabinet and was hardened when S.G. Holland became the new leader of the Opposition in November 1940. But the New Zealand government felt that it should have been consulted before Britain became committed to a campaign that could only be fought if Anzac troops were made available. Wavell was to claim that Freyberg, the New Zealand commander, as well as Blamey had been consulted and was aware of the dangers.[69]

Peter Fraser, the New Zealand Prime Minister, left for London at this juncture, and was in Cairo during part of the Crete battle. He spent a portion of the summer in London, and attended the war cabinet, without taking the high profile affected by Menzies. What was achieved was that it was accepted that Dominion contingents should have greater recognition as such, and that Freyberg had the right to communicate with his own government, which Blamey had earlier secured.[70]

The contrast with Australia was even greater in respect of the growing Japanese threat. The New Zealand government, which had opposed the closing of the Burma Road, also set its face against any

[67] F.L.W. Wood, *The New Zealand People at War* (Wellington, 1958), pp. 138 – 42.
[68] Ibid., 144 ff, (quotation on p. 155).
[69] Ibid., 174 ff.
[70] Ibid., pp. 188 – 90.

further attempts at appeasement, and took the view that only the certainty of general resistance would deter the Japanese. For this reason they advocated a formal guarantee to the Dutch East Indies.[71]

India: the continuing search for a solution

The events of May-June 1940 affected India both because its military contribution seemed likely to become more important with the increasingly central role of the Middle East and because it seemed possible for Congress to exploit Britain's difficulties to extract political concessions on its own terms.[72] It was also evident that India would become an important contributor to the Empire's war supplies in spite of the hesitations expressed by the Australian Prime Minister.[73] Of indirect significance for India was the fact that Britain was inevitably more and more dependent on the United States as a more than friendly neutral and as a hoped-for ally. The vague appeal that the idea of Indian self-government had long possessed for some Americans could now be formulated in terms of India's need to be brought more fully and more willingly into the war effort, and pressures could be detected that were only to find their full expression after the United States itself became a belligerent.[74]

During the period between June 1940 and the early Japanese successes after Pearl Harbor, which included the conquest of Burma and hence a threat to the integrity of India itself, British policy was the fruit of the interaction between four individuals representing different and sometimes opposite points of view. The Viceroy, Linlithgow, had no illusions about the task he faced. India was not like the Dominions,

---

[71] Ibid., ch. XV, 'The Impact of the Pacific'.

[72] For a narrative of the political developments in the period see Gowher Rizvi, *Linlithgow and India* (London, 1978), 151 ff; B.R. Tomlinson, *The Indian National Congress and the Raj*, pp. 149 – 53. For Nehru's role see S. Gopal, *Nehru*, vol. I, pp. 259 – 77.

[73] In October 1940 an 'Eastern Group Conference' met at New Delhi and set up two new organisations with headquarters in India, the Central Provision Office and the Central Supply Council. John Glendevon, *The Viceroy at Bay*, p. 191.

[74] For an American view of the last stages of the Raj, arguing that the idea of a gradual handing over of power was unreal, that Gandhi succeeded in creating a national movement (apart from the Muslims) which could do more than take over a running concern, and actually create a new order based on different principles, and that it was the 'Quit India' movement in 1942 which was decisive, see Francis G. Hutchins, *India's Revolution: Gandhi and the Quit India Movement* (Cambridge, Mass., 1973). It is an interpretation that ignores what actually happened between 1942 and 1947 and the effect on Britain of the war itself and the changing balance of world power. For a very different view of these years as witnessed in Delhi see the account in Nirad C. Chaudhuri, *Thy hand, Great Anarch* (London, 1987).

a natural part of a British association of nations, but a conquered country in which Britain retained its hold through the exercise in the last resort of her military might. Whatever the future destiny of the country, he could not, while the war was on, make changes in its running which might jeopardise the successful prosecution of the war. In so far as he could attend to Indian affairs amid all the other pressures upon his time and energies, Churchill took a similar line, though one tinged with a more romantic view of Britain's role and an even greater unwillingness to see it abandoned. At the other end of the scale stood Clement Attlee, who represented the Labour Party's belief that there must be a reasonable solution based on liberal principles that could be expected to appeal to Indians as much as to anyone else. Amery, who likewise looked to the eventual evolution of India into a fully self-governing Dominion, had to act as the channel of communication between Churchill and the Viceroy and endeavour to make his influence felt through the assiduity of his attention to the issues. Revealing as are these differences between individuals, it must be kept in mind that the Churchill government in respect of India acted as a unit, with Attlee going along with its actual decisions even when back-bench Labour opinion was more sympathetic to Indian claims.[75]

[75] 'India and Burma have no natural association with the Empire, from which they are alien by race, history and religion, and for which as such neither of them have any affection, and both are in the Empire because they are conquered countries which [have] been brought there by force, kept there by our controls, and which hitherto it has suited to remain under our protection. I suspect that the moment they think that we may lose the war, or take a bad knock, their leaders would be much more concerned to make terms with the victor at our expense than to fight for the ideals to which so much lip-service is given.' Linlithgow to Amery, 21 January 1942, *The Transfer of Power*, vol. I (London, H.M.S.O., 1970), pp. 44 – 50. A strong defence of Linlithgow is that in the biography by his son, Lord Glendevon, *The Viceroy at Bay*. Less sympathetic is the sketch in W.R. Louis, *The Last Three Viceroys* (London, 1987). Attlee commented on these remarks by Linlithgow: 'This is an astonishing statement to be made by a Viceroy. It sounds more like an extract from an anti-imperialist propaganda speech. If it were true it would form the greatest possible condemnation of our rule in India and would amply justify the action of every extremist in India. But it is not the whole truth. All India was not the fruits of conquest: large parts of it came under our rule to escape from tyranny and anarchy. The history of at least 150 years has forged close links between India and the United Kingdom. It is one of the great achievements of our rule in India that, even if they do not entirely carry them out, educated Indians do accept British principles of justice and liberty. We are condemned by Indians not by the measure of Indian ethical conceptions but by our own, which we have taught them to accept.' 'The Indian Political Situation', memorandum by Attlee, 2 February 1942, *The Transfer of Power*, vol. I, pp. 110 – 12. A treatment favourable to the Labour Party approach and to Congress is in R.J. Moore, *Churchill, Cripps and India, 1939–1945* (Oxford, 1979). Knowing the Labour Party's close links with Congress, particularly through Stafford Cripps, it is not surprising that Jinnah tried to win them over to his side. Glendevon, op. cit., p. 195. But the Labour leaders continued to underestimate Jinnah's potential strength and remained close to Congress in their constitutional thinking. On the Labour Party's attitudes to India during the coalition see P.S.Gupta, *Imperialism and the British Labour Movement*, pp. 266 – 74.

Increasingly, the key advice received by the Indian government, and through it by the war cabinet, was that of its military advisers, notably the Commander-in-Chief India, who had always held a key position. Linlithgow was successful in getting General Auchinleck, with his intimate knowledge of the Indian scene, appointed to the post at the beginning of 1941; but when Churchill's discontent with Wavell's conduct of the Middle Eastern campaign came to a head, Wavell was in June 1941 replaced by Auchinleck and himself took up the Indian appointment, a post which he was to retain until he replaced Linlithgow as Viceroy in 1943.

All political questions arising in India had to be looked at from the point of view of their probable impact upon the country's defence. Dealing with Congress on this issue was complicated by its own divisions and uncertainties. Some leaders were prepared to limit their non-cooperation with the authorities after June 1940; Gandhi himself tried and failed to convert Congress to the view that the tactics of 'non-violence' developed as part of the struggle against the British should become its policy if India itself was threatened with invasion. Congress' own offer to the British was to postpone the demand for the implementation of independence until after the war, provided that in the meantime they set up a 'National Government'. But what a National Government would mean without a complete constitutional upheaval and whether such a government would behave like the Dominion governments as an active partner in the war effort was left unclear, although the continuance in authority of a British commander-in-chief was part of the suggested agreement.

Linlithgow himself was convinced that a mere rejection of the Congress proposals was insufficient, and the terms of a new British offer were worked out by himself and Amery with occasional interventions from Churchill. The upshot was the 'August Offer'.[76] Dominion status for India after the war was declared to be the objective; a representative body would be called to devise a constitution, with guarantees offered to the Muslims against a system that would be unacceptable to them. Meanwhile, representative Indians would be invited to join the Viceroy's Executive Council and the War Advisory Committee.

[76] *India and the War*, statement issued with the Authority of His Majesty's Government by the Governor General, 8 August 1940 (Cmd 6219). Published in *The Transfer of Power*, vol. I, Appendix 1.

Congress and the other main parties rejected the August Offer; Gandhi was reinstated in the Congress leadership with supreme authority; the offer of co-operation in the war effort was withdrawn and civil disobedience renewed. In turn, the government prepared for action against Congress, although Amery secured the watering down of the Viceroy's more drastic proposals. Even so, the powers used were sufficient for the arrest of many of the leaders of the anti-war civil disobedience campaign formally launched in November.

Although the mobilisation of India for the war was maintained, there was once again political deadlock. A conference of Indian Liberal leaders in March proposed a new formula for advance towards a largely Indian government, but neither Congress nor the Muslim League were involved, and in this situation it offered no way forward for the Viceroy. The Secretary of State's reaction to the proposals had as its main effect the consolidation of Jinnah's position as leader of the Muslim community.[77] In June the Viceroy proceeded to implement his own original offer by recasting his Executive Council with an Indian majority. At the same time a National Defence Council was formed, bringing about an association between the Central Government, the Provinces, and the Princely States, although here also the political pressures could not be avoided. In September Jinnah forced the Muslim Prime Ministers of Bengal, Assam and the Punjab to resign from the Defence Council.[78] But the civil disobedience campaign gradually lost momentum, and by the beginning of December it was found possible to release the last of those still detained. The guarded optimism that Linlithgow had expressed in the summer might be regarded as reasonable enough.[79]

Meanwhile, the portents of United States intervention were beginning to be sensed. The direct representation of India at Washington and of the U.S. government in New Delhi had been under negotiation since April 1941, with both sides aware of the implications for the constitutional position.[80] In May the influential Under-Secretary of State, Adolf Berle, suggested that the United States government use the negotiation to propose that India be brought 'into the partnership

---

[77] D.A. Low, 'The Mediator's Moment: Sir Tej Bahadur Sapru and the Antecedents to the Cripps Mission to India, 1940–1942', *JICH*, vol. XII (1984), pp. 145–64.
[78] Glendevon, op. cit., p. 202.
[79] See for instance Linlithgow's private letter to Smuts, 13 July 1941: *Smuts Papers*, vol. VI, pp. 312–4.
[80] *FRUS*, 1941, vol. III, pp. 170–6.

of nations on terms equal to those of the other members of the British Commonwealth'. From London the Ambassador, Winant, argued along the same lines, on the ground that the charges of imperialism brought against the British in India hindered the United States from supporting Britain. And the head of the Division of Near Eastern Affairs in the State Department voiced similar views. Caution was urged by Sumner Welles on the ground that any major constitutional change would create disturbances in India with which the British would be unable to cope, and thus actually damage the war effort. He also claimed that apart from limited groups the matter was not one of major interest to American public opinion. A different view was conveyed to the Secretary of State by the U.S. Commissioner in India, who wrote that India did not consider herself as fighting for her interests as a nation and felt that she was being called upon to defend an Empire in which she was not received as an independent partner.[81]

Except in relation to supplies for the 'Eastern Group', India's concerns were not closely followed in the Dominions. Anti-imperialists in Canada might take much the same line as their counterparts in the United States, but for the Canadian government there were domestic considerations to take into account. Amery suggested in November 1940 that Canada and India exchange High Commissioners. But in a memorandum to the Prime Minister strongly tinged with pro-Congress sentiment, Skelton pointed out that such a gesture would have little relevance unless franchise restrictions on Indians in Canada were lifted. Mackenzie King, in a note on the memorandum, summed it up: 'Let sleeping dogs lie. Don't rouse agitation in B[ritish] C[olumbia] in order to keep down one in India', and the idea was rejected. If the franchise question was raised it would be hard not to consider the much larger numbers of Chinese and Japanese settlers.[82] In April, the sending of a Trade Commissioner from India to Canada was agreed upon.

Pearl Harbour, Singapore and eclipse

The destruction of so much of the American Pacific Fleet at Pearl

[81] Memorandum by Berle, 5 May 1941; Winant to Secretary of State, 1 August and 4 November 1941; Memorandum by Wallace Murray, 7 November 1941; Welles to Secretary of State, 15 November 1941: ibid., pp. 176 – 89.
[82] Skelton to Mackenzie King, 20 January 1941, DCER, vol. VII, pp. 19 – 20.

Harbor on 7 December 1941 altered the presuppositions on which all the planning of a future war with Japan had been based. The loss of the *Prince of Wales* and *Repulse* three days later exposed the hollowness of British planning for the defence of Malaya and above all the 'Totem' of Singapore. It meant a new look at the whole world conflict, and this was undertaken when Churchill and Roosevelt conferred in the United States in December and January.[83] The setbacks to the Allied cause which followed thick and fast and culminated on 15 February 1942 in the surrender at Singapore were accompanied by a series of improvisations in the machinery for the command of allied forces in the south-west Pacific and the Indian Ocean.[84] What they eventually amounted to was the incorporation of Australia and New Zealand in the mainly American effort to carry the war back northwards, and to Britain's responsibility being for the present the defence of Burma, shortly to be lost, and of the Indian sub-continent. The main decisions were made in Washington by the Combined Chiefs of Staff and their political masters. The Dominions might formally be given an advisory role in London, but it was on Washington that they had to set their sights, now and for the future.

In the rapid movement of events and amid the political tensions created by the Dominion losses in manpower and the perceived threat to their own security, it is not surprising that renewed doubts were cast on the capacity of Britain's leadership. Of the Dominions whose forces were directly involved, this was less true of Canada. But the fact that two battalions of Canadian troops whom it had been agreed to send to Hong Kong as recently as 2 October 1941 were taken prisoner when the colony surrendered on 25 December was bound to be resented, since the Canadian government had been assured that the Japanese would be attacking the Soviet Union rather than the western powers.[85] New Zealand, which had pressed for greater firmness

[83] J.M.A. Gwyer, *Grand Strategy*, vol. III, pt. 1, chs XI-XIV, and J.R.M. Butler, *Grand Strategy*, vol. III, pt. 2, chs XVI, XVII, XIX and XX give the full sequence of events and negotiations. Churchill's own account is in his *The Second World War*, vol. III, chs 33 – 6. See also Gilbert, op. cit., VII, ch. 2.

[84] For the Singapore story see S. Woodburn Kirby, *Singapore: the chain of disaster* (London, 1971). It has since been made known that the Japanese were fully aware of the absence of an integrated defence plan for Singapore and of the weakness of the British position by a German intelligence coup in December 1940. See Christopher Andrew, 'The affair of the weighted canvas bag that didn't sink', *The Listener* (London), 2 January 1986.

[85] C.P. Stacey, *Arms, Men and Governments*, 42, and *A Date with History*. pp. 200 – 1; Pickersgill, op. cit., vol. I, pp. 351 – 4. Churchill visited Ottawa during his North American sojourn in December 1941 and relations between him and Mackenzie King seem to have been friendly.

against Japan and had not shared Australian beliefs in the possibilities of an accommodation, had not sustained direct losses and does not appear to have made much of Britain's miscalculations.[86]

It was from Australia, as might be expected, that the greatest pressure was exerted for more say in policy, and that the recriminations were most vocal, particularly after the losses sustained by Australian troops in the retreat through Malaya, at Singapore and in Java. The Australian government could point to the warnings it had uttered frequently about the state of Singapore's defences, most particularly in the air.[87] It had not shared Churchill's undoubted underestimate of Japan's war-making capacity, and when Churchill defended his own record in opposing appeasement and the neglect of British defences in the pre-war years, it was insufficient to exonerate the British for what had happened more recently. Churchill's argument that forces and equipment had had to be held in the Middle East or sent to the Russians until war actually broke out in the Far East because of the danger from a pincer movement against Egypt by Rommel in the west and by Germans coming through the Caucasus against Persia, Syria and Iraq, could be read as clearly confirming the priority he attached to the Middle East. It was perhaps understandable that Curtin should reply that, just as Churchill had correctly foreseen events in Europe, so the Australians had seen the trend of the Pacific situation more clearly than it had been perceived in London.[88] The British government even now felt that Australian advice would not be useful to the war cabinet on matters other than those directly affecting Australia.[89] Certainly it could not accept Curtin's suggestion of trying to persuade the Russians to enter the war against Japan by making territorial concessions to her, not only in the Far East, but in Iran and Europe as well.[90]

A still more outspoken criticism of Churchill was made by Curtin's Minister for External Affairs, Evatt, to Stafford Cripps, then about to take up his position as Lord Privy Seal and Leader of the House of Commons. He now added to Australia's complaints against the British

Ibid., 325 ff.
[86] F.L.W. Wood, op. cit., ch. XV.
[87] *DAFP*, vol. V, pp. 313 – 4, 330 – 1.
[88] Churchill to Curtin, 19 January 1942; Curtin to Churchill, 21 January 1942: ibid., pp. 445 – 7, 456.
[89] For Australia's claim to a bigger say see Earle Page to Curtin, 1 January 1942, ibid., 398 ff.
[90] Ibid., pp. 311 – 2, 377, 491.

government the suggestion that the talks between the U.S. Secretary of State and the Japanese special envoy, Kurusu, which were the prelude to Pearl Harbour, would have led to Japan's acceptance of a *modus vivendi* but for the obstruction of the U.K. government, and that Britain was deliberately trying in the new Pacific Council to separate Australia, which was included, from China, which was not.[91]

India was equally threatened by the spread of the war to the Far East. 'Now we are really up against it', wrote Amery to Linlithgow. 'You, with your terribly inadequate provision against air attack, will have to manage somehow against air raids on Eastern India and perhaps on your coastal ports.'[92] The menace was rapidly to grow even greater, and if India were to be attacked the issue of the willingness of its political spokesmen to co-operate in her defence was bound to seem even more crucial. Such certainly appeared to be the case in American eyes. It was directly raised during Churchill's visit to Washington in December 1941 – January 1942 by the President himself, and received a characteristically robust reply. Although Churchill believed that he had dissuaded Roosevelt from further intervention, the incident marked the beginning of the direct involvement of the United States in India's affairs. The next step was the appointment of an economic and war supply mission, one of whose members, Louis Johnson, was to be the personal representative of the President.[93]

The close patronage by the Americans of the Chinese President, Chiang Kai-shek, also indicates that his visit to India early in February 1942 must be regarded as an aspect of American policy. While ostensibly intended to encourage the Indians to take part in the common resistance to Japanese aggression, the way in which Chiang insisted upon meeting the leaders of Congress as well as British and Indian officials suggested that he saw himself as a possible mediator on the Indian political scene.[94]

[91] Evatt to Cripps, 16 February 1942, ibid., pp. 525 – 7. The editors refer on Britain's attitude to the Hull-Kurusu talks to Sir Llewellyn Woodward's *British Foreign Policy in the Second World War*, vol. II, (London, 1971). But his account does not suggest that British objections were a substantial cause of the breakdown. Indeed, it is clear that there were no proposals which the Americans were prepared to make, particularly in respect of China, which could have satisfied the elements who were by now dominant in Japan.

[92] Glendevon, op. cit., p. 215.

[93] Moore, op. cit., p. 47; *FRUS*, 1942, vol. I, 593 ff.

[94] See the correspondence about the visit in *The Transfer of Power*, vol. I. After his visit Chiang had his unfavourable comments on the British handling of India conveyed to Roosevelt. *FRUS*, 1942, vol. I, pp. 605 – 6.

Meanwhile the Atlantic Charter, whose relevance to the Empire had never been accepted by Churchill, came to the fore again with the American proposal that a United Nations declaration be promulgated, committing its signatories to the principles of the Charter. Before its signature and publication on 1 January 1942, two questions had to be resolved. It was necessary for the British to persuade the Americans that India should be allowed to be a signatory as, although not fully self-governing, her individual role in international relations had been accepted ever since Versailles. It was also the view of the war cabinet that, as on previous occasions, the countries of the British Commonwealth should be grouped together among the signatories and not appear individually according to their place in the alphabetic order. But on this point the British were overruled. The Australians, who had unsuccessfully argued for the exclusion of India, supported the Americans over the order of listing.[95]

In India itself the resolutions of the Congress Working Committee, the 'Bardoli resolutions' of 30 December, did not appear to point a way to the co-operation of Congress with the war effort, since they did little more than repeat its well-known demands.[96] Another proposal from Sapru and the Indian Liberals also seemed an inadequate basis for a settlement. Amery for his part was unprepared to go beyond the 'August offer'. What was important was that co-operation between the British and Indian governments should be as effective as possible, and to that end it was proposed that a member of the Viceroy's Executive should be appointed in London together with a representative of the Princes, and should, like the Dominion Prime Ministers, attend meetings of the War Cabinet relevant to their own concerns. This suggestion was agreed to early in February.[97] Meanwhile the offer of Sapru and the Indian Liberals still required a reply, and out of the consideration of this question came Churchill's announcement on 11 February (reiterating Britain's commitment to Dominion status for India as soon as possible after the war) that Stafford Cripps would

[95] Ibid., pp. 1 – 27; Woodward, op. cit., vol. II, pp. 210 – 19; Curtin to Casey, 30 December 1941, *DAFP*, vol. V, p. 386. In a published article in December 1941 Curtin had written: 'Australia looks to America, free of any pangs as to our traditional links or kinship with the United Kingdom.' Edwards, op. cit., p. 156.

[96] The Resolutions are printed in *The Transfer of Power*, vol. I, Appendix III.

[97] Sapru to Laithwaite, 2 January 1942; Amery to Churchill, 22 January 1942; Linlithgow to Amery, 30 January 1942; Amery to Linlithgow, 8 February 1942: ibid., pp. 3 – 5, 54, 93, 131 – 3.

shortly be visiting India to pursue the efforts for a political settlement.[98]

With that announcement, the process of handing over power in India took another and probably irrevocable step. The further unravelling of the diplomatic unity of the Commonwealth through the United Nations Declaration was perhaps of less moment. In any event, it was the fall of Singapore four days after Churchill's announcement on India that was by far the most important symbol of the new situation. As an American historian has pointed out, 'The sinking of *Prince of Wales* and *Repulse* together with the fall of Singapore brought an end to the illusion of both the power and prestige of the British Empire in the Far East.'[99] It is not a judgement with which one can quarrel.

[98] Low, loc. cit.; Moore, op. cit., ch. 4.
[99] W.R. Louis, 'The Road to Singapore: British Imperialism in the Far East, 1932 – 1942', in W.J. Mommsen and L. Kettenacker (eds), *The Fascist Challenge and the Policy of Appeasement* (London, Allen & Unwin, 1983), p. 385.

Chapter 15

SIGNPOSTS TO THE FUTURE

Singapore, the turning point

The fall of Singapore and the circumstances in which it fell must be given prominence in any account of the concluding phase of the British Empire. It has been plausibly suggested that the series of miscalculations, both in London and on the spot, and in particular the slowness of the local command to react to the rapidly changing military position, can only be explained in psychological terms,[1] though, to be fair, an equal sense of puzzlement still affects those who would explain the failure of the United States to foresee and provide against the attack on Pearl Harbor. And it is possible to question whether the emphasis given to Singapore in the present context is excessive. It is certainly the case that no-one in London, however worried about the immediate prospects, took the view that the Empire-Commonwealth as a working system of power had now come to an end.

Indeed, as soon as the fear of defeat at the hands of Germany and her allies began to diminish and as soon therefore as the bureaucratic machine began to look towards the post-war needs of British defence, it was again taken for granted that it would be possible to rely on the resources of the entire Empire, and to make plans embracing their use.[2] Again, it could be pointed out that in fact after the defeat of Japan all Britain's Asian possessions were restored to her rule and that almost all remained in that situation until independence inside or outside the Commonwealth was voluntarily conceded.[3] It has subsequently been tempting to pass over the events of the war and to see the

[1] See Norman Dixon, *On the Psychology of Military Incompetence* (London, 1976).
[2] See the useful material in Julian Lewis, *Changing Direction: British Military Planning for Post-War Strategic Defence, 1942–1947* (London, 1988). For British efforts after the war to keep India within the structure of Commonwealth defence see R.J. Moore, *The Making of the New Commonwealth* (Oxford, 1987), pp. 14–15, 198–9.
[3] Hong Kong, which had no physical capacity for independence, remains under British rule, but is to be 'restored' to China in 1997 when the lease of the New Territories runs out.

process of national emancipation as a continuous one. And this has been particularly true of nationalist leaders both in Asia and Africa, who have tried to ascribe the achievement of independence to the efforts and struggle of their own peoples, but also of British leaders justifying the transformation to the British themselves.[4] And this point of view was particularly strongly voiced by those historians who saw the Commonwealth continuing to fulfil a valuable role politically, a thesis easier to maintain in the early post-war decades than it was to be later on.[5]

The transition in Britain from general acceptance of an imperial system and the need to maintain it to the view that national 'self-determination' was the over-riding principle in international relations to which everything was subordinate was not completed all at once. Many even of the leaders of the post-war Labour government were not at once converted.[6] Others, with their eyes fixed upon the need for domestic reform and reconstruction, regarded the colonial legacy as a burden and a bore.[7]

What is true is that once the new orthodoxy prevailed, historians tended to underestimate the cost of imperial liquidation to Britain's former subjects or wards and the extent to which the gloomy prognostications of the 'die-hards' had been borne out in an all too painful fashion. The massacres that accompanied the coming of independence to the Indian subcontinent were obliterated in people's

---

[4] 'While we could not foresee, even at the end of the war, the rapidity with which the dissolution of the old system would come about, we knew in our hearts that the process was inevitable and right.' Harold Macmillan, *Memoirs*, vol. III, *Tides of Fortune*, (London, Macmillan, 1969), p. xv.

[5] 'When the transfer of power was completed, energies which political leaders had previously devoted to the cause of hastening independence were released for direction towards more productive ends. It is our study (and our pride) that they have sometimes been used to develop new forms of Commonwealth co-operation which are more effective than those sponsored under the old Imperial control. Political goodwill will enable administrative co-operation to continue.' C.E. Carrington, *The Liquidation of the British Empire* (London, Harrap, 1961), p. 87.

[6] 'Bevin like everyone else hates the idea of our leaving India, but like everyone else has no real alternative to suggest... Both he and [A.V.] Alexander are really imperialists and dislike any idea of leaving India'. Diary entry, 24 December 1946, in Penderel Moon (ed.), *Wavell, The Viceroy's Journal*, (London, Oxford University Press, 1973), p. 399.

[7] On being offered the post of Secretary of State for the Colonies, Hugh Dalton wrote in his diary on 28 February 1950: 'I had a horrid vision of pullulating, poverty stricken diseased nigger communities for whom one can do nothing in the short run and who, the more one tries to help them, are querulous and ungrateful; of Malaya and a futile military campaign; of white settlers reactionary and troublesome in their way as the niggers... of Parliamentary questions by pro-native cranks and anti-native capitalists...'. B. Pimlott (ed.), *The Politicial Diary of Hugh Dalton* (London, Cape, 1986), pp. 472 – 3.

minds by the historic nature of the event.[8] Nor has much attention been paid to the loss of life in the wars in the subcontinent since that time, or in Sri Lanka, or the wide recrudescence of terrorism. It is rarely pointed out that the departure of the British from Palestine with no attempt at a peaceful handover to their successors was the proximate if not the ultimate cause of the subsequent series of wars in that region.[9] The travails of post-independence Nigeria, Uganda or the Sudan, for instance, are all too frequently played down. And this is to talk only in terms of direct loss of life through internecine warfare, to the accompaniment of massacres and famine. It overlooks the actual economic rundown of many of the formerly colonial economies and the general inability of the newly independent States to maintain constitutional methods of decision-making, let alone the 'Westminster model'.

The British and 'imperial overstretch'

When one does ask why the British retreat took place, it is of course possible for those with a broad sweep in their historical thinking to fit the British experience into an overarching theory of the rise and fall of Empires, to link together economic and technical supremacies as generating military and political power, and to show how the demands made by the latter result universally in modern experience in what has been well-styled 'imperial overstretch'.[10] Others, while finding such a perspective of great heuristic utility, may prefer to await the wisdom given by a lengthier perspective.[11]

Whether the past of the British Empire itself can assist the process of interpretation is also open to question. Modern students of the fate of the First British Empire, like those who have studied more recent events, have called attention to the fact that it was changes in the colonies rather than in the policies of the mother-country that were

[8] For a personal account of the effects of partition in India see Penderel Moon, *Divide and Quit* (London, 1961).
[9] For the background and immediate consequences see W.R. Louis, *The British Empire in the Middle East, 1945-1951* (Oxford, 1984).
[10] See Paul Kennedy, *The Rise and Fall of the Great Powers: Economic Change and Military Conflict, 1500 to 2000* (London, 1988). Professor Kennedy's work appeared when the present volume was in its final stages of preparation.
[11] Gibbon, after defending the British government's handling of the American colonists, wrote: 'Having supported the British, I must destroy the Roman Empire.' But he did not draw any parallels. S. Lutnick, 'Edward Gibbon and the Decline of the First British Empire', *Studies in Burke and his Time* (Lubbock, Texas), vol. X (1968 – 9).

decisive: the expansion and collapse of the First British Empire was 'the consequence of a series of profound upheavals and challenges on the periphery, and not the emergence of a new attitude in the metropolis'.[12]

It is certainly suggestive that what brought the issue of imperial relationships to the fore in the eighteenth century was the increasing cost of defence and the size of the debt incurred in order to defend the colonies in the Seven Years War, and the difficulty of finding a formula for collective defence expenditure when some colonies felt themselves to be so much more vulnerable than others.[13] In the twentieth century the problem presented itself differently, in that Dominion contributions (and even, to a considerable extent, Indian contributions) to defence were a matter for negotiation, not for the exercise of Parliamentary sovereignty, which had been abandoned as part and parcel of the emergence of Dominion status.

But of course the parallel is anyhow incomplete, since the ultimate threat to the Empire and its constituent parts was now seen to be in Europe itself, in that demands for Dominion assistance could be viewed as asking for contributions to maintaining a European policy for which the Dominions were not responsible. As the Prime Minister of Canada put it,

> The idea that every twenty years this country should automatically and as a matter of course take part in a war overseas for democracy or self-determination of other small nations, that a country which has all it can do to run itself should feel called upon to save periodically a continent that cannot run itself and to these ends risk the lives of its people, risk bankruptcy and political disunion, seems to many a nightmare and sheer madness.[14]

When the war did come, all the members of the Commonwealth except Eire were engaged, and together faced a series of defeats and retreats that showed up the failure to match strategy to power, and by implication either that the task was impossible or that the central organs of imperial policy and the procedures by which they operated

[12] R.W.Tucker and D.C. Hendrickson, *The Fall of the First British Empire* (Baltimore, 1982), p. 6. The relations between changes in the metropolis and those on the periphery is one of the themes of Phillip Darby, *The Three Faces of Imperialism* (New Haven and London, 1987).

[13] Tucker and Hendrickson, op. cit., pp. 77 – 87.

[14] Speech by Mackenzie King, 30 March 1939, quoted in W. Blair Neatby, *William Lyon Mackenzie King*, vol. III (Toronto, Methuen, 1976), p. 300.

were unsuited to their task. Appeasement did produce what its advocates had claimed it would, a (more or less) united Empire at the point of challenge; but it had not produced a strategy for actually winning the war. The war was won with Britain as a junior partner in the victorious alliance, and the Empire consequently survived, though with much of its emotional and intellectual underpinning removed. Both Russian and American participation proved necessary for victory, and neither power had the preservation of the British Empire high up on its list of objectives.[15] It could nevertheless be claimed that while the course of the war and its cost to Britain in particular must be held responsible for the rapidity with which the imperial system was dissolved – to all intents and purposes in two decades from its end – the seeds of the intellectual changes in the metropolis that were important for the nature and speed of the imperial debacle were present in the inter-war decades and may have owed as much to the impact of the first world war as to that of the second conflict.

Inter-imperial strains

The strains of inter-imperial relations in the second world war were to some extent prefigured at the Paris Peace Conference of 1919, when the Dominion statesmen Hughes, Botha and Sir Joseph Ward indicated that Lloyd George's apparent willingness to meet President Wilson's wishes at the expense of the Dominions' objectives was liable to bring about the disruption of the Empire. They felt that they had been made much of during the war when their troops were needed but were now not being consulted as they should be.[16] Yet consultation, as events were to prove, implied commitments which the Dominions were anxious to avoid.

Dominion residents in Britain in the inter-war period might also suffer from a feeling that they were not regarded as equals. A Canadian

[15] For a major assessment of Anglo-American relations in this respect see Christopher Thorne, *Allies of a Kind: The United States, Britain and the War against Japan* (London, 1978). Roosevelt's anti-imperialism as a factor in his rejection of Churchill's wish for a more intimate Anglo-American relationship is dealt with in H.B. Ryan, *The Vision of Anglo-America: The US-UK Alliance and the Emerging Cold War, 1943–1946* (Cambridge, 1987). For some reflections on these issues see my essay 'The End of the British Empire and the Assumption of worldwide commitments by the United States', in W.R. Louis and H. Bull (eds), *The Special Relationship: Anglo-American Relations since 1945* (Oxford, 1986).
[16] Entries for 30 January and 1 April 1919 in J. McEwen (ed.), *The Riddell Diaries* (London 1988), pp. 255 – 6, 264.

at Oxford found that there people did indeed use the word 'Dominion'; but when he went to camp with the Officers' Training Corps he found that the army talked of the colonies and colonials. By the time Canadian troops came to be stationed in Britain in the second world war, this particular obstacle had been overcome; but sensitivities remained.[17]

How far Britain itself was imperially-minded in the inter-war period is a difficult question to answer. The first signs of retreat – the Montagu – Chelmsford Reforms, the Milner declaration on Egypt, and the Irish Treaty – did evoke a considerable hostile reaction:

> How is it that the once great Conservative Party, formerly supposed to stand for loyalty, for patriotism, for all the sounder and saner elements in public life, has become the aider and abetter of a Government which is throwing Egypt and India to the wolves, while surrendering our naval superiority first to the United States, and then to Japan, and abandoning Ireland to the rule of a gang of bloodstained murderers?[18]

But in the Baldwin era that followed such voices were less and less audible and such views found fewer and fewer adherents.[19] Churchill's campaign against the India bill in the 1930s was only a coda to the imperialist protest.

It was in part the case that the appeal of service as understood by the pre – 1914 servants of empire had lost its strength:

> Before the Great War my generation served men who believed in the righteousness of the vocation to which they had been called, and we shared their belief. They were the priests and we the acolytes of a cult – pax Britannica – for which we worked happily and if need be died gladly. Curzon at his best was our spokesman and Kipling at his noblest our inspiration.[20]

It was certainly not the Dominions that provided such inspiration. When in January 1940 Churchill made a speech to the House of Commons detailing *inter alia* the help coming from the Dominions

[17] C.P. Stacey, *A Date with History*, p. 35.

[18] H.F. Whyatt in the *National Review* (London), vol.77, (1921), p. 767.

[19] A good deal of pro-imperial sentiment was propagated from official quarters, especially among the young, but its impact must be considered doubtful. See J. Mackenzie, *Propaganda and Empire* (Manchester, 1984).

[20] Arnold Wilson, *South West Persia: A Political Officer's Diary* (London, Oxford University Press, 1941), introduction.

and colonies, he found his audience unreceptive. 'For some reason', noted his secretary, 'no subject is more boring to the average Englishman than the British Empire.'[21] Churchill himself was not, except for India, an imperial statesman.

The Empire and Anglo-American Relations

Churchill was of course well aware of the hostility of the American administration to the British Empire, both in respect of its pressure for immediate concessions to the Indian nationalist movement and for the dissolution of all special economic ties between members of the Commonwealth.[22] But, convinced as he was that the war could not be won without the Americans, Churchill continued to give relations with the American President an absolute priority in thought and action.

The importance attached by Churchill to his relationship with Roosevelt was quite different from his attitude to the Dominion Prime Ministers.[23] It was only in association with the United States that the other English-speaking democracies could, in Churchill's view, play a leading role in the world.[24] There was little sympathy for Smuts' view that the Commonwealth could be strengthened to form the core of a new world organisation to replace the League.[25] Nor could such scepticism be marvelled at when even suggestions from Smuts and the Australian Prime Minister, Curtin, that consultation within the Commonwealth might be made more effective raised the bogy of 'centralisation' in the minds of Canadian Liberals.[26]

A lack of commitment

By the non-verbal tests of imperial commitment, Britain in the inter-

---

[21] Diary entry for 16 January 1940, in John Colville, *The Fringes of Power* (London, Hodder & Stoughton, 1985), p. 71.

[22] The story is fully set out in William Roger Louis, *Imperialism at Bay, 1941–1945: the United States and the decolonisation of the British Empire* (Oxford, 1977).

[23] On the occasion of Churchill's visit to Ottawa in December 1941 his doctor noted of Churchill's attitude to his host: 'The two men are of course quite friendly, but the P.M. is not really interested in Mackenzie King.' The careful wooing of Roosevelt was another matter. Diary entry, 31 December 1941, in Lord Moran, *Winston Churchill: The Struggle for Survival, 1940–1965* (London, Constable, 1966), p. 19.

[24] See e.g. Churchill's conversation with Mackenzie King on 5 September 1941: J.W. Pickersgill, *The Mackenzie King Record*, vol. I, (Toronto, 1960), p. 253.

[25] See e.g. Smuts to Dawson, 26 January 1940, in Lothian Papers, Box 160.

[26] R. Cook, *The Politics of John W. Dafoe and the Free Press* (Toronto, 1969), p. 279.

war period again offers negative evidence. Lord Milner was reported as having been in the habit of saying that 'the only power capable of destroying the British Empire was the British Treasury'.[27] And the evidence for its purblind parsimony is abundant enough.

If the political right and the Whitehall establishment were not imperially minded, it is hardly suprising to find that the left were overtly hostile. Almost all the literature that was applauded by the intelligentsia was suffused by revulsion against empire and the militarism that was believed to be its necessary counterpart.[28] It is of course true that the intelligentsia represented a minority viewpoint even on the political left. The Labour Party was, as has been seen, on the whole indifferent to most of the empire; it does not seem to have had any close relationship with its sister-parties in Australia and New Zealand.[29] In respect of the colonial empire its sympathies for the indigenous peoples rather than settler communities did not amount to a demand for a rapid devolution of power. The exception was India. Sympathies with Congress were to be found among the Labour leadership and between the passing of the 1935 Government of India Act and the outbreak of war there were close contacts between Nehru and important figures in the Labour Party, notably Attlee.[30] In this sense, 1947 did no more than confirm the Labour Party's established position, even though it had to accept partition as the price of carrying its policy into effect. And it is noteworthy that, even at this late date, the basic debate between Attlee and Churchill was carried on in terms of what was best for India, not in terms of the impact of Indian independence on Britain's world role.[31]

It has been suggested that the blame for partition must ultimately lie with Gandhi and Congress, who made it impossible to proceed

[27] Grigg to H.R. Blood, Governor of the Gambia, 14 September 1943: Grigg Papers, 1939–1945.B.

[28] 'Looking back on "Bloomsbury" I have little doubt that however civilizing its influence, it was politically speaking a liability...Its contempt of all existing politicians and its tendency to retreat into an ivory tower was, I believe, partly responsible for many talented and potentially politically minded younger people coming to the conclusion that some form of communism was England's only hope...I merely observe that the retreat from Empire was vigorously fostered and assisted by the Bloomsbury set.' *The Memoirs of Lord Gladwyn* (London, Weidenfeld and Nicolson, 1972), p. 34.

[29] This is the more surprising since it was members of the British working class who were most likely to have relatives or friends in the 'white Dominions'. Corelli Barnett, *The Collapse of British Power* (London, 1972), p. 80.

[30] See Trevor Burridge, *Attlee, a Political Biography* (London, 1985), 270 ff.

[31] Barnett, op. cit., 134 ff.

with an orderly progress towards full Dominion status.[32] But the reason why such a transfer of power did not take place in this way can also be seen as a consequence of the gap created between rulers and ruled by the pervading consciousness of racial prejudice. In the view of Indians this consciousness was enhanced by the British victory in the first world war.[33] But, if this is the case, it was not a departure from a philosophy of imperial government that had its roots in the nineteenth century, when it was held that social aloofness from those governed was essential to the authority of the rulers, and the only safeguard against the corruption they condemned both in local society and in the case of their predecessors. Such a philosophy was of course exemplified in the life-style of the rulers, which corresponded to an aristocratic model, though the individuals concerned were themselves from middle-class backgrounds in Britain itself.[34] What was true of India was inevitably still truer of colonial situations where the material and cultural gaps were even wider. In this sense it could be said that it was the Empire that made the British governing class, rather than the other way round. And to accept this argument would require one at least to modify the familiar thesis that the Empire provided an alternative set of values which enabled the British ruling class to avoid confrontation with the problems of industrial development and competition, which were neglected to an extent sufficient to explain Britain's loss of power.[35]

Clearly, in the light of such beliefs, there were unlikely to be any important consequences from such intermixture of the races as took place. Anglo-Indians (Eurasians) were the objects of prejudice on both sides, and their upward mobility was severely confined. If Gladstone was correct in saying that 'no conquest has ever been permanent unless followed by an amalgamation',[36] then the Empire outside the

[32] James Halliday, (pseud.), *A Special India* (London, 1968); the author, who had long family connections with India, served in the I.C.S. from 1926 to 1947.

[33] N.R. Bonarjee, *Under Two Masters*, p. 74. For an account of the last period of British rule critical of the British attitudes towards Indians but unsympathetic to the Nationalist movement, and giving a very different view of Gandhi, Nehru and Mountbatten to the conventional one, see Nirad C. Chaudhuri, *Thy Hand, Great Anarch* (London, 1987). Paul Scott's series of novels, the *Raj Quartet*, provides valuable insights into the psychology of the situation.

[34] The whole subject of relations between the British and their Indian subjects is treated at length in K. Ballhatchet, *Race, Sex and Class: Imperial Attitudes and Policies and their Critics, 1793–1905* (London, 1980).

[35] For a recent restatement of this position see Corelli Barnett, *The Audit of War* (London, 1986), p. 221. See also M. Weiner, *English Culture and the Decline of the Industrial Spirit* (Cambridge, 1981).

[36] Quoted by Stephen Koss in *John Morley at the India Office* (New Haven and London, 1969), p. 182.

area of British settlement was inevitably a transitory phenomenon. Indeed, where India was concerned the most obvious parallel would seem to be that with the Crusaders' Latin Kingdom of Jerusalem, where a European ruling and trading class, supported through taxation of the local peasantry, neither mixed with the indigenous population nor attempted to convert them. Little impact upon the crusaders was made by the local languages and cultures. Only diet and dress were affected. And after the departure of the Latins only the ruins of their castles testified to their one-time presence.[37] Of course, a more simple colonial structure of this kind meant fewer requirements for collaborators; by contrast, the modern European Empires inevitably involved finding such collaborators among the indigenous peoples, whether one is thinking of the Indianisation of the I.C.S. or of the African 'chiefs'.[38]

It is possible in retrospect to see that an imperial system which in part depended upon the assumed willingness of individual sovereign nations to co-operate to the full (which was not assisted by the assumptions of innate superiority on one side and the lurking suspicions of unequal treatment on the other), and in part upon retaining the allegiance of collaborators torn at by growing nationalist sentiments, was essentially fragile. It demanded on the part of the British political elite an ability to see things in imperial terms which, as has been seen, did not come naturally to its members unless they were directly involved in imperial matters.[39]

The Empire, Asia and Europe: conflicts of interest

Because Europe was closer at hand and could pose more of a threat,

[37] See J. Prawer, *The Latin Kingdom of Jerusalem* (London, 1973).

[38] Ronald Robinson, 'Non-European Foundations of European Imperialism; sketch for a theory of collaboration' in R. Owen and B. Sutcliffe, *Studies in the Theory of Imperialism* (London, 1962), and the same author's 'The Excentric Idea of Imperialism with or without Empire', in W.J. Mommsen and J. Osterhammel, *Imperialism and After* (London, 1986).

[39] At the height of the 1931 financial crisis a dedicated imperialist wrote: 'I am very much struck by the fact that in all the talk this morning about the crisis and our patriotic duty, I have not found a single reference to the Empire – not in the *Times*, not even in the *Daily Express*. The habit of limiting the patriotic appeal to what concerns this island is growing rapidly.' Grigg to Neville Chamberlain, 29 September 1931, Grigg Papers. The record of the National Government gave him no comfort: 'There is not a man (in the Cabinet) who understands the idiom of Imperial partnership or really thinks seriously about it. They talk about the Empire as landsmen talk about the sea. The Empire is difficult. So is the sea. But sailors love the difficulties of the sea though they often dread them, and it is dangerous for a National Government in this country to be both devoid of sea sense and insular.' Grigg to J.L. Garvin, 11 April 1934, ibid.

British statesmen were, as the Dominion leaders rightly suspected, always likely to give precedence to European considerations. One thing which those three very different characters, Smuts, Mackenzie King and Menzies, had in common was an abiding mistrust of the French.

Here again, the pivotal nature of the events surrounding the fall of Singapore become clear. But for self-control by the political leaders in both Britain and Australia, both the use of Australian troops in the defence of Malaya and their handling there as well as the surrender might have created much ill-will.[40] Even so, an immediate impetus was given to Australia's increasing lack of confidence in the imperial tie. Both Australia and New Zealand expressed discontent with any idea that their contribution to the making of allied strategy should be confined to representation in a Pacific Council in London and successfully demanded direct access to the Americans upon whom they now depended. But it was not only immediate defence that was at issue. For both countries, but perhaps especially for Australia, the Pacific War was a turning point in their entire national histories. As an Australian historian has written, Pearl Harbor and the sinking of the *Prince of Wales* and *Repulse* 'marked for Australia the waning of an era in which history or tradition was dominant and the emergence of a new era when geography was probably as crucial as history'.[41] The British inheritance was less significant henceforth than Australia's location in relation to Asia.

While, at the level of the armed forces and of supply, intimate co-operation continued between the United Kingdom and the Dominions, the tendency to disaggregation was in fact irreversible, once the inability of British sea-power to protect the Dominions had become patent. Australia and New Zealand could only look to the United States to protect them against Japan in the immediate present, and against future dangers dimly perceived. The two Dominions also acquired international personalities in the full sense for the first time, and Australia was to play an important if temporary role as a

---

[40] On 18 March 1942 Churchill told a private meeting of junior ministers that the loss of Singapore was 'the greatest military disaster in the history of the British Army. The Australians were very bitter about it. There was a retort to them, but he could not make it publicly as it would not ease matters. There were 17,300 Australian troops in Singapore. Only 280 were reported as being killed. Troops ought to be able to withstand a casualty rate of 30 to 35% before surrendering.' Kevin Jefferys (ed.), *Labour and the Wartime Coalition: From the Diary of James Chuter Ede 1941–1945* (London, Historians Press, 1987), p. 65.
[41] Geoffrey Blainey, *The Tyranny of Distance* (Melbourne, Macmillan, 1966), p. 208.

spokesman for the smaller powers in the San Francisco Conference that set up the United Nations Organisation.[42]

Canada: between two powers

Canadian developments were less dramatic, since the need to strike a balance between the British and the American influence had been apparent for so long. But the war did point to the fact of being a neighbour of the United States as the dominant consideration for Canada in both economic life and defence. The British connection was increasingly seen as of value largely as preventing Canada's total absorption by her much more powerful ally. Canadians had felt that their interests and opinions were not given due weight in spite of their considerable contribution to the allied war effort. And this was, as a percipient Canadian diplomat realised soon after the United States entered the war, an inevitable consequence of the now close relationship between the United Kingdom and the United States:

> With the entry of the United States into the war we are not as well placed to influence the conduct of the war as we were when the United States was neutral. Canadian influence can be greatest when there is a divergence of policy between the United Kingdom and the United States. Now that they are partners we become only a junior member of the partnership.[43]

It could of course be added that Canada was always likely to be less effective in wartime than her material and human resources might have made one expect because it was in wartime that the stresses imposed upon her political system by her multinational composition were most likely to come to the fore. Very considerable efforts had to be expended by the government on retaining sufficient political support to be effective externally. Out of reach of any serious enemy threat, Canadians could not be expected to treat victory as essential for national survival, as was true by and large of the British after Dunkirk. Churchill could concentrate his energies on this sole

---

[42] It is worth noting that the United Nations Declaration of 1 January 1942 was signed by Australia, Canada, India, New Zealand and South Africa according to their places in the alphabetical order in the general list of signatories, and were not grouped together as had been the case with the Treaty of Versailles. Text in *FRUS*, 1942, vol. I, pp. 25 – 6.

[43] Hume Wrong (from Washington) to L.B. Pearson, 3 February 1942: quoted by Granatstein, op. cit., p. 296.

objective in a way impossible for Mackenzie King. The fact that King won his election in 1945 while Churchill lost his, is perhaps not unrelated to this fact.

The full emergence of Canada as an important power of the middle rank could only come with the peace, and for a few brief years Canada was a major factor both on the wider international scene and in the creation of the North Atlantic Alliance, though as the cold war hardened, its particular role tended to fall into the background.

India, the Middle East and Africa: contrasts in imperial decline

The revelation of Britain's declining strength following upon Japan's entry into the war was no less important for that part of the Empire still directly ruled from London. It is no accident that the date chosen to open the series of documents illustrating Britain's relinquishment of her Indian empire was January 1942.[44] It took some time to realise that the difference that this made was much greater than that made by the changed position of the old Dominions. They, like Britain, were to take their places in a new combination of powers led by the United States and basically committed to free economies and (except for South Africa) liberal democracy. The successor states to the Indian Empire and those states that came into being on its periphery felt no such automatic commitment to values originating in the western world. It can be argued that the extension of the franchise in India prior to independence had weakened those elements in Indian society upon whose continued collaboration Britain might more reliably have depended. But the movement towards democracy was inherent in the British presence. In any event, the seeds of non-alignment were clearly present in Nehru's thinking well before the outbreak of war.

If the defence of India was no longer Britain's direct concern, the empire in the Middle East that had grown up in order to facilitate such defence had also lost its principal historic *raison d'être*. So much was proved by the decade between Indian independence and 'Suez'. The final irony was that of the successor states in the region, only Israel, the final victim in Ernest Bevin's day of the British penchant for Arabs, attempted to acclimatise in that inhospitable region the legal and constitutional legacy of British rule and retained a strong inclination to the West.

[44] N. Mansergh, *The Transfer of Power, 1942–1947*, vols. I-XII (London, 1970 – 81).

Retreat in sub-Saharan Africa and in the Caribbean was less directly the product of the 1942 débâcle and is a separate story, even though the political consciousness of Africans was (as in the first world war) given another jolt forwards. For some time after the war, it looked as though the time-scale for independence in Africa would be quite a lengthy one, partly for economic reasons and partly because of the new commitment to 'paternalistic' development.[45]

What happened in the rest of Africa was also affected by the final triumph of Boer nationalism in South Africa in the election of 1948, and its subsequent acquisition of republican status outside the Commonwealth. It also marks the transition in the realm of thought generally to a new and specific concept of 'race relations', meaning now only relations between whites and non-whites. It is worth reminding oneself of how far one has travelled by pointing out that not only had race relations in Southern Africa previously meant the contest between Briton and Boer, but that in Canada, as late as the second world war, it was still used to describe relations between anglophones and francophones.[46]

It will be for a younger scholar to carry out the original intention of writing a third volume of *Imperial Sunset*, to deal with the period from 1942 to 1961 or soon thereafter, which might be entitled *The Great Retreat*. But the time for that may not have come. Not that the documents are lacking; as with so many aspects of recent history, the historian is more likely to be overwhelmed by the documentation than to feel he is faced with a shortage. The difficulty is one of perspective. It is all too close at hand and excites too many passions. Despite the plausible contention that Britain's entry into the European Communities marked both an end of the Empire story and of particular economic and other ties to Commonwealth countries, we do not know how far we can be certain that Britain's imperial instincts are quenched for ever. Foreigners, particularly the French, are not sure. The French have not only shown more tenacity in hanging on to their empire and in substituting for it a new version of 'informal

[45] The present writer took part in university courses after the war designed to prepare young men for roles as 'district officers', etc., in countries destined shortly to become independent. See R. Symonds, *Oxford and Empire* (London, 1986).
[46] On the impact of the Japanese conquests and occupation upon race relations in Asia see Christopher Thorne, *The Issue of War: States, Societies and the Far Eastern Conflict of 1941–1945* (London, 1985).

empire', they also seem convinced that the British are still capable of Machiavellian devices in pursuit of the same goals.

In 1976 Britain and France agreed to give independence to the condominium of the New Hebrides in 1985. It was later brought forward to 1980. A French deputy wrote that the reason was that France had been engaged in a massive educational programme, which by 1982 would have produced a francophone majority. Great Britain, Australia and New Zealand had pressed for the date to be earlier so that a government based on an anglophone majority would take over on independence, as indeed happened.[47] Fable or not, the story helps to direct attention to what matters most in imperial history – the will to Empire, or the lack of it.[48]

[47] R.A. Foster, 'Vanuatu: The end of an episode of schizophrenic colonialism', *The Round Table*, no. 280, (October 1980), pp. 367 – 73.
[48] Some may feel that the Falklands War in 1982 and Britain's willingness to complicate relations with Spain, a fellow member of the European Community, for the sake of Gibraltar suggest the lingering on into the 1980s of a modicum of imperial sentiment. British policy in both cases could be and was justified by the principle of self-determination; the same, *mutatis mutandis*, could be said of policy towards Northern Ireland, a relic of an earlier Empire of settlement.

CHRONOLOGY

1921	January 3	First Indian parliament meets
	February 4	James Craig elected Ulster leader
	February 8	Jan Christian Smuts gains majority in South African election
	February 9	Government of India Act comes into operation
	March	Conference of British and Dominion naval officers at Penang
	March 4	Harding inaugurated as President of U.S.A.
	March 8	French troops occupy Rhineland towns in protest against non-repayment of reparations
	March 16	Anglo-Russian trade treaty signed
	March 18	Treaty of Riga signed
	April 2	Chelmsford succeeded by Reading as Viceroy
	April 19	Government of Ireland Act comes into force
	June – August	Imperial conference
	June 7	First Parliament of Northern Ireland opens
	June 24	Lloyd George invites De Valera to negotiate
	July 9	Anglo-Irish truce announced
	July 11	President Harding summons Washington Conference
	November 12 – 6 February 1922	Washington Naval Conference
	November 21	Treaty signed between Britain and Afghanistan
	November – December	Prince of Wales visits India

	December 6	Anglo-Irish Treaty signed
	December 13	Four Power Pacific Treaty signed
	December 29	United States, British Empire, France, Italy and Japan sign Washington Treaty to limit naval armaments
1922	January 7	Dail approves Anglo-Irish Treaty
	January 26	Legislative council of Southern Rhodesia accepts draft constitution conferring limited self-government
	February 6	Treaty of Washington signed
	February 28	Allenby Declaration of formal independence for Egypt
	March 16	Britain recognises Kingdom of Egypt; joint Anglo-Egyptian sovereignty over Sudan
	June 30	'Churchill' white paper on Palestine
	July 24	League of Nations passes Palestine mandate
	September	'Chanak affair'
	September 10	Anglo-Russian commercial treaty
	September 11	British mandate declared in Palestine
	October 5	Treaty of Alliance with King Faisal
	October 11	Pact of Mundania ends Chanak crisis
	October 24	Dail accepts constitution for Irish Free State
	October 30	Benito Mussolini forms fascist government in Italy
	November 19 – July 24, 1923	Lausanne Conference
	December 6	Irish Free State comes into formal existence
	December 7	Northern Ireland parliament votes against inclusion in Irish Free State
	December 17	Last British troops leave southern Ireland
1923	April 30	End of Irish civil war
	July 24	Treaty of Lausanne with Turkey

	August 2	President Harding dies; succeeded by Calvin Coolidge
	September 29	Middle East mandates come into force
	October 26 – November 8	Imperial conference
	November 8 – 9	Nazi putsch in Munich
1924	January 21	Death of Lenin
	February 1	Britain recognises U.S.S.R.
	March 18	Decision not to proceed with Singapore naval base announced
1925	April 28	Churchill announces reintroduction of Gold Standard
	May 1	Cyprus declared a British Crown Colony
	May 4 – June 17	Geneva conference on arms and war
	June 11	Dominions Office separated from Colonial Office
	October 5 – 16	Locarno conference
	October 25	Locarno treaties signed
1926	March	Creation of Empire Marketing Board announced
	May 3 – 12	General strike
	May 23	Lebanon declared a republic by France
	June 5	Anglo-Turkish agreement on Mosul
	August 31	Russia and Afghanistan make treaty of neutrality and non-aggression
	October 19 – November 23	Imperial conference
1927	January 31	End of Allied military control of Germany
	May 13	German economic system collapses: 'Black Friday'
	May 31	Britain makes treaty with King Faisal and accepts enlarged Saudi Arabia

	June 20 – August 7	Washington naval conference
	October	Labour Party conference pledges party's support for Dominion Home Rule for India
	December 27	Stalin takes effective power in Russia after expulsion of Trotsky from Communist Party
1928	July 31	Agreement on Iraqi oilfields
	October 6	Chiang-Kai-shek elected President of China
	November 7	Hoover elected President of United States
1929	July	Beaverbrook launches Empire Free Trade crusade
	August	Hague conference agrees to relieve Germany of allied control
	October 23 – 24	'Wall Street crash'
	December	Round Table conference on Dominion status for India
1930	April 3 – 22	London Conference on Naval Disarmament: Britain, United States and Japan sign Treaty of London
	June 24	Simon Report on India published
	June 30	Last Allied troops leave German soil
	October 1	Britain restores Wei-hai-wei to China
	October 1 – November 14	Imperial Conference
	November 12 – January 31	Conference on Government of India in London
1931	March 4	Lord Irwin (Viceroy) and Gandhi make Delhi pact
	August 24	MacDonald forms National Government
	September 18	Japanese forces invade Manchuria

388

	September 21	Britain abandons Gold Standard
	October – November	Second session of Round Table Conference on Government of India
	December 11	Statute of Westminster
1932	February 2	Geneva Disarmament Conference opens
	June 16 – July 9	Lausanne conference: German reparations virtually ended
	July 21 – August 20	Imperial Conference in Ottawa
	September 14	Germany leaves Geneva Disarmament Conference
	October 3	Iraq achieves full independence as member of League of Nations on ending of mandate
	November 8	F.D.Roosevelt elected President of United States
	December 11	Germany returns to Geneva Disarmament Conference
1933	January	De Valera terminates British annuity payments; Anglo-Irish trade war begins
	January 30	Hitler becomes chancellor of Germany
	March 4	Roosevelt inaugurated: makes 'New Deal' speech
	April 30	United States abandons Gold Standard
	May 3	Irish Government abolishes Oath of Allegiance to Crown
	June – July	World Economic Conference in London
	September 30	Empire Marketing Board dissolved
	October 14	Germany withdraws from Geneva Disarmament Conference
	October 21	Germany leaves League of Nations
	November	Cabinet tacitly abandons 'Ten Year Rule'
1934	June 11	Geneva Disarmament conference fails
	August 19	Hitler takes sole power as Fuhrer
	October 23 – December 19	London Naval Disarmament Conference

	December 21	Anglo-Irish coal-and-cattle pact
1935	January 9	Anglo-Indian trade agreement
	March 4	British rearmament announced
	March 16	Hitler introduces conscription; Germany repudiates Versailles disarmament clauses
	May	Jubilee of George V; Dominion Prime Ministers meet in London
	June 7	Baldwin becomes Prime Minister
	August 2	Government of India Act passed
	October 3	Italian armies attack Abyssinia
	November 29	Hoare-Laval pact published, and proposal abandoned
1936	January 20	Death of George V; accession of Edward VIII
	February 17	Anglo-Irish trade agreement
	March 7	Hitler enters the Rhineland
	April 28	Accession of Faruk as King of Egypt
	May 1	Haile Selassie abdicates in Abyssinia
	July 16	Outbreak of Spanish Civil War
	August 24	Germany adopts conscription
	August 26	Anglo-Egyptian treaty of alliance
	December 11	Edward VIII abdicates; accession of George VI
1937	May	Imperial Conference
	May 26	Egypt enters League of Nations
	June 14	Ireland passes new constitution
	July 7	Peel Commission recommends partition of Palestine
		Fighting renewed between China and Japan
1938	February	Singapore graving dock opened
	March 11 – 13	Anschluss: Hitler annexes Austria
	April 25	Anglo-Irish economic agreement; 'Treaty ports' ceded by Britain to Ireland

	September	'Munich crisis'
	October 2	Japan withdraws from League of Nations
	November 17	Agreement on tariff reductions between United Kingdom, United States and Canada.
1939	January	I.R.A. begins terrorist campaign against Britain
	March 15	Break-up of Czechoslovakia
	March 28	Spanish civil war ends
	March 31	Britain gives guarantee to Poland
	April 13	Britain and France guarantee independence of Greece and Rumania
	April 27	Britain introduces conscription
	May 17	White paper on Palestine
	May 22	'Pact of steel': formal German-Italian alliance
	May 23	Parliament approves plan for independence of Palestine
	August 23	Molotov-von Ribbentrop pact
	August 25	Britain and Poland make formal mutual assistance pact
	September 1	Germany invades Poland
	September 3	Britain, Australia, India and France declare war on Germany; Chamberlain forms War Cabinet
	September 6	South Africa declares war on Germany
	September 10	Canada declares war on Germany
	October 6	Britain and France reject Hitler's peace offer
	November 30	Russia attacks Finland
1940	March 12	Finland concludes armistice with Russia
	April 9	Hitler occupies Denmark and invades Norway
	May 10	Germany invades Holland, Belgium and France
	May 27 – June 3	'Dunkirk evacuation'

	June 10	Mussolini declares war on France and Britain
	June 16	Pétain forms government in France
	June 17 – 23	Russia occupies Baltic states
	June 22	Franco-German armistice
	July 10 – September 15	Battle of Britain
	July	Hitler orders preparations for invasion of Britain
	September 7 – May 16, 1941	'The Blitz'
	September 17	Hitler postpones invasion of Britain
	September 27	Japan adheres to Axis Pact
	December 29	Britain takes economic sanctions against Eire
1941	March 11	United States passes Lend-Lease Act
	March 30	Rommel attacks British forces in North African desert
	May 5	Haile Selassie restored to power
	May 27	British forces withdraw from Crete
	June 8	Britain and Free French issue declaration of independence for Syria and Lebanon
	June 22	Hitler attacks Russia
	July 12	Anglo-Russian mutual aid agreement
	July 28	Japanese troops move into Indo-China
	August 14	Churchill and Roosevelt make 'Atlantic Charter' agreement
	August 25	Britain and Russia invade Iran
	December 7	Japan attacks U.S. fleet at Pearl Harbour
	December 11	Germany and Italy declare war on United States
	December 25	Surrender of Hong Kong
1942	January 1	'United Nations' declaration against separate peace
	February 15	Surrender of Singapore

U.K. and Dominion Prime Ministers

GREAT BRITAIN

1916 – 22	David Lloyd George
1922 – 3	Arthur Bonar Law
1923 – 4	Stanley Baldwin
1924	(Jan.-Nov.) James Ramsay MacDonald
1924 – 9	Stanley Baldwin
1929 – 35	James Ramsay MacDonald
1935 – 7	Stanley Baldwin
1937 – 40	Neville Chamberlain
1940 – 5	Winston Churchill

AUSTRALIA

1915 – 23	W.M. Hughes
1923 – 9	S.M. Bruce
1929 – 32	J.H. Scullin
1932 – 9	J.A. Lyons
1939 – 41	Robert Menzies
1941	(Aug.-Oct.) A.W. Fadden
1941 – 9	John Curtin

CANADA

1921 – 6	W.L. Mackenzie King
1926	(June-Sept.) Arthur Meighen
1926 – 30	W.L. Mackenzie King
1930 – 5	R.B. Bennett
1935 – 48	W.L. Mackenzie King

IRISH FREE STATE

1922 – 32	William Cosgrave
1932 – 48	Eamon de Valera

NEW ZEALAND

1912 – 25	William Massey
1925 – 8	William Coates

1928 – 30	Joseph Wood
1930 – 5	G.W. Forbes
1935 – 40	Michael Savage
1940 – 45	Peter Fraser

SOUTH AFRICA

1919 – 24	Jan Christian Smuts
1924 – 39	J.B.M. Hertzog
1939 – 48	Jan Christian Smuts

BIOGRAPHICAL NOTES

Allenby, Field-Marshal Edmund H.H. (1861 – 1936), cr. 1st Viscount 1918. Commander-in-Chief Egyptian Expeditionary Force, 1917 – 19; High Commissioner for Egypt, 1919 – 25.

Amery, Rt Hon. Leopold Stennett (1873 – 1955). Unionist M.P. 1911 – 45. Parliamentary Under-Secretary for Colonies 1919 – 21, First Lord of Admiralty 1922 – 4, Secretary of State for Colonies 1924 – 9, and Secretary of State for Dominion Affairs 1925 – 9, Secretary of State for India and Burma 1940 – 45.

Bennett, Rt Hon. Richard Bedford (1870 – 1947). Leader of Canadian Conservative Party 1927 – 38; Canadian Prime Minister and Minister for External Affairs and Finance 1930 – 35.

Birkenhead, Earl of, (1872 – 1930) F.E. Smith, cr. 1st Earl 1922. Unionist M.P. 1906 – 19. Attorney General 1915 – 19; Secretary of State for India 1922 – 4, 1924 – 8.

Bruce, Rt. Hon. Stanley Melbourne (1883 – 1967), cr. 1st Viscount Bruce of Melbourne 1947. Prime Minister of Australia and Minister for External Affairs 1923 – 9, Australian Minister in London 1932 – 3, Australian High Commissioner in London 1933 – 45.

Cameron, Sir Donald (1872 – 1948). Colonial Civil Service, 1890 – 1924; Governor of Tanganyika 1925 – 31, Governor of Nigeria 1931 – 5.

Casey, Richard Gardiner (1890 – 1976), cr. Baron Casey 1960. Liason Officer between Australian Government and British Foreign Office, 1924 – 7, 1927 – 31; Australian Minister to U.S.A. 1940 – 42; British Minister resident in the Middle East and member of War Cabinet, 1942 – 3.

Chamberlain, Rt Hon. Neville (1869 – 1940). Conservative M.P. 1918 – 40. Chancellor of Exchequer 1923 – 4, 1931 – 7; Prime Minister 1937 – 40; Lord President of the Council 1940.

De Valera, Eamon (1882 – 1975). President of Sinn Fein 1917 – 26. Founded Fianna Fail party 1926, and president until 1959. Prime Minister of Ireland 1932 – 48, 1951 – 4, 1957 – 9. President of Ireland 1959 – 73.

Eden, (Robert) Anthony (1897 – 1957), cr. 1st Earl of Avon, 1961. Conservative M.P. 1923 – 57. Parliamentary Private Secretary to Austen Chamberlain 1926 – 9, Parliamentary Under-Secretary for Foreign Affairs, 1931 – 3; Minister for League of Nations Affairs 1935; Foreign Secretary 1935 – 8, 1940 – 5, 1951 – 5; Dominions Secretary 1939 – 40; Secretary of State for War 1940; Prime Minister 1955 – 7.

Gandhi, Mohandas Karamchand (1869 – 1948). Campaigned for Indian settlers in South Africa, 1908 – 15; returned to India 1915; started Satyagraha movement 1918 and non-cooperation campaign 1920; leader of Indian National Congress to 1934.

Hailey, William Malcolm Hailey, (1872 – 1969), cr. 1st Baron Hailey, 1936. Joined I.C.S. 1895. Governor of Punjab 1924 – 8, of United Provinces 1928 – 30 and 1931 – 4. Director, African Research Survey, 1935 – 8; member of Permanent Mandates Commission, League of Nations, 1935 – 8.

Halifax, Earl of (1881 – 1959), Edward Frederick Lindley Wood, Lord Irwin, 3rd Viscount, cr. 1st Earl 1944. Colonial Under-Secretary 1922 – 4, Viceroy of India 1926 – 31, Secretary of State for War 1935, Foreign Secretary 1938 – 40, British Ambassador to United States 1941 – 6.

Henderson, Sir Nevile Meyrick (1882 – 1942). Acting British High Commissioner in Constantinople, 1922 – 4; Minister at Cairo, 1924; British Ambassador in Berlin, April 1937-September 1939.

Hertzog, General James Barry Munnik (1866 – 1942). Prime Minister of South Africa 1924 – 39, leader of Nationalist Party and founder and leader of United South African National Party, 1933 – 9.

Hoare, Rt Hon. Sir Samuel John Gurney (1880 – 1959), cr. 1st Viscount Templewood 1944. Conservative M.P. 1910 – 44. Secretary of State for Air 1922 – 4, 1924 – 9, 1940; India Secretary 1931 – 5; Foreign Secretary 1935. Special Ambassador to Spain 1940 – 44.

Howard, Esme William (1863 – 1939), cr. 1st Baron Howard of Penrith 1930. British Ambassador to USA 1924 – 30.

Inskip, Thomas Walker Hobart (1876 – 1947), cr. 1st Viscount Caldecote 1939. Conservative MP 1918 – 29, 1931 – 9. Minister for Co-Ordination of Defence 1936 – 9; Dominions Secretary January – September 1939, May-October 1940.

Jinnah, Mahomed Ali (1876 – 1948). President of All India Muslim League 1916, 1920 and 1934 – 47; President of Pakistan Constituent Assembly, 1947 – 8.

Lloyd, Lord (1879 – 1941), George Ambrose Lloyd, cr. 1st Baron Lloyd 1925. M.P. (Con.) 1910 – 18, 1924 – 5. Colonial Secretary 1940 – 1.

Loraine, Sir Percy (1880 – 1961). Extensive diplomatic experience, including Secretariat of Paris Peace Conference 1919, British Minister to Persia 1921 – 6, High Commissioner for Egypt and Sudan 1929 – 33; Ambassador to Turkey, 1933 – 9, to Italy 1939 – 40.

Lugard, F.J.D. (1858 – 1945), Baron Lugard (1928). High Commissioner for Northern Nigeria 1900 – 06; Governor of Hong Kong 1907 – 12; Governor of Nigeria 1912 – 19; British member of Permanent Mandates Commission, League of Nations, 1922 – 36.

Luke, Sir Harry (1884 – 1969). Assistant Governor of Jerusalem, 1920 – 24; Colonial Secretary of Sierra Leone 1924 – 8; Chief Secretary of Palestine 1928 – 30; Lieutenant-Governor of Malta 1930 – 38; Governor of Fiji and High Commissioner for the Western Pacific, 1938 – 42.

Lyons, Rt Hon. Joseph Aloysius (1879 – 1939). Founder and leader of United Australia Party 1931. Prime Minister of Australia 1932 – 9.

MacDonald, Malcolm John (1901 – 81). Son of J. Ramsay MacDonald. Labour then National Labour M.P. 1929 – 35, 1936 – 45. Under Secretary for Dominions 1931 – 5, Secretary of State for Colonies June – November 1935, 1938 – 40; U.K. High Commissioner in Canada 1941 – 6.

MacMichael, Sir Harold (1882 – 1969). Civil secretary of the Sudan 1926 – 33; Governor of Tanganyika 1933 – 7; High Commissioner for Palestine and Trans-Jordan 1938 – 44.

Menzies, Sir Robert Gordon (1894 – 1978). Held various Australian ministerial posts, 1932 – 9; Prime Minister of Australia 1939 – 41, 1949 – 66.

Nehru, Shri Jawaharlal (1889 – 1964). Son of Pandit Motilal Nehru. Member of all-India Congress Committee from 1918; joined non-violent, non-cooperation movement under Gandhi 1920; General Secretary of Congress Committee 1929; suceeded father as president of Congress 1929; President of Indian National Congress 1936, 1937, 1946, 1951 – 4; President of All-India states Peoples Conference 1939; Prime Minister of India and Minister for External Affairs 1947 – 64.

Olivier, Sydney (1859 – 1943), cr. 1st Baron Olivier 1924. Colonial Service 1882 – 1913, including considerable experience in West Indies; Secretary of State for India 1924.

Passfield, Lord (1859 – 1947), Sidney Webb, cr. 1st Baron Passfield 1929. Dominions Secretary 1929 – 30, Colonial Secretary 1929 – 31.

Peel, William Robert Wellesley, Viscount, cr. 1st Earl 1929, (1867 – 1937). Secretary of State for India 1922 – 4, 1928 – 9; member of Indian Round Table Conference 1931 – 2; chairman of Burma Round Table Conference 1931 – 2; chairman of Royal Commission on Palestine 1936 – 7.

Plumer, Field-Marshal Henry Charles Onslow (1857 – 1932), cr. 1st Baron Plumer 1929. Governor of Malta 1919 – 24; High Commissioner for Palestine 1925 – 8.

Runciman, Walter (1870 – 1949), cr. 1st Viscount Runciman 1937. Liberal M.P. 1898 – 1900, 1902 – 18, 1924 – 9, National Liberal M.P. 1931 – 7. President of Board of Trade 1931 – 7; Head of Mission to Czechoslovakia 1938.

Salisbury, James Edward Hubert Gascoyne Cecil, 4th Marquess, (1861 – 1947). Under Secretary for Foreign Affairs 1900 – 3; Lord Privvy Seal 1903 – 5, President Board of Trade 1905, Lord President of the Council 1922 – 4; deputy chairman of Committee of Imperial Defence, 1922 – 4.

Samuel, Sir Herbert (1870 – 1963). Herbert Louis Samuel, 1st Viscount Samuel, cr. 1937. M.P. (Liberal) 1902 – 18, 1929 – 35. British High Commissioner in Palestine, 1920 – 5; leader of Liberal Party 1931 – 5.

Swinton, Lord (1884 – 1972): born Philip Lloyd-Graeme, changed name to Cunliffe-Lister 1924, cr. 1st Viscount Swinton 1935. Secretary to Overseas Trade Department 1921 – 2, President of Board of Trade 1922 – 4, 1924 – 9, Aug-Nov 1931; Secretary of State for Colonies 1931 – 5; Secretary of State for Air, 1935 – 8.

Thomas, Rt Hon. James Henry (1874 – 1949). Labour then National Labour M.P. 1910 – 36. Secretary of State for Colonies 1924, 1931, 1935 – 6; Secretary of State for Dominions 1930 – 35.

Trenchard, Hugh Montague (1873 – 1956). Cr. 1st Viscount Trenchard 1936. Entered army 1893; Chief of Air Staff 1918 – 29; Marshal of Royal Air Force 1927.

Wavell, Field-Marshal Archibald Percival (1883 – 1950). Knighted 1939, cr. 1st Earl Wavell 1947. Commander in Palestine and Jordan 1937 – 8, Commander-in-Chief Middle East 1939 – 41, Commander-in-Chief India 1941 – 3, Supreme Commander S.W. Pacific January-March 1942; Governor – General and Viceroy of India 1943 – 7.

Wedgwood Josiah (1872 – 1943), cr. 1st Baron Wedgwood 1942. Liberal then Labour M.P. 1906 – 42. Vice-chairman of Labour Party 1921 – 4.

Weizmann, Chaim (1874 – 1952). President of World Zionist Organisation and Jewish Agency for Palestine 1921 – 31, 1935 – 46; first President of State of Israel, 1949.

INDEX

Page and footnote numbers printed in italics refer to biographical details of the subject of the entry.